Analyzing Financial and Economic Data with R

Marcelo S. Perlin (marcelo.perlin@ufrgs.br)

Second Edition - 2020-02-15

Analyzing Financial and Economic Data with R

by **Marcelo Scherer Perlin**

© 2020 Marcelo S. Perlin. All rights reserved.

Independent publication. Printed on demand by Amazon.com. Online edition with first six chapters available at: *htttps://www.msperlin.com/afedR/*

Cover:	Rubens Lima - https://capista.com.br
Proofreader:	Various
ISBN (print):	9781710627312
ISBN (ebook):	-

History of editions:

2017-05-01   First edition
2020-02-15   Second edition

While the author has used good faith efforts to ensure that the instructions and code contained in this work are accurate, the author disclaims all responsibility for errors or omissions, including without limitation responsibility for damages resulting from the use of or reliance on this work and its resulting code. The use of the information contained in this work is at your own risk. If any code in this book is subject to open source licenses or the intellectual property rights of others, complying with such rights and licenses is your responsibility as a user.

Contents

About New Edition   9

Preface   11
     Supplement Material 13
     Content for Instructors 14

1 Introduction   15
     1.1 What is R 16
     1.2 Why Choose R 16
     1.3 What Can You Do With R and RStudio? 17
     1.4 Installing R 18
     1.5 Installing RStudio 20
     1.6 Resources in the Web 22
     1.7 Structure and Organization 23
     1.8 Exercises 24

2 Basic Operations in R   27
     2.1 Working With R 27
     2.2 Objects in R 29
     2.3 International and Local Formats 30
     2.4 Types of Files in R 31

	2.5 Explaining the RStudio Screen	32
	2.6 Running Scripts from RStudio	36
	2.7 Testing and Debugging Code	38
	2.8 Creating Simple Objects	39
	2.9 Creating Vectors	41
	2.10 Knowing Your Environment and Objects	42
	2.11 Displaying and Formatting Output	45
	2.12 Finding the Size of Objects	49
	2.13 Selecting Elements from an Atomic Vector	52
	2.14 Removing Objects from the Memory	56
	2.15 Displaying and Setting the Working Directory	57
	2.16 Canceling Code Execution	59
	2.17 Code Comments	59
	2.18 Looking for Help	61
	2.19 R Packages	63
	2.20 Using Code Completion with *tab*	69
	2.21 Interacting with Files and the Operating System	72
	2.22 Exercises	79

3 Writing Research Scripts — 81
	3.1 Stages of Research	81
	3.2 Folder Structure	83
	3.3 Important Aspects of a Research Script	86
	3.4 Exercises	88

4 Importing Data from Local Files — 89
	4.1 *csv* files	90
	4.2 *Excel* Files (*xls* and *xlsx*)	97
	4.3 *RData* and *rds* Files	102
	4.4 *fst* files	104
	4.5 SQLite Files	107

		4.6	Unstructured Data and Other Formats	110
		4.7	How to Select a Format	113
		4.8	Exercises	114

5 Importing Data from the Internet   117

	5.1	Package `GetQuandlData`	118
	5.2	Package `BatchGetSymbols`	124
	5.3	Package `simfinR`	130
	5.4	Package `tidyquant`	138
	5.5	Package `Rbitcoin`	141
	5.6	Other Packages	143
	5.7	Accessing Data from Web Pages (*webscraping*)	143
	5.8	Exercises	148

6 Dataframes and other objects   151

	6.1	`Dataframes`	152
	6.2	`Lists`	180
	6.3	`Matrices`	190
	6.4	Exercises	198

7 Basic Object Classes   201

	7.1	Numeric Objects	201
	7.2	Character Objects	219
	7.3	Factor Objects	233
	7.4	Logical Objects	240
	7.5	Date and Time	243
	7.6	Missing Data - `NA` (*Not available*)	259
	7.7	Exercises	263

8 Programming and Data Analysis — 265

- 8.1 R Functions 265
- 8.2 Using `for` Loops 276
- 8.3 Conditional Statements (`if`, `else`, `switch`) 283
- 8.4 Using `apply` Functions 286
- 8.5 Using package `purrr` 301
- 8.6 Data Manipulation with Package `dplyr` 309
- 8.7 Exercises 314

9 Cleaning and Structuring Data — 317

- 9.1 The Format of a `dataframe` 317
- 9.2 Converting `lists` into `dataframes` 322
- 9.3 Removing Outliers 327
- 9.4 Inflation and Price Data 334
- 9.5 Modifying Time Frequency and Aggregating Data 337
- 9.6 Exercises 338

10 Creating and Saving Figures with `ggplot2` — 341

- 10.1 The `ggplot2` Package 342
- 10.2 Using Graphics Windows 343
- 10.3 Creating Figures with Function `qplot` 344
- 10.4 Creating Figures with Function `ggplot` 346
- 10.5 Using Themes 355
- 10.6 Creating Panels with `facet_wrap` 359
- 10.7 Using the Pipeline 362
- 10.8 Creating Statistical Graphics 364
- 10.9 Saving Graphics to a File 373
- 10.10 Exercises 374

11 Financial Econometrics with R — 377

- 11.1 Linear Models (OLS) 378
- 11.2 Generalized Linear Models (GLM) 395
- 11.3 Panel Data Models 402
- 11.4 Arima Models 412
- 11.5 GARCH Models 418
- 11.6 Regime Switching Models 425
- 11.7 Dealing with Several Models 437
- 11.8 Exercises 443

12 Reporting Results — 447

- 12.1 Reporting Tables 448
- 12.2 Reporting Models 451
- 12.3 Creating Reports with *RMarkdown* 454
- 12.4 Exercises 459

13 Optimizing Code — 461

- 13.1 Optimizing your Programming Time 461
- 13.2 Optimizing Code Speed 465
- 13.3 Exercises 481

About New Edition

Since the first edition of this book in 2017, many things have changed. The second edition of the book complements and extends the previous material, considering new ways to use Rstudio, new R packages written by me and others, as well as the feedback from the first edition.

However, the format of the book has changed significantly. The order of chapters is now aligned with the steps of data-based research, from importing tables, cleaning it, testing hypotheses and presenting results. Thus, the reader can follow through the chapters according to his own work. Another important change is the alignment with the `tidyverse` tools – a set of packages that greatly facilitate the use of R –, especially for data importation and manipulation. Some native R functions are presented when necessary, but only when a `tidyverse` counterpart does not exist.

Three new chapters were added to this book, including a dedicated piece to the process of reporting research output and the use of the *RMarkdown* technology. The final chapter now discusses code optimization by presenting the best code practices and simple strategies to improve work efficiency.

For all R teachers in the world, this and all future editions of the book will include class material such as end-of-chapter and dynamic exercises with solutions and *RMarkdown* slides with the content of **all** chapters. All teaching material is publicly available in the internet[1] and released with a generous MIT license[2]. So, if you are an R tutor in finance or economics, feel free to use and modify the teaching material to your liking. However, if you do so, please make sure that you cite the original source.

I hope you enjoy reading this book and, based on its content you can find ways to improve your data analysis. Your feedback is always important and

---

[1] https://www.msperlin.com/blog/publication/2020_book-afedr-en/
[2] https://opensource.org/licenses/MIT

you can reach me at *marceloperlin@gmail.com*. This book is a special and lifelong project and I will keep improving it as much as I can over the years.

Preface

Since you are reading this book, you are likely a data analyst looking for alternative and more efficient ways to add value to your organization, an undergraduate or graduate student in your first steps learning data science, or an experienced researcher, looking for new tools to use in your work. Be assured that you are in the right place. **This book will teach you to use R and RStudio for data analysis in finance and economics**.

The material in this book started out as class slides from my work as a university teacher and researcher in the south of Brazil. Moreover, by observing students learning and using R in the classroom, I frequently see the positive impact that it has on their careers. They can autonomously do complex data tasks with their computers, providing a better and more comprehensive analysis to help the decision-making process in their organizations. They spend less time doing repetitive and soul-crushing spreadsheet data chores and more time thinking about their analysis and learning new tools. This book attempts to go beyond the classroom and reach an international and more diversified audience.

Another motivation for writing this book is my personal experience using code from other researchers. Usually, the code is not well-organized, lacks clarity, and, possibly, only works in the computer of its author! After being constantly frustrated, I realized the work required to figure out the code of other researchers would take more time than writing the procedure myself. These cases hurt the development of science, as one of its basic principles is the **reproducibility of experiments**. In the case of a computer-intensive field, such as empirical finance and economics, the underlying research code should run without effort in other people's computers. As researchers are expected to be good writers, it should also be expected that their code is in a proper format and readable by other people. With this book, I will tackle this problem by presenting a code structure focused on scientific reproducibility, organization, and usability.

In this book, we will not work on the advanced uses of R. The content will be limited to simple and practical examples. One challenge of writing this book was defining the boundary between introductory and advanced material. Wherever possible, I gradually dosed the level of complexity. For readers interested in learning advanced features of the program and its inner workings, I suggest the work of Venables et al. (2004), Teetor (2011) and Wickham (2014).

This is what you'll learn from this book:

Using R and RStudio In chapter 01 we will discuss the use of R as a programming platform designed to solve data-related problems in finance and economics. In chapter 02 we will explore basic commands and many functionalities of R and RStudio that will increase your productivity.

Importing financial and economic data In chapters 04 and 05 we will learn to import data from local files, such as an Excel spreadsheet, or the internet, using specialized packages that can download financial and economic data such as stock prices, economic indices, the US yield curve, corporate financial statements, and many others.

Cleaning, structuring and analyzing the data with R In chapters 06 and 07 we will concentrate our study on the ecosystem of basic and advanced classes of objects within R. We will learn to manipulate objects such as numeric vectors, dates and whole tables. In chapters 08 and 09 we'll study to use the programming tools to solve data-related problems such as cleaning and structuring messy data. In chapter 11 we will learn applications of the most common econometric models used in finance and economics including linear regression, generalized linear model, Arima model and others. Creating a visual analysis of data

In chapter 10 we'll learn to use functions from package `ggplot2` to create clever visualizations of our datasets, including the most popular applications in finance and economics, time series and statistical plots.

Reporting your results In chapter 12 we will see how to report our data analysis using specialized packages and the *RMarkdown* technology. It includes the topic of presenting and exporting tables, figures and models to a written report.

Writing better and faster code In the last chapter of the book we discuss best programming practices with R. We will look at how to profile code and search for bottlenecks and improving execution time with caching strategies using package `memoize`, C++ code with `Rcpp` and parallel computing with `furrr`.

Supplement Material

All the material used in the book, including code examples separated by chapters, is publicly available on the Internet and distributed with an R package called afedR. It includes data files and several functions that can make it easier to run the examples of the book. If you plan to write some code as you read the book, this package will greatly help your journey.

If you want to use the internet to install the package in your computer, you simply need to execute a couple of lines of code in R. Also, to do that, you just need to copy and paste these commands into RStudio prompt (bottom left of screen, with a ">" sign) and press enter for each command. Be aware you'll need R and RStudio installed in your computer (see section 1.4 for details).

```
# install devtools dependency
install.packages('devtools')

# install book package
devtools::install_github('msperlin/afedR')
```

What this code will do is to install package devtools, a required dependency for installing a package from Github, which is where the book bundle is hosted. After that, a call to devtools::install_github('msperlin/afedR') will install the package in your computer.

After installing the book package afedR, you can copy all book files to a local folder by simply executing the following command in R:

```
afedR::afedR_get_book_files(path_to_copy = '~')
```

The previous code will unzip the book file into your "Documents/afedR-files" folder, as the tilda (~) is a shortcut to your "Documents" directory. The package also includes several other functions that will be used throughout the book. If you prefer the old-fashioned way of using an internet page, you can find and download the zip file in the book site[3].

A suggestion, before you read the rest of the book: go to the book website and search for the related links page at the bottom. There you will find all internet addresses highlighted in the text, including the links for the installation of R and RStudio.

---

[3]https://www.msperlin.com/blog/static/afedr-files/afedr_files.zip

Content for Instructors

If you are an R instructor, you'll find plenty of material you can use with your classes. I made sure you get everything you need:

Static end of chapter exercises Every chapter in this book includes exercises that your students can practice. The solutions are available as .Rmd files in its source and the compiled version.

RMarkdown slides Slides from the book are also available in source and compiled form for **all** chapters. There you'll find plenty of content to help you build an R class from scratch. Fell free to modify the files as needed, just make sure you cite the original source.

Dynamic R exercises Collection of dynamic R exercises built on top of the R package `exams`. This technology can produce unique exercises for each of your students. Functions for compiling the exercises and grading them are available within the book package. Have a look in this blog post[4] for instructions on how to use it with your students.

All of this content is released with the MIT license, so feel free to use and abuse it, as long as you give the credits to the original author. You can find the content within the book package `afedR` (see previous instructions on installation) or directly at the book site[5].

I hope you enjoy this book and find it useful for your work.

Good reading!

Marcelo S. Perlin

---

[4] https://www.msperlin.com/blog/post/2019-12-02-dynamic-exercises-afedr/
[5] https://www.msperlin.com/blog/publication/2020_book-afedr-en/

Chapter 1

Introduction

In the digital era, information is abundant and accessible. From the ever-changing price of financial contracts to the unstructured data of social media websites, the high volume of information creates a strong need for data analysis in the workplace. A company or organization benefit immensely when it can create a bridge between raw information from its environment and making strategic decisions. Undoubtedly, this is a prolific time for professionals skilled in using the right tools for acquiring, storing, and analyzing data.

In particular, datasets related to Economics and Finance are widely available to the public. International and local institutions, such as central banks, government research agencies, financial exchanges, and many others, provide their data publicly, either by legal obligation or to foment research. Whether you are looking into statistics for a particular country or a company, most information is just two clicks away. By analyzing this information efficiently and effortlessly, you'll be able to offer valuable insights to your team.

Not surprisingly, fields with abundant access to data and practical applications, such as economics and finance, it is expected that a graduate student or a data analyst has learned at least one programming language that allows him/her to do his work efficiently. **Learning how to program is becoming a requisite for the job market**. In this setup, the role and contribution of R shine. In these sections, I will explain what R is and why you should use it.

1.1 What is R

R is a programming language specially designed to resolve statistical problems and display graphical representations of data. R is a modern version of S, a programming language originally created in Bell Laboratories (formerly AT&T, now Lucent Technologies). The base code of R was developed by two academics, **Ross Ihaka** and **Robert Gentleman**, resulting in the programming platform we have today. For anyone curious about the name, the letter R was chosen due to the common first letter of the name of their creators.

Today, R is almost synonymous with data analysis, with a large user base and consolidated modules. It is likely that researchers from various fields, from economics to biology, find in R significant preexisting code that facilitates their analysis.

On the business side, large and established companies, such as *Google* and *Microsoft*, already adopted R as the internal language for data analysis. R is maintained by **R Foundation**[1] and the **R Consortium**[2], a collective effort to fund projects for extending the programming language.

1.2 Why Choose R

Learning a new programming language requires a lot of time and effort. Perhaps you're wondering why you should choose R and invest time in learning it. Here are the main arguments.

First, **R is a mature and stable platform, continuously supported and intensively used in the industry**. When choosing R, you will have the computational background not only for an academic career in scientific research but also to work as a data analyst in private organizations. Due to its open license, you can use R anywhere. Also, the strong support from the community means it is very unlikely the R platform will ever fade away or be substituted. Depending on your career choices, R might be the only programming language you ever need to learn.

Learning R is easy. My experience in teaching R allows me to confidently state that students, even those with no programming experience, have no problem learning the language and using it to create their own code. The language is intuitive and certain rules and functions can be extended to

---

[1] https://www.r-project.org/foundation/
[2] https://www.r-consortium.org/

different cases. For example, the function `print` is used to show the contents of an object on the screen. You can use it for any kind of object. So, by learning the main concept, you'll be able to apply it in different scenarios. Once you understand how the software expects you to think, it is easy to discover new features starting from a previous logic. This generic notation facilitates the learning process.

The engine of R and the interface of RStudio creates a highly productive environment. The graphical interface provided by RStudio facilitates the use of R and increases productivity by introducing new features to the platform. By combining both, the user has at his disposal many tools that facilitate the development of research scripts and other projects.

CRAN Packages allow the user to do many different things with R. We will soon learn that we can import external code directly into R as individual modules (packages) and use it for different purposes. These packages extend the basic language of R and enable the most diverse functionalities. You can, for example, use R to write and publish a book, build and publish a blog, create exams with dynamic content, write random jokes and poems (seriously!), send emails, access and collect data from the internet, and many other features. It is truly impressive what you can do with just a couple of lines of code in R.

R is compatible with different operating systems and it can interface with different programming languages. If you need to execute code from another programming language, such as *C++*, *Python*, *Julia*, it is easy to integrate it with R. Therefore, the user is not restricted to a single programming language and can easily use features and functions from others. For example, the C++ code is well known for its superior speed in numerical tasks. From an R script, you can use package `Rcpp` to write a C++ function and effortlessly use it within your R code.

R is free! The main software and all its packages are free. A generous license motivates the adoption of the R language in a business environment, where obtaining individual and collective licenses of commercial software can be costly. This means you can take R anywhere you go.

1.3 What Can You Do With R and RStudio?

R is a fairly complete programming language and any computational problem can be solved based on it. Given the adoption of R for different areas of knowledge, the list is extensive. With finance and economics, I will be highlighting these possibilities:

- Substitute and improve data-intensive tasks from spreadsheet-like software;

- Develop routines for managing and controlling investment portfolios and executing financial orders;

- Creating tools for calculating and reporting economic indices such as inflation and unemployment;

- Performing empirical data research using statistical techniques, such as econometric models and hypothesis testing;

- Create dynamic *websites* with the `shiny` package, allowing anyone in the world to use a computational tool created by you;

- Automate the process of writing technical reports with the **RMarkdown** technology;

Moreover, public access to packages developed by users further expands these capabilities. The CRAN views website[3] offers a *Task Views* panel for the topic of Finance[4] and Econometrics[5]. There you can find the main packages to perform specific operations such as importing financial data from the internet, estimating econometric models, calculation of different risk estimates, among many other possibilities. Reading this page and the knowledge of these packages is essential for those who intend to work in Finance and Economics. It is worth noting, however, that the complete list of packages is much larger.

1.4 Installing R

Before going any further, let's install the required software on your computer. The most direct and practical way to install R is to direct your browser to R website[6] and click the *Download* link in the left side of the page, as shown in Figure 1.1.

---

[3] https://cran.r-project.org/web/views
[4] https://cran.r-project.org/web/views/Finance.html
[5] https://cran.r-project.org/web/views/Econometrics.html
[6] http://www.r-project.org/

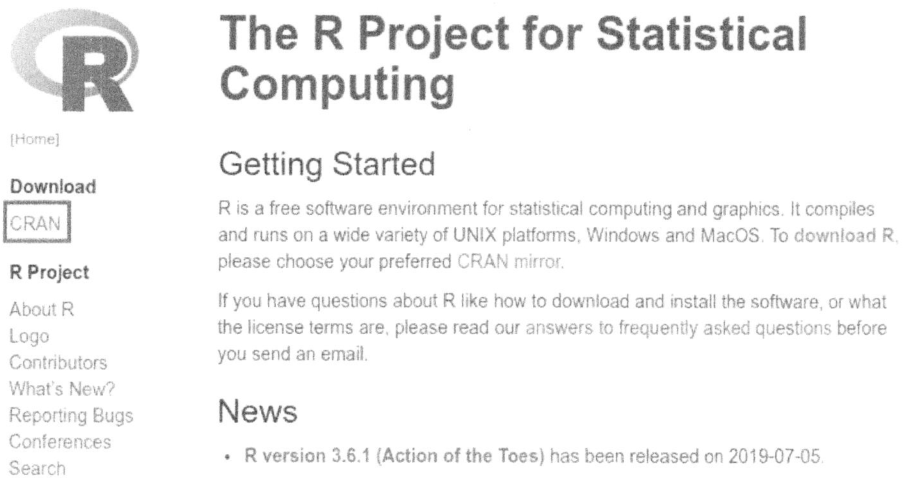

1.4. INSTALLING R

Figure 1.1: Initial page for downloading R

The next screen gives you a choice of the mirror to download the installation files. The CRAN repository (*R Comprehensive Archive network*) is mirrored in various parts of the world. You can choose one of the links from the nearest location to you. If undecided, just select the mirror *0-Cloud* (see Figure 1.2), which will automatically take you to the nearest location.

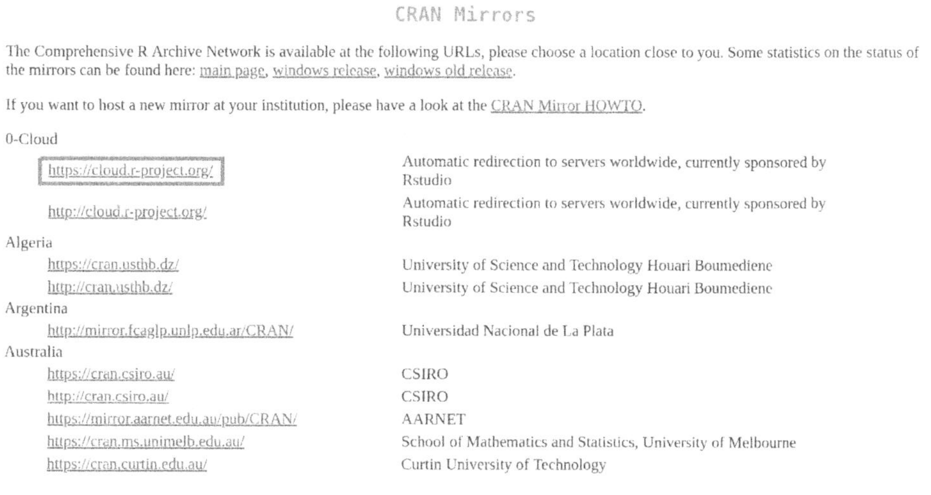

Figure 1.2: Choosing the CRAN mirror

The next step involves selecting your operating system, likely to be *Windows*. From now on, due to the greater popularity of this platform, we will focus on installing R in Windows. The instructions for installing R in other operating systems can be easily found online. Regardless of the underlying platform, using R is about the same. There are a few exceptions, especially when R interacts with the file system. In the content of the book, special care was taken to choose functions that work the same way in different operating systems. A few exceptions are highlighted throughout the book. So, even if you are using a Mac or a flavor of Linux, you can take full advantage of the material presented here.

Figure 1.3: Choosing the operating system

After clicking the link *Download R for Windows*, as in Figure 1.3, the next screen will show the following download options: *base*, *contrib*, *old.contrib* and *RTools*. The first (*base*), should be selected. It contains the download link to the executable installation file of R in *Windows*.

If the user is interested in creating and distributing their own R packages, *RTools* should also be installed. For most users, however, this should not be the case. If you don't intend to write packages, you can safely ignore *Rtools* for now. The links to *contrib* and *old.contrib* relate to files for the current and old releases of R packages and can also be ignored. We will discuss the use of packages in the next chapter.

After clicking the link *base*, the next screen will show the link to the *download* of the R installation file (Figure 1.5). After downloading the file, open it and follow the steps in the installation screen. At this time, no special configuration is required. I suggest keeping all the default choices and simply hit *accept* in the displayed dialogue screens. After the installation of R, it is strongly recommended to install RStudio, which will be addressed next.

1.5 Installing RStudio

The base installation of R includes its own *GUI* (graphical user interface), where we can write and execute code. However, this native interface has several limitations. RStudio substitutes the original GUI and makes access to R

1.5. INSTALLING RSTUDIO

Figure 1.4: Installation options

Figure 1.5: Downloading R

more practical and efficient. One way to understand this relationship is with an analogy with cars. While R is the engine of the programming language, RStudio is the body and instrument panel, which significantly improves the user experience. Besides presenting a more attractive look, RStudio also adds several features that make the life of a programmer easier, allowing the creation of projects and packages, creation of dynamic documents, among others.

The installation of RStudio is simpler than that of R. The files are available in RStudio website[7]. After accessing the page, click *Download RStudio* and then *Download RStudio Desktop*. After that, just select the installation file relative to the operating system on which you will work. This option is probably *WINDOWS Vista 7/8/10*. Note that, as well as R, RStudio is also available for alternative platforms.

I emphasize that using RStudio is not essential to develop programs in R. Other interfaces are available and can be used. However, in my experience, RStudio is the interface that offers a vast range of features for the language and is widely used, which justifies its choice.

1.6 Resources in the Web

The R community is vivid and engaging. There are many authors, such as myself[8], that constantly release material about R in their blogs. It includes the announcement of new packages, posts about data analysis in real life, curiosities, rants, and tutorials. R-Bloggers[9] is a website that aggregates these blogs, making it easier for anyone to access and participate. I strongly recommend to sign up for the R-Bloggers feed in RSS[10], Facebook[11] or Twitter[12]. Not only you'll be informed of what is happening in the R community, but also learn a lot by reading other people's code and articles.

Learning and using R can be a social experience. Several conferences and user-groups are available in many countries. You can find the complete list in this link[13]. I also suggest looking in social platforms for local R groups in your region.

---

[7] https://www.rstudio.com/
[8] https://www.msperlin.com/blog
[9] https://www.r-bloggers.com/
[10] https://feeds.feedburner.com/RBloggers
[11] https://www.facebook.com/rbloggers/?fref=ts
[12] https://twitter.com/Rbloggers
[13] https://jumpingrivers.github.io/meetingsR/index.html

1.7 Structure and Organization

This book presents a practical approach to using R in finance and economics. To get the most out of this book, I suggest you first seek to understand the code shown, and only then, try using it on your own computer. Whenever you find a piece of code that you do not understand, go on and study it. At first, it might seem like a daunting task but, with time, be confident that the learning process will get a lot easier as the code blocks start to make sense.

Learning to program in a new platform is like learning a foreign spoken language: the use in day-to-day problems is imperative to create fluency. All the code and data used in this book is available with the installation of package **afedR** (see the preface for instructions on how to install it). I suggest you test the code on your computer and *play* with it, modifying the examples and checking the effect of changes in the outputs. Whenever you have a computational problem, try using R to solve it. You'll stumble and make mistakes at first. But I guarantee that, soon enough, you'll be able to write complex data tasks effortlessly.

Throughout the book, every demonstration of code will have two parts: the R code and its output. The output is nothing more than the result of the commands on the screen. All inputs and outputs code will be marked in the text with a special format. See the following example:

```
# create a list
L <- list('abc', 1:5, 'dec')

# print list
print(L)
```

```
R> [[1]]
R> [1] "abc"
R>
R> [[2]]
R> [1] 1 2 3 4 5
R>
R> [[3]]
R> [1] "dec"
```

For the previous chunk of code, lines `L <- list('abc', 1:5, 'dec')` and `print(L)` are actual commands given to R. The output of this simple piece of code is the on-screen presentation of the contents of object L. The symbol `R>` is used for any code output. Notice also that inline comments are set with the symbol `#`. Anything on the right side of `#` is not evaluated by R. These comments serve as written notes about the code.

The code can also be spatially organized using newlines. This is a common strategy around arguments of functions. The next chunk of code is equivalent to the previous and will run the exact same way. Notice how we used a new line to vertically align the arguments of function `list`. You'll soon see that, throughout the book, this type of vertical alignment is constantly used.

```
# create a list
L <- list('abc',
          1:5,
          'dec')

# print list
print(L)

R> [[1]]
R> [1] "abc"
R>
R> [[2]]
R> [1] 1 2 3 4 5
R>
R> [[3]]
R> [1] "dec"
```

The code also follows a well-defined structure. One decision in writing computer code is how to name objects and how to structure it. It is recommended to follow a clear pattern, so it is easy to maintain over time and be used and understood by others. For this book, a mixture of the author's personal choices with the coding style suggested by Google[14] was used. The reader, however, may choose the structure he finds more efficient and aesthetically pleasing. Like many things in life, this is a choice. We will get back at discussing code structure in chapter 13.

1.8 Exercises

1. Use Google to search for R groups in your region. Verify if there are frequent meetings and, if you so desire, go to one and make new

---

[14]https://google.github.io/styleguide/Rguide.xml

1.8. EXERCISES

friends.

2. Once you have R and RStudio installed, head over to the CRAN package website[15] and search for computer technologies that you use in your current work. For example, if you use Google Sheets[16] extensively in your work, you'll soon find there is a package in CRAN that can interact with it by creating and reading cloud-based spreadsheets.

3. If you work in an institution with data infrastructure, talk to the IT department and seek to understand what type of data technology is being currently used. Check if it's possible, from R, to connect to the databases of your company and import the tables. No need for writing any code yet, just make sure the technology is available.

4. Head over to the RBloggers[17] website and search for a topic of your interest, such as, "Tennis" or "investments". Read at least two or three articles that interest you.

---

[15]https://cloud.r-project.org/web/packages/available_packages_by_date.html
[16]https://www.google.com/sheets/about/
[17]https://www.r-bloggers.com/

Chapter 2

Basic Operations in R

It is important to understand how to work with R and RStudio efficiently before you develop your data analysis. This includes understanding the RStudio interface, basic R commands, file extensions, available shortcuts and the autocomplete feature of RStudio.

In this section, we will go through the initial steps from the viewpoint of someone who has never worked with R and possibly never had contact with other programming languages. Those already familiar with the software may not find novel information here and, therefore, I suggest skipping to the next section. However, it is recommended, that you at least check the discussed topics so you can confirm your knowledge about the features of the software and how to use them for working smarter and not harder. This is especially true for RStudio, which offers several tools to increase your productivity.

2.1 Working With R

The greatest difficulty new user experiences when developing routines in R is the format of work – the so-called development cycle. Our interaction with computers has been simplified over the years and we are currently comfortable with the *point&click* format. That is, if you want to perform an operation on the computer, just point the *mouse* to the specific location on the screen and click a button. Visual cues in a series of steps allow the execution of complex tasks. But, you need to be aware that this form of interaction is just one layer above what actually happens. Behind all these *clicks*, there is a command being executed on your computer. Any common task such as opening a *pdf* file, a spreadsheet document, directing a *browser* to a web page has an underlying call to a code.

The "point&click" format of visual and motor interaction has its benefits in facilitating and popularizing the use of computers. However, it is not flexible and effective when working with computational procedures such as data analysis. By knowing the commands available to the user and how to execute them, it is possible to create a file containing several instructions in sequence and, in the future, simply request that the computer **execute** this file using the recorded procedures. There is no need to do a "scripted" point&click operation. You spend some time writing the program but, in the future, it will always execute the recorded procedure in the same way.

In the medium and long term, there is a significant gain in productivity between the use of a *script* (sequence of commands) and a *point&click* type of interface. Going further, the risk of human error in executing the procedure is almost nil because the commands and their required sequence of execution are recorded in the text file and will always be executed in the same way. This is one of the main reasons programming languages are popular in science. All steps of data-based research, including results, can be replicated.

In using R, the ideal format of work is to merge the mouse movement with commands. R and RStudio have some functionality with the *mouse*, but their capacity is optimized when we perform operations using code. When a group of commands is performed in a smart way, we have an R script that should preferably produce something important to us at the end of its execution. In finance and economics, this can be the current price of a stock, the value of an economic index such as inflation, the result of academic research, among many other possibilities.

Like other software, R allows us to import data and export files. We can use code to import a dataset stored in a local file – or the web–, analyze it and paste the results into a technical report. We can use RStudio and the *RMarkdown* technology to write a dynamic report, where code and content are integrated. For example, the book you're reading was written using the `bookdown` package (Xie, 2016). The content of the book is compiled with the execution of the R codes and their outputs are recorded in the scope of the text. All figures and data tasks in the book can be updated with the execution of a simple command. Needless to say that by using the capabilities of R and RStudio, you will work smarter and faster.

The final product of working with R and RStudio will be an R script that produces elements for a data report. A good example of a simple and polished R script can be found at this link[1]. Open it and you'll see the content

---

[1] https://github.com/msperlin/afedR/raw/master/inst/extdata/others/S_

of a file with extension .R that will download stock prices of two companies and create a plot and a table. By the end of the book, you can understand what is going on in the code and how it gets the job done. Even better, you'll be able to improve it. Soon, you'll learn to execute the code on your own computer. If impatient, simply copy the text content of the link to a new RStudio R script, save it, and press `control + shift + enter`.

2.2 Objects in R

In R, everything is an object, and each type of object has its properties. For example, the daily closing prices of the IBM stock can be represented as a numerical vector, where each element is a price recorded at the end of a trading day. Dates related to these prices can be represented as text (*string*) or as a unique `Date` class. Finally, we can represent the price data and the dates together by storing them in a single object of type `dataframe`, which is nothing more than a table with rows and columns. These objects are part of the R ecosystem, and through their manipulation, we take full advantage of the software.

While we represent data as objects in R, a special type is a `function`. It stores a pre-established manipulation of other objects available to the user. R has an extremely large number of functions, which enable the user to perform a wide range of operations. For example, the basic commands of R, available in the package `base`, adds up to a total of 1229 functions.

Each function has its own name and a programmer can write their own functions. For example, the `mean` function is a procedure that calculates the average values of a vector. If we wanted to calculate the average value of the sequence `1, 2, 3, 4, 5`, simply insert the following command in the *prompt* (left bottom side of RStudio's screen) and press *enter*:

```
x <- mean(1:5, na.rm = TRUE)
```

The colon symbol (*:*) in `1:5` creates a sequence starting at 1 and ending at 5. The `mean` function is used with start and end parentheses. These parentheses serve to highlight the entries (*inputs*), that is, the information sent to the function to produce something that will be saved in object `x`. Note that each entry is separated by a comma, as in `my_fct(input1, input2, input3, ...)`. We also set option `na.rm = TRUE`. This is a specific directive

---

Example_Script.R

for the `mean` function to ignore any element of type `NA` (*not available*) if they exist. An `NA` value can be problematic, as we will soon learn.

Functions are at the heart of R and we will dedicate a large part of this book to them. You can use the available functions or write your own. You can also publish functions as a package and let other people use your code. We will reply to the topic of creating and using custom functions in chapter 8.

2.3 International and Local Formats

Before explaining the use of R and RStudio, it is important to highlight some rules of formatting numbers, Latin characters and dates.

decimal: Following an international notation, the decimal point in R is defined by the period symbol (.), as in `2.5` and not a comma, as in `2,5`. If this is not standard in your country, you'll have issues when importing local data from text files. Sometimes, such as with storing data in Microsoft Excel files, the conversion happens automatically in the importing process. This, however, is generally an exception. As a general rule of using R, only use commas to separate the inputs of a function. Under no circumstances should the comma symbol be used as the decimal point separator. Always give priority to the international format because it will be compatible with the vast majority of data.

Latin characters: Due to its international standard, R has problems understanding Latin characters, such as the cedilla and accents. If you can, avoid it, and do not use Latin characters in the names of your variables or files. In the content of character objects (text), you can use them without problems as long as the encoding of the script is correctly specified (e.g. UTF-8, Latin1). I strongly recommend the use of the English language for writing code and defining object names. This automatically eliminates the use of Latin characters and facilitates the usability of the code by people outside of your country.

date format: Dates in R are structured according to the ISO 8601[2] format. It follows the `YYYY-MM-DD` pattern, where `YYYY` is the year in four numbers, `MM` is the month and `DD` is the day. An example is 2020-02-08. This, however, may not be the case in your country. When importing local data sets, make sure the dates are in this format. If necessary, you can convert any date to the ISO format. Again, while you can work with your local format of dates in R,

---

[2] https://www.iso.org/iso-8601-date-and-time-format.html

2.4. TYPES OF FILES IN R

it is best advised to use the international notation. The conversion between one format and another is quite easy and will be presented in chapter 7.

If you want to learn more about your local format in R, use the following command by typing it in the prompt and pressing enter:

```
Sys.localeconv()
```

```
R>       decimal_point       thousands_sep            grouping
R>               "."                  ""                  ""
R>      int_curr_symbol     currency_symbol mon_decimal_point
R>              "BRL "                "R$"                ","
R> mon_thousands_sep        mon_grouping        positive_sign
R>               "."            "\003\003"                  ""
R>       negative_sign      int_frac_digits          frac_digits
R>               "-"                  "2"                  "2"
R>       p_cs_precedes       p_sep_by_space       n_cs_precedes
R>               "1"                  "1"                  "1"
R>      n_sep_by_space         p_sign_posn         n_sign_posn
R>               "1"                  "1"                  "1"
```

The output of `Sys.localeconv()` shows how R interprets decimal points and the thousands separator, among other things. As you can see from the previous output, this book was compiled using the Brazilian notation for the currency but uses the dot point for decimals. As already noted earlier, I feel that it is a good policy to follow the international notation, especially for the decimal point. If necessary, you can change your local format to the US/international notation using the following command.

```
Sys.setlocale("LC_ALL", "English")
```

However, one thing that is worth noting is the fact that you'll need to run this command every time that R starts or incorporate it in the initialization of the software.

2.4 Types of Files in R

Like any other programming platform, R has a file ecosystem and each type of file has a different purpose. In the vast majority of cases, however, the work will focus mostly on a couple of types. Next, I describe various file extensions. The items in the list are ordered by importance. Note that we omit graphic files such as *.png*, *.jpg*, *.gif* and data storage/spreadsheet files (*.csv*, *.xlsx*, ..) among others, as they are not exclusive to R.

Files with extension *.R*: text files containing R code. Besides, these are the files we will spend most of our time. They contain the sequence of commands that configures the main script and subroutines of the data research. Examples: *Script-stock-research.R*, *R-fcts.R*.

Files with extension *.RData* or *.rds*: files that store data in the native format. These files are used to save/write objects created in different sessions into your hard drive. For example, you can use a *.rds* file to save a table after processing and cleaning up the raw database. By *freezing* the data in a local file, we can later load it for subsequent analysis. Examples: *cleaned-inflation-data.rds*, *model-results.RData*.

Files with extension *.Rmd* and *.md*: files used for editing dynamic documents in the *RMarkdown* and *markdown* formats. Using these files allows the creation of documents where text and code output are integrated into the same document. In chapter 12 we have a dedicated section for RMarkdown, which will explore this functionality in detail. Example: *investment-report.Rmd*.

Files with extension *.Rproj*: contain files for editing projects in RStudio, such as a new R package, a *shiny* application or a book. While you can use the functionalities of RStudio projects to write R scripts, it is not a necessity. For those interested in learning more about this functionality, I suggest the RStudio manual[3]. Example: *project-retirement.Rproj*.

2.5 Explaining the RStudio Screen

After installing the two programs, R and RStudio, open RStudio by double-clicking its icon. Moreover, you should understand that R also has its own interface and this often causes confusion. You should find the correct shortcut for RStudio by going through your software folders. In Windows, you can search for RStudio using the *Start* button and typing *Rstudio*.

After opening RStudio, the resulting window should look like Figure 2.1.

Note that RStudio automatically detected the installation of R and initialized your screen on the left side.

If you do not see something like this on the screen of RStudio:

---

[3] https://support.rstudio.com/hc/en-us/articles/200526207-Using-Projects

2.5. EXPLAINING THE RSTUDIO SCREEN

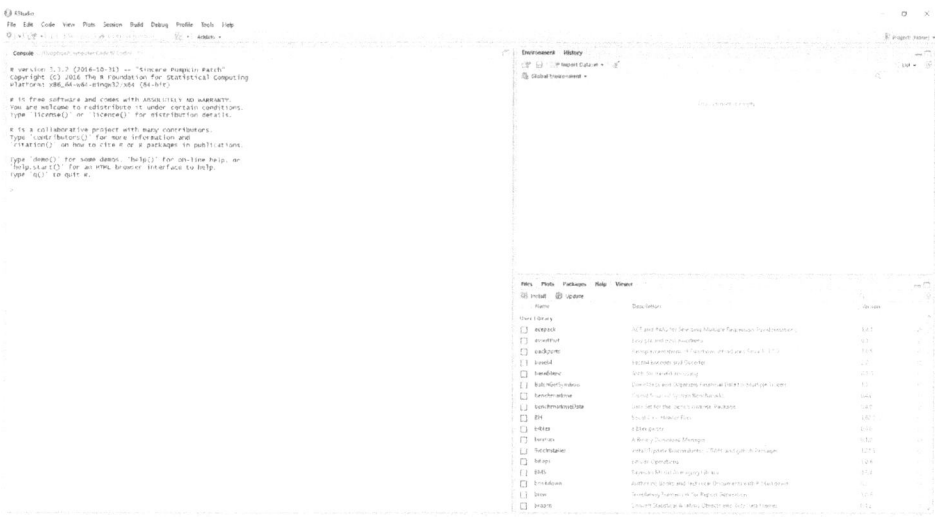

Figure 2.1: The RStudio screen

```
R version 3.6.1 (2019-07-05) -- "Action of the Toes"
Copyright (C) 2019 The R Foundation for Statistical Computing
Platform: x86_64-w64-mingw32/x64 (64-bit)

R is free software and comes with ABSOLUTELY NO WARRANTY.
You are welcome to redistribute it under certain conditions.
Type 'license()' or 'licence()' for distribution details.

  Natural language support but running in an English locale

R is a collaborative project with many contributors.
Type 'contributors()' for more information and
'citation()' on how to cite R or R packages in publications.

Type 'demo()' for some demos, 'help()' for on-line help, or
'help.start()' for an HTML browser interface to help.
Type 'q()' to quit R.
```

then R was not installed correctly. Repeat the installation steps in the previous chapter and confirm the startup message on the lower left side of RStudio.

As a first exercise, click *file*, *New File*, and *R Script*. A text editor should appear on the left side of the screen. It is there that we will spend most of our time developing code. Commands are executed sequentially, from top to bottom. A side note, all *.R* files created in RStudio are just text files and can be edited anywhere. It is not uncommon for experienced programmers to use specific software to write code and another to run it.

After the previous steps in RStudio, the resulting screen should look like the image in Figure 2.2. The main items/panels of the RStudio screen in are:

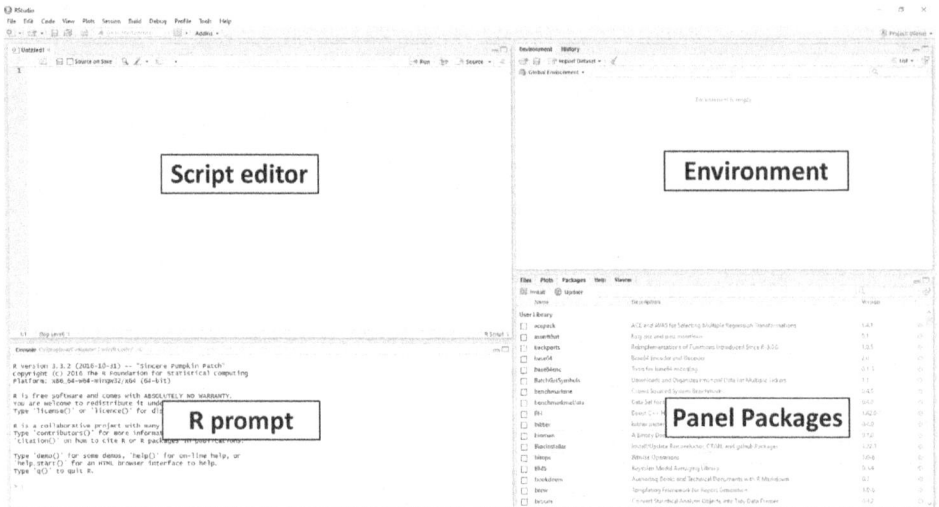

Figure 2.2: Explaining the RStudio screen

Script Editor: located on the left side and above the screen. This panel is used to write scripts and functions, mostly on files with the *.R* extension;

R prompt: on the left side and below the script editor. It displays the *prompt*, which can also be used to give commands to R. The main purpose of the prompt is to test code and display the results of the commands entered in the script editor;

Environment: located on the top-right of the screen. Shows all objects, including variables and functions currently available to the user. Also note a *History* panel, which shows the history of commands previously executed by the user;

Panel Packages: shows the packages installed and loaded by R. Here you have four tabs: *Files*, to load and view system files; *Plots*, to view statistical figures created in R; *Help* to access the help system and *Viewer* to display dynamic and interactive results, such as a web page.

As an introductory exercise, let's initialize two objects in R. Inside the prompt (lower left side), insert these commands and press *enter* at the end of each. The `<-` symbol is nothing more than the result of joining < (less

2.5. EXPLAINING THE RSTUDIO SCREEN

than) with the - (minus sign). The ' symbol represents a single quotation mark and, in the computer keyboard, it is found under the escape (*esc*) key.

```
# set x
x <- 1

# set y
y <- 'My humble text'
```

If done correctly, notice that two objects appeared in the *environment* panel, one called `x` with a value of 1, and another called `y` with the text content `"My humble text"`. You should have noticed how we used specific symbols to define objects `x` and `y`. The use of double quotes (" ") or single quotes (' ') defines objects of the class `character`. Numbers are defined by the value itself. As will be discussed later, understanding R object classes are important as each has a different behavior within the R code. After executing the previous commands, the *history tab* has been updated.

Now, let's show the values of `x` on the screen. To do this, type the following command:

```
# print contents of x
print(x)
```

R> [1] 1

The `print` function is one of the main functions for displaying values in the *prompt* of R. The text displayed as `[1]` indicates the index of the first line number. To verify this, enter the following command, which will show a lengthy sequence of numbers on the screen:

```
# print a sequence
print(50:100)
```

```
R>  [1] 50 51 52 53 54 55 56 57 58 59 60 61
R> [13] 62 63 64 65 66 67 68 69 70 71 72 73
R> [25] 74 75 76 77 78 79 80 81 82 83 84 85
R> [37] 86 87 88 89 90 91 92 93 94 95 96 97
R> [49] 98 99 100
```

Here, we use the colon symbol in `50:100` to create a sequence starting at 50 and ending at 100. Note that, on the left side of each line, we have the values [1], [13], and [25]. These represent the index of the first element presented in the line. For example, the fifteenth element of `50:100` is 64.

2.6 Running Scripts from RStudio

Now, let's combine all the previously typed codes into a single file by copying and pasting all commands into the editor's screen (upper left side). The result looks like Figure 2.3.

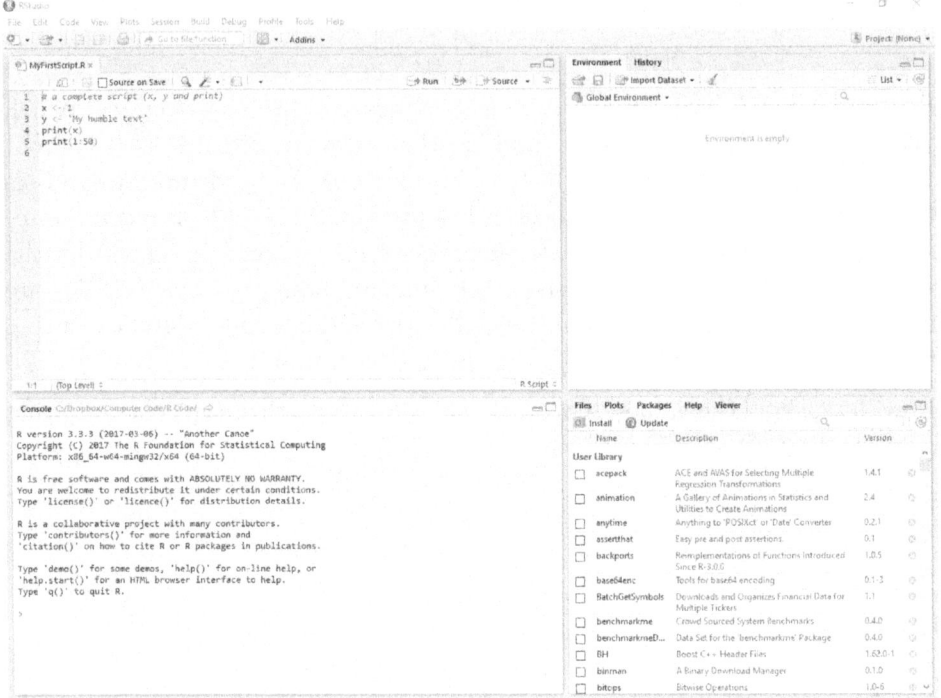

Figure 2.3: Example of an R script

After pasting all the commands in the editor, save the .R file to a personal folder where you have read and write permissions. In Windows, one possibility is to save it in the `My Documents` folder with a name like `'my_first_script.R'`. This saved file, which at the moment does nothing special, records the steps of a simple algorithm that creates several objects and shows their content. In the future, this file can take an expressive size by containing all stages of the data analysis such as importing data, cleaning it, performing the data analysis and exporting tables and figures.

2.6.1 RStudio shortcuts

In RStudio, there are some predefined and time-saving shortcuts for running code from the editor. To execute an entire script, simply press **control +**

2.6. RUNNING SCRIPTS FROM RSTUDIO

shift + s. This is the *source* command. With RStudio open, I suggest testing this key combination and checking how the code saved in a *.R* file is executed. The output of the script is shown in the prompt of R. The result in RStudio should look like Figure 2.4.

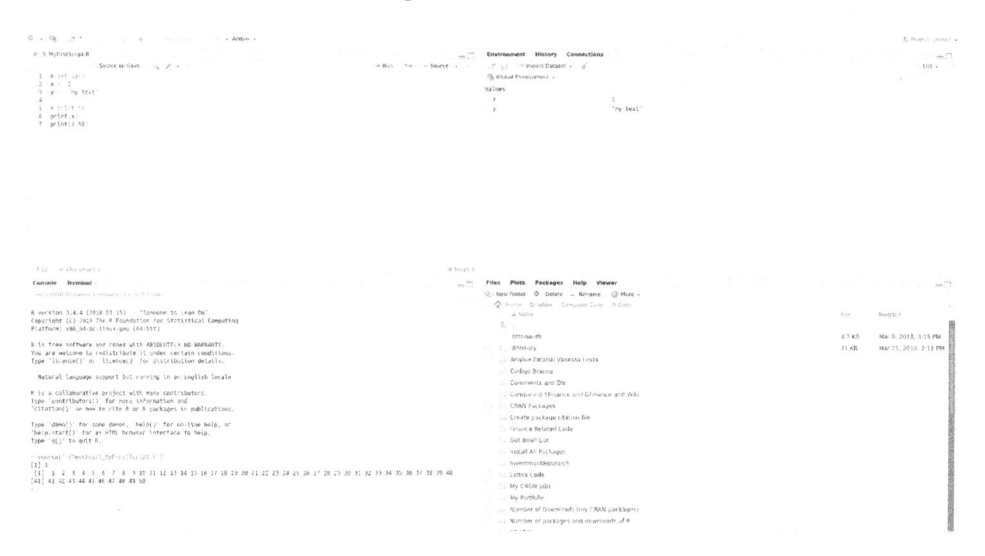

Figure 2.4: Example of a R script after execution

Another way of executing code is with the shortcut **control + enter**, which will only execute the line where the cursor is located. This shortcut is very useful in developing scripts because it allows each line of the code to be tested. As an example of usage, point the cursor to the `print(x)` line and press *control + enter*. As you will notice, only the line `print(x)` was executed and the cursor moves to the next line. Therefore, before running the whole script, you can test it line by line and check for possible errors.

Next, I highlight these and other RStudio shortcuts, which are also very useful.

control + shift + s executes (source) the current RStudio file;
control + shift + enter executes the current file with echo, showing the commands on the prompt;
control + enter executes the selected line, showing on-screen commands;
control + shift + b executes the codes from the beginning of the file to the cursor's location;
control + shift + e executes the codes of the lines where the cursor is until the end of the file.

I suggest using these shortcuts from day one, creating a healthy habit. Those who like to use the *mouse*, an alternate way to execute code is to click the *source* button in the upper-right corner of the code editor.

If you want to run code in a *.R* file within another *.R* file, you can use the `source` command. For example, imagine that you have the main script with your data analysis and another script that performs some support operation such as importing data to R. These operations have been dismembered as a way of organizing the code.

To run the support *script*, just call it with function `source` in the main script, as in the following code:

```
# execute import script
source('import-data.R')
```

Here, all code in `import-data.R` will be executed. This equals manually opening file `import-data.R` and hitting *control + shift + s*.

It's worth knowing that you can set your own shortcuts. For that, search for the "Tools" option in the Rstudio's navigation bar and click on "Modify Keyboard Shortcuts".

2.7 Testing and Debugging Code

Developing code follows a cycle. At first, you will write a command line on a script, try it using *control + enter* and check the output. A new line of code is written once the previous line worked as expected. A moving cycle is clear, writing code is followed by line execution, followed by result checking, modify and repeat if necessary. This is a normal and expected process. You need to make sure that every line of code is correctly specified before moving to the next one.

When trying to find an error in a preexisting script, R offers some tools for controlling and assessing its execution. This is especially useful when you have a long and complicated script. The simplest and easiest tool that R and RStudio offer is code breakpoint. In RStudio, you can click on the left side of the script editor and a red circle will appear, as in Figure 2.5.

This red circle indicates a flag that will force the code to stop at that line. You can use it to test existing code and check its objects at a certain part of the execution. Pausing the code at a certain point might seem strange for a starting programmer but, for large scripts, with many functions and complex code, it is a necessity. When the execution hits the breakpoint,

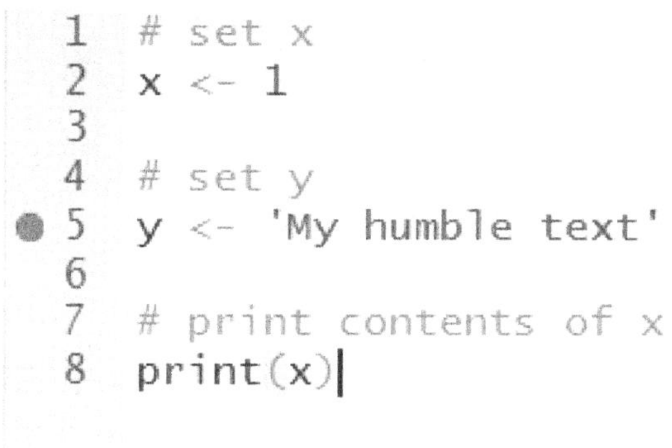

2.8. CREATING SIMPLE OBJECTS

```
1   # set x
2   x <- 1
3
4   # set y
5   y <- 'My humble text'
6
7   # print contents of x
8   print(x)
```

Figure 2.5: Example of breakpoint in an R script

the prompt will change to `Browse[1]>` and you'll be able to try new code and verify the content of all current objects. From the Console, you have the option to continue the execution to the next breakpoint or stop it. The same result can be achieved using a function `browser`. Have a look:

```
# set x
x <- 1

# set y
y <- 'My humble text'

browser()

# print contents of x
print(x)
```

The practical result is the same as using RStudio's red circle, but it gives you more control for the case of several commands in the same line.

2.8 Creating Simple Objects

One of the most basic and most used commands in R is the creation of objects. As shown in previous sections, you can define an object using the `<-` command, which is verbally translated to *assign*. For example, consider the following code:

```
# set x
x <- 123

# set my_x, my_y and my_z in one line
my_x <- 1; my_y <- 2; my_z <- 3
```

We can read this code as *the value 123 is assigned to x*. The direction of the arrow defines where the value is stored. For example, using `123 -> x` also works, although this is not recommended as the code becomes less readable. Moreover, notice that you can create objects within the same line by separating the commands using a semi-colon.

Using an arrow symbol `<-` for object definition is specific to R. The reason for this choice was that, at the time of conception of the *S* language, keyboards had a specific key that directly defined the arrow symbol. This means that the programmer only had to hit one key in the keyboard to set the *assign* symbol. Modern keyboards, however, are different. If you find it troublesome to use this symbol, you can use a shortcut as well. In *Windows*, the shortcut for the symbol `<-` is `alt` plus `-`.

Most programming languages uses a equality symbol (=) to define objects and, often, this creates confusion. When using R, you can also define objects with =, as in `x = 123`, however, no one should ever recommend it. The equality symbol has a special use within an R code as it defines function arguments, as in `my_1 <- fct(arg1 = 1, arg2 = 3)`. For now, just remember to use `<-` for defining objects. We will learn more about functions and using the equality symbol in a future chapter.

The name of the object is important in R. With the exception of very specific cases, the user can name objects as he likes. This freedom, however, can work against you. It is desirable to set short object names that make sense to the content of the script and which are simple to understand. This facilitates the understanding of the code by other users and is part of the suggested set of rules for structuring code. Note that all objects created in this book have nomenclature in English and specific format, where the white space between nouns are replaced by an underscore, as in `my_x <- 1` and `name_of_file <- 'my_data_file.csv'`. We will get back at code structure in chapter 13.

R executes the code looking for objects available in the environment, including functions. You also need to be aware that R is case sensitive. Likewise, object `m` differs from `M`. If we try to access an object that does not exist, R will return an error message and halt the execution of the rest of the code. Have a look:

2.9. CREATING VECTORS

```
print(z)
```

```
R> Error in print(z): object 'z' not found
```

The error occurred because the object z does not exist in the current environment. If we create a variable z as z <- 321 and repeat the command print(z), we will not have the same error message.

2.9 Creating Vectors

In the previous examples, we created simple objects such as x <- 1 and x <- 'ABC'. While this is sufficient to demonstrate the basic commands in R, in practice, such commands are very limited. A real problem of data analysis will certainly have a greater volume of information.

When we gather many elements of the same class, such as numeric, into a single object, the result is an atomic vector. An example would be the representation of a series of daily stock prices as an atomic vector of the class numeric. Once you have a vector, you can manipulate it any way you want.

Atomic vectors are created in R using the c command, which comes from the verb *combine*. For example, if we want to combine the values 1, 2 and 3 in a single object, we can do it with the following command:

```
# create numeric atomic vector
x <- c(1, 2, 3)

# print it
print(x)
```

```
R> [1] 1 2 3
```

The c command works the same way for any other class of object, such as *character*:

```
# create character atomic vector
y <- c('text 1', 'text 2', 'text 3', 'text 4')

# print it
print(y)
```

```
R> [1] "text 1" "text 2" "text 3" "text 4"
```

The only restriction on the use of the c command is that all elements must have the same class. If we insert data from different classes in a call to c(), R will try to mutate all elements into the same class following its own logic. If the conversion of all elements to a single class is not possible, an error message is returned. Note the following example, where numeric values are set in the first and second element of x and a character in the last element.

```
# a mixed vector
x <- c(1, 2, '3')

# print result of forced conversion
print(x)
```

```
R> [1] "1" "2" "3"
```

The values of x are all of type character. The use of class command confirms this result:

```
# print class of x
class(x)
```

```
R> [1] "character"
```

2.10 Knowing Your Environment and Objects

After using various commands, further development of an R script requires you to understand what objects are available and if their content is as expected. You can find this information simply by looking at the *environment* tab in the upper right corner of RStudio. However, there is a command that shows the same information in the prompt. In order to know what objects are currently available in R's memory, you can use the command ls. Note the following example:

2.10. KNOWING YOUR ENVIRONMENT AND OBJECTS

```
# set some objects
x <- 1
y <- 2
z <- 3

# print all objects in the environment
print(ls())
```

```
R> [1] "x" "y" "z"
```

Objects x, y and z were created and are available in the current working environment. If we had other objects, they would also appear in the output to ls.

To display the content of each object, just enter the names of objects and press **enter** in the *prompt*:

```
# print objects by their name
x
```

```
R> [1] 1
```

```
y
```

```
R> [1] 2
```

```
z
```

```
R> [1] 3
```

Typing the object name on the screen has the same effect as using the print command. In fact, when executing the sole name of a variable in the prompt or script, R internally passes the object to the print function.

In R, all objects belong to a class. As previously mentioned, to find the class of an object, simply use the class function. In the following example, x is an object of the class numeric, y is a text (character) object and fct_example is a function object.

```r
# set objects
x <- 1
y <- 'a'
fct_example <- function(){}

# print their classes
print(class(x))
```

```
R> [1] "numeric"
```

```r
print(class(y))
```

```
R> [1] "character"
```

```r
print(class(fct_example))
```

```
R> [1] "function"
```

Another way to learn more about an object is to check its textual representation. Every object in R has this property and we can find it with function `str`:

```r
# set vec
x <- 1:10
# print the textual representation of a vector
print(str(x))
```

```
R>  int [1:10] 1 2 3 4 5 6 7 8 9 10
R> NULL
```

We find that object `x` is a vector of class `int` (integer). Function `str` is particularly useful when trying to understand the details of a more complex object, such as a `dataframe` or a `list`.

2.11 Displaying and Formatting Output

You can show the value of an R object on the screen in two ways. You can either enter its name in the prompt or use the `print` function. Explaining it further, the `print` function focuses on the presentation of objects and can be customized for any type. For example, if we had an object of a class called `My_Table` to represent a specific type of table, we could create a function called `print.My_Table` that would show a table on the screen with a special format for the rows and column names. Function `print`, therefore, is oriented towards presenting objects and the user can customize it for different classes. The `base` package, which is automatically initialized with R, contains several `print` functions for various kinds of objects, such as `numeric` and `character`.

However, there are other specific functions to display text in the prompt. The main one is `cat` (*concatenate and print*). This function takes a text as input, processes it for specific symbols and displays the result on the screen. Function `cat` is far more powerful and customizable than `print`.

For example, if we wanted to show the text, The value of x is equal to 2 on-screen using a numerical object, we could do it as follows:

```
# set x
x <- 2

# print customized message
cat('The value of x is', x)
```

```
R> The value of x is 2
```

You can also customize the screen output using specific commands. For example, if we wanted to break a line in the screen output, we could do it through the use of the reserved character \n:

```
# set text with break line
my_text <- ' First Line,\n Second line'

# print it
cat(my_text)
```

```
R>  First Line,
R>  Second line
```

Note that the use of `print` would not result in the same effect as this command displays the text as it is, without processing it for specific symbols:

```
print(my_text)
```

```
R> [1] " First Line,\n Second line"
```

Another example in the use of specific commands for text is to add a *tab* space with the symbol `\t`. See an example next:

```r
# set text with tab
my_text <- 'before-> \t inside \t <-after'

# concatenate and print it!
cat(my_text)
```

```
R> before->        inside        <-after
```

We've only scratched the surface of the possible ways to manipulate text output. More details are found in the official R manual[4].

2.11.1 Customizing the Output

Another way to customize text output is by using specific functions to manipulate objects of class `character`. For that, there are two very useful functions: `paste` and `format`.

Function `paste` *glues* a series of character objects. It is a very useful function and will be used intensively for the rest of the examples in this book. Consider the following example:

```r
# set some text objects
my_text_1 <- 'I am a text'
my_text_2 <- 'very beautiful'
my_text_3 <- 'and informative.'

# paste all objects together and print
cat(paste(my_text_1, my_text_2, my_text_3))
```

---

[4]https://cran.r-project.org/doc/manuals/R-lang.html#Literal-constants

2.11. DISPLAYING AND FORMATTING OUTPUT

```
R> I am a text very beautiful and informative.
```

The previous result is not far from what we did in the example with the `print` function. Note, however, that the `paste` function adds a space between each text. If we did not want this space, we could use the function `paste0` as in:

```
# example of paste0
cat(paste0(my_text_1, my_text_2, my_text_3))
```

```
R> I am a textvery beautifuland informative.
```

Another very useful possibility with the `paste` function is to insert a text or symbol between the junction of texts. For example, if we wanted to add a comma (,) between each item to be pasted, we could do this by using the input option `sep` as follows:

```
# example using the argument sep
cat(paste(my_text_1, my_text_2, my_text_3, sep = ', '))
```

```
R> I am a text, very beautiful, and informative.
```

If we had an atomic vector with all elements to be glued in a single object, we could achieve the same result using the `collapse` argument. See an example next.

```
# set character object
my_text <-c('I am a text', 'very beautiful', 'and informative.')

# example of using the collapse argument in paste
cat(paste(my_text, collapse = ', '))
```

```
R> I am a text, very beautiful, and informative.
```

Another key feature of the `paste` command is that also works for vectors. For example, let's say I needed to create a series of text objects containing the phrase "My value is equal to X", where "X" goes from 1 to 10. We can do the following:

```
# set size and vector
my_size <- 10
my_vec <- 1:my_size

# define string vector
my_str <- paste0('My value is equal to ', my_vec)

# print it
print(my_str)
```

```
R>  [1] "My value is equal to 1"
R>  [2] "My value is equal to 2"
R>  [3] "My value is equal to 3"
R>  [4] "My value is equal to 4"
R>  [5] "My value is equal to 5"
R>  [6] "My value is equal to 6"
R>  [7] "My value is equal to 7"
R>  [8] "My value is equal to 8"
R>  [9] "My value is equal to 9"
R> [10] "My value is equal to 10"
```

Going forward, command `format` is used to format numbers and dates. It is especially useful when we want to represent numbers in a more visually appealing way. By definition, R presents a set number of digits after the decimal point:

```
# example of decimal points in R
cat(1/3)
```

```
R> 0.3333333
```

If we wanted only two digits on the screen, we could use the following code:

```
# example of using the format on numerical objects
cat(format(1/3, digits=2))
```

```
R> 0.33
```

Likewise, if we wanted to use a scientific format in the display, we could do the following:

2.12. FINDING THE SIZE OF OBJECTS

```
# example of using a scientific format
cat(format(1/3, scientific=TRUE))
```

R> 3.333333e-01

Function `format` has many more options. If you need your numbers to come out in a specific way, have a look at the help manual for this function. It is also a generic function and can be used for many types of objects.

This section only covers a small part of string manipulation. We will study it more deeply in chapter 7.

2.12 Finding the Size of Objects

In R, an object size can mean different things but most likely it is defined as the number of individual elements that constitute the object. This information serves not only to assist the programmer in checking possible code errors but also to know the length of iteration procedures such as *loops*, which will be treated in a later chapter of this book.

In R, the size of an object can be checked with the use of four main functions: `length`, `nrow`, `ncol` and `dim`.

Function `length` is intended for objects with a single dimension, such as atomic vectors:

```
# create atomic vector
x <- c(2, 3, 3, 4, 2,1)

# get length of x
n <- length(x)

# display message
cat('The length of x is ', n)
```

R> The length of x is 6

For objects with more than one dimension, such as a matrix, use functions `nrow`, `ncol` and `dim` (dimension) to find the number of rows (first dimension) and the number of columns (second dimension). See the difference in usage below.

```
# create a matrix
M <- matrix(1:20, nrow = 4, ncol = 5)

# print matrix
print(M)
```

```
R>       [,1] [,2] [,3] [,4] [,5]
R> [1,]    1    5    9   13   17
R> [2,]    2    6   10   14   18
R> [3,]    3    7   11   15   19
R> [4,]    4    8   12   16   20
```

```
# calculate size in different ways
my_nrow <- nrow(M)
my_ncol <- ncol(M)
my_n_elements <- length(M)

# display message
cat('The number of lines in M is ', my_nrow)
```

```
R> The number of lines in M is  4
```

```
cat('The number of columns in M is ', my_ncol)
```

```
R> The number of columns in M is  5
```

```
cat('The number of elements in M is ', my_n_elements)
```

```
R> The number of elements in M is  20
```

The `dim` function shows the dimension of the object, resulting in a numeric vector as output. This function should be used when the object has more than two dimensions. In practice, however, such cases are rare as most data-related problems can be solved with a bi-dimensional representation. An example is given next:

2.12. FINDING THE SIZE OF OBJECTS

```
# get dimension of M
my_dim <- dim(M)

# print it
print(my_dim)
```

R> [1] 4 5

In the case of objects with more than two dimensions, we can use the `array` function to create the object and `dim` to find its size. Have a look at the next example:

```
# create an array with three dimensions
my_array <- array(1:9, dim = c(3, 3, 3))

# print it
print(my_array)
```

```
R> , , 1
R>
R>      [,1] [,2] [,3]
R> [1,]    1    4    7
R> [2,]    2    5    8
R> [3,]    3    6    9
R>
R> , , 2
R>
R>      [,1] [,2] [,3]
R> [1,]    1    4    7
R> [2,]    2    5    8
R> [3,]    3    6    9
R>
R> , , 3
R>
R>      [,1] [,2] [,3]
R> [1,]    1    4    7
R> [2,]    2    5    8
R> [3,]    3    6    9
```

```r
# display its dimensions
print(dim(my_array))
```

```
R> [1] 3 3 3
```

An important note here is that **the use of functions `length`, `nrow`, `dim` and `ncol` are not intended to discover the number of letters in a text**. This is a common mistake and you should be aware of it. For example, if we had a `character` type of object and we use the `length` function, the result would be the following:

```r
# set text object
my_char <- 'abcde'

# print result of length
print(length(my_char))
```

```
R> [1] 1
```

This occurred because the `length` function returns the number of elements in an object. In this case, `my_char` has only one element. To find out the number of characters in the object, we use the `nchar` function as follows:

```r
# find the number of characters in an character object
print(nchar(my_char))
```

```
R> [1] 5
```

2.13 Selecting Elements from an Atomic Vector

After creating an atomic vector of a class, it is possible that the user is interested in only one or more elements of it. For example, if we were updating the value of an investment portfolio, our interest is only for the latest price of the stocks. All values from other dates are not relevant to our analysis and therefore could be safely ignored.

The selection of *pieces* of an atomic vector is called indexing and it is accomplished with the use of square brackets (`[ ]`). Consider the following example:

2.13. SELECTING ELEMENTS FROM AN ATOMIC VECTOR

```
# set x
my_x <- c(1, 5, 4, 3, 2, 7, 3.5, 4.3)
```

If we wanted only the third element of my_x, we use the bracket operator as follows:

```
# get the third element of x
elem_x <- my_x[3]

# print it
print(elem_x)
```

```
R> [1] 4
```

Indexing also works using vectors containing the desired locations. If we are only interested in the last and penultimate values of my_x, we use the following code:

```
# set vector with indices
my_idx <-  (length(my_x)-1):length(my_x)

# get last and penultimate value of my_x
piece_x_1 <- my_x[my_idx]

# print it
print(piece_x_1)
```

```
R> [1] 3.5 4.3
```

A cautionary note: **a unique property of the R language is that if a non-existing element of an object is accessed, the program returns the value NA (*not available*)**. See the next example code, where we attempt to obtain the fourth value of a vector with only three components.

```
# set object
my_vec <- c(1, 2, 3)

# print non-existing fourth element
print(my_vec[4])
```

```
R> [1] NA
```

This is important because NA elements are contagious. That is, anything that interacts with NA will also become NA. The lack of treatment of these errors can lead to problems that are difficult to identify. In other programming languages, attempting to access non-existing elements generally returns an error and cancels the execution of the rest of the code. In the case of R, given that access to non-existent elements does not generate an error or *warning* message, it is possible that this will create a problem in other parts of the script due to the cascade effect: anything that interacts with an NA value will turn into another NA. **You should always pay attention every time that NA values are found unexpectedly**. A manual inspection in the length and indexation of vectors may be required.

The use of indices is very useful when you are looking for items of a vector that satisfy some condition. For example, if we wanted to find out all values in my_x that are greater than 3, we could use the following command:

```
# find all values in my_x that is greater than 3
piece_x_2 <- my_x[my_x>3]

# print it
print(piece_x_2)
```

```
R> [1] 5.0 4.0 7.0 3.5 4.3
```

It is also possible to index elements by more than one condition using the logical operators & and | (*or*). For example, if we wanted the values of my_x greater than 2 **and** lower than 4, we could use the following command:

```
# find all values of my_x that are greater than 2 and lower then 4
piece_x_3 <- my_x[ (my_x > 2) & (my_x < 4) ]
print(piece_x_3)
```

```
R> [1] 3.0 3.5
```

Likewise, if we wanted all items that are lower than 3 **or** greater than 6, we use:

2.13. SELECTING ELEMENTS FROM AN ATOMIC VECTOR

```r
# find all values of my_x that are lower than 3 or higher than 6
piece_x_4 <- my_x[ (my_x < 3) | (my_x > 6) ]

# print it
print(piece_x_4)
```

```
R> [1] 1 2 7
```

Moreover, logic indexing also works with the interaction of different objects. That is, we can use a logical condition in one object to select items from another:

```r
# set my_x and my.y
my_x <- c(1, 4, 6, 8, 12)
my_y <- c(-2, -3, 4, 10, 14)

# find all elements of my_x where my.y is higher than 0
my_piece_x <- my_x[my_y > 0 ]

# print it
print(my_piece_x)
```

```
R> [1]  6  8 12
```

Looking more closely at the indexing process, it is worth noting that, when we use a data indexing condition, we are in fact creating a variable of the `logical` type. This object takes only two values: `TRUE` and `FALSE`. Have a look in the code presented next, where we create a `logical` object, print it and present its class.

```r
# create a logical object
my_logical <- my_y > 0

# print it
print(my_logical)
```

```
R> [1] FALSE FALSE  TRUE  TRUE  TRUE
```

```
# find its class
class(my_logical)
```

```
R> [1] "logical"
```

Logical objects are very useful whenever we are testing a particular condition on a data set. We will learn more about this and other basic classes in chapter 7.

2.14 Removing Objects from the Memory

After creating several variables, the R environment can become full of used and disposable content. In this case, it is desirable to clear the memory to erase objects that are no longer needed. Generally, this is accomplished at the beginning of a script, so that every time the script runs, the memory will be cleared before any calculation. In addition to cleaning the computer's memory, it also helps to avoid possible errors in the code. In most cases, cleaning the working environment should be performed only once at the beginning of the script.

For example, given an object x, we can delete it from memory with the command rm, as shown next:

```
# set x
x <- 1

# remove x
rm('x')
```

After executing the command rm('x'), the value of x is no longer available in the R session. In practical situations, however, it is desirable to clean up all the memory used by all objects created in R. We can achieve this goal with the following code:

```
rm(list = ls())
```

The term list in rm(list = ls()) is a function argument of rm that defines which objects will be deleted. The ls() command shows all the currently available objects. Therefore, by chaining together both commands, we erase

2.15 Displaying and Setting the Working Directory

all current objects available in the environment. As mentioned before, it is a good programming policy to clear the memory before running the script. However, you should only wipe out all of R's memory if you have already saved the results of interest or if you can replicate them.

Like other programming platforms, **R always works in a directory**. If no directory is set, a default value is used when R starts up. It is based on the working directory that R searches for files to load data or other R scripts. It is in this directory that R saves any output if we do not explicitly define a path on the computer. This output can be a graphic file, text or a spreadsheet. **It is a good programming policy is to change the working directory to the same place where the *script* is located**.

The simplest way of checking the current working directory is looking at RStudio's prompt panel. At the top, in a small font and just below the word "Console", you'll see the working path. Using code, we can check the current working directory with function `getwd`:

```
# get current dir
my_dir <- getwd()

# display it
print(my_dir)
```

```
R> C:/Dropbox/06-My Books/afedR-ed2/Book Content
```

The result of the previous code shows the folder in which this book was written and compiled. As you can see, the book files are saved in a subfolder of my Dropbox directory. From the path, you should also realize that I'm working in a Windows OS. The root directory `C:/` gives that information away.

The change of the working directory is performed with the `setwd` command. For example, if we wanted to change our working directory to *C:/My Research/*, simply type in the *prompt*:

```
# set where to change directory
my_d <- 'C:/My Research/'

# change it
setwd(my_d)
```

After changing the directory, importing and saving files in the *C:/My Research/* folder will be a lot easier.

As for simple cases such as the above, remembering the directory name is not difficult. In practical cases, however, the working directory can be in a deeper directory of the file system. A simple and very efficient way of setting the working directory is using the *autocomplete* feature of RStudio. Explained briefly, we can use the *tab* key in the keyboard to navigate the computer's folders within RStudio. Give it a try with the following steps:

1) Write command `setwd('')` in a script as it is, with an empty content for the inner character;

2) Place your cursor between the ' symbols;

3) Press the *tab* key.

Now you'll be able to see your folders in a small window and use the arrows and *enter* key to navigate. The autocomplete feature of RStudio goes much deeper than that. We will learn more about it in a future section of this chapter.

Another, more modern, way of setting the directory is to use the RStudio API package, which contains a set of functions that only work inside RStudio and provides information about current file, project and many more. To find out the path of the current R script being edited in RStudio and set the working directory to there, you can write:

```
my_path <- dirname(rstudioapi::getActiveDocumentContext()$path)
setwd(my_path)
```

This way, the script will change the directory to its own location, no matter where you copy it. Be aware, however, that this trick only works in RStudio's script editor and within a saved file. It will not work from the prompt.

Once you are working on the same path as the script, using relative paths is preferable. For example, if you are working in a folder that contains a subdirectory called `data`, you can enter this sub-folder with the code:

```
# change to subfolder
setwd('data')
```

Another possibility is to go to a previous level of the directory using .., as in:

```
# change to the previous level
setwd('..')
```

So, if you are working in directory `C:/My Research/` and execute the command `setwd('..')`, the current folder becomes `C:/`, which is one level below `C:/My Research/`.

2.16 Canceling Code Execution

Whenever R is running some code, a visual cue in the shape of a small red circle in the right corner of the *prompt* will appear. If you read it, the text shows the *stop* word. This button is not only an indicator of running code but also a shortcut for canceling its execution. Another way to cancel an execution is to point the mouse to the *prompt* and press the *escape (esc)* button from the keyboard.

To try it out, run the next chunk of code in RStudio and cancel its execution using *esc*.

```
for (i in 1:100) {
  cat('\nRunning code (please make it stop by hitting esc!)')
  Sys.sleep(1)
}
```

In the previous code, we used a `for` loop and function `Sys.sleep` to display the message `'\nRunning code (please make it stop by hitting ESC!)'` one hundred times, every second. For now, do not worry about the code and functions used in the example. We will discuss the use of loops in chapter 8.

2.17 Code Comments

In R, comments are set using the hashtag symbol `#`. Anything after this symbol will not be processed by R. This gives you the freedom to write whatever you want within the script. An example:

```
# this is a comment (R will not parse it)
# this is another comment (R will again not parse it)

x <- 'abc' # this is an inline comment
```

Comments are an effective way to communicate any important information that cannot be directly inferred from the code. In general, you should avoid using comments that are too obvious or too generic:

```
# read CSV file
df <- read.csv('data/data_file.csv')
```

As you can see, it is quite obvious from the line `df <- read.csv('..')` that the code is reading a .csv file. The name of the function already states that. So, the comment was not a good one as it did not add any new information to the user. A better approach at commenting would be to set the author, description of the script and better explain the origin and last update of the data file. Have a look:

```
# Script for reproducing the results of JOHN (2019)
# Author: Mr data analyst (dontspamme@emailprovider.com)
# Last script update: 2020-01-10
#
# File downloaded from www.site.com/data-files/data_file.csv
# The description of the data goes here
# Last file update: 2020-01-10

df <- read.csv('data/data_file.csv')
```

So, by reading the comments, the user will know the purpose of the script, who wrote it and the date of the last edit. It also includes the origin of the data file and the date of the latest update. If the user wants to update the data, all he has to do is go to the referred website and download the new file.

Another productive use of comments is to set sections in the code, such as in:

```
# Script for reproducing the results of JOHN (2019)
# Author: Mr data analyst (dontspamme@emailprovider.com)
# Last script update: 2020-01-10
```

```
#
# File downloaded from www.site.com/data-files/data_file.csv
# The description of the data goes here
# Last file update: 2020-01-10

# Clean data ------------------------
# - remove outliers
# - remove unnecessary columns

# Create descriptive tables ----------


# Estimate models --------------------


# Report results ---------------------
```

The use of a long line of dashes (-) at each section of the code is intentional. It causes RStudio to identify and bookmark the sections, with a link to them at the bottom of the script editor. Test it yourself, copy and paste the above code into a new R script, save it, and you'll see that the sections appear on a button between the editor and the prompt. Such a shortcut can save plenty of time in lengthy scripts.

If you share code with other people, you'll soon realize that comments are essential and expected. They help transmit information that is not available from the code. This is one way of a discerning novice from experienced programmers, the later is always very communicative in its comments (sometimes too much!).

A note here, throughout the book you'll see that the code comments are, most of the time, a bit obvious. This was intentional as clear and direct messages are important for new users, which is part of the audience of this book.

2.18 Looking for Help

A common task in the use of R is to seek help. Even advanced users often seek instructions on specific tasks, whether it is to better understand the details of some functions or simply to study a new procedure. The use of the R help system is part of the everyday routine with the software and you should master it as soon as possible.

You can get help by using the *help* panel in RStudio or directly from the *prompt*. Simply enter the question mark next to the object on which you want help, as in `?mean`. In this case, object `means` is a function and the use of the `help` command will open a panel on the right side of RStudio.

In R, the help screen of a function is the same as shown in Figure 2.6. It presents a general description of the function, explains its input arguments and the format of the output. The help screen follows with references and suggestions for other related functions. More importantly, examples of usage are given last and can be copied to the prompt or script in order to accelerate the learning process.

---

mean {base}   R Documentation

Arithmetic Mean

Description

Generic function for the (trimmed) arithmetic mean.

Usage

```
mean(x, ...)

## Default S3 method:
mean(x, trim = 0, na.rm = FALSE, ...)
```

Arguments

- x   An R object. Currently there are methods for numeric/logical vectors and date, date-time and time interval objects. Complex vectors are allowed for `trim = 0`, only.
- trim   the fraction (0 to 0.5) of observations to be trimmed from each end of x before the mean is computed. Values of trim outside that range are taken as the nearest endpoint.
- na.rm   a logical value indicating whether NA values should be stripped before the computation proceeds.

Figure 2.6: Help screen for function mean

If we are looking for help for a given text and not a function name, we can use double question marks as in `??"standard deviation"`. This operation will search for the occurrence of the term in all packages of R and it is very useful to learn how to perform a particular task. In this case, we looked for the available functions to calculate the standard deviation of a vector.

As a suggestion, the easiest and most direct way to learn a new function is by trying out the examples in the manual. This way, you can see which type of input objects the function expects and what type of output it gives. Once you have it working, read the help screen to understand if it does exactly what you expected and what are the options for its use. If the function performs the desired procedure, you can copy and paste the example for your own *script*, adjusting where necessary.

Another very important source of help is the Internet itself. Sites like stackoverflow and specific *mailing lists* and blogs, whose content is also on the Internet, are a valuable source of information. If you find a problem that could not be solved by reading the standard help files, the next logical step is to seek a solution using your error message or the description of the problem in search engines. In many cases, your problem, no matter how specific it is, has already occurred and has been solved by other users. In fact, it is more surprising **not** to find the solution for a programming problem on the internet, than the other way around.

2.19 R Packages

One of the greatest benefits of using R is its package collection. A package is nothing more than a group of procedures aimed at solving a particular computational problem. R has at its core a collaborative philosophy. Users provide their codes for others to use. And, most importantly, **all packages are free**. For example, consider a case where the user is interested in accessing data about historical inflation in the USA. He can install and use an R module that is specifically designed for importing data from central banks and research agencies.

Every function in R belongs to a package. When R initializes, packages `stats`, `graphics`, `grDevices`, `utils`, `datasets`, `methods` and `base` are loaded by default. Almost every function we have used so far belongs to the package `base`. R packages can be accessed and installed from different sources. The main being **CRAN** (*The Comprehensive R Archive network*), and **Github**. It's worth knowing that the quantity and diversity of R packages increase every day.

CRAN is the official repository of R and it is built by the community. Anyone can send a package. However, there is an evaluation process to ensure that certain strict rules about code format and safety are respected. For those interested in creating and distributing packages, a clear and easy to learn the material on how to create and send packages to CRAN is presented on the site R packages[5]. Complete rules are available on the CRAN website[6].

The suitability of the code to CRAN standards is the developer's responsibility. My personal experience, sending and publishing a package on CRAN

---

[5] http://r-pkgs.had.co.nz/intro.html
[6] https://cran.r-project.org/web/packages/policies.html

demands a significant amount of work, especially in the first submission. After that, it becomes a lot easier. Don't be angry if your package is rejected. My own packages were rejected several times before entering CRAN. Listen to what the maintainers tell you and try fixing all problems before resubmitting. If you're having issues that you cannot solve or find a solution on the Internet, look for help in the R-packages mailing list[7]. You'll be surprised at how accessible and helpful the R community can be.

The complete list of packages available on CRAN, along with a brief description, can be accessed at the packages section of the R site[8]. A practical way to check if there is a package that does a specific procedure is to load the previous page and search in your *browser* for a keyword of interest (e.g. "SEC data"). If there is a package that does what you want, it is very likely that the keyword is used in the description field.

Another important source for finding packages is the CRAN Task Views[9]. There you can find the collection of noteworthy packages for a given area of expertise. See the *Task Views* screen in Figure 2.7.

	CRAN Task Views
Bayesian	Bayesian Inference
ChemPhys	Chemometrics and Computational Physics
ClinicalTrials	Clinical Trial Design, Monitoring, and Analysis
Cluster	Cluster Analysis & Finite Mixture Models
DifferentialEquations	Differential Equations
Distributions	Probability Distributions
Econometrics	Econometrics
Environmetrics	Analysis of Ecological and Environmental Data
ExperimentalDesign	Design of Experiments (DoE) & Analysis of Experimental Data
ExtremeValue	Extreme Value Analysis
Finance	Empirical Finance
Genetics	Statistical Genetics
Graphics	Graphic Displays & Dynamic Graphics & Graphic Devices & Visualization
HighPerformanceComputing	High-Performance and Parallel Computing with R
MachineLearning	Machine Learning & Statistical Learning
MedicalImaging	Medical Image Analysis
MetaAnalysis	Meta-Analysis
Multivariate	Multivariate Statistics
NaturalLanguageProcessing	Natural Language Processing
NumericalMathematics	Numerical Mathematics
OfficialStatistics	Official Statistics & Survey Methodology
Optimization	Optimization and Mathematical Programming
Pharmacokinetics	Analysis of Pharmacokinetic Data
Phylogenetics	Phylogenetics, Especially Comparative Methods
Psychometrics	Psychometric Models and Methods
ReproducibleResearch	Reproducible Research
Robust	Robust Statistical Methods

Figure 2.7: Task View screen

A popular alternative to CRAN is Github[10]. Unlike the former, Github imposes soft restrictions on the code and, because of this and its version control system, it is a popular choice by developers. In practice, it is very common for developers to maintain a development version on Github and the

---

[7]https://www.r-project.org/mail.html
[8]https://cran.r-project.org/web/packages/available_packages_by_date.html
[9]https://cran.r-project.org/web/views/
[10]https://github.com/

2.19. R PACKAGES

official version in CRAN. When the development version reaches a certain stage of maturity, it is then sent to CRAN.

The most interesting part of this is that the Github packages can be accessed and installed directly from the prompt using the internet. To find out the current amount of packages on CRAN, type and execute the following commands in the prompt:

```r
# get a matrix with available packages
df_cran_pkgs <- available.packages()

# find the number of packages
n_cran_packages <- nrow(df_cran_pkgs)

# print it
print(n_cran_packages)
```

```
R> [1] 15344
```

If you are wondering which package to use, simply select the one closest to you. Currently, 2020-02-08 17:46:43, there are 15344 packages available on the CRAN servers, a very impressive mark for the community of developers as a whole.

You can also check the amount of locally installed packages in R with the `installed.packages` command:

```r
# find number of packages currently installed
n_local_packages <- nrow(installed.packages())

# print it
print(n_local_packages)
```

```
R> [1] 451
```

In this case, the computer in which the book was written has 451 packages currently installed. Notice that, even as an experienced researcher and R programmer, I'm only using a small fraction of all packages available in CRAN! The number of installed packages is probably different from yours. Give it a try with the command `installed.packages()`!

2.19.1 Installing Packages from CRAN

To install a package, simply use the command `install.packages`. You only need to do it once for each new package. As an example, we will install a package called `readr` that will be used in future chapters. Note that we defined the package name in the installation as if it were text with the use of quotation marks (" ").

```
# install package readr
install.packages("readr")
```

That's it! After executing this simple command, package `readr` and all of its dependencies will be installed and the functions related to the package will be ready for use once the package is loaded in a script. If the installed package is dependent on another package, R detects this dependency and automatically installs the missing packages. Thus, all the requirements for using the installed package will already be satisfied and everything will work perfectly. It is possible, however, that a package has an external dependency. As an example, the package `RndTexExams` depends on the existence of a LaTeX installation. These cases are usually announced in the description of the package and an error informs that a requirement is missing. External dependencies for R packages are not common, but they do happen.

2.19.2 Installing Packages from Github

To install a package hosted in Github, you must first install the *devtools* package, available on CRAN:

```
# install devtools
install.packages('devtools')
```

After that, use the function `devtools::install_github` to install a package directly from Github. In the following example, we will install the development version of package `dplyr`:

```
# install ggplot2 from github
devtools::install_github("hadley/dplyr")
```

Note that the username of the developer is included in the input string. In this case, the *hadley* name belongs to the developer of `ggplot2`, Hadley Wickham. Throughout the book, you will notice that this name appears several times. Hadley is a prolific and competent developer of several popular R packages and currently works for RStudio.

2.19.3 Loading Packages

Within a script, use the function `library` to load a package, as in the following example.

```
# load package readr
library(readr)
```

After running this command, all functions of the package will be available to the user. In this case, it is not necessary to use " " to load the package. If the package you want to use is not available, R will throw an error message. See an example next, where we try to load a non-existing package called `unicorn`.

```
library(unicorn)
```

Remember this error message. It will appear every time a package is not found. If you got the same message when running code from this book, you need to check what are the required packages of the example and install them using `install.packages`, as in `install.packages('unicorn')`.

Alternatively, if you use a specific package function and do not want to load all functions from the same package, you can do it with the use of double colons::', as in the following example.

```
# example of using a function without loading package
fortunes::fortune(10)
```

```
R>
R> Overall, SAS is about 11 years behind R and S-Plus in
R> statistical capabilities (last year it was about 10
R> years behind) in my estimation.
R>    -- Frank Harrell (SAS User, 1969-1991)
R>       R-help (September 2003)
```

Here, we use function `fortune` from the package `fortunes`, which shows on screen a potentially funny phrase chosen from the R mailing list. For our example, we selected message number 10. One interesting use of the package `fortune` is to display a random joke every time R starts and, perhaps, lighten up your day. As mentioned before, R is fully customizable. You can find many tutorials on how to achieve this effect by searching on the web for "customizing R startup".

Another way of loading a package is by using the `require` function. A call to `require` has a different behavior than a call to `library`. Whenever you try to load an uninstalled package with the `library` function, it returns an error. This means that the script stops and no further code are evaluated. As for `require`, if a package is not found, it returns an object with value `FALSE` and the rest of the code is evaluated. So, in order to avoid code being executed without its explicit dependencies, it is best advised to always use `library` for loading packages in R scripts.

The use of `require` is left for loading up packages inside of functions. If you create a custom function that requires procedures from a particular package, you must load the package within the scope of the function. For example, see the following code, where we create a new function called `fct_example` that depends on the package `quantmod`:

```
fct_example <- function(x){

  require(quantmod)

    df <- getSymbols(x, auto.assign = F)
    return(df)
}
```

In this case, the first time that `fct_example` is called, it loads up the package `quantmod` and all of its functions. Using `require` inside a function is a good programming policy because the function becomes self-contained, making it easier to use it in the future. This was the first time where the complete definition of a function in R is presented. Do not worry about it for now. We will explain it further in chapter 8.

2.19.4 Upgrading Packages

Over time, it is natural that packages available on CRAN are upgraded to accommodate new features, correct bugs and adapt to changes. Thus, it is recommended that users update their installed packages to a new version over the internet. In R, this procedure is quite easy. A direct way of upgrading packages is to click the button *Update* located in the package panel, lower right corner of RStudio, as shown in Figure 2.8.

The user can also update packages through the prompt. Simply type command `update.packages()` and hit *enter*, as shown below.

2.20. USING CODE COMPLETION WITH TAB

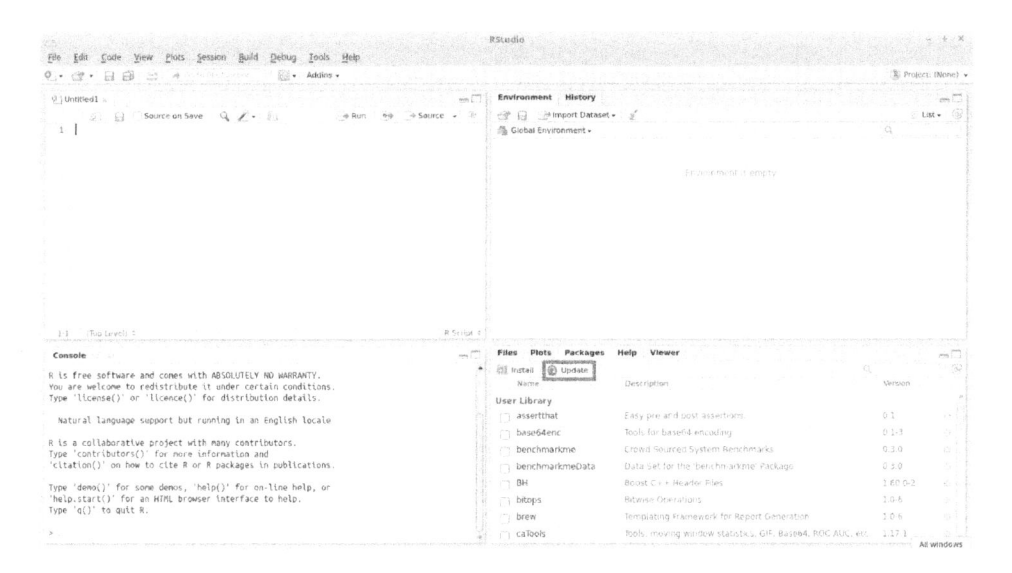

Figure 2.8: Updating R packages

```
# update all installed packages
update.packages()
```

The command `update.packages` compares the version of the installed packages with the versions available in CRAN. If it finds any difference, the new versions are downloaded and installed. After running the command, all packages will be synchronized with the versions available in CRAN.

2.20 Using Code Completion with *tab*

A very useful feature of RStudio is *code completion*. This is an editing tool that facilitates the search of object names, packages, function arguments, and files. Its usage is very simple. After you type any first letter in the keyboard, just press *tab* (left side of the keyboard, above *capslock*) and a number of options will appear. See Figure 2.9 where, after entering the *f* letter and pressing *tab*, a small window appears with a list of object names that begin with that letter.

The autocomplete feature is self-aware and will work differently depending on where it is called. As such, it works perfectly for searching for packages. For that, type `library()` in the prompt or editor, place the cursor in between the parentheses and press *tab*. The result should look something like Figure 2.10, shown next.

```
Type 'demo()' for some demos, 'help()' for on-line help, or
'help.start()' for an HTML browser interface to help.
Type 'q()' to quit R.

> f|
```

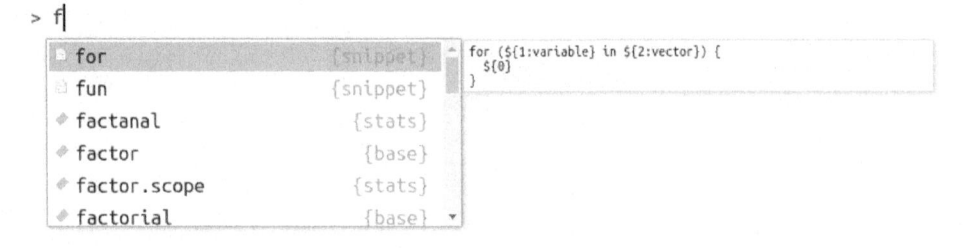

for	{snippet}
fun	{snippet}
factanal	{stats}
factor	{base}
factor.scope	{stats}
factorial	{base}

```
for (${1:variable} in ${2:vector}) {
    ${0}
}
```

Figure 2.9: Usage of autocomplete for object name

```
Type 'demo()' for some demos, 'help()' for on-line help, or
'help.start()' for an HTML browser interface to help.
Type 'q()' to quit R.

> library(r)
```

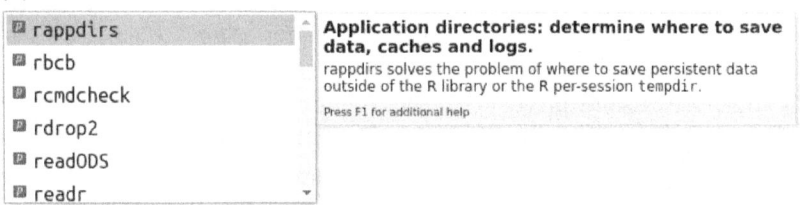

| rappdirs |
| rbcb |
| rcmdcheck |
| rdrop2 |
| readODS |
| readr |

Application directories: determine where to save data, caches and logs.
rappdirs solves the problem of where to save persistent data outside of the R library or the R per-session tempdir.
Press F1 for additional help

Figure 2.10: Usage of autocomplete for packages

2.20. USING CODE COMPLETION WITH TAB

Note that a description of the package or object is also offered by the code completion tool. This greatly facilitates the day to day work as the memorization of package names and R objects is not an easy task. The use of the *tab* decreases the time to look up names, also avoiding possible coding errors.

The use of this tool becomes even more beneficial when objects and functions are named with some sort of pattern. In the rest of the book, you will notice that objects tend to be named with the prefix *my*, as `my_x`, `my_num`, `my_df`. Using this naming rule (or any other) facilitates the lookup for the names of objects created by the user. You can just type `my_`, press *tab*, and a list of objects will appear.

As mentioned in the previous section, you can also find files and folders on your computer using *tab*. To try it, write the command `my_file <- ""` in the prompt or a script, point the cursor to the middle of the quotes and press the *tab* key. A screen with the files and folders from the current working directory should appear, as shown in Figure 2.11.

```
Type 'demo()' for some demos, 'help()' for on-line help, or
'help.start()' for an HTML browser interface to help.
Type 'q()' to quit R.

> my_file <- '|'
                01-CRAN Packages
                02-Finance Code
                03-Bibliometric Code
                04-Personal Code
                05-About R and others
                06-Unused and Old
```

Figure 2.11: Usage of autocomplete for files and folders

The use of autocomplete is also possible for finding the name and description of function arguments. To try it out, write `cat()` and place the mouse cursor inside the parentheses. After that, press *tab*. The result should be similar to Figure 2.12. By using *tab* inside of a function, we have the names of all arguments and their description – a mirror of the information found in the help files.

Likewise, you can also search for a function within a package with *tab*. For that, simply type the name of the package followed by two commas, as in

```
Type 'demo()' for some demos, 'help()' for on-line help, or
'help.start()' for an HTML browser interface to help.
Type 'q()' to quit R.

> cat()
```

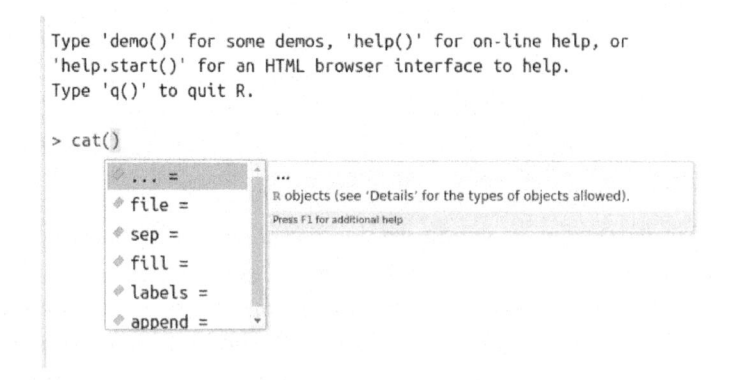

Figure 2.12: Usage of autocomplete for function arguments

`readr::`, and press *tab*. The result should be similar to Figure 2.13

```
Type 'demo()' for some demos, 'help()' for on-line help, or
'help.start()' for an HTML browser interface to help.
Type 'q()' to quit R.

> readr::
```

Figure 2.13: Usage of autocomplete for finding functions within a package

Summing up, using code completion will make you more productive. You'll find names of files, objects, arguments, and packages much faster. Use it as much as you can and form a habit out of it.

2.21 Interacting with Files and the Operating System

As you are learning R, soon enough you'll find a data-related problem with a demand for interacting with files on the computer, either by creating new folders, decompressing and compressing files, listing and removing files from the hard drive of the computer or any other type of operation. R has full support for such type of operation. You can pretty much automate any type of computer task if so needed.

2.21.1 Listing Files and Folders

To list files from your computer, use function `list.files`, where the `path` argument sets the directory to list the files from. For the compilation of the book, I've created a directory called *data*. This folder contains all the data needed to recreate the book's examples. You can check the files in the sub-folder `data` with the following code:

```
# list files in data folder
my_files <- list.files(path = "data", full.names = TRUE)
print(my_files)
```

```
R>   [1] "data/batchgetsymbols_parallel_example.rds"
R>   [2] "data/BGS_Cache"
R>   [3] "data/FileWithLatinChar_ISO-8859-9.txt"
R>   [4] "data/FileWithLatinChar_UTF-8.txt"
R>   [5] "data/Financial Sample.xlsx"
R>   [6] "data/grunfeld.csv"
R>   [7] "data/MySQLiteDatabase.SQLITE"
R>   [8] "data/pride_and_prejudice.txt"
R>   [9] "data/SP500_Excel.xlsx"
R>  [10] "data/SP500_long_yearly_2010-01-01_2019-11-04.rds"
R>  [11] "data/SP500-Stocks_long.csv"
R>  [12] "data/SP500-Stocks_wide.csv"
R>  [13] "data/SP500-Stocks-WithRet.rds"
R>  [14] "data/SP500.csv"
R>  [15] "data/SQLite_db.SQLITE"
R>  [16] "data/temp_file.xlsx"
R>  [17] "data/temp_fst.fst"
R>  [18] "data/temp_rds.rds"
R>  [19] "data/temp_writexl.xlsx"
R>  [20] "data/temp_xlsx.xlsx"
R>  [21] "data/temp.csv"
R>  [22] "data/temp.fst"
R>  [23] "data/temp.RData"
R>  [24] "data/temp.rds"
R>  [25] "data/temp.txt"
R>  [26] "data/temp.xlsx"
R>  [27] "data/top25babynames-by-sex-2005-2017.csv"
R>  [28] "data/UCI_Credit_Card.csv"
```

There are several files with different extensions in this directory. These files contain data that will be used in future chapters. When using `list.files`, it is recommended to set input `full.names` as TRUE. This option makes sure that the names returned by the function contain the full path. It facilitates further manipulation, such as reading and importing information from data files. It is worth noting that you can also list the files recursively, that is, list all files from all sub-folders contained in the original address. To check it, try using the following code in your computer:

```
# list all files for all subfolders (IT MAY TAKE SOME TIME...)
list.files(path = getwd(), recursive = T, full.names = TRUE)
```

The previous command will list all files in the current folder and sub-folders. Depending on the current working directory, it may take some time to run it all. If you executed it, be patient or just cancel it pressing *esc* in your keyboard.

To list folders (directories) on your computer, use the command `list.dirs`. See below.

```
# store names of directories
my_dirs <- list.dirs(recursive = F)

# print it
print(my_dirs)
```

```
R>  [1] "./_book"              "./_bookdown_files"
R>  [3] "./.Rproj.user"        "./afedR_ed_02_cache"
R>  [5] "./afedR_ed_02_files"  "./BGS_Cache"
R>  [7] "./css"                "./data"
R>  [9] "./ebook files"        "./eqs"
R> [11] "./fig_ggplot"         "./figs"
R> [13] "./ftp files"          "./GetEdgarData-cache"
R> [15] "./html code"          "./images"
R> [17] "./latex"              "./many_datafiles"
R> [19] "./many_datafiles_2"   "./mem_cache"
R> [21] "./Other chapters"     "./quandl_cache"
R> [23] "./Scripts"            "./simfin_cache"
R> [25] "./tabs"
```

The command `list.dirs(recursive = F)` listed all directories of the current path without recursion. The output shows the directories used to write the book. It includes the output directory of the book (`./_book`), the directory with the data (`./data`), among others. In this same directory, you can

2.21. INTERACTING WITH FILES AND THE OPERATING SYSTEM

find the chapters of the book, organized by files and based on the *RMarkdown* language (`.Rmd` file extension). To list only files with the extension `.Rmd`, we can use the `pattern` input in function `list.files` as follows:

```
# list all files with the extension .Rmd
list.files(pattern = "*.Rmd")
```

```
R>   [1] "_Welcome.Rmd"
R>   [2] "00a-About-new-edition.Rmd"
R>   [3] "00b-Preface.Rmd"
R>   [4] "01-Introduction.Rmd"
R>   [5] "02-Basic-operations.Rmd"
R>   [6] "03-Research-scripts.Rmd"
R>   [7] "04-Importing-exporting-local.Rmd"
R>   [8] "05-Importing-internet.Rmd"
R>   [9] "06-Data-structure-objects.Rmd"
R>  [10] "07-Basic-objects.Rmd"
R>  [11] "08-Programming.Rmd"
R>  [12] "09-Cleaning-data.Rmd"
R>  [13] "10-Figures.Rmd"
R>  [14] "11-Models.Rmd"
R>  [15] "12-Reporting-results.Rmd"
R>  [16] "13-Optimizing-code.Rmd"
R>  [17] "14-References.Rmd"
R>  [18] "afedR_ed_02.Rmd"
R>  [19] "index.Rmd"
```

The files presented above contain all the contents of this book, including this specific paragraph, located in file `02-Basic-operations.Rmd`!

2.21.2 Deleting Files and Directories

You can also use an R session to delete files and directories from your computer. This might come in handy when dealing with disposable data files. Use these commands with responsibility. If not careful, you can easily break the operating system of your computer.

You can delete files with command `file.remove`:

```r
# create temporary file
my_file <- 'data/tempfile.csv'
write.csv(x = data.frame(x=1:10),
          file = my_file)

# delete it
file.remove(my_file)
```

R> [1] TRUE

Remember that you must have permission from your operating system to manipulate the hard drive and delete a file. In the previous chunk of code, the returned value TRUE tells us that the operation was successful.

To delete directories and all their elements, we use `unlink`:

```r
# create temp dir
dir.create('temp')

# create a file inside of temp
my_file <- 'temp/tempfile.csv'
write.csv(x = data.frame(x=1:10),
          file = my_file)

unlink(x = 'temp', recursive = TRUE)
```

Notice that, unlike `file.remove`, function `unlink` returns nothing. If needed, we can check if the deletion of a directory was successful with command `dir.exists`:

```r
dir.exists('temp')
```

R> [1] FALSE

As expected, the directory was not found.

2.21.3 Downloading Files from the Internet

We can also use R to download files from the Internet with function `download.file`. See the following example, where we download an Excel spreadsheet from Microsoft's website:

```
# set link
link_dl <- 'go.microsoft.com/fwlink/?LinkID=521962'
local_file <- 'data/temp_file.xlsx' # name of local file

download.file(url = link_dl,
              destfile = local_file)
```

Using `download.file` is quite handy when you are working with Internet data that is constantly updated. Just re-download the file with data at the beginning of the *script*. After that, we could continue the code by reading the downloaded file and performing our analysis.

One trick worth knowing is that you can also download files from cloud services such as Dropbox[11] and Google Drive[12]. So, if you need to send a data file to a large group of people and update it frequently, just pass the file link from the cloud service. This way, any local change in the data file in your computer will be reflected for all users with the file link.

2.21.4 Using Temporary Files and Directories

An interesting aspect of R is that every new session is linked to a temporary folder within the computer. This folder is used to store any disposable files and folders generated by R. The location of this directory is available with `tempdir`:

```
windows_tempdir <- tempdir()
print(windows_tempdir)
```

```
R> C:\Users\NAME\AppData\Local\Temp\Rtmp8E
```

The name of the temporary directory, in this case 'Rtmp8E', is randomly defined at the start of every new R session. When the computer is rebooted, all temporary directories are deleted.

---
[11]https://www.dropbox.com/
[12]https://drive.google.com/

The same dynamic is found for file names. If you want to use a temporary random name for some reason, use `tempfile`:

```
windows_tempfile <- tempfile(pattern = 'temp_',
                             fileext = '.xlsx')
cat(windows_tempfile)
```

```
R> C:\Users\NAME\AppData\Local\Temp\Rtmp8E\temp_4365730565.xlsx
```

You can also set its extension and name:

```
windows_tempfile <- tempfile(pattern = 'temp_',
                             fileext = '.csv')
cat(windows_tempfile)
```

```
R> C:\Users\NAME\AppData\Local\Temp\Rtmp8E\temp_43664e87729.csv
```

As a practical case of using temporary files and folders, let's *download* the Excel worksheet from Microsoft into a temporary folder and read its content for the first five rows:

```
# set link
link_dl <- 'go.microsoft.com/fwlink/?LinkID=521962'
local_file <- tempfile(fileext = '.xlsx', tmpdir = tempdir())

download.file(url = link_dl,
              destfile = local_file)

df_msft <- readxl::read_excel(local_file)

print(head(df_msft))
```

```
R> # A tibble: 6 x 16
R>   Segment Country Product `Discount Band` `Units Sold`
R>   <chr>   <chr>   <chr>   <chr>                  <dbl>
R> 1 Govern~ Canada  Carret~ None                   1618.
R> 2 Govern~ Germany Carret~ None                   1321
R> 3 Midmar~ France  Carret~ None                   2178
R> 4 Midmar~ Germany Carret~ None                    888
R> 5 Midmar~ Mexico  Carret~ None                   2470
```

```
R> 6 Govern~ Germany Carret~ None                         1513
R> # ... with 11 more variables: `Manufacturing
R> #   Price` <dbl>, `Sale Price` <dbl>, `Gross
R> #   Sales` <dbl>, Discounts <dbl>, Sales <dbl>,
R> #   COGS <dbl>, Profit <dbl>, Date <dttm>, `Month
R> #   Number` <dbl>, `Month Name` <chr>, Year <chr>
```

The example Excel file contains the sales report of a company. Do notice that the imported file becomes a `dataframe` in our R session, a table like an object with rows and columns.

By using `tempfile`, we do not need to delete (or worry) about the downloaded file because it will be removed from the computer's hard disk when the system is rebooted.

2.22 Exercises

1. Create a new R script, set a name and save it to a personal folder. Now, use the script to define two objects: one containing a number between 1 and 100 and another with the text of your name (eg `'John'`). Within RStudio, execute the script with RStudio keyboard shortcuts (*control + enter* and *control + shift + enter*).

2. Within the previous script, display the following phrase in the *prompt* of R: "`My name is ....`". Tip: use functions `cat` and `paste0`.

3. Within the same script, print the current working directory of your R session (see function `getwd`, as in `print(getwd())`). Now, modify the working directory to your *Desktop* area and display the following message: `'My desktop address is ....'`. Tip: use the autocomplete feature of RStudio with the tab key for quickly finding the desktop folder.

4. Use R to download the book zip file available at this link[13]. Save it as a file in the temporary session folder (see `tempfile` function).

5. Use the `unzip` function to unzip the downloaded file from the previous exercise to a desktop folder called `'Book files'`. How many files are available? Tip: use argument `recursive = TRUE` with `list.files` to make sure you use subfolders in your search.

---

[13]https://www.msperlin.com/blog/static/afedr-files/afedr_files.zip

6. Every time you install a new R package, all related files are locally stored in a specific directory of your computer. Using the command `Sys.getenv('R_LIBS_USER')` and `list.dirs`, list all directories in the root of this folder. How many did you find?

7. On the same subject, create a variable called `pkg_files` that contains all files in all subdirectories of the folder containing the files of the different packages available at `Sys.getenv('R_LIBS_USER')`. On average, how many files are needed for each package?

8. Use function `install.packages` to install package `BatchGetSymbols` in your computer. After the installation, use function `BatchGetSymbols` from the same package to download price data for the IBM stock in the previous 15 days from today. Tip: You can use the function `Sys.Date()` to find out the current date and use `Sys.Date() - 15` to figure out the start of the previous 15 days from today.

9. Using the `devtools` package, install the development version of the `ggplot2` package in the Hadley Hickman repository. Load the package using `library` and create a simple plot with code `qplot(y = rnorm(10), x = 1:10)`.

10. CHALLENGE - Using your programming ability with R, count the number of files in every folder in the "Documents" directory. Using the prompt, display the five folders with the largest number of files.

Chapter 3

Writing Research Scripts

So far we learned how to use R for basic tasks such as interacting with the computer, creating simple vectors and downloading files from the internet. Although, before we import large volume tables into R and analyze them, we need to discuss the structure of a research script and, more specifically, how to organize our work efficiently.

An organized code facilitates sharing and future use. As a research code becomes larger and complex, organization is a necessity. In this chapter, I will suggest a way to organize files and folders. So, I recommend that you follow these guidelines – or at least your own version of them – in every project you work on.

3.1 Stages of Research

Unlike other software designs, every research script has clear consecutive steps to achieve its goal.

1. **Importation of data**: Raw (original) data is imported from a local file or the internet. At this stage, no manual data manipulation, such as renaming columns names at a .csv file, should happen. The raw data should be imported "as it is". Save any required and reproducible manipulation for the next stage.

2. **Cleaning and structuring the data**: The raw data imported in the previous step is further cleaned and structured according to the need of the research. Abnormal records and errors in observations

can be removed or treated. The structure of the data can also be manipulated, binding different datasets and adding other variables of interest. Preferably, at the end of this stage, there should be a couple of final datasets that will be used in the next stage.

3. **Visual analysis and hypothesis testing**: After cleansing and structuring the data, the work continues with implementing the visual analysis and hypothesis testing. Here, you can create graphical representations of the data for your audience and use statistical tools, such as econometric models, to test a particular hypothesis. This is the *heart* of the research and the stage most likely to take more development time.

4. **Reporting the results**: The final stage of a research script is reporting the results. Likely, we will be exporting selected tables and figures from R to a text processing software such as Latex, Writer (LibreOffice) or Word (Microsoft).

Each of the mentioned steps can be structured in a single *.R* script or in several separate files. Using multiple files is preferable when the first steps of the research demand significant processing time. For example, in importing and organizing a large volume database, it is worth the trouble to separate the code in different files. It will be easier to find bugs and maintain the code. Each script will do one job, and do it well.

A practical example would be the analysis of a large dataset of financial transactions. Importing and cleansing the data takes plenty of computer time. A smart organization is to insert these primary data procedures in a *.R* file and save the final objects of this stage in an external file. This local archive serves as a bridge to the next step, hypothesis testing, where the previously created file with clean data is imported. Every time a change is made to the hypothesis testing script, it is unnecessary to rebuild the whole dataset. This simple organization of files saves a lot of time. The underlying logic is simple, isolate the parts of the script that demand more computational time – and less development –, and connect them to the rest of the code using external data files.

If you are working with multiple files, one suggestion is to create a naming structure that informs the steps of the research in an intuitive way. An example would be to name the data importing code as `01-Import-and-clean-data.R`, the modeling code as `02-build-report-models.R` and so on. The practical effect is that using a number in the first letter of the filenames clarifies the order of execution. We can also create a *master* script called `0-run-it-all.R` or `0-main.R` that runs (`source`) all other scripts. So, every time we make an update to the original data, we can simply run `0-run-it-all.R` and will have the new results, without the need to run each script individually.

3.2 Folder Structure

A proper folder structure also benefits the reproducibility and organization of research. In simple scripts, with a small database and a low number of procedures, it is unnecessary to spend much time thinking about the organization of files, just place all files in the same directory. This is certainly the case for most of the code in this book. More complex programs, with several stages of data cleansing, hypothesis testing, and several sources of data, organizing the file structure is essential.

A suggestion for an effective folder structure is to create a single directory and, within it, create subdirectories for each input and output element. For example, you can create a subdirectory called `data`, where all the original data will be stored, a directory `fig` and `tables`, where figures and tables with final results will be exported. If you are using many custom-written functions in the scripts, you can also create a directory called `R-Fcts` and save all files with function definitions at this location. As for the root of the directory, you should only find the main research scripts there. An example of a file structure that summarizes this idea is:

```
/Capital Markets and Inflation/
    /data/
        stock_indices.csv
        inflation_data.csv
    /figs/
        SP500_and_inflation.png
    /tables/
        Table1_descriptive_table.tex
        Table2_model_results.tex
    /R-Fcts/
        fct_models.R
        fct_clean_data.R
    0-run-it-all.R
    1-import-and-clean-data.R
    2-run-research.R
```

The research code should also be self-contained, with all files available within a sub-folder of the root directory. If you are using many different R packages, it is advisable to add a comment in the first lines of `0-run-it-all.R` that indicates which packages are necessary to run the code. The most friendly way to inform it is by adding a commented line that installs all required packages, as in `#install.packages('pkg1', 'pkg2', ...)`. So, when someone receives the code for the first time, all he (or she) needs to do is uncomment the line and execute it. External dependencies and steps for their installation should also be informed.

The benefits of this directory format are as follows. If you need to share the code with other researchers, simply compress the directory to a single file and send it to the recipient. After decompressing the file, the structure of the folder immediately informs the user were to change the original data, the order of execution of the scripts in the root folder, and where the outputs are saved. The same benefit goes when you reuse your code in the future, say three years from now. By working smarter, you will be more productive, spending less time with repetitive and unnecessary steps.

An example for the content of file `0-run-it-all.R` would be:

```r
# clean up workspace
rm(list=ls())

# close all figure windows created with x11()
graphics.off()

# load packages
library(pkg1)
library(pkg2)
library(pkg3)

# change directory
my_dir <- dirname(rstudioapi::getActiveDocumentContext()$path)
setwd(my_dir)

# list functions in 'R-Fcts'
my_R_files <- list.files(path='R-Fcts',
                         pattern = '*.R',
                         full.names=TRUE)

# Load all functions in R
sapply(my_R_files, source)

# Import data script
```

3.2. FOLDER STRUCTURE

```
source('01-import-and-clean-data.R')

# run models and report results
source('02-run-research.R')
```

This is the first time we use functions `graphics.off` and `sapply`. The first one simply closes all windows used to display a figure. In a research script, sometimes you may have many graphical windows opened and it is wise to close them all. Command `sapply` will apply a function, in this case `source`, to a series of elements. Here, the practical effect is that all files located at folder `R-Fcts` and with extension *.R* will be executed. In chapter 8 we will learn more about `sapply` and its variants.

Notice that, assuming all packages are installed, no extra step is needed to run the above code successfully on another computer. We could also automate the copy of the figure and table files used in the report with `file.copy`. From there, you can create a link in the text for each figure file. As an example, in LaTeX, you can include a figure file with the command `\includegraphics{file_name_here}`. You can also create a direct link for the figure file in the research folder, although this method is not recommended since it creates an external dependency on the written report. Either way, whenever the main code is executed, all research figures will be automatically updated in the text. If needed, you can also produce table files in different formats using packages `xtable` (Dahl, 2016) and `texreg` (Leifeld, 2013). We will go deeper into this subject in chapter 12.

Another way of setting up directories in a research script is by using an RStudio project. For that, open RStudio and go to *File*, *New Project*, *New Directory*, and choose a folder and project name. RStudio will create a file with the *.RProj* extension in the chosen directory. Every time you want to work on the project, just open the project file in RStudio.

The benefit of this approach is that it is unnecessary to change the directory in the code. The project automatically changes it to the location of the *.RProj* file. Various information is saved, including the history of files being edited, a history of project commands, among other things. Besides that, custom options for the project can also be made. It's worth noting that *.RProj* file is pure text and editable. You can open it in any text editor of your operating system and see how it stores many startup options for R.

3.3 Important Aspects of a Research Script

In this section I'll be making some suggestions for how you can conduct research with R. Making it clear, these are personal positions from my experience as a researcher and teacher. Many points raised here are specific to the academic environment but can be easily extended to the practice of research outside universities. In short, these are suggestions I wish I knew when I first started my career.

Firstly, **know your data!**. I can't stress enough how this is important! The first instinct of every passionate data analyst when encountering a new set of tables is to immediately import it into R and perform an analysis. However, a certain level of caution is needed. Every time you come across a new set of data, ask yourself how much you **really** know about this data:

- How was the data collected? To what purpose?
- How do the available data compare with data used in other studies?
- Is there any possibility of bias within the data collection?

Furthermore, you need to remember that the ultimate goal of any research is communication. Thus, it is very likely that you will report your results to people who will have an informed opinion about the subject, including the sources and individualities of different datasets. The worst case scenario is when a research effort of three to six months in between coding and writing is nullified by a simple lapse in data checking. Unfortunately, this is not uncommon.

As an example, consider the case of analyzing the long term performance of companies in the retail business. For that, you gather a recent list of available companies and download financial records about their revenue, profit and adjusted stock price for the past twenty years. Well, the problem here is in the selection of the companies. By taking those that are available today, you missed all companies that went bankrupt during the 20 year period. By looking only at companies that stayed active during the whole period, you indirectly selected those that are profitable and presented good performance. This is a well-known effect called **survival bias**. The right way of doing this research is gathering a list of companies in the retail business twenty years ago and keep track of those that went bankrupt and those that stayed alive.

The message is clear. **Be very cautious about the data you are using**. Your raw tables stand at the base of the research. A small detail that goes unnoticed can invalidate your whole work. If you are lucky and the database

3.3. IMPORTANT ASPECTS OF A RESEARCH SCRIPT

is accompanied by a written manual, break it down to the last detail. If the information is not clear, do not be shy about sending questions to the responsible party. Likewise, if there is an inevitable operational bias in your dataset, be open and transparent about it.

The second point here is the code. After you finish reading this book, you will have the knowledge to conduct research with R. The computer will be a powerful ally in making your research ideas come true, no matter how gigantic they may be. However, **a great power comes with great responsibility**. Likewise, you need to be aware that a single misplace line in a code can easily bias and invalidate your research.

Remember that analyzing data is your profession and **your reputation is your most valuable asset**. If you have no confidence in the produced code, do not publish or communicate your results. The code is entirely your responsibility and no one else's. Check it as many times as necessary. Always be skeptical about your own work:

- Do the descriptive statistics of the variables faithfully report the database?
- Is there any relationship between the variables that can be verified in the descriptive table?
- Do the main findings of the research make sense to the current literature of the subject? If not, how to explain them?
- Is it possible that a *bug* in the code has produced the results?

I'm constantly surprised by how many studies submitted to respected periodicals can be denied publication based on a simple analysis of the descriptive table. Basic errors in variable calculations can be easily spotted with a trained eye. The process of continuous evaluation of your research will not only make you stronger as a researcher but will also serve as practice for peer evaluation, much used in academic research. If you do not have enough confidence to report results, test your code extensively. If you have already done so and are still not confident, identify the lines of code you have doubts and seek help with a colleague or your advisor, if there is one. The latter is a strong ally who can help you in dealing with problems he/she already had.

All of the research work is, to some extent, based on existing work. Today it is extremely difficult to carry out ground-breaking research. Knowledge is built in the form of blocks, one over the other. There is always a collection of literature that needs to be consulted. Particularly in the case of data research. Therefore, you should always compare your results with the results already presented in the subject, especially when it is replicated. If the main results are not similar to those found in the literature, one should ask himself: could a code error have created this result?

I clarify that it is possible that the results of research differ from those of the literature, but the opposite is more likely. Knowledge of this demands care with your code. *Bugs* and code errors are quite common, especially in early versions of scripts. As a data analyst, it is important to recognize this risk and manage it.

3.4 Exercises

1. Imagine a survey regarding your household budget over time. Data is stored as separate spreadsheets, one for each year, from 2009 to 2019. The objective of the research is to understand if it is possible to buy a home property in 5 years. Based on this, detail the elements in each stage of the study as a sequence, from importing the data to constructing the report.

2. Based on the previous exercise, create a folder structure on your computer to accommodate the research. Create dummy files with no content for each subdirectory (see folder structure at section 3.2). Note that the creation of the directories can be done with function `dir.create`.

Chapter 4

Importing Data from Local Files

Surely, the very first step of an R script is getting your data into R. In this chapter, we will learn to import and export data available as local files in the computer. Although the task is not particularly difficult, a good data analyst should understand the different characteristics of file formats and how to take the best advantage of them in every situation. While some are best suited for sharing and collaboration, others can offer a significant boost in reading and writing speeds.

Here we will draw a comprehensive list of file formats for importing and exporting data, including:

- Text data with comma-separated values (*csv*);
- Microsoft Excel (*xls*, *xlsx*);
- R native files (*RData*, *rds*);
- `fst` format;
- SQLite;
- Unstructured text data.

The first lesson in importing data from local files is that the location of the file must be explicitly stated in the code. The path of the file is then passed to a function that will read the file. Remember from the previous chapter, which you can use for the *autocomplete* feature of RStudio to set the path (see section 2.20). An example:

```
my_file <- 'C:/My Research/data/SP500_Data.csv'
```

Note the use of forwarding slashes (/) to designate the file directory. Relative references also work, as in:

```
my_file <- 'data/SP500_Data.csv'
```

Here, it is assumed that in the current working folder there is a directory called **data** and, inside of it, a file called SP500_Data.csv. If the file path is simply its name, such as in `my_file <- 'SP500_Data.csv'`, it is implicitly assumed that the file is located in the root of the working directory. From the previous chapter, recall you can use **setwd** to change the working folder to where the work is being done and simply use the relative path of the data file. An example:

```
setwd('C:/My Research')
my_file <- 'data/SP500_Data.csv'
```

Another very important point here is that **the data will be imported and exported in R as an object of type dataframe**. That is, a table contained in an Excel or *.csv* file will become a **dataframe** object in R. When we export data, the most common format is this same type of object. Conveniently, **dataframes** are nothing more than tables, with rows and columns.

Each column in the **dataframe** will have its own class, the most common being numeric (*numeric*), text (*character*), factor (*factor*) and date (*Date*). When importing the data, **it is imperative that each column is represented in the correct class**. A vast amount of errors can be avoided by simply checking the column classes in the **dataframe** resulting from the import process. For now, we only need to understand this basic property of **dataframes**. We will study the details of this object in chapter 6.

4.1 *csv* files

Consider the data file called SP500.csv. It contains daily closing prices of the SP500 index from 2010-01-01 until 2019-01-01. Since SP500.csv is a simple text file, you can open it in any text editor and check its contents.

Here we will use package **afedR** for grabbing the file and copying it to your local folder. If you followed the instructions in the book preface chapter, you should have package **afedR** already installed. If not, execute the following code:

4.1. CSV FILES

```
# install devtools dependency
install.packages('devtools')

# install book package
devtools::install_github('msperlin/afedR')
```

Once you installed package **afedR**, file SP500.csv and all other data files used in the book were downloaded from Github. The package also includes functions for facilitating the reproduction of all code examples. Command `afedR::afedR_get_data_file` will return the local path of a book data file by its name.

Let's copy SP500.csv to your "My Documents" folder with the following code using the tilde (~) shortcut:

```
my_f <- afedR::afedR_get_data_file('SP500.csv')
file.copy(from = my_f, to = '~' )
```

Now, if it is your first time working with *.csv* files, use a file browser (Explorer in Windows) and open SP500.csv in the "My Documents" folder with any text editor software such as Notepad. The first lines of SP500.csv, also called header lines, show the column names. Following international standards, rows are set using line breaks, and all columns are separated by commas (,).

The content of SP500.csv is very standard. However, you should be aware this is not always the case. So, if you want to avoid the common issues, I suggest that you use a set of steps that can avoid most problems in importing data from *.csv* files:

1) Check the existence of text before the actual data. A standard *.csv* file will only have the contents of a table but, sometimes, you will find a header text with some details about the data. In R, you can control how many lines you skip in the *csv* reading function;

2) Verify the existence of names for all columns and if those names are readable;

3) Check the symbol for column separation. Normally it is a comma, but you never know for sure;

4) For the numerical data, verify the decimal symbol. R will expect it to be a dot. If necessary, you can adjust this information in the CSV reading function.

5) Check the encoding of the text file. Normally it is one of UTF-8, Latin1 (ISO-8859) or Windows 1252. These are broad encoding formats and should suffice for most languages. Whenever you find strange symbols in the text columns of the resulting `dataframe`, the problem is due to a difference in encoding. While the file is encoded in a specific format, R is reading it with a different encoding structure. Windows users can check the encoding of a text file by opening it in Notepad++[1]. The information about the encoding will be available in the bottom right corner of the Notepad++ editor. However, you need to be aware that Notepad++ is not part of the Windows installation and you might need to install it on your computer. Linux and Mac users can find the same information in any advanced text editor software such as Kate[2].

Whenever you find an unexpected text structure in a *.csv* file, use the arguments of the *csv* reading function to import the information correctly. As a rule of thumb, **never modify raw .csv data manually**. It is far more efficient to use the R code to deal with different structures of *.csv* files. It takes a bit of work, but such a policy will save you a lot of time in the future as, in a couple of weeks, you are likely to forget how you manually cleaned that *.csv* file for your R script. Whenever you need to update the data file, the code will automatically manage all problems.

4.1.1 Importing Data

The `base` package of R includes a native function called `read.csv` for importing data from *.csv* files. However, we will prefer the `tidyverse` alternative, `readr::read_csv`, as it is more efficient and easier to work with. In short, the benefit is that it reads the data very quickly, and it uses clever rules for defining the classes of imported columns.

This is the first package from the `tidyverse` that we will use. Before doing so, it is necessary to install it in your R session. A simple way of installing all `tidyverse` packages as a bundle is as follows:

```
install.packages('tidyverse')
```

After running the previous code, all `tidyverse` packages will be installed on your computer. You should also keep in mind that aspects such installation might take a while. Once it finishes, let's load the `tidyverse` set of packages.

---

[1] https://notepad-plus-plus.org/
[2] https://kate-editor.org/

4.1. CSV FILES

```r
# load library
library(tidyverse)
```

Back to importing data from *.csv* files, to load the contents of file SP500.csv in R, use the `readr::read_csv` function.

```r
# set file to read
my_f <- afedR::afedR_get_data_file('SP500.csv')

# read file
my_df_sp500 <- read_csv(my_f)
```

```
R> Parsed with column specification:
R> cols(
R>   ref.date = col_date(format = ""),
R>   price.close = col_double()
R> )
```

```r
# print it
print(head(my_df_sp500))
```

```
R> # A tibble: 6 x 2
R>   ref.date   price.close
R>   <date>           <dbl>
R> 1 2010-01-04       1133.
R> 2 2010-01-05       1137.
R> 3 2010-01-06       1137.
R> 4 2010-01-07       1142.
R> 5 2010-01-08       1145.
R> 6 2010-01-11       1147.
```

The contents of the imported file are set as a `dataframe` object in R. As mentioned in the previous chapter, each column of a `dataframe` has a class. We can check the classes of `my_df_sp500` using function `glimpse` from package `dplyr`, which is also part of the `tidyverse`. This function is an improved version of `base:str`, also showing a textual representation of R objects. Let's use it:

```
# Check the content of dataframe
glimpse(my_df_sp500)
```

```
R> Observations: 2,264
R> Variables: 2
R> $ ref.date   <date> 2010-01-04, 2010-01-05, 2010-...
R> $ price.close <dbl> 1132.99, 1136.52, 1137.14, 114...
```

Note that the column of dates (`date`) was imported as a `Date` vector and the closing prices as numeric (`dbl`, double accuracy). This is exactly what we expected. Internally, function `read_csv` identifies columns classes according to their content.

Notice how the previous code presented a message entitled `Parsed with column specification: ....` This message shows how the function sets the attributes of the columns by reading the first 1000 lines of the file. Column `ref.date` was imported as `date` and column `price.close` was imported as `double` (numeric). We can use this information in our own code by copying the text and assigning it to a variable. Have a look:

```
# set cols from import message
my_cols <- cols(ref.date = col_date(),
                price.close = col_character() )

# read file with readr::read_csv
my_df_sp500 <- read_csv(my_f, col_types = my_cols)
```

As an exercise, Let's import the same data, but use a `character` class for column `date`:

```
# set cols from import message
my_cols <- cols(ref.date = col_character(),
                price.close = col_character() )

# read file with readr::read_csv
my_df_sp500 <- read_csv(my_f, col_types = my_cols)

# glimpse the dataframe
glimpse(my_df_sp500)
```

4.1. CSV FILES

```
R> Observations: 2,264
R> Variables: 2
R> $ ref.date    <chr> "2010-01-04", "2010-01-05", "2...
R> $ price.close <chr> "1132.98999", "1136.52002", "1...
```

As expected, both columns are of class `character`. So, a possible set of steps using `readr::read_csv` is, first, to read the file without arguments in `read_csv`, copy the default column classes from the output message, add it as argument `col_types`, and re-execute the script. This is handy when the imported file has several columns and manually defining each column class requires lots of typing.

There is also a simpler way of using the classes defined by `read_csv`, just set `col_types = cols()`. This way you don't need to manually copy and paste the message from `read_csv`. See it in use next:

```
# read file with readr::read_csv
my_df_sp500 <- read_csv(my_f,
                        col_types = cols())

# glimpse the dataframe
glimpse(my_df_sp500)
```

```
R> Observations: 2,264
R> Variables: 2
R> $ ref.date    <date> 2010-01-04, 2010-01-05, 2010-...
R> $ price.close <dbl> 1132.99, 1136.52, 1137.14, 114...
```

Going further, `read_csv` has several other input options such as:

- change the format of the import data, including symbols for decimal places and encoding (`locale` option);
- change column names (argument `col_names`);
- skip n lines before importation (`skip` option);
- custom definition for NA values (`na` option)

among many other possibilities. Package `readr` also provides several other functions for specific import situations. If the `read_csv` function does not solve your problem in reading some structured text file, surely another function of this package will.

4.1.2 Exporting Data

To write a *.csv* file, use the `readr::write_csv` function. First, we create a new dataframe with some random data:

```
# set the number of rows
N <- 100

# set dataframe
my_df <- data.frame(y = runif(N),
                    z = rep('a',N))

# print it
print(head(my_df))
```

```
R>           y z
R> 1 0.1256810 a
R> 2 0.2773001 a
R> 3 0.8029237 a
R> 4 0.5474154 a
R> 5 0.2333112 a
R> 6 0.2305196 a
```

And now we use `write_csv` to save it in a new *.csv* file:

```
# set file out
f_out <- 'data/temp.csv'

# write to files
write_csv(x = my_df,
          path = f_out)
```

In the previous example, we save the object `my_df` into a file with path `data/temp.csv`. We can read it back and check its contents using `read_csv` once again:

```
# read it
my_df_imported <- read_csv(f_out)

# print first five rows
print(head(my_df_imported))
```

4.2. EXCEL FILES (XLS AND XLSX)

```
R> # A tibble: 6 x 2
R>        y z
R>    <dbl> <chr>
R> 1 0.126 a
R> 2 0.277 a
R> 3 0.803 a
R> 4 0.547 a
R> 5 0.233 a
R> 6 0.231 a
```

As we can see, the data imported from the file is identical to the one created in the previous code chunk.

4.2 *Excel* Files (*xls* and *xlsx*)

Although it is not an efficient or portable data storage format, Excel is a very popular software due to its spreadsheet-like capacities. It is not uncommon for data to be stored and distributed in this format, especially in the finance industry.

The downside of using Excel files for storing data is its low portability and the longer time required to read and write it. This may not be a problem for small tables, but when handling a large volume of data, using Excel files can be very frustrating, and it is not advised. If you can, avoid the use of Excel files in your work cycle.

4.2.1 Importing Data

R does not have a native function for importing Excel files; therefore, we must install and use packages to perform this operation. There are several options, but the main packages are `XLConnect` (Mirai Solutions GmbH, 2016), `xlsx` (Dragulescu, 2014), `readxl` (Wickham, 2016a) and `tidyxl` (Garmonsway, 2017).

Despite their similar goals, each package has its peculiarities. If reading Excel files is important to your work, I strongly advise the study of each package. For example, package `tidyxl` was specially designed to read unstructured Excel files, where the desired information is not contained in a tabular format. Package `XLConnect` allows the user to open a live connection and control an Excel file from R, making it possible to export and send data, format cells, create graphics in Excel, and more.

In this section, we will give priority to package `readxl`, one of the most straightforward packages to use. It also does not require the installation of external software such as *Java*. Let's start with an example. Consider a file called SP500-Excel.xlsx that contains the same SP500 data. We can import the information from the file using function `read_excel` from `readxl`:

```
library(readxl)

# set excel file
my_f <- afedR::afedR_get_data_file('SP500_Excel.xlsx')

# read excel file
my_df <- read_excel(my_f, sheet = 'Sheet1')

# print classes
print(sapply(my_df, class))
```

```
R> $ref.date
R> [1] "POSIXct" "POSIXt"
R>
R> $price.close
R> [1] "numeric"
```

```
# print with head (first five rows)
print(head(my_df))
```

```
R> # A tibble: 6 x 2
R>   ref.date            price.close
R>   <dttm>                    <dbl>
R> 1 2010-01-04 00:00:00       1133.
R> 2 2010-01-05 00:00:00       1137.
R> 3 2010-01-06 00:00:00       1137.
R> 4 2010-01-07 00:00:00       1142.
R> 5 2010-01-08 00:00:00       1145.
R> 6 2010-01-11 00:00:00       1147.
```

As we can see, one benefit of using Excel files is that the column's classes are directly inherited. If the classes are correct in the Excel file, then they will automatically be correct in R. In our case, the date column of file SP500_Excel.xlsx was correctly set as a `dttm` object, a special type of `DateTime` class. Likewise, even if the Excel file used commas for decimals, the import process would still succeed as the conversion is handled internally.

4.2. EXCEL FILES (XLS AND XLSX)

4.2.2 Exporting Data

Exporting a `dataframe` to an Excel file is also easy. Again, no native function in R performs this procedure. We can, however, use packages `xlsx` and `writexl`. A requisite for using `xlsx` is the installation of Java JDK in the operating system. For Windows users, visit the Java site[3] and install the software. After that, install `xlsx` with command `install.packages('xlsx')` and try loading it with `library(xlsx)`. If you got an error message about *Java* , try rebooting your system.

An example of `xlsx` usage is given next:

```
library(xlsx)

# create dataframe
N <- 50
my_df <- data.frame(y = seq(1,N), z = rep('a',N))

# set excel file
f_out <- 'data/temp.xlsx'

# write to excel
write.xlsx(x = my_df, file = f_out, sheetName = "my df")
```

If you want to save several `dataframes` into several worksheets of the same Excel file, you must use the input option `append=TRUE` in the call to `write.xlsx`. Otherwise, the function will create a new file on each call and erase all previous content. See the following example, where we export two `dataframes` for two different sheets in the same Excel file:

```
# create two dataframes
N <- 25
my_df_A <- data.frame(y = seq(1, N),
                      z = rep('a', N))

my_df_B <- data.frame(z = rep('b', N))

# set file out
f_out <- 'data/temp.xlsx'

# write in different sheets
```

---

[3] https://www.java.com/pt_BR/

```
write.xlsx(x = my_df_A,
           file = f_out,
           sheetName = "my df A")

write.xlsx(x = my_df_B,
           file = f_out,
           sheetName = "my df B",
           append = TRUE )
```

After executing the code, we can open the excel files and check their contents to see that they mirror the artificial data.

As for package `writexl`, its innovation is that a Java installation is not needed. Writing speed is also significantly increased. See an example next.

```
library(writexl)
# set number of rows
N <- 25

# create random dfs
my_df_A <- data.frame(y = seq(1, N),
                      z = rep('a', N))

write_xlsx(x = my_df_A,
           path = f_out)
```

In order to compare writing performance, let's calculate the difference of time from `xlsx` to `writexl`:

```
library(writexl)
library(readxl)
library(xlsx)

# set number of rows
N <- 2500

# create random dfs
my_df_A <- data.frame(y = seq(1,N),
                      z = rep('a',N))

# set files
```

4.2. EXCEL FILES (XLS AND XLSX)

```r
my_file_1 <- 'data/temp_writexl.xlsx'
my_file_2 <- 'data/temp_xlsx.xlsx'

# test export
time_write_writexl <- system.time(write_xlsx(x = my_df_A,
                                              path = my_file_1))

time_write_xlsx <- system.time(write.xlsx(x = my_df_A,
                                           file = my_file_2))

# test read
time_read_readxl <- system.time(read_xlsx(path = my_file_1 ))
time_read_xlsx <- system.time(read.xlsx(file = my_file_2,
                                         sheetIndex = 1 ))
```

And now we show the results:

```r
# results
my_formats <- c('xlsx', 'readxl')
results_read <- c(time_read_xlsx[3], time_read_readxl[3])
results_write<- c(time_write_xlsx[3], time_write_writexl[3])

# print text
my_text <- paste0('\nTime to WRITE dataframe with ',
                  my_formats, ': ',
                  format(results_write, digits = 4),
                  ' seconds', collapse = '')
cat(my_text)

my_text <- paste0('\nTime to READ dataframe with ',
                  my_formats, ': ',
                  format(results_read, digits = 4),
                  ' seconds', collapse = '')
cat(my_text)
```

```
R>
R> Time to WRITE dataframe with xlsx: 2.055 seconds
R> Time to WRITE dataframe with readxl: 0.010 seconds
R> Time to READ dataframe with xlsx: 3.298 seconds
R> Time to READ dataframe with readxl: 0.008 seconds
```

As we can see, even for low-volume data, a dataframe with 2500 rows and 2 columns, the run-time difference is significant. If you are working with large spreadsheets, the use of packages `readxl` and `writexl` for reading and writing Excel files is strongly recommended.

4.3 *RData* and *rds* Files

R offers native formats to write objects to a local file. The great benefit of using both native formats, *RData*, and *rds*, is that the saved file is compact and its access is very fast. The downside is the low portability, i.e., it's difficult to use the files in other software.

The difference between *RData* and *rds* is that the first can save many R objects in a single file, while the latter only one. This, however, is not a hard restriction for the *rds* format as we can incorporate several objects into a single one using a `list`, a special type of object. In practice, a *rds* file can store as many objects as needed.

4.3.1 Importing Data

To create a new *.RData* file, use the `save` function. See the following example, where we create a *.RData* file with some content, clear R's memory, and then load the previously created file:

```
# set a object
my_x <- 1:100

# set name of RData file
my_file <- 'data/temp.RData'

# save it
save(list = c('my_x'), file = my_file)
```

We can verify the existence of the file with the `file.exists` function:

```
# check if file exists
file.exists(my_file)
```

```
R> [1] TRUE
```

4.3. RDATA AND RDS FILES

As expected, file temp.RData is available.

Importing data from .rds files is very similar. For that we use function readr::read_rds:

```
# set file path
my_file <- 'data/temp.rds'

# load content into workspace
my_y <- read_rds(path = my_file)
```

Comparing the code between using .RData and .rds files note that the .rds the format allows the explicit definition of the output object. The contents of my_file in read_rds is saved in my_y. When we use the load function for *RData* files, we cannot name the output directly. This is particularly inconvenient when you need to modify the name of the imported object.

As a suggestion, give preference to the *.rds* format, which is more practical, resulting in cleaner code. The difference in speed between one and the other is minimal. The benefit of importing multiple objects into the same RData format file becomes irrelevant when using list objects, which can incorporate other objects into its content. We will see more details about this type of object in chapter 6.

4.3.2 Exporting Data

We can create a new *RData* file with command save:

```
# set vars
my_x <- 1:100
my_y <- 1:100

# write to RData
my_file <- 'data/temp.RData'
save(list = c('my_x', 'my_y'),
     file = my_file)
```

We can check if the file exists with function file.exists:

```
file.exists(my_file)
```

R> [1] TRUE

The result is TRUE as expected.

As for *.rds* files, we save it with function `readr::write_rds`:

```
# set data and file
my_x <- 1:100
my_file <- 'data/temp.rds'

# save as .rds
write_rds(x = my_x,
          path = my_file)

# read it
my_x2 <- read_rds(path = my_file)

# test equality
print(identical(my_x, my_x2))
```

```
R> [1] TRUE
```

Command `identical` tests if both objects are equal. Again, as expected, we find the result to be TRUE.

4.4 *fst* files

The *fst* format[4] is specially designed to enable quick writing and reading time from tabular data, with minimal disk space. Using this format is particularly beneficial when working with large databases in powerful computers. The trick here is the use of all computer cores to import and export data, while all other formats only use one. If you have a computer with several cores, the gain in speed is impressive, as we will soon learn.

4.4.1 Importing Data

Using *fst* file is very simple and similar to the previous cases. We use function `read_fst` from package `fst` to read files:

---

[4]http://www.fstpackage.org/

4.4. FST FILES

```r
library(fst)

# set file location
my_file <- afedR::afedR_get_data_file('temp.fst')

# read fst file
my_df <- read_fst(my_file)

# check contents
glimpse(my_df)
```

```
R> Observations: 1,000
R> Variables: 1
R> $ x <dbl> 0.24521684, 0.25430881, 0.79129094, 0.23...
```

As with the other cases, the data from file temp.fst is available in the workspace.

4.4.2 Exporting Data

We use function `fst::write_fst` to save dataframes in the *fst* format:

```r
library(fst)

# create dataframe
N <- 1000
my_file <- 'data/temp.fst'
my_df <- data.frame(x = runif(N))

# write to fst
write_fst(x = my_df, path = my_file)
```

4.4.3 Timing the *fst* format

As a test of the potential of the `fst` format, we will now time the read and write time between `fst` and `rds` for a large table: 5,000,000 rows and 2 columns. We will also report the size of the resulting file.

```r
library(fst)

# set number of rows
N <- 5000000

# create random dfs
my_df <- data.frame(y = seq(1,N),
                    z = rep('a',N))

# set files
my_file_1 <- 'data/temp_rds.rds'
my_file_2 <- 'data/temp_fst.fst'

# test write
time_write_rds <- system.time(write_rds(my_df, my_file_1 ))
time_write_fst <- system.time(write_fst(my_df, my_file_2 ))

# test read
time_read_rds <- system.time(readRDS(my_file_1))
time_read_fst <- system.time(read_fst(my_file_2))

# test file size (MB)
file_size_rds <- file.size(my_file_1)/1000000
file_size_fst <- file.size(my_file_2)/1000000
```

And now we check the results:

```r
# results
my_formats <- c('.rds', '.fst')
results_read <- c(time_read_rds[3], time_read_fst[3])
results_write<- c(time_write_rds[3], time_write_fst[3])
results_file_size <- c(file_size_rds , file_size_fst)

# print text
my_text <- paste0('\nTime to WRITE dataframe with ',
                  my_formats, ': ',
                  results_write, ' seconds', collapse = '')
cat(my_text)

my_text <- paste0('\nTime to READ dataframe with ',
                  my_formats, ': ',
```

```
                      results_read, ' seconds', collapse = '')
cat(my_text)

my_text <- paste0('\nResulting FILE SIZE for ',
                  my_formats, ': ',
                  results_file_size, ' MBs', collapse = '')
cat(my_text)


R>
R> Time to WRITE dataframe with .rds: 0.0539999999999985 seconds
R> Time to WRITE dataframe with .fst: 0.0289999999999999 seconds
R> Time to READ dataframe with .rds: 0.0399999999999991 seconds
R> Time to READ dataframe with .fst: 0.0249999999999986 seconds
R> Resulting FILE SIZE for .rds: 20.003538 MBs
R> Resulting FILE SIZE for .fst: 7.136797 MBs
```

The difference is very impressive! The `fst` not only reads and writes faster but also results in smaller file sizes. Be aware, however, this result is found in a 16 core computer in which the book was compiled. You may not be able to replicate the same result in a more modest machine. The message here is clear if you are working with high volume data with good hardware, the preference to the *fst* format is justified.

4.5 SQLite Files

The use of *.csv* or *.rds* files for storing objects has its limits as the size of the files increases. If you are waiting a long time to read a `dataframe` from a file or if you are only interested in a small portion of a large table, you should look for alternatives. Likewise, if you are working in a network of computers from your institution and many people are using the same tables, it makes sense to keep and distribute the information from a central server. This way, every user can access the same information concurrently.

This brings us to the topic of **database software**. These specific programs usually work with a query language, called *SQL (Structured Query Language)*. It allows the user to read portions of the data and even manipulate it efficiently. Many options of database software integrate nicely with R. The list includes **MySQL**, **SQLite** and **MariaDB**. Here, we will provide a quick tutorial on this topic using SQLite, which is the easiest one to work.

Before moving to the examples, we need to understand how to use database software. First, R will connect to the database and return a connection object. Based on this connection, we will send queries for importing data using the *SQL* language. The main advantage is we can have a large database of, let's say, 10 GB and only load a small portion of it in R. This operation is also very quick, allowing efficient access to the available tables.

4.5.1 Importing Data

Assuming the existence of an SQLite file in the computer, we can import its tables with package RSQLite:

```
library(RSQLite)

# set name of SQLITE file
f_sqlite <- afedR::afedR_get_data_file('SQLite_db.SQLITE')

# open connection
my_con <- dbConnect(drv = SQLite(), f_sqlite)

# read table
my_df <- dbReadTable(conn = my_con,
                     name = 'MyTable1') # name of table in sqlite

# print with str
glimpse(my_df)
```

```
R> Observations: 1,000,000
R> Variables: 2
R> $ x <dbl> 0.82994084, 0.72794196, 0.22151907, 0.68...
R> $ G <chr> "A", "B", "A", "A", "B", "A", "B", "A", ...
```

It worked. The dataframe from the table MyTable1 is exactly as expected.

Another example of using SQLite is with the actual SQL statements. Notice, in the previous code, we used the function dbReadTable to get the contents of all rows in table MyTable1. Now, let's use an SQL command to get from MyTable2 only the rows where the G column is equal to A.

4.5. SQLITE FILES

```r
# set sql statement
my_SQL_statement <- "select * from myTable2 where G='A'"

# get query
my_df_A <- dbGetQuery(conn = my_con,
                     statement = my_SQL_statement)

# disconnect from db
dbDisconnect(my_con)

# print with str
print(str(my_df_A))
```

```
R> 'data.frame':    499919 obs. of  2 variables:
R>  $ x: num  0.235 0.773 0.721 0.2 0.323 ...
R>  $ G: chr  "A" "A" "A" "A" ...
R> NULL
```

It also worked, as expected.

In this simple example, we can see how easy it is to create a connection to a database, retrieve tables, and disconnect. If you have to work with large tables, which, in my opinion, is any database that occupies more than 4 GB of your computer memory, it is worth moving it to proper database software. You'll be able to retrieve data faster, without the need of loading the whole database in the computer's memory. If you have a server available in your workplace, I strongly advise learning how to connect to it and use the SQL language to your advantage. There are many other ways you can query and manipulate data using SQL. Several tutorials are available in the internet.

4.5.2 Exporting Data

As an example of exporting data to an SQLite file, let's first create an SQLite database. For that, we will set two large `dataframes` with random data and save both in an SQLite file using the package `RSQLite`.

```r
library(RSQLite)

# set number of rows in df
N = 10^6
```

```
# create simulated dataframe
my_large_df_1 <- data.frame(x=runif(N),
                            G= sample(c('A','B'),
                                      size = N,
                                      replace = TRUE))

my_large_df_2 <- data.frame(x=runif(N),
                            G = sample(c('A','B'),
                                       size = N,
                                       replace = TRUE))

# set name of SQLITE file
f_sqlite <- 'data/SQLite_db.SQLITE'

# open connection
my_con <- dbConnect(drv = SQLite(), f_sqlite)

# write df to sqlite
dbWriteTable(conn = my_con, name = 'MyTable1',
             value = my_large_df_1)
dbWriteTable(conn = my_con, name = 'MyTable2',
             value = my_large_df_2)

# disconnect
dbDisconnect(my_con)
```

The `TRUE` output of `dbWriteTable` indicates everything went well. A connection was opened using function `dbConnect`, and the `dataframes` were written to an SQLite file, called data/SQLite_db.SQLITE. Unlike other database software, SQLite stores data and configurations from a single file, without the need of a formal server. Also, notice how we disconnected from the database using the function `dbDisconnect`.

4.6 Unstructured Data and Other Formats

The previous packages and functions are sufficient for getting most of the work done. Nevertheless, it is worth mentioning that R can also import data from other formats such as SPSS, Stata, Matlab, among many others.

4.6. UNSTRUCTURED DATA AND OTHER FORMATS 111

If that is your case, I suggest a thorough study of the `foreign` package (R Core Team, 2015).

Another example is the case of unstructured data stored in text files. Let's explore it.

4.6.1 Importing Data

You can read the contents of a text file with function `readr::read_lines`:

```
# set file to read
my_f <- afedR::afedR_get_data_file('pride_and_prejudice.txt')

# read file line by line
my_txt <- read_lines(my_f)

# print 50 characters of first fifteen lines
print(str_sub(string = my_txt[1:15],
              start = 1,
              end = 50))
```

```
R>  [1] "The Project Gutenberg EBook of Pride and Prejudice"
R>  [2] ""
R>  [3] "This eBook is for the use of anyone anywhere at no"
R>  [4] "almost no restrictions whatsoever.  You may copy i"
R>  [5] "re-use it under the terms of the Project Gutenberg"
R>  [6] "with this eBook or online at www.gutenberg.org"
R>  [7] ""
R>  [8] ""
R>  [9] "Title: Pride and Prejudice"
R> [10] ""
R> [11] "Author: Jane Austen"
R> [12] ""
R> [13] "Posting Date: August 26, 2008 [EBook #1342]"
R> [14] "Release Date: June, 1998"
R> [15] "Last Updated: March 10, 2018"
```

In this example, file pride_and_prejudice.txt contains the whole content of the book *Pride and Prejudice* by Jane Austen, freely available in the Gutenberg[5] project. We imported the entire content of the file as a `character`

---
[5]http://www.gutenberg.org/

vector named `my_txt`. Each element of `my_txt` is a line from the raw text file. Based on it, we can calculate many things such as the number of lines in the book and the number of times that the name `'Bennet'`, one of the protagonists, appears in the text:

```r
# count number of lines
n_lines <- length(my_txt)

# set target text
name_to_search <- 'Bennet'

# set function for counting words
fct_count_bennet <- function(str_in, target_text) {

  require(stringr)


  n_words <- length(str_locate_all(string = str_in,
                                   pattern = target_text)[[1]])

  return(n_words)
}

# use fct for all lines of Pride and Prejudice
n_times <- sum(sapply(X = my_txt,
                      FUN = fct_count_bennet,
                      target_text = name_to_search))

# print results
my_msg <- paste0('The number of lines found in the file is ',
                 n_lines, '.\n',
                 'The word "', name_to_search, '" appears ',
                 n_times, ' in the book.')
cat(my_msg)
```

R> The number of lines found in the file is 13427.
R> The word "Bennet" appears 664 in the book.

In the example, we once again used `sapply`. In this case, it allowed us to use a function for each element of `my_txt`. We searched and counted the number of times the word "Bennet" was found. Notice we could simply change `name_to_search` for any other name if we wanted to.

4.6.2 Exporting Data

A typical case of exporting unstructured text is saving the log record of a procedure. This is quite simple. Using function `readr::write_lines`, use the input `path` to set the name of the local file and `x` for the actual textual content.

```
# set file
my_f <- 'data/temp.txt'

# set some string
my_text <- paste0('Today is ', Sys.Date(), '\n',
                  'Tomorrow is ', Sys.Date()+1)

# save string to file
write_lines(x = my_text, path = my_f, append = FALSE)
```

In the previous example, we created a simple text object and saved it in data/temp.txt. We can check the result with the `readr::read_lines` function:

```
print(read_lines(my_f))
```

```
R> [1] "Today is 2020-02-08"    "Tomorrow is 2020-02-09"
```

As we can see, it worked as expected.

4.7 How to Select a Format

The choice of file format is an important topic and might actually be a time-saver at your work. In that decision, we must consider three points:

- speed of reading and write operations;
- size of the resulting file;
- compatibility with other software and operating systems.

Usually, the use of *csv* files easily satisfies these requirements. A *csv* file is nothing more than a text file that can be opened, viewed, and imported into any other statistical software. This makes it easy to share it with other people. Also, the size of *csv* files is usually not restrictive and, if needed, it can be compressed using the *zip* function. For these reasons, the use of *csv* files for importing and exporting data is preferable in the vast majority of situations.

In the specific case of working with bulky tables, I suggest the `fst` format. It allows extremely fast access to the data. The downside is that the data loses its portability. Going further, if your work involves multiple tables or access to small portions of the data at each stage of the research, I suggest using SQLite files.

4.8 Exercises

1. Create a dataframe with the following code:

```
my_N <- 10000
my_df <- data.frame(x = 1:my_N,
                    y = runif(my_N))
```

Export the resulting dataframe to each of the following formats: csv, rds, xlsx e fst.

Which format took more computer space? Tip: You can use function `file.size` to check the resulting file sizes.

2. Improve the previous code by measuring the execution time needed to record all data in the different formats. Which one had the minimum writing time? Tip: Use function `system.time` for measuring execution time.

3. Within the previous code, change the value of `my_N` to 1000000 and re-execute the code. Does this change modify the answers to the two previous questions? How?

4. Using functions `afedR::afedR_get_data_file` and `readr::read_csv`, read the contents of the book file `'SP500-Stocks_long.csv'`. How many columns and how many rows you find in this table?

5. At link https://eeecon.uibk.ac.at/~zeileis/grunfeld/Grunfeld.csv you can find the CSV file for the *Grunfeld* data. This is a particularly famous table due to its use as a benchmark data in econometric models. Using function `readr::read_csv`, read this file using the direct link in `read_csv`. How many rows do you find in the resulting `dataframe`?

6. **CHALLENGE** - In the following link:

https://perso.telecom-paristech.fr/eagan/class/igr204/data/nat1900-2017.tsv

you can find data about all baby names in France from 1900 to 2017. But, the data comes with a caveat: all columns are separated by a tab symbol. After reading the manual for `readr::read_delim`, import the information from this file on your computer. How many rows does the file contain?

Chapter 5

Importing Data from the Internet

It can be said that one of the great advantages of R is a large amount of data that can be imported using the internet. In fact, you can download and update a whole database within the script, which means that you can avoid all the tedious work of manual data collection. It also becomes easy to share reproducible code, as anyone can feasibly download the same tables with a single line of code.

In this chapter, I will describe and give examples of the most important and reliable packages for data importation in the fields of finance and economics. It is a small, but comprehensive list of packages that cover a large range of research topics. The list includes:

GetQuandlData (Perlin, 2019a) Imports economical and financial data from the Quandl platform.
BatchGetSymbols (Perlin, 2016) Imports adjusted and unadjusted stock price data from Yahoo Finance.
simfinR (Perlin, 2019b) Imports financial statements and adjusted stock prices from the SimFin project[1].
tidyquant (Dancho and Vaughan, 2019) Imports several financial information about stock prices and fundamental data.
Rbitcoin (Gorecki, 2014) Imports data for cryptocurrencies.

---

[1]https://simfin.com/

5.1 Package `GetQuandlData`

Quandl is an established and comprehensive platform that provides access to a series of free and paid data. Several central banks and research institutions provide free economic and financial information on this platform. I strongly recommend browsing the available tables from the Quandl website[2]. It is likely that you'll find datasets that you're familiar with.

In R, package `Quandl` (Raymond McTaggart et al., 2019) is the official extension offered by the company and available in CRAN. However, the package has some issues (see blog post here[3]) and it is uncomfortable to work with the `tidyverse` collection of packages. The alternative package `GetQuandlData` (Perlin, 2019a) is, in my humble and biased opinion as an author, a better alternative.

The **first and mandatory** step in using `GetQuandlData` is to register a user at the Quandl website. Soon after, go to *account settings* and click *API KEY*. This page should show a code, such as `Asv8Ac7zuZzJSCGxynfG`. Copy it to the clipboard (*control + c*) and, in R, define a character object containing the copied content as follows:

```
# set FAKE api key to quandl
my_api_key <- 'Asv8Ac7zuZzJSCGxynfG'
```

This API key is unique to each user, and the one presented here will not work on your computer. You'll need to get your own API key to run the examples of the book. After finding and setting your key, go to Quandl's website and use the search box to look for the symbol of the time series of interest. As an example, we will use data for gold prices in US dollars, with a Quandl code equivalent to `'WGC/GOLD_DAILY_USD'`. Do notice that the structure of a Quandl code is always the same, with the name of the main database at first, and the name of table second, separated by a forward slash (/).

Now, with the API key and the Quandl symbol, we use function `get_Quandl_series` to download the data from 1980-01-01 to 2019-01-01:

```
library(GetQuandlData)
library(tidyverse)

# set symbol and dates
```

---

[2] https://www.quandl.com/
[3] https://www.msperlin.com/blog/post/2019-10-01-new-package-getquandldata/

5.1. PACKAGE GETQUANDLDATA

```r
my_symbol <- c('Gold Prices in EURO' = 'WGC/GOLD_DAILY_USD')
first_date <- as.Date('1980-01-01')
last_date <- as.Date('2019-01-01')

# get data!
df_gold <- get_Quandl_series(id_in = my_symbol,
                             api_key = my_api_key,
                             first_date = first_date,
                             last_date = last_date)

# check it
glimpse(df_gold)
```

```
R> Observations: 10,384
R> Variables: 4
R> $ series_name <chr> "Gold Prices in EURO", "Gold P...
R> $ ref_date    <date> 2019-10-18, 2019-10-17, 2019-...
R> $ value       <dbl> 1490.00, 1492.65, 1485.10, 148...
R> $ id_quandl   <chr> "WGC/GOLD_DAILY_USD", "WGC/GOL...
```

Notice how we set the name of the time series inline `id_in = c('Gold Prices in EURO' = my_symbol)`. The name of the element becomes the value of column `series_name` in `df_gold`. If we had more time series, they would be stacked in the same table, but with different `series_name` value.

Worth knowing that other `Quandl` API options are available with inputs `order`, `collapse` and `transform`. If using `Quandl` is important to your work, I strongly recommend reading the available parameters for querying data[4]. Several choices for data transformations can be passed to function `get_Quandl_series`.

As an inspection check, let's plot the prices of Gold in USD over time. Here we will use the package `ggplot2` to create the figure. For now, you don't need to worry about the plotting code, because we have chapter 10, which is fully dedicated to this topic.

```r
library(ggplot2)

# plot prices with ggplot2
p <- ggplot(df_gold, aes(x = ref_date, y = value)) +
```

---

[4]https://docs.quandl.com/docs/parameters-2

```
  geom_line() +
  labs(y = 'Prices (USD)',
       x = '',
       title = 'Prices of Gold',
       subtitle = paste0(first_date, ' to ', last_date),
       caption = 'Data from Quandl') +
  theme_bw()

# print it
print(p)
```

Prices of Gold
1980-01-01 to 2019-01-01

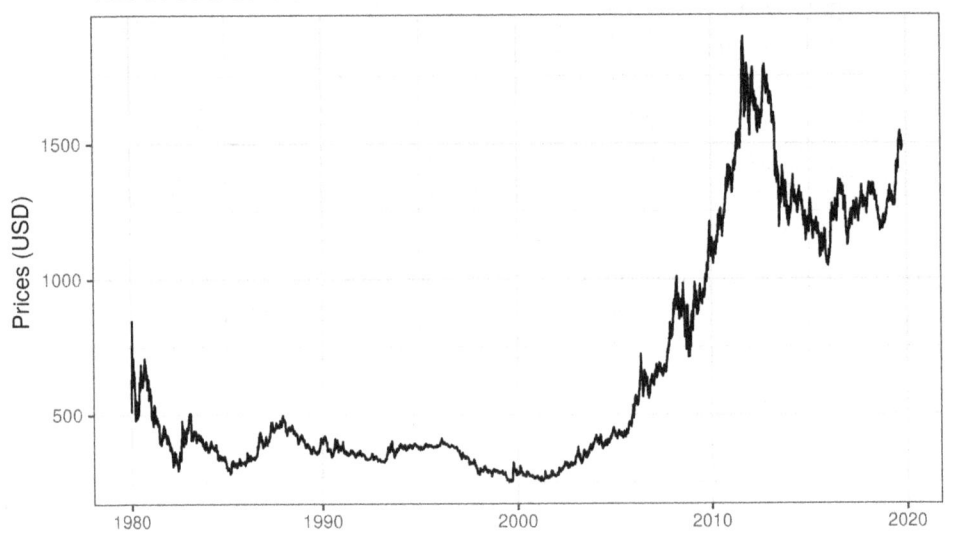

Data from Quandl

Overall, gold prices were fairly stable between 1980 and 2000, reaching a spike after 2010. One possible explanation is the higher demand for safer assets, such as gold, after the 2009 financial crisis. However, gold was never an efficient long term investment. To show that, let's calculate its compound annual return from 1980-01-01 to 2019-10-18:

```
# sort the rows
df_gold <- df_gold %>%
  arrange(ref_date)
```

5.1. PACKAGE GETQUANDLDATA

```
total_ret <- last(df_gold$value)/first(df_gold$value) - 1
total_years <- as.numeric(max(df_gold$ref_date) - 
                         min(df_gold$ref_date) )/365

comp_ret_per_year <- (1 + total_ret)^(1/total_years) - 1

print(comp_ret_per_year)
```

R> [1] 0.02718761

We find the result that Gold prices in USD compounded in a rate equal to 2.719% per year. This is not an impressive investment result by any means. As a comparison, the annual inflation for the US in the same period is 3.184. This means that by buying gold in 1980, the investor received less than the inflation as a nominal return, resulting in losing purchasing power.

5.1.0.1 Fetching many time series

When asking for multiple time series from Quandl, package GetQuandlData stacks all the data in a single dataframe, making it easier to work with the tidyverse tools. As an example, let's look at Quandl database RATEINF, which contains a time series of inflation rates around the world. First, we need to see what are the available datasets:

```
library(GetQuandlData)
library(tidyverse)

# databse to get info
db_id <- 'RATEINF'

# get info
df_db <- get_database_info(db_id, my_api_key)

glimpse(df_db)
```

```
R> Observations: 26
R> Variables: 8
R> $ code         <chr> "CPI_ARG", "CPI_AUS", "CPI_CA...
R> $ name         <chr> "Consumer Price Index - Argen...
R> $ description  <chr> "Please visit <a href=http://...
```

```
R> $ refreshed_at <dttm> 2020-02-08 02:13:22, 2020-02...
R> $ from_date    <date> 1988-01-31, 1948-09-30, 1989...
R> $ to_date      <date> 2013-12-31, 2019-12-31, 2019...
R> $ quandl_code  <chr> "RATEINF/CPI_ARG", "RATEINF/C...
R> $ quandl_db    <chr> "RATEINF", "RATEINF", "RATEIN...
```

Column `name` contains the description of tables. If we dig deeper, we'll find the following names:

`print(unique(df_db$name))`

```
R>  [1] "Consumer Price Index - Argentina"
R>  [2] "Consumer Price Index - Australia"
R>  [3] "Consumer Price Index - Canada"
R>  [4] "Consumer Price Index - Switzerland"
R>  [5] "Consumer Price Index - Germany"
R>  [6] "Consumer Price Index - Euro Area"
R>  [7] "Consumer Price Index - France"
R>  [8] "Consumer Price Index - UK"
R>  [9] "Consumer Price Index - Italy"
R> [10] "Consumer Price Index - Japan"
R> [11] "Consumer Price Index - New Zealand"
R> [12] "Consumer Price Index - Russia"
R> [13] "Consumer Price Index - USA"
R> [14] "Inflation YOY - Argentina"
R> [15] "Inflation YOY - Australia"
R> [16] "Inflation YOY - Canada"
R> [17] "Inflation YOY - Switzerland"
R> [18] "Inflation YOY - Germany"
R> [19] "Inflation YOY - Euro Area"
R> [20] "Inflation YOY - France"
R> [21] "Inflation YOY - UK"
R> [22] "Inflation YOY - Italy"
R> [23] "Inflation YOY - Japan"
R> [24] "Inflation YOY - New Zealand"
R> [25] "Inflation YOY - Russia"
R> [26] "Inflation YOY - USA"
```

What we want is the `'Inflation YOY - *'` datasets, which contain the year-on-year inflation rates for different countries. Let's filter the `dataframe` to keep the series with the yearly inflation, and select four countries:

5.1. PACKAGE GETQUANDLDATA

```
selected_series <- c('Inflation YOY - USA',
                     'Inflation YOY - Canada',
                     'Inflation YOY - Euro Area',
                     'Inflation YOY - Australia')

# filter selected countries
idx <- df_db$name %in% selected_series
df_db <- df_db[idx, ]
```

Now we grab the data using get_Quandl_series:

```
my_id <- df_db$quandl_code
names(my_id) <- df_db$name
first_date <- '2010-01-01'
last_date <- Sys.Date()

df_inflation <- get_Quandl_series(id_in = my_id,
                                  api_key = my_api_key,
                                  first_date = first_date,
                                  last_date = last_date)

glimpse(df_inflation)


R> Observations: 400
R> Variables: 4
R> $ series_name <chr> "Inflation YOY - Australia", "...
R> $ ref_date    <date> 2019-12-31, 2019-09-30, 2019-...
R> $ value       <dbl> 1.8, 1.7, 1.6, 1.3, 1.8, 1.9, ...
R> $ id_quandl   <chr> "RATEINF/INFLATION_AUS", "RATE...
```

And, finally, we create an elegant plot to see the behavior of the inflation rates in the selected countries:

```
p <- ggplot(df_inflation, aes(x = ref_date, y = value/100)) +
  geom_col() +
  labs(y = 'Inflation YOY (%)',
       x = '',
       title = 'Inflation in the World',
       subtitle = paste0(first_date, ' to ', last_date),
       caption = 'Data from Quandl') +
```

```
scale_y_continuous(labels = scales::percent) +
facet_wrap(~series_name) +
theme_bw()
```

```
print(p)
```

Inflation in the World
2010-01-01 to 2020-02-08

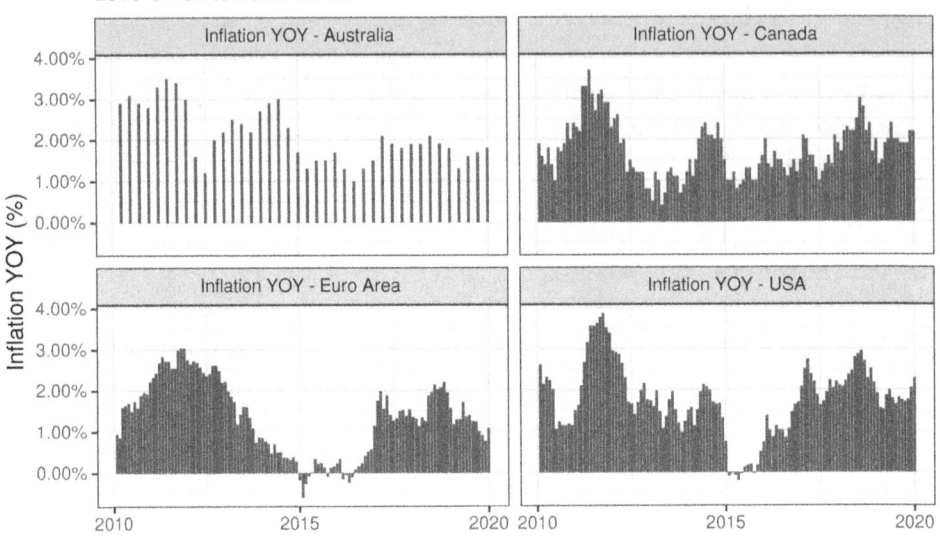

Data from Quandl

As you can see, the `GetQuandlData` output is formatted to work well with the `tidyverse` tools.

5.2 Package `BatchGetSymbols`

Package `BatchGetSymbols` (Perlin, 2016) is all about downloading stock price data from Yahoo Finance. Unlike other packages, `BatchGetSymbols` focuses on large batch downloads of structured and clean/tidy data. Its main features are:

Cleanliness and organization: All financial data from different *tickers* is kept in the same `dataframe` in a format that facilitates further analysis using packages from `tidyverse`.

5.2. PACKAGE BATCHGETSYMBOLS

Control of import errors: All download errors are registered in the output. If a particular stock does not have available data in Yahoo finance, it will be skipped and all other stock data are still downloaded and returned to the user;

Comparison of dates to a benchmark: Individual asset data is compared to data available for a benchmark, usually a market index. If the number of missing dates exceeds a certain limit set by the user, the stock is removed from the final dataframe. Moreover, you can set the minimal accepted volume of data for each stock, removing all stock cases with a low number of rows.

Caching system: By default, all imported data is locally saved using a clever caching system. Whenever the user repeats a data query, the cache system is used. If the desired data is not available in the cache, the function will only download the missing data. This significantly increases data access speed while minimizing the use of an Internet connection;

Access to *tickers* in market indices: The package includes functions to download the SP500 composition. This makes it easy to import data for a large number of stocks. You can, for example, download prices for all stocks constituents of the SP500 index.

Use of multiple cores: If the user is downloading a large batch of stock data, an option for parallel execution is available. The practical effect is, depending on the number of cores in the computer, a significant decrease in total download time.

Flexible output format: The package also offers functions to modify the format of the data. If you need the wide format dataframe, such as a price matrix where tickers are columns and prices are rows, all you need to do is call function `BatchGetSymbols::reshape.wide`. Likewise, changing the frequency of the data is also possible. You can, for example, download weekly or monthly prices.

As an example of usage, let's download the prices of four stocks in the previous five years using function `BatchGetSymbols`. We choose these companies: Microsoft (MSFT), Google (GOOGL), JP Morgan (JPM) and General Electric (GE).

In the call to function `BatchGetSymbols`, we set arguments `thresh.bad.data = 0.95` and `bench_ticker = '^GSPC'`. These choices make sure that all returned data have at least 95% of valid prices when compared to data from the SP500 index (ticker `'^GSPC'`).

```
library(BatchGetSymbols)

# set tickers
tickers <- c('MSFT','GOOGL','JPM','GE')

# set dates
first_date <- Sys.Date()-5*365
last_date <- Sys.Date()
thresh_bad_data <- 0.95    # sets percent threshold for bad data
bench_ticker <- '^GSPC'    # set benchmark as ibovespa
cache_folder <- 'data/BGS_Cache' # set folder for cache

l_out <- BatchGetSymbols(tickers = tickers,
                         first.date = first_date,
                         last.date = last_date,
                         bench.ticker = bench_ticker,
                         thresh.bad.data = thresh_bad_data,
                         cache.folder = cache_folder)
```

The output of `BatchGetSymbols` is an object of type `list`, which was not yet presented in this book. For now, all you need to know is that a `list` is a container for other objects. We will further study this class in chapter 6.

Back to our example, object `l_out` has two elements, a table called `df.control` and another table called `df.tickers`. We can access each element using operator $, such as in `l_out$df.control`. The first table, `df.control`, contains the result of the download process. As previously mentioned, the package not only downloads the data but also keeps track of possible errors and missing values. Let's check the content of this table.

```
# print result of download process
print(l_out$df.control)
```

```
R> # A tibble: 4 x 6
R>   ticker src   download.status total.obs
R>   <chr>  <chr> <chr>               <int>
R> 1 MSFT   yahoo OK                   1260
R> 2 GOOGL  yahoo OK                   1260
R> 3 JPM    yahoo OK                   1260
R> 4 GE     yahoo OK                   1260
R> # ... with 2 more variables:
R> #   perc.benchmark.dates <dbl>,
```

5.2. PACKAGE BATCHGETSYMBOLS

```
R> #   threshold.decision <chr>
```

Column `threshold.decision` from `df.control` shows that all tickers were valid, and we got 1260 valid observations (rows) for each company.

As for the actual financial data, it is contained in element `df.tickers` of `l_out`. Let's have a look:

```
# print df.tickers
glimpse(l_out$df.tickers)
```

```
R> Observations: 5,040
R> Variables: 10
R> $ price.open         <dbl> 42.24, 42.74, 42.65, 4...
R> $ price.high         <dbl> 42.74, 42.77, 42.65, 4...
R> $ price.low          <dbl> 42.21, 42.18, 42.21, 4...
R> $ price.close        <dbl> 42.36, 42.60, 42.38, 4...
R> $ volume             <dbl> 31381100, 29670700, 38...
R> $ price.adjusted     <dbl> 38.15845, 38.37465, 38...
R> $ ref.date           <date> 2015-02-09, 2015-02-1...
R> $ ticker             <chr> "MSFT", "MSFT", "MSFT"...
R> $ ret.adjusted.prices <dbl> NA, 0.0056657966, -0.0...
R> $ ret.closing.prices <dbl> NA, 0.0056656514, -0.0...
```

As expected, we find information about stock prices and traded volume. Notice it also includes column `ticker`, which contains the symbols of the stocks. In the tidy format, each stock has a chunk of data that is pilled in top of each other. Later, in chapter 8, we will use this column to split the data and build summary tables.

To inspect the data, let's look at its prices with `ggplot2`.

```
library(ggplot2)

p <- ggplot(l_out$df.tickers, aes(x = ref.date,
                                  y = price.adjusted)) +
  geom_line() + facet_wrap(~ticker, scales = 'free_y') +
  scale_y_continuous(labels = format.cash) +
  labs(x = '',
       y = 'Stock Adjusted Prices',
       title = 'Prices of four stocks',
       caption = 'Data from Yahoo Finance') +
```

```
theme_bw()
```

```
print(p)
```

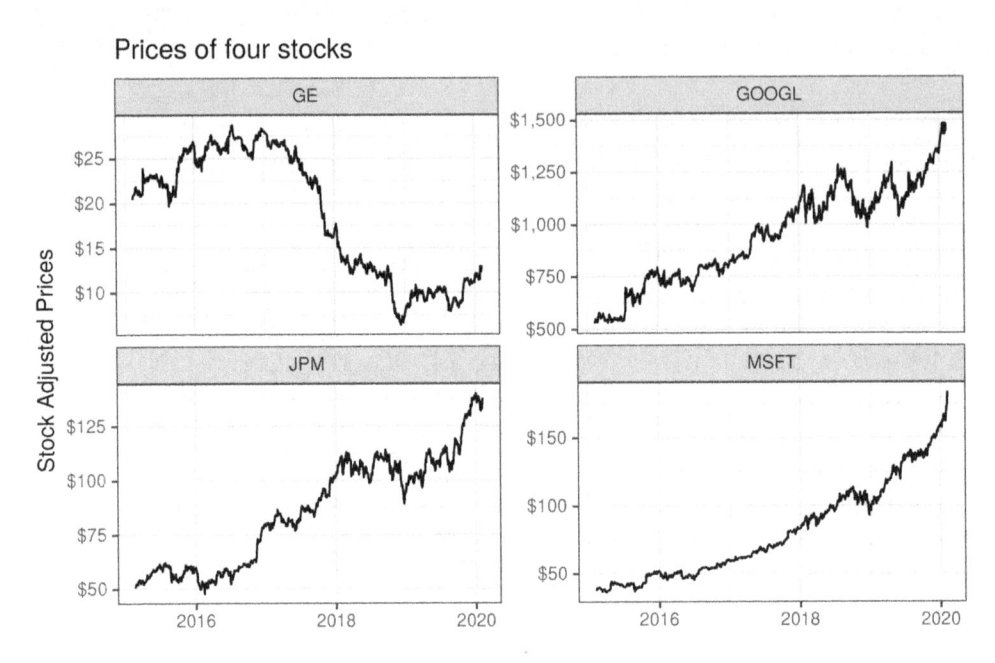

Prices of four stocks

Data from Yahoo Finance

We see that General Eletric (GE) stock was not kind to its investors. Someone that bought the stock at its peak in mid-2016 has found its current value at less than half. Now, when it comes to the GOOGL, JPM and MSFT, we see an upward increase in stock prices. These are profitable and competitive companies in their sectors and not surprisingly, the stock prices surged over time.

Now, let's look at an example of a large batch download of stock prices. For that, we had to find the group of tickers of stocks that currently belong to the SP500 index with function `BatchGetSymbols::GetSP500Stocks` first. After that, we simply pass the vector of tickers to `BatchGetSymbols`. We will also use parallel computing to speed up the importation:

```
library(BatchGetSymbols)

# set tickers
df_SP500 <- GetSP500Stocks()
```

5.2. PACKAGE BATCHGETSYMBOLS

```
sp500_tickers <- df_SP500$Tickers

# set dates
first_date <- '2010-01-01'
last_date <- '2019-01-01'
thresh_bad_data <- 0.95     # sets percent threshold for bad data
bench_ticker <- '^GSPC'     # set benchmark as ibovespa
cache_folder <- 'data/BGS_Cache' # set folder for cache

# set number of cores (half of available cores)
future::plan(future::multisession,
             workers = floor(parallel::detectCores()/2))

l_out <- BatchGetSymbols(tickers = sp500_tickers,
                         first.date = first_date,
                         last.date = last_date,
                         bench.ticker = bench_ticker,
                         thresh.bad.data = thresh_bad_data,
                         cache.folder = cache_folder,
                         do.parallel = TRUE)
```

And now we check the resulting data:

```
glimpse(l_out$df.tickers)
```

```
R> Observations: 1,027,664
R> Variables: 10
R> $ price.open         <dbl> 83.09, 82.80, 83.88, 8...
R> $ price.high         <dbl> 83.45, 83.23, 84.60, 8...
R> $ price.low          <dbl> 82.67, 81.70, 83.51, 8...
R> $ price.close        <dbl> 83.02, 82.50, 83.67, 8...
R> $ volume             <dbl> 3043700, 2847000, 5268...
R> $ price.adjusted     <dbl> 64.09430, 63.69284, 64...
R> $ ref.date           <date> 2010-01-04, 2010-01-0...
R> $ ticker             <chr> "MMM", "MMM", "MMM", "...
R> $ ret.adjusted.prices <dbl> NA, -0.0062636148, 0.0...
R> $ ret.closing.prices <dbl> NA, -0.0062635150, 0.0...
```

We get a table with 1027664 rows in `l_out$df.tickers`. Looking deeper into `l_out$df.control` we find that, out of 505 tickers, only 454 passed the consistency check. This is a fairly sized table. Notice how easy it was to get that large volume of data from Yahoo Finance into an R session.

5.3 Package `simfinR`

SimFin[5] is a special project for making financial data as accessible as possible. It works by gathering data from different stock exchanges and financial reports, cleaning and verifying it against official records, and distributing the tables from an API (*access point interface.*). From its own website:

> Our core goal is to make financial data as freely available as possible because we believe that having the right tools for investing/research shouldn't be the privilege of those that can afford to spend thousands of dollars per year on data.

The platform is free, with a daily limit of 2000 api calls. This is not bad and should suffice for most users. If you need more calls, the premium version[6] is just 10 euros a month, a fraction of what other data vendors usually request.

Package `simfinR` facilitates importing data from the SimFin API. First, it makes sure the requested data exists and only then calls the api. As usual, all api queries are saved locally using package `memoise`. This means that the second time you ask for a particular data about a company/year, the function will load a local copy, and will not call the web api.

The release version of the package `simfinR` is available in CRAN. You can install it with command `install.packages('simfinR')`.

5.3.1 Example 01 - Apple Inc Annual Profit

The first step in using `simfinR` is registering at the SimFin website. Once done, click on Data Access[7]. It should now show an API key such as `'rluwSlN304NpyJeBjlxZPspfBBhfJR4o'`. Save it in an R object for later use.

```
my_api_key <- 'rluwSlN304NpyJeBjlxZPspfBBhfJR4o'
```

You need to be aware that the **API key in `my_api_key` will not work for you**. You need to get your own to execute the examples.

With the API key in hand, the second step is to find the numerical id of the company of interest. For that, we can find all available companies and their respective ids and ticker with `simfinR_get_available_companies`.

---

[5] https://simfin.com/
[6] https://simfin.com/simfin-plus
[7] https://simfin.com/data/access/api

5.3. PACKAGE SIMFINR 131

```r
library(simfinR)
library(tidyverse)

# get info
df_info_companies <- simfinR_get_available_companies(my_api_key)

# check it
glimpse(df_info_companies)
```

```
R> Observations: 2,710
R> Variables: 3
R> $ simId  <int> 171401, 901704, 901866, 45730, 378251, 8...
R> $ ticker <chr> "ZYXI", "ZYNE", "ZVO", "ZUMZ", "ZTS", "Z...
R> $ name   <chr> "ZYNEX INC", "Zynerba Pharmaceuticals, I...
```

Digging deeper into the dataframe, we find that the numerical id of Apple is 111052. Let's use it to download the annual financial information since 2009.

```r
id_companies <- 111052 # id of APPLE INC
type_statements <- 'pl' # profit/loss
periods = 'FY' # final year
years = 2009:2018

df_fin_FY <- simfinR_get_fin_statements(
  id_companies,
  type_statements = type_statements,
  periods = periods,
  year = years,
  api_key = my_api_key)

glimpse(df_fin_FY)
```

```
R> Observations: 580
R> Variables: 13
R> $ company_name   <chr> "APPLE INC", "APPLE INC", "APPLE...
R> $ company_sector <chr> "Computer Hardware", "Computer H...
R> $ type_statement <fct> pl, pl, pl, pl, pl, pl, pl, pl, ...
R> $ period         <fct> FY, FY, FY, FY, FY, FY, FY, FY, ...
R> $ year           <int> 2009, 2009, 2009, 2009, 2009, 20...
```

```
R> $ ref_date       <date> 2009-12-31, 2009-12-31, 2009-12...
R> $ acc_name       <chr> "Revenue", "Sales & Services Rev...
R> $ acc_value      <dbl> 4.2905e+10, NA, NA, NA, -2.5683e...
R> $ tid            <chr> "1", "3", "5", "6", "2", "7", "8...
R> $ uid            <chr> "1", "0", "0", "0", "2", "0", "0...
R> $ parent_tid     <chr> "4", "1", "1", "1", "4", "2", "2...
R> $ display_level  <chr> "0", "1", "1", "1", "0", "1", "1...
R> $ check_possible <lgl> FALSE, FALSE, FALSE, FALSE, FALS...
```

And now we plot the results of the Net Income (profit/loss) for all years:

```
net_income <- df_fin_FY %>%
            dplyr::filter(acc_name == 'Net Income')

p <- ggplot(net_income,
           aes(x = ref_date, y = acc_value)) +
  geom_col()   +
  labs(title = 'Yearly Profit of APPLE INC',
       x = '',
       y = 'Yearly Profit',
       subtitle = '',
       caption = 'Data from simfin <https://simfin.com/>') +
  theme_bw()

print(p)
```

5.3. PACKAGE SIMFINR

Yearly Profit of APPLE INC

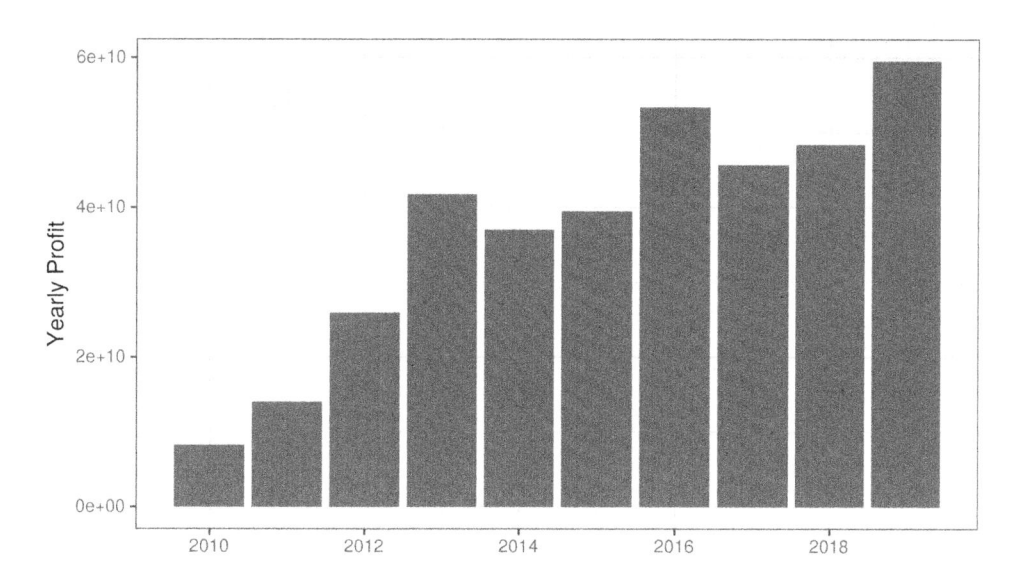

Data from simfin <https://simfin.com/>

Not bad! Apple has been doing very well over the years. We can also grab data for all quarters and get more detailed information:

```
type_statements <- 'pl' # profit/loss
periods = c('Q1', 'Q2', 'Q3', 'Q4') # final year
years = 2009:2018

df_fin_quarters <- simfinR_get_fin_statements(
  id_companies,
  type_statements = type_statements,
  periods = periods,
  year = years,
  api_key = my_api_key)

glimpse(df_fin_quarters)
```

```
R> Observations: 2,320
R> Variables: 13
R> $ company_name    <chr> "APPLE INC", "APPLE INC", "APPLE...
R> $ company_sector  <chr> "Computer Hardware", "Computer H...
R> $ type_statement  <fct> pl, pl, pl, pl, pl, pl, pl, pl, ...
R> $ period          <fct> Q1, Q1, Q1, Q1, Q1, Q1, Q1, Q1, ...
```

```
R> $ year           <int> 2009, 2009, 2009, 2009, 2009, 20...
R> $ ref_date       <date> 2009-03-31, 2009-03-31, 2009-03...
R> $ acc_name       <chr> "Revenue", "Sales & Services Rev...
R> $ acc_value      <dbl> 1.188e+10, NA, NA, NA, -7.373e+0...
R> $ tid            <chr> "1", "3", "5", "6", "2", "7", "8...
R> $ uid            <chr> "1", "0", "0", "0", "2", "0", "0...
R> $ parent_tid     <chr> "4", "1", "1", "1", "4", "2", "2...
R> $ display_level  <chr> "0", "1", "1", "1", "0", "1", "1...
R> $ check_possible <lgl> FALSE, FALSE, FALSE, FALSE, FALS...
```

And plot the results:

```
net_income <- df_fin_quarters %>%
              filter(acc_name == 'Net Income')

p <- ggplot(net_income,
            aes(x = period, y = acc_value)) +
  geom_col() + facet_grid(~year, scales = 'free') +
  labs(title = 'Quarterly Profit of APPLE INC',
       x = 'Quarters',
       y = 'Net Profit',
       caption = 'Data from simfin') +
  theme_bw()

print(p)
```

5.3. PACKAGE SIMFINR

Quarterly Profit of APPLE INC

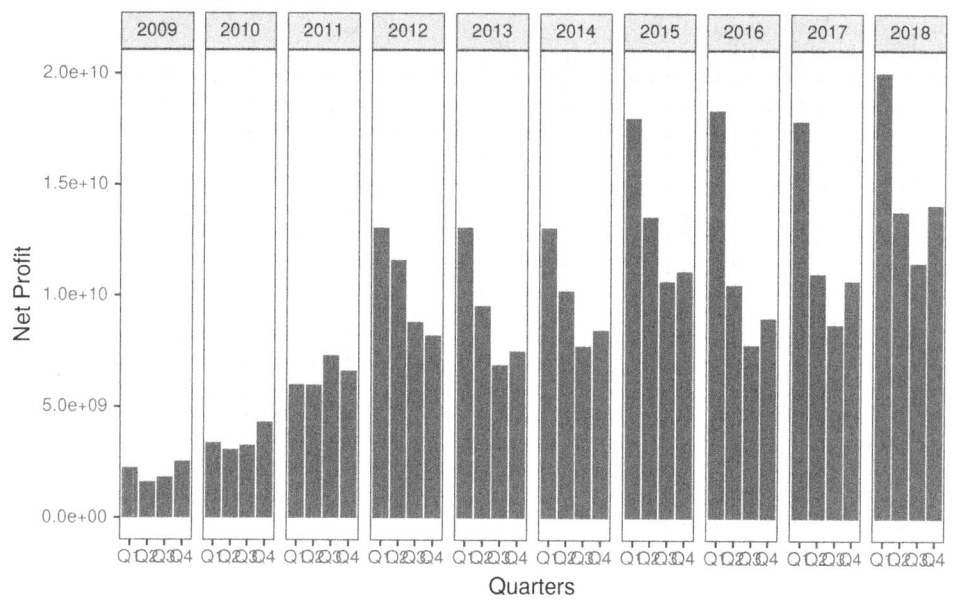

Data from simfin

Nice and impressive profit record. The first quarter (Q1) seems to present the best performance, probably due to the effect of Christmas in the retail business. Apple sells quality products at a premium price. Not surprisingly, many people want the new iphone for Christmas and that translates into more sells in the month of december, which are registered at the first quarter of the year.

5.3.2 Example 02 - Quarterly Net Profit of Many Companies

Package `simfinR` can also fetch information for many companies in a single call. Let's run another example by selecting four random companies and creating the same previous graph:

```
set.seed(5)
my_ids <- sample(df_info_companies$simId, 4)
type_statements <- 'pl' # profit/loss
periods = 'FY' # final year
years = 2010:2018

df_fin <- simfinR_get_fin_statements(
```

```
                id_companies = my_ids,
                type_statements = type_statements,
                periods = periods,
                year = years,
                api_key = my_api_key)

net_income <- df_fin %>%
              filter(acc_name == 'Net Income')

p <- ggplot(net_income,
            aes(x = ref_date, y = acc_value)) +
  geom_col() +
  labs(title = 'Annual Profit/Loss of Four Companies',
       x = '',
       y = 'Net Profit/Loss',
       caption = 'Data from simfin') +
  facet_wrap(~company_name, scales = 'free_y') +
  theme_bw()

print(p)
```

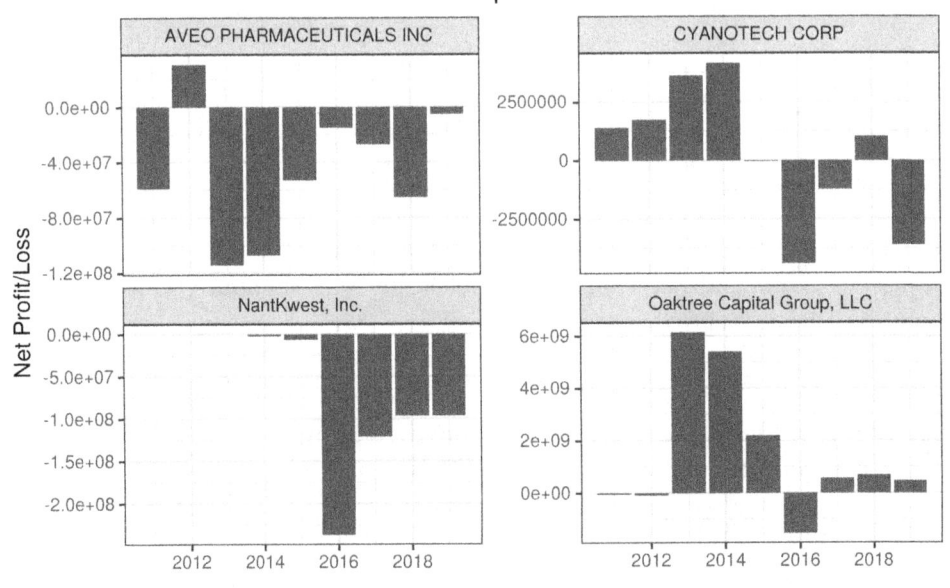

5.3. PACKAGE SIMFINR

5.3.3 Example 03: Fetching price data

The simfin project also provides prices of stocks, adjusted for dividends, splits and other corporate events. Have a look:

```
set.seed(5)
my_ids <- sample(df_info_companies$simId, 4)
type_statements <- 'pl' # profit/loss
periods = 'FY' # final year
years = 2009:2018

df_price <- simfinR_get_price_data(id_companies = my_ids,
                                    api_key = my_api_key)

p <- ggplot(df_price,
            aes(x = ref_date, y = close_adj)) +
  geom_line() +
  labs(title = 'Adjusted stock prices for four companies',
       x = '',
       y = 'Adjusted Stock Prices',
       caption = 'Price data from simfin') +
  facet_wrap(~company_name, scales = 'free_y') +
  theme_bw()

print(p)
```

Adjusted stock prices for four companies

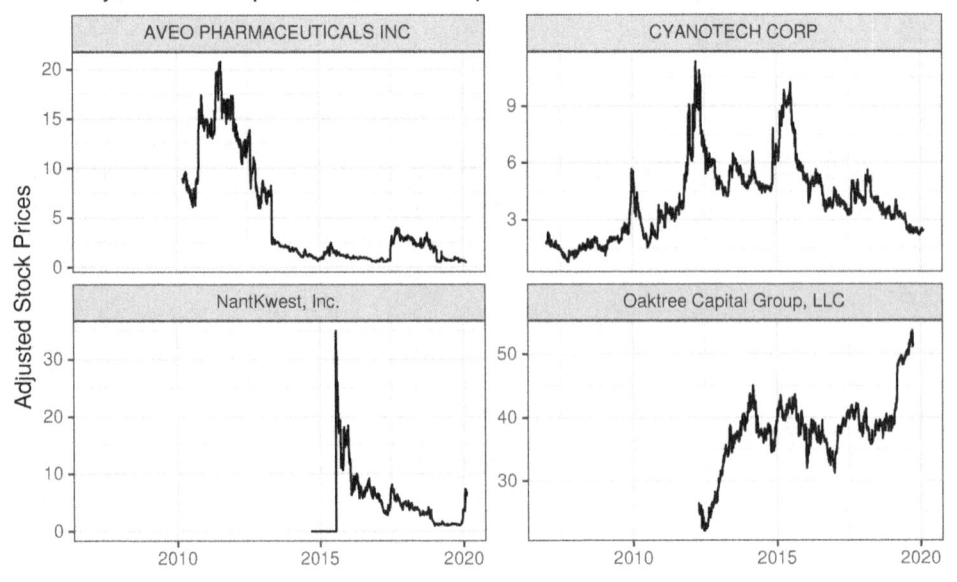

Price data from simfin

As you can see, the data is comprehensive and should suffice for many different corporate finance research topics.

5.4 Package `tidyquant`

Package `tidyquant` (Dancho and Vaughan, 2019) provides functions related to financial data acquisition and analysis. It is an ambitious project that offers many solutions in the field of finance. As you might suspect, `tidyquant` is designed to interact well with the *tidyverse* format, also known as the *long* format, discussed in chapter 6.

The package includes functions for obtaining financial data from the web, manipulation of such data, and the calculation of performance measures of portfolios.

In its current version, `tidyquant` has 47 functions. Let's look at its main functionalities. First, we will obtain price data for Apple stocks (AAPL) using function `tq_get`.

```
library(tidyquant)

# set stock and dates
```

5.4. PACKAGE TIDYQUANT

```
ticker <- 'AAPL'
first_date <- '2019-01-01'
last_date <- Sys.Date()

# get data with tq_get
df_prices <- tq_get(ticker,
                    get = "stock.prices",
                    from = first_date,
                    to = last_date)

glimpse(df_prices)
```

```
R> Observations: 278
R> Variables: 7
R> $ date     <date> 2019-01-02, 2019-01-03, 2019-01-...
R> $ open     <dbl> 154.89, 143.98, 144.53, 148.70, 1...
R> $ high     <dbl> 158.85, 145.72, 148.55, 148.83, 1...
R> $ low      <dbl> 154.23, 142.00, 143.80, 145.90, 1...
R> $ close    <dbl> 157.92, 142.19, 148.26, 147.93, 1...
R> $ volume   <dbl> 37039700, 91312200, 58607100, 547...
R> $ adjusted <dbl> 155.2140, 139.7535, 145.7195, 145...
```

As we can see, except for column names, the price data has a similar format to the one we got with `BatchGetSymbols`. This is not surprising as both share the same origin, Yahoo Finance.

One interesting aspect of `tidyquant` is the same function, `tq_get`, can be used to download other financial information from different sources, such as Google Finance, Morning Star, FRED, and Oanda. Likewise, we can access to information about US stock exchanges using function `tq_exchange`. In the next chunk of code, we find information about all stocks traded in the NYSE (New York Securities Exchange) market.

```
# get stocks in NYSE
df_nyse <- tq_exchange("NYSE")

glimpse(df_nyse)
```

```
R> Observations: 3,094
R> Variables: 7
R> $ symbol          <chr> "DDD", "MMM", "WBAI", "WUB...
```

```
R> $ company          <chr> "3D Systems Corporation", ...
R> $ last.sale.price  <dbl> 10.920, 160.080, 6.600, 58...
R> $ market.cap       <chr> "$1.29B", "$92.08B", "$283...
R> $ ipo.year         <dbl> NA, NA, 2013, 2013, NA, NA...
R> $ sector           <chr> "Technology", "Health Care...
R> $ industry         <chr> "Computer Software: Prepac...
```

We find 3094 stocks for 13 sectors and 133 different industries. Notice how we could use the ticker vector with `tidyquant::tq_get` or `BatchGetSymbols` to download price data for **all stocks** traded in the NYSE exchange.

We can also get information about components of an index using function `tq_index`. The available market indices are:

```
# print available indices
print(tq_index_options())
```

```
R> [1] "DOW"       "DOWGLOBAL" "SP400"    "SP500"
R> [5] "SP600"
```

Let's get information for `"DOWGLOBAL"`.

```
# get components of "DOWJONES"
print(tq_index("DOWGLOBAL"))
```

```
R> # A tibble: 156 x 8
R>    symbol company identifier sedol  weight sector
R>    <chr>  <chr>   <chr>      <chr>   <dbl> <chr>
R>  1 AAPL   Apple ~ 03783310   2046~ 0.00941 Infor~
R>  2 GE     Genera~ 36960410   2380~ 0.00872 Indus~
R>  3 6752-~ Panaso~ 657270     6572~ 0.00853 Consu~
R>  4 MSFT   Micros~ 59491810   2588~ 0.00848 Infor~
R>  5 ADBE   Adobe ~ 00724F10   2008~ 0.00836 Infor~
R>  6 VWS-DK Vestas~ 596465     5964~ 0.00812 Indus~
R>  7 NG-GB  Nation~ BDR05C     BDR0~ 0.00807 Utili~
R>  8 TSM    Taiwan~ 87403910   2113~ 0.00805 Infor~
R>  9 INTC   Intel ~ 45814010   2463~ 0.00802 Infor~
R> 10 UNH    United~ 91324P10   2917~ 0.00794 Healt~
R> # ... with 146 more rows, and 2 more variables:
R> #   shares_held <dbl>, local_currency <chr>
```

5.5 Package Rbitcoin

We only looked into a few functions from the package `tidyquant`. It also offers solutions for the usual manipulations, such as calculating returns and functions for portfolio analytics. You can find more details about this package in its website[8].

5.5 Package Rbitcoin

Given the lasting popularity of crypto-currencies, another package worth mentioning is `RBitcoin`. It allows access to trade data from several Bitcoin exchanges. Here, let's show a simple example of importing trade data from the `'Kraken'` exchange, using Euro as the currency.

```
library(Rbitcoin)

# set mkt, currency pair and type of action
mkt <- "kraken"
currency <- c("BTC","EUR")
action <- 'trades'

# import data
my_l <- market.api.process(market = mkt,
                           currency_pair = currency,
                           action = action)

# print it
print(my_l)


R> $market
R> [1] "kraken"
R>
R> $base
R> [1] "BTC"
R>
R> $quote
R> [1] "EUR"
R>
R> $timestamp
R> [1] "2020-02-08 17:47:13 -03"
R>
```

---
[8] https://business-science.github.io/tidyquant/

```
R> $market_timestamp
R> [1] NA
R>
R> $trades
R>                       date   price      amount
R>    1: 2020-02-08 19:10:43  9014.5  0.00974144
R>    2: 2020-02-08 19:10:43  9014.5  0.00812514
R>    3: 2020-02-08 19:10:45  9014.5  0.01786661
R>    4: 2020-02-08 19:10:49  9014.5  0.00338062
R>    5: 2020-02-08 19:10:51  9014.5  0.01070249
R>   ---
R>  996: 2020-02-08 20:45:33  9027.5  0.04000000
R>  997: 2020-02-08 20:45:50  9027.5  0.00400997
R>  998: 2020-02-08 20:46:02  9027.4  0.01038062
R>  999: 2020-02-08 20:47:03  9027.5  0.00698638
R> 1000: 2020-02-08 20:47:03  9027.5  0.80000000
R>                      tid  type
R>    1:               <NA>  ask
R>    2:               <NA>  ask
R>    3:               <NA>  ask
R>    4:               <NA>  ask
R>    5:               <NA>  ask
R>   ---
R>  996:               <NA>  bid
R>  997:               <NA>  bid
R>  998:               <NA>  bid
R>  999:               <NA>  bid
R> 1000: 1581194823167614322 bid
```

The output of `market.api.process` is a `list` object with information about Bitcoin in the `'Kraken'` market. The actual trades are available in the `trade` slot of `my_l`. Let's have a look at its content:

`glimpse(my_l$trades)`

```
R> Observations: 1,000
R> Variables: 5
R> $ date   <dttm> 2020-02-08 19:10:43, 2020-02-08 19...
R> $ price  <dbl> 9014.5, 9014.5, 9014.5, 9014.5, 901...
R> $ amount <dbl> 0.00974144, 0.00812514, 0.01786661,...
R> $ tid    <chr> NA, NA, NA, NA, NA, NA, NA, NA, NA,...
R> $ type   <chr> "ask", "ask", "ask", "ask", "ask", ...
```

It includes price and time information for the past 1000 trades. The package also includes functions for looking into the order book of each market and managing Bitcoin wallets. One can find more details about the functionalities of the package in its website[9].

5.6 Other Packages

In CRAN, you'll find many more packages for importing financial datasets in R. In this section, we focused on packages, which are free and easy to use. Interface with commercial data sources is also possible. Several companies provide APIs for serving data to their clients. Packages such as `Rblpapi` (Bloomberg), `IBrokers` (Interactive Brokers), `TFX` (TrueFX), `rdatastream` (Thomson Dataworks) can make R communicate with these commercial platforms. If the company you use is not presented here, check the list of packages in CRAN[10]. It is very likely you'll find what you need.

5.7 Accessing Data from Web Pages (*webscraping*)

Packages from the previous section make it easy to import data directly from the web with a single line of code. However, in many cases, the information of interest is not available through a package, but on a web page. Fortunately, we can use R to read the HTML data and import the desired information into an R session. The main advantage is that every time we execute the R code, we get the same content as the target website.

The process of extracting information from web pages is called *webscraping*. Depending on the structure and technology used on the internet page, importing its content can be as trivial as a single line in R or a complex process, taking hundreds of lines of code. Let's look at two simple examples; first, we will retrieve tabular information about the SP500 index from Wikipedia and, second, we will extract current inflation and interest rate from the Reserve Bank of Australia (RBA) website.

---

[9]https://github.com/jangorecki/Rbitcoin
[10]https://cran.r-project.org/

144   CHAPTER 5. IMPORTING DATA FROM THE INTERNET

5.7.1 Scraping the Components of the SP500 Index from Wikipedia

In its website, Wikipedia offers a section[11] about the components of the SP500 index. This information is presented in a tabular format, Figure 5.1.

Figure 5.1: Mirror of Wikipedia page on SP500 components

The information on this web page is constantly updated, and we can use it to import information about the stocks belonging to the SP500 index. Before delving into the R code, we need to understand how a webpage works. Briefly, a webpage is nothing more than a lengthy HTML code interpreted by your browser. A numerical value or text presented on the website can usually be found within the code. This code has a particular tree-like structure with branches and classes. Moreover, every element of a webpage has an address, called *xpath*. In chrome and firefox browsers, you can see the actual code of a webpage by using the mouse to right-click any part of the webpage and selecting *View page source*.

The first step in webscraping is finding out the location of the information you need. In Chrome, you can do that by right-clicking in the specific location of the number/text on the website and selecting *inspect*. This will open an extra window in the browser. Once you do that, right-click in the selection and chose *copy* and *copy xpath*. In Figure 5.2, we see a mirror of what you should be seeing in your browser.

Here, the copied *xpath* is:

---

[11]https://en.wikipedia.org/wiki/List_of_S%26P_500_companies

5.7. ACCESSING DATA FROM WEB PAGES (WEBSCRAPING)

Figure 5.2: Finding xpath from website

```
'//*[@id="mw-content-text"]/table[1]/thead/tr/th[2]'
```

This is the address of the header of the table. For the whole content of the table, including header, rows, and columns, we need to set an upper level of the HTML tree. This is equivalent to address //*[@id="MW-content-text"]/table[1].

Now that we have the location of what we want, let's load package rvest (Wickham, 2016b) and use functions read_html, html_nodes and html_table to import the desired table into R:

```
library(rvest)

# set url and xpath
my_url <- 'https://en.wikipedia.org/wiki/List_of_S%26P_500_companies'
my_xpath <- '//*[@id="mw-content-text"]/div/table[1]'

# get nodes from html
out_nodes <- html_nodes(read_html(my_url),
                        xpath = my_xpath)

# get table from nodes (each element in
# list is a table)
df_SP500_comp <- html_table(out_nodes)

# isolate it
df_SP500_comp <- df_SP500_comp[[1]]

# change column names (remove space)
```

```
names(df_SP500_comp) <- make.names(names(df_SP500_comp))

# print it
glimpse(df_SP500_comp)
```

```
R> Observations: 505
R> Variables: 9
R> $ Symbol                 <chr> "MMM", "ABT", "ABBV", "AB...
R> $ Security               <chr> "3M Company", "Abbott Lab...
R> $ SEC.filings            <chr> "reports", "reports", "re...
R> $ GICS.Sector            <chr> "Industrials", "Health Ca...
R> $ GICS.Sub.Industry      <chr> "Industrial Conglomerates...
R> $ Headquarters.Location  <chr> "St. Paul, Minnesota", "N...
R> $ Date.first.added       <chr> "", "1964-03-31", "2012-1...
R> $ CIK                    <int> 66740, 1800, 1551152, 815...
R> $ Founded                <chr> "1902", "1888", "2013 (18...
```

Object `df_SP500_comp` contains a mirror of the data from the Wikipedia website. The names of the columns require some work. However, the data is intact and could be further used in a script. Notice how the output is the exact same data as the previous use of function `BatchGetSymbols::GetSP500Stocks`. By executing command `edit(BatchGetSymbols::GetSP500Stocks)` you'll see that the source of data is the same and the code is similar to the one we just executed.

5.7.2 Scraping the Website of the Reserve Bank of Australia

As another example of webscraping with R, let's import information from the Reserve Bank of Australia. When accessed in 2019-07-25, its home page[12] mirrors Figure 5.3.

The website presents several information such as current news and interest rates. Let's assume we are interested in the information about the current cash/bank rate and inflation, right upper corner of the webpage.

The first step of *webscrapping* is finding out the *xpath* of the information we want. Using the procedure described in the previous example, we find out the address of both values, market rate and current inflation:

---

[12]http://www.rba.gov.au/

5.7. ACCESSING DATA FROM WEB PAGES (WEBSCRAPING)

Figure 5.3: Website for the Reserve Bank of Australia

```
xpath_inflation <- '//*[@id="content"]/section[1]/div/div[2]/p'
xpath_int_rate <- '//*[@id="content"]/section[1]/div/div[1]/p'
```

A difference from the previous example is we are not importing a table, but a simple text from the website. For that, we use function `html_text` and not `html_table`. The full code and its output are presented next.

```
library(rvest)

# set address of RBA
my_url <- 'https://www.rba.gov.au/'

# read html
html_code <- read_html(my_url)

# set xpaths
xpath_inflation <- '//*[@id="content"]/section[1]/div/div[2]/p'
xpath_int_rate <- '//*[@id="content"]/section[1]/div/div[1]/p'

# get inflation from html
my_inflation <- html_text(html_nodes(html_code,
                                     xpath = xpath_inflation ))
```

```
# get interest rate from html
my_int_rate <- html_text(html_nodes(x = html_code,
                                    xpath = xpath_int_rate ))
```

And now we print the result:

```
# print result
cat("\nCurrent inflation in AUS:", my_inflation)
```

```
R>
R> Current inflation in AUS: 1.3%
```

```
cat("\nCurrent interest rate AUS:", my_int_rate)
```

```
R>
R> Current interest rate AUS: 1.00%
```

Using *webscraping* techniques can become a strong ally of the researcher. It can give you access to an immense amount of information available on the web. However, each scenario of *webscraping* is particular. It is not always the case you can import data directly and easily as in previous examples.

Another problem is that the webscrapping code depends on the structure of the website. Any simple change in the *html* structure and your code will fail. You should be aware that maintaining a *webscraping* code can demand significant time and effort from the developer. If possible, you should always check for alternative sources of the same information.

Readers interested in this topic should study the functionalities of packages `rvest` (Wickham, 2016b), `XML` (Lang and the CRAN Team, 2016), `RSelenium` (Harrison, 2016) and `splashr` (available in Github[13]). Each one of these is best suited to sove a particular webscraping problem.

5.8 Exercises

1. Using the `BatchGetSymbols` package, download price data for Tesla, Inc. (TSLA) in the last two years. What is the lowest adjusted price you can find? What is the date with the lowest price? Tip: Use function `which.min` to find the position of the minimum price.

---

[13]https://github.com/hrbrmstr/splashr

5.8. EXERCISES

2. Use `tidyquant::tq_get` to download historical values for the SP500 index (^GSPC) since 1950 until today. What is the annual compound rate of return for the index?

3. Use the Quandl search box[14] to find available databases for your country. This includes databases from Central Banks and research agencies. Cite those that are most popular and most likely to be used in your work.

4. Create a profile on the Quandl website[15]. Using `GetQuandlData`, download unemployment data for Brazil using the Central Bank of Brazil Statistical Database. What is the latest value of this series?

5. What is the latest value of EUR Bitcoin at BTC? Use trade price data information from the `Kraken` exchange to solve the exercise.

---

[14] https://www.quandl.com/search
[15] https://www.quandl.com/

Chapter 6

Dataframes and other objects

In R, everything is an object with its own properties. A `numeric` vector can interact with other `numeric` objects in operations such as multiplication, division, and addition. This is not true for objects of the `character` class, where mathematical properties are not valid or intuitive – it does not make sense to add a numeric value to a text or to divide a text for other text. But, the `character` class has other properties, such as allowing the user to look for a specific chunk of characters, splitting parts of a text, and replacing specific characters, among many other possibilities. **One of the most important aspects of working with R is learning the functionalities of the object classes**.

The basic object classes in R include numeric values, characters (text), factors, dates, among many other cases. However, base classes are stored in more complex data structures, such as **dataframes** (tables) and lists. Such an organization makes the job of manipulating data a lot easier. Imagine, for example, conducting a study using price and volume data for five hundred stocks. If we used one numeric object – a vector – for each stock's volume and price, we would have one thousand objects to handle in our *environment*. Although it is possible to work this way, the resulting code would be disorganized, difficult to understand, and prone to errors – the so-called spaguetti code[1]. So twisted and tangled that it becomes difficult to use and maintain.

To avoid that, a simpler way to organize our data is to create an object named `my_data` and allocate prices and volumes there. All the information needed to perform the study would be in this object, facilitating the import

---

[1]https://en.wikipedia.org/wiki/Spaghetti_code

and export of data. Our code would also be simpler and more structured as would only need to manipulate one object – a table, expanding it with new variables or relating it to other tables. Said that, let's have a closer look at objects for structuring datasets, including `dataframes`, `lists` and `matrices`.

6.1 Dataframes

Without a doubt, the `dataframe` class is the most used and most important object to understand while learning R. You will spend most of your time manipulating one or many `dataframes` to get the result you need. A `dataframe` is simply a table with rows and columns. It allows for each column to have a different class. We can organize text data into a dataframe along with numbers, for example. This flexibility makes the `dataframe` an efficient object to represent heterogeneous datasets. Internally, a dataframe is a special type of `list`, where each column is an atomic vector.

A `dataframe` can organize our work significantly. The tabular structure of a `dataframe` forces the data to be *paired*, where each row is a different data point with several pieces of information (columns). This simple data structure can accommodate an infinite variety of information. As new data points arrive, the number of rows increases. When a new variable is inserted in the analysis, we simply add a new column to the existing table.

Another positive aspect of using the `dataframe` class in R is that several functions expect a `dataframe` as input. For example, the data manipulation package `dplyr` and the graphical package `ggplot2` work from a `dataframe` only. Operations of importing and exporting information are mostly `dataframe` oriented. Without a doubt, `dataframes` are at the centre of functionalities in R, and you **must** master the manipulation of this object.

6.1.1 Creating `dataframes`

The `dataframe` object is one of R's native classes and is implemented in the `base` package. We can, for example, create a `dataframe` with function `base::data.frame`. However, the `tidyverse` universe offers its own version of a dataframe, called `tibble`. Converting a dataframe to `tibble` is internal and automatic. A `tibble` object is more flexible than native `dataframes`, making it significantly easier to use. Following our preference for the `tidyverse` functions, from now on we will use `tibbles` as our version of `dataframes`.

6.1. DATAFRAMES

We call function `tibble::tibble` to create a `dataframe`. Notice that function `tibble:data_frame` does the same job, but has been deprecated. This means that developers of the `tibble` package will give preference to the `tibble` function in the future and, as users, we should follow the recommendation. We will now use this function for creating a `dataframe` with financial data of different stocks.

```
library(tidyverse)

# set tickers
tickers <- c(rep('AAP',5),
             rep('COG', 5),
             rep('BLK', 5),
             rep('CAM',5) )

# set a date vector
dates <- as.Date(rep(c("2010-01-04", "2010-01-05", "2010-01-06",
                       "2010-01-07", "2010-01-08"), 4) )

# set prices
prices <- c(40.38,  40.14,  40.49,  40.48,  40.64,
            46.23,  46.17,  45.97,  45.56,  45.46,
            238.58, 239.61, 234.67, 237.25, 238.92,
            43.43,  43.96,  44.26,  44.5,   44.86)

# create tibble/dataframe
my_df <- tibble(tickers, dates, prices)

# print its first 5 rows
print(head(my_df))
```

```
R> # A tibble: 6 x 3
R>   tickers dates      prices
R>   <chr>   <date>      <dbl>
R> 1 AAP     2010-01-04   40.4
R> 2 AAP     2010-01-05   40.1
R> 3 AAP     2010-01-06   40.5
R> 4 AAP     2010-01-07   40.5
R> 5 AAP     2010-01-08   40.6
R> 6 COG     2010-01-04   46.2
```

We used the function `rep` to replicate and facilitate the creation of the raw data for the `dataframe` object. Notice how all our data is now stored in a single object, facilitating access and organization of the resulting code. The content of `my_df` can also be viewed in the RStudio interface. To do so, click on the object name in the *environment* tab, top right of the screen. After that, a viewer will appear on the main screen of the program, as in 6.1.

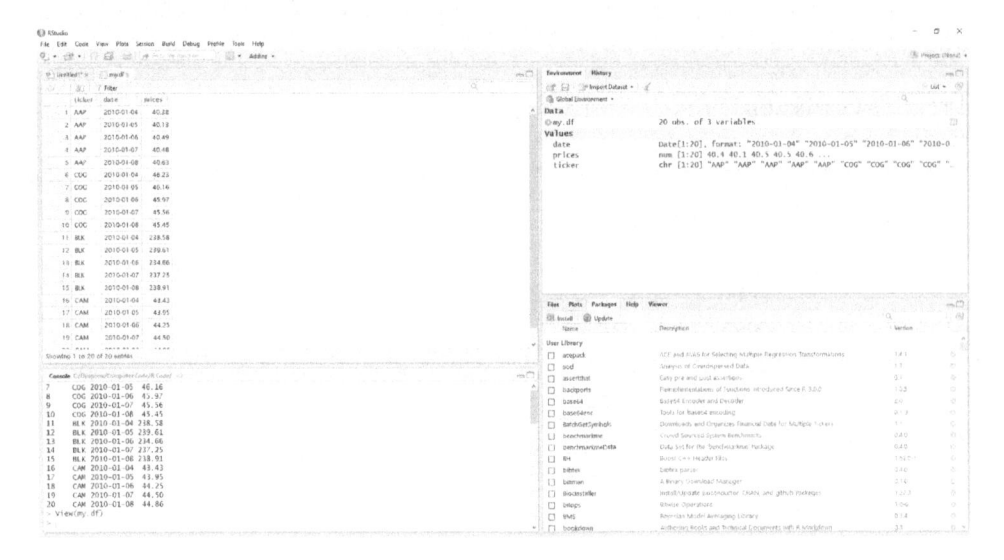

Figure 6.1: Example of viewing a dataframe in RStudio

The advantage of using the viewer is that you can explore the data and easily sort the columns by clicking on their names. For those who like to use the prompt, you can open the viewer with function `View`, as in `View(my_df)`.

6.1.2 Inspecting a Dataframe

Once you have a dataframe in your R session, the following and **mandatory** step is to check its contents. With time, this should become a healthy habit in your work. We need to be aware of these items:

- Properly defined column's names and classes;
- Correct number of rows and columns;
- The existence (or not) of missing data (`NA`).

We often have no control over how we get our data and errors in column names are very common. With that in mind, having meaningful column names that are intuitive, easy to access and without special characters is essential. Therefore, the first step in checking a `dataframe` is to analyze the names of columns and, if necessary, adjust the code. As a rule, **never**

6.1. DATAFRAMES

touch the content of raw tables, always use code to further manipulate the data.

It is also very important to make sure that the classes of columns from the imported `dataframe` are correctly specified. Otherwise, future column operations may cause an error. For example, if a column of numeric values is imported with the text class (`character`), any mathematical operation with that column will cause an error. **Checking column's classes right after importing the data are imperative** and will save you a lot of time.

We should also check for the number of `NA` values in the different columns. Whenever you find a large proportion of `NA` values in the imported table, you should find out what is going on and if the information is being correctly imported. As mentioned in the previous chapter, `NA` values are contagious and will turn anything it touches into another `NA`.

Back to the code, one of the most recommended functions for familiarizing yourself with a `dataframe` is `dplyr::glimpse`. It shows the name and class of the columns and the number of rows/columns. We used and abused this function in previous chapters. Here's a simple example:

```
# check content of my_df
glimpse(my_df)
```

```
R> Observations: 20
R> Variables: 3
R> $ tickers <chr> "AAP", "AAP", "AAP", "AAP", "AAP",...
R> $ dates   <date> 2010-01-04, 2010-01-05, 2010-01-0...
R> $ prices  <dbl> 40.38, 40.14, 40.49, 40.48, 40.64,...
```

Usually, the use of `glimpse` is sufficient to check if the data import process has succeeded. However, a deeper analysis can also help to understand how each column varies in the imported data and if that makes sense to our problem. Here comes the role of the `base::summary` function:

```
# check variation my_df
summary(my_df)
```

```
R>     tickers              dates
R>  Length:20          Min.   :2010-01-04
R>  Class :character   1st Qu.:2010-01-05
R>  Mode  :character   Median :2010-01-06
```

```
R>                    Mean   :2010-01-06
R>                    3rd Qu.:2010-01-07
R>                    Max.   :2010-01-08
R>      prices
R>  Min.   : 40.14
R>  1st Qu.: 42.73
R>  Median : 45.16
R>  Mean   : 92.08
R>  3rd Qu.: 93.34
R>  Max.   :239.61
```

The objective of summary is to provide a grasp of the content for each column of the dataframe. Notice that summary interprets each column differently. For the first case, column ticker, a *character* vector, it shows only its length. But, for column prices, a numeric vector, it presents its maximum, minimum, median and quartiles. We can use a simple call to base::summary for inspecting the contents of all columns. For example, an extreme observation (*outlier*) could easily be identified by analyzing the output of summary.

A more visual way of inspecting dataframes is with package inspectdf (Rushworth, 2019). Based on it, we can plot figures that show different information such as the number of NA by column, the statistical distribution of numeric data, among other cases. Here we'll use the same example data and investigate properties of it.

```
library(inspectdf)

# inspect categories of columns
show_plot(inspect_cat(my_df))
```

6.1. DATAFRAMES

Frequency of categorical levels in df::my_df
Gray segments are missing values

dates	2010-01-04	2010-01-05	2010-01-06	2010-01-07	2010-01-08
tickers	AAP	BLK		COG	

```
# inspect NA values
show_plot(inspect_na(my_df))
```

Prevalence of NAs in df::my_df
df::my_df has 3 columns, of which 0 have missing values

```
# inspect memory size of columns
show_plot(inspect_mem(my_df))
```

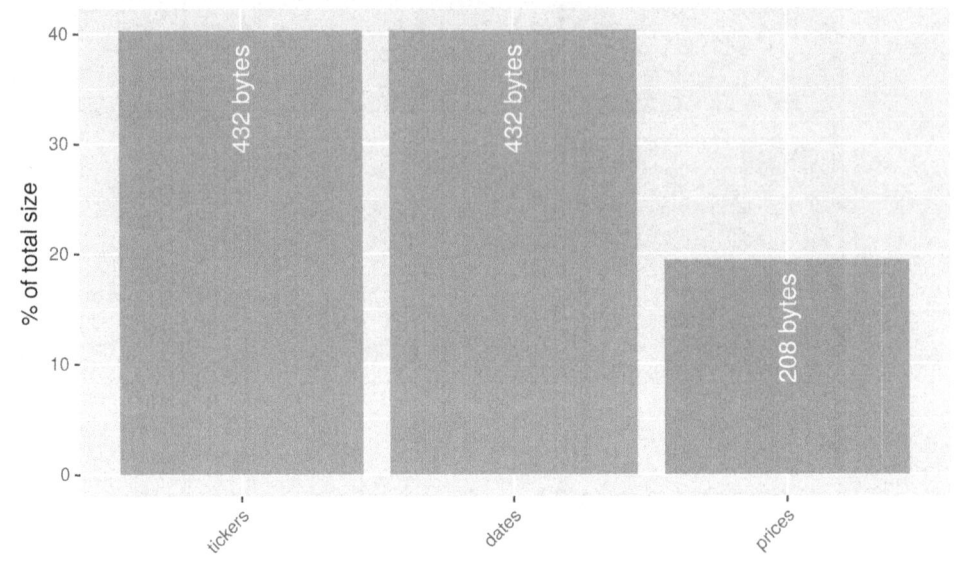

Column sizes in df::my_df

df::my_df has 3 columns, 20 rows & total size of 2 Kb

- tickers: 432 bytes
- dates: 432 bytes
- prices: 208 bytes

If you prefer visual analysis, **inspectdf** can be of great help in better understanding the content of a **dataframe**. From the previous example, we have the categorical levels of all columns of **my_df**, the number of **NA** by column and the size of each column in hard disk space.

6.1.3 The *pipeline* Operator (%>%)

An important feature of the **tidyverse** universe is the extensive use of the *pipeline* operator, first proposed by Bache and Wickham (2014) in package **magrittr** and defined by symbol **%>%**. The *pipeline* operator allows data operations to be performed sequentially and in a modular fashion, increasing readability and maintainability of the resulting code.

Imagine a situation where we have three functions to be applied to a **dataframe**. Each function depends on the output of another function. This requires chaining your calls, so one output feeds an object to the next call. Using the *pipeline* operator, we can write the **dataframe** manipulation procedure with the following code:

6.1. DATAFRAMES

```
my_tab <- my_df %>%
  fct1(arg1) %>%
  fct2(arg2) %>%
  fct3(arg3)
```

We use symbol %>% at the end of each line to "glue" the operations. The `fct*` functions are operations performed at each step. The `arg*` objects are just arguments (options) for each function call. The result of each code line is passed to the next function sequentially. Thus, there is no need to create intermediate objects. To compare, here are two ways to perform the same operation **without** the *pipeline* operator:

```
# version 1
my_tab <- fct3(fct2(fct1(my_df,
                        arg1),
                   arg2),
              arg1)
```

```
# version 2
temp1 <- fct1(my_df, arg1)
temp2 <- fct2(temp1, arg2)
my_tab <- fct3(temp1, arg3)
```

Notice how the alternatives result in a messy code structure. Version one is the ugliest. You need to pay attention to understand the code. You probably haven't noticed, but both codes have typos and would cause a bug. For the first, the last `arg1` argument should be `arg3` and, in the second, the `fct3` function is using the `temp1` dataframe and not `temp2`. This example shows how using *pipelines* makes the code more elegant and readable. From now on we will use the pipeline operator extensively.

6.1.4 Accessing Columns

To discover the names of the columns of a `dataframe`, we have two functions, `names` and `colnames`, with the exact same behavior:

```
# get names of columns with names
names(my_df)
```

```
R> [1] "tickers" "dates"    "prices"
```

```
colnames(my_df)
```

```
R> [1] "tickers" "dates"   "prices"
```

Both can also modify column names:

```
# set temp df
temp_df <- my_df

# change names
names(temp_df) <- paste('Col', 1:ncol(temp_df))

# check names
names(temp_df)
```

```
R> [1] "Col 1" "Col 2" "Col 3"
```

In this example, the way we use **names** differs greatly from other R functions. Here, we use the function on the left side of the **assign** symbol (<-). Internally, we are defining an attribute of the **temp_df** object, the name of its columns.

To access a particular column of a **dataframe**, we can use operator $ or the name/position of the column with brackets. See next:

```
# isolate columns of df
my_tickers <- my_df$tickers
my_prices <- my_df['prices']
my_dates <- my_df[ ,2]

# print the results
print(head(my_tickers))
```

```
R> [1] "AAP" "AAP" "AAP" "AAP" "AAP" "COG"
```

```
print(head(my_prices))
```

6.1. DATAFRAMES

```
R> # A tibble: 6 x 1
R>   prices
R>    <dbl>
R> 1  40.4
R> 2  40.1
R> 3  40.5
R> 4  40.5
R> 5  40.6
R> 6  46.2
```

```
print(head(my_dates))
```

```
R> # A tibble: 6 x 1
R>   dates
R>   <date>
R> 1 2010-01-04
R> 2 2010-01-05
R> 3 2010-01-06
R> 4 2010-01-07
R> 5 2010-01-08
R> 6 2010-01-04
```

It's worth knowing that, internally, dataframes are stored as `lists`, where each element is a column. This is important because some properties of `lists` also work for `dataframes`. One example is using a double bracket (`[[ ]]`) for selecting columns:

```
# select column in dataframe with list notation
print(my_df[[2]])
```

```
R>  [1] "2010-01-04" "2010-01-05" "2010-01-06"
R>  [4] "2010-01-07" "2010-01-08" "2010-01-04"
R>  [7] "2010-01-05" "2010-01-06" "2010-01-07"
R> [10] "2010-01-08" "2010-01-04" "2010-01-05"
R> [13] "2010-01-06" "2010-01-07" "2010-01-08"
R> [16] "2010-01-04" "2010-01-05" "2010-01-06"
R> [19] "2010-01-07" "2010-01-08"
```

To access specific rows and columns of a `dataframe`, use single brackets with atomic vectors that indicate positions:

```
# accessing rows 1:5, column 2
print(my_df[1:5, 2])
```

```
R> # A tibble: 5 x 1
R>   dates
R>   <date>
R> 1 2010-01-04
R> 2 2010-01-05
R> 3 2010-01-06
R> 4 2010-01-07
R> 5 2010-01-08
```

```
# accessing rows 1:5, columns 1 and 2
print(my_df[1:5, c(1,2)])
```

```
R> # A tibble: 5 x 2
R>   tickers dates
R>   <chr>   <date>
R> 1 AAP     2010-01-04
R> 2 AAP     2010-01-05
R> 3 AAP     2010-01-06
R> 4 AAP     2010-01-07
R> 5 AAP     2010-01-08
```

```
# accessing rows 1:5, all columns
print(my_df[1:5, ])
```

```
R> # A tibble: 5 x 3
R>   tickers dates      prices
R>   <chr>   <date>     <dbl>
R> 1 AAP     2010-01-04  40.4
R> 2 AAP     2010-01-05  40.1
R> 3 AAP     2010-01-06  40.5
R> 4 AAP     2010-01-07  40.5
R> 5 AAP     2010-01-08  40.6
```

Column selection can also be performed using names, as in the following example:

6.1. DATAFRAMES

```
# selecting rows 1 to 3, columns 'ticker' and 'prices'
print(my_df[1:3, c('tickers', 'prices')])
```

```
R> # A tibble: 3 x 2
R>   tickers prices
R>   <chr>    <dbl>
R> 1 AAP      40.4
R> 2 AAP      40.1
R> 3 AAP      40.5
```

Or, using the pipeline operator and function `dplyr::slice` and `dplyr::select`:

```
my.temp <- my_df %>%
  select(tickers, prices) %>%
  slice(1:3) %>%
  glimpse()
```

```
R> Observations: 3
R> Variables: 2
R> $ tickers <chr> "AAP", "AAP", "AAP"
R> $ prices  <dbl> 40.38, 40.14, 40.49
```

6.1.5 Modifying a `dataframe`

To create new columns in a dataframe, simply use function `dplyr::mutate` and the *pipeline* operator.

```
# add columns with mutate
my_df <- my_df %>%
  mutate(ret = prices/lag(prices) -1,
         seq_1 = 1:nrow(my_df),
         seq_2 =  seq_1 +9) %>%
  glimpse()
```

```
R> Observations: 20
R> Variables: 6
R> $ tickers <chr> "AAP", "AAP", "AAP", "AAP", "AAP",...
R> $ dates   <date> 2010-01-04, 2010-01-05, 2010-01-0...
```

```
R> $ prices   <dbl> 40.38, 40.14, 40.49, 40.48, 40.64,...
R> $ ret      <dbl> NA, -0.0059435364, 0.0087194818, -...
R> $ seq_1    <int> 1, 2, 3, 4, 5, 6, 7, 8, 9, 10, 11,...
R> $ seq_2    <dbl> 10, 11, 12, 13, 14, 15, 16, 17, 18...
```

All new columns are defined as arguments in `dplyr::mutate`. Also note we use the `price` column to construct `ret`, the daily return of prices. A special case here is the creation of column `seq_2` based on `seq_1`, that is, even before it is explicitly calculated, it is possible to use the new column to create another one.

Another, more traditional way of creating new columns is using operator $:

```
# add new column with base R
my_df$seq_3 <- 1:nrow(my_df)

# check it
glimpse(my_df)
```

```
R> Observations: 20
R> Variables: 7
R> $ tickers  <chr> "AAP", "AAP", "AAP", "AAP", "AAP",...
R> $ dates    <date> 2010-01-04, 2010-01-05, 2010-01-0...
R> $ prices   <dbl> 40.38, 40.14, 40.49, 40.48, 40.64,...
R> $ ret      <dbl> NA, -0.0059435364, 0.0087194818, -...
R> $ seq_1    <int> 1, 2, 3, 4, 5, 6, 7, 8, 9, 10, 11,...
R> $ seq_2    <dbl> 10, 11, 12, 13, 14, 15, 16, 17, 18...
R> $ seq_3    <int> 1, 2, 3, 4, 5, 6, 7, 8, 9, 10, 11,...
```

Therefore, you can use $ to either access or modify a dataframe.

Going further, if we try to create a column with the number of elements different than the number of rows of the target `dataframe`, an error will appear.

```
my_df <- my_df %>%
    mutate(seq_3 = 1:100) %>%
    glimpse()
```

```
R> Error: Column `seq_3` must be length 20 (the number of rows) ...
```

6.1. DATAFRAMES

However, due to the simplified recycling rule, we can use single values to fill up a whole column:

```
my_df <- my_df %>%
  mutate(seq_3 = 1) %>%
  glimpse()
```

```
R> Observations: 20
R> Variables: 7
R> $ tickers <chr> "AAP", "AAP", "AAP", "AAP", "AAP",...
R> $ dates   <date> 2010-01-04, 2010-01-05, 2010-01-0...
R> $ prices  <dbl> 40.38, 40.14, 40.49, 40.48, 40.64,...
R> $ ret     <dbl> NA, -0.0059435364, 0.0087194818, -...
R> $ seq_1   <int> 1, 2, 3, 4, 5, 6, 7, 8, 9, 10, 11,...
R> $ seq_2   <dbl> 10, 11, 12, 13, 14, 15, 16, 17, 18...
R> $ seq_3   <dbl> 1, 1, 1, 1, 1, 1, 1, 1, 1, 1, 1, 1...
```

To remove columns from a `dataframe`, use function `dplyr::select` with the minus symbol for the undesired columns:

```
# removing columns
my_df.temp <- my_df %>%
  select(-seq_1, -seq_2, -seq_3) %>%
  glimpse()
```

```
R> Observations: 20
R> Variables: 4
R> $ tickers <chr> "AAP", "AAP", "AAP", "AAP", "AAP",...
R> $ dates   <date> 2010-01-04, 2010-01-05, 2010-01-0...
R> $ prices  <dbl> 40.38, 40.14, 40.49, 40.48, 40.64,...
R> $ ret     <dbl> NA, -0.0059435364, 0.0087194818, -...
```

Using base R, the traditional way of removing columns is to allocate a single value NULL to its contents:

```
# set temp df
temp_df <- my_df

# remove cols
temp_df$prices <- NULL
```

```
temp_df$dates    <- NULL
temp_df$ret      <- NULL
temp_df$tickers  <- NULL

# check it
glimpse(temp_df)
```

```
R> Observations: 20
R> Variables: 3
R> $ seq_1 <int> 1, 2, 3, 4, 5, 6, 7, 8, 9, 10, 11, 1...
R> $ seq_2 <dbl> 10, 11, 12, 13, 14, 15, 16, 17, 18, ...
R> $ seq_3 <dbl> 1, 1, 1, 1, 1, 1, 1, 1, 1, 1, 1, 1, ...
```

6.1.6 Filtering rows of a dataframe

A fairly common dataframe operation in R is to filter rows according to one or more conditions. For example, if we only wanted data from the 'COG' stock, we could use the filter function to filter the table:

```
# filter df for single stock
my_df.temp <- my_df %>%
  filter(tickers == 'COG') %>%
  glimpse()
```

```
R> Observations: 5
R> Variables: 7
R> $ tickers <chr> "COG", "COG", "COG", "COG", "COG"
R> $ dates   <date> 2010-01-04, 2010-01-05, 2010-01-0...
R> $ prices  <dbl> 46.23, 46.17, 45.97, 45.56, 45.46
R> $ ret     <dbl> 0.137549213, -0.001297859, -0.0043...
R> $ seq_1   <int> 6, 7, 8, 9, 10
R> $ seq_2   <dbl> 15, 16, 17, 18, 19
R> $ seq_3   <dbl> 1, 1, 1, 1, 1
```

We can go further and also filter data for 'COG' and dates after '2010-01-05':

6.1. DATAFRAMES

```r
# filter df for single stock and date
my_df.temp <- my_df %>%
  filter(tickers == 'COG',
         dates > as.Date('2010-01-05')) %>%
  glimpse()
```

```
R> Observations: 3
R> Variables: 7
R> $ tickers <chr> "COG", "COG", "COG"
R> $ dates   <date> 2010-01-06, 2010-01-07, 2010-01-08
R> $ prices  <dbl> 45.97, 45.56, 45.46
R> $ ret     <dbl> -0.004331817, -0.008918860, -0.002...
R> $ seq_1   <int> 8, 9, 10
R> $ seq_2   <dbl> 17, 18, 19
R> $ seq_3   <dbl> 1, 1, 1
```

Here we used symbol == to test for equality in column `ticker` and *greater than* (>) for selecting the rows where the dates are after 2010-01-05. There are plenty more operators for all kinds of logical conditions. We will study these in chapter 7.

6.1.7 Sorting a `dataframe`

After creating or importing a `dataframe`, we can sort its rows according to the values of any column. A common case where a sort operation is needed is when financial or economic data is imported, but the dates are not ascending. Depending on the situation, it may be easier – or expected – to deal with data where the dates are always increasing along the rows, from top to bottom. The sorting operation in `dataframes` is performed using function `dplyr::arrange` or `base::order`.

As an example, consider creating a `dataframe` with these values:

```r
# set new df
my_df <- tibble(col1 = c(4, 1, 2),
                col2 = c(1, 1, 3),
                col3 = c('a','b','c'))

# print it
print(my_df)
```

```
R> # A tibble: 3 x 3
R>    col1  col2 col3
R>   <dbl> <dbl> <chr>
R> 1    4     1 a
R> 2    1     1 b
R> 3    2     3 c
```

We use function `dplyr::arrange` and the *pipeline* operator to order the whole `dataframe` by the ascending values of column `col1`:

```
# sort ascending, by col1
my_df <- my_df %>%
  arrange(col1) %>%
  print()
```

```
R> # A tibble: 3 x 3
R>    col1  col2 col3
R>   <dbl> <dbl> <chr>
R> 1    1     1 b
R> 2    2     3 c
R> 3    4     1 a
```

We can also sort by descending values using `desc`:

```
# sort descending, col1 and col2
my_df <- my_df %>%
  arrange(desc(col1)) %>%
  print()
```

```
R> # A tibble: 3 x 3
R>    col1  col2 col3
R>   <dbl> <dbl> <chr>
R> 1    4     1 a
R> 2    2     3 c
R> 3    1     1 b
```

And, for multiple columns, using extra arguments in `arrange`:

6.1. DATAFRAMES

```r
# sort ascending, by col2 and col1
my_df <- my_df %>%
  arrange(col2, col1) %>%
  print()
```

```
R> # A tibble: 3 x 3
R>    col1  col2 col3
R>   <dbl> <dbl> <chr>
R> 1     1     1 b
R> 2     4     1 a
R> 3     2     3 c
```

As for base R, function `order` returns the position of the elements for the sorted vector. With the first column of `my_df`, the positions of the elements in ascending order are:

```r
# set index with positions of ascending order in col1
idx <- order(my_df$col1)

# print it
print(idx)
```

```
R> [1] 1 3 2
```

Therefore, when using the output of function `order` as an index of an existing `dataframe`, you get a new version of the `dataframe`, where all rows are set according to the ascending values of a particular column. See an example next:

```r
# order my_df by col1
my_df.2 <- my_df[order(my_df$col1), ]

# print result
print(my_df.2)
```

```
R> # A tibble: 3 x 3
R>    col1  col2 col3
R>   <dbl> <dbl> <chr>
R> 1     1     1 b
R> 2     2     3 c
R> 3     4     1 a
```

This operation may also be performed considering more than one column. See the following example, where we sort the rows of `my_df` using columns `col2` and `col1`.

```
# sort df with col2 and col1
my_df.3 <- my_df[order(my_df$col2, my_df$col1), ]

# print result
print(my_df.3)
```

```
R> # A tibble: 3 x 3
R>    col1  col2 col3
R>   <dbl> <dbl> <chr>
R> 1    1    1  b
R> 2    4    1  a
R> 3    2    3  c
```

6.1.8 Combining and Aggregating `dataframes`

In the practice of manipulating data, often you must aggregate multiple `dataframes` into a single one. This usually happens when the heterogeneous data is imported from different sources and we must bind them into a single table. In the simplest case of combining `dataframes`, we join them according to the rows (vertically) or columns (horizontally). For that, we have functions `dplyr::bind_rows` (alternative to `base::rbind`) and `dplyr::bind_cols` (alternative to `base::cbind`). Examples of usage are given next.

```
# set two dfs with same colnames
my_df_1 <- tibble(col1 = 1:5,
                  col2 = rep('a', 5))
my_df_2 <- tibble(col1 = 6:10,
                  col2 = rep('b', 5))

# bind them by rows
my_df <- bind_rows(my_df_1, my_df_2)

# print result
print(my_df)
```

6.1. DATAFRAMES

```
R> # A tibble: 10 x 2
R>     col1 col2
R>    <int> <chr>
R>  1     1 a
R>  2     2 a
R>  3     3 a
R>  4     4 a
R>  5     5 a
R>  6     6 b
R>  7     7 b
R>  8     8 b
R>  9     9 b
R> 10    10 b
```

Notice that, in the previous example, the names of columns are the same between my_df_1 and my_df_2. Function dplyr::bind_rows is very clever and will search for shared names and correctly bind the data, even if the column positions are different. If we swapped the positions of the columns, there would be no change in the result of the bind operation.

Another interesting aspect of dplyr::bind_rows is that, if the names of the columns don't match, the unmatched columns will return a NA result (not available). This means we can bind tables with different column names:

```
# set two df with different colnames
my_df_1 <- tibble(col1 = 1:5,
                  col2 = rep('a', 5))
my_df_2 <- tibble(col1 = 6:10,
                  col3 = rep('b', 5))

# bind them by rows (NA values for missing cols)
my_df <- bind_rows(my_df_1,
                   my_df_2)

# print result
print(my_df)
```

```
R> # A tibble: 10 x 3
R>    col1 col2  col3
R>   <int> <chr> <chr>
R> 1     1 a     <NA>
R> 2     2 a     <NA>
```

```
R>  3    3 a    <NA>
R>  4    4 a    <NA>
R>  5    5 a    <NA>
R>  6    6 <NA> b
R>  7    7 <NA> b
R>  8    8 <NA> b
R>  9    9 <NA> b
R> 10   10 <NA> b
```

For the case of column bind with function `dplyr::bind_cols`, the names of the columns must be different, but the number of rows must be the same:

```r
# set two dfs
my_df_1 <- tibble(col1 = 1:5,
                  col2 = rep('a', 5))
my_df_2 <- tibble(col3 = 6:10,
                  col4 = rep('b', 5))

# column bind dfs
my_df <- cbind(my_df_1, my_df_2)

# print result
print(my_df)
```

```
R>   col1 col2 col3 col4
R> 1   1    a    6    b
R> 2   2    a    7    b
R> 3   3    a    8    b
R> 4   4    a    9    b
R> 5   5    a   10    b
```

Sometimes, aggregating different tables won't be as easy as simply row or column binding. For example, imagine you have data for annual unemployment rates in one `dataframe` and data for monthly inflation in another. There, you can't just bind their columns as their frequency and number of rows are different. The solution is to use an index – a vector of dates – that relates both tables.

For that, you can use functions `dplyr::join*` to merge two dataframes using one or more indexes. This includes `dplyr::inner_join`, `dplyr::left_join`, `dplyr::full_join`, and many others. The main difference between them is how you treat the row cases without a match.

6.1. DATAFRAMES

For example, `dplyr::inner_join` keeps only the data where it finds a matching index, while `dplyr::full_join` keep everything from both tables and fills the missing information with `NA` values. Let's have a closer look by using a practical example of both.

```
# set df
my_df_1 <- tibble(date = as.Date('2016-01-01')+0:10,
                  x = 1:11)

my_df_2 <- tibble(date = as.Date('2016-01-05')+0:10,
                  y = seq(20,30, length.out = 11))
```

Please do notice that both dataframes share a column called `date`, which will be automatically used as a matching index.

```
# aggregate tables
my_df <- inner_join(my_df_1,
                    my_df_2)

glimpse(my_df)
```

```
R> Observations: 7
R> Variables: 3
R> $ date <date> 2016-01-05, 2016-01-06, 2016-01-07, ...
R> $ x    <int> 5, 6, 7, 8, 9, 10, 11
R> $ y    <dbl> 20, 21, 22, 23, 24, 25, 26
```

Now with `dplyr::full_join`:

```
# aggregate tables
my_df <- full_join(my_df_1,
                   my_df_2)

glimpse(my_df)
```

```
R> Observations: 15
R> Variables: 3
R> $ date <date> 2016-01-01, 2016-01-02, 2016-01-03, ...
R> $ x    <int> 1, 2, 3, 4, 5, 6, 7, 8, 9, 10, 11, NA...
R> $ y    <dbl> NA, NA, NA, NA, 20, 21, 22, 23, 24, 2...
```

Notice the difference in the number of rows from one to the other. When using `dplyr::full_join`, all unmatched cases are set to `NA`.

If we had **dataframes** with different column names, we can also set the index explicitly with argument **by** of `dplyr::*_join`. See the next example, where we set different column names and still match the data using a vector of dates:

```
# set df
my_df_3 <- tibble(ref_date = as.Date('2016-01-01')+0:10,
                  x = 1:11)


my_df_4 <- tibble(my_date = as.Date('2016-01-05')+0:10,
                  y = seq(20,30, length.out = 11))

# join by my_df.3$ref.date and my_df.4$my.date
my_df <- inner_join(my_df_3, my_df_4,
                    by = c('ref_date' = 'my_date'))

glimpse(my_df)
```

```
R> Observations: 7
R> Variables: 3
R> $ ref_date <date> 2016-01-05, 2016-01-06, 2016-01-...
R> $ x        <int> 5, 6, 7, 8, 9, 10, 11
R> $ y        <dbl> 20, 21, 22, 23, 24, 25, 26
```

Whenever you need to combine tables that share information, use one of the `dplyr::*_join` functions. The decision of how to treat the unmatched cases will depend on the problem you're analyzing.

6.1.9 Extensions of the `dataframe` Class

As mentioned in the previous chapter, one benefit of using R is the existence of a range of packages designed to deal with specific problems. This is also true for extensions of the basic data structure. While the `tibble` class is a good solution for most cases, sometimes, it can make more sense to store the data in a specific type of custom object. Over time, several solutions have been developed.

For example, it is common in economic and financial research to work with numeric data indexed by time. We can store this data in a matrix format,

6.1. DATAFRAMES

so each line represents dates and each column represents a variable. With this structure, time operations, such as period aggregations, are easier to perform. This is the main idea of package `xts` (Ryan and Ulrich, 2014). The great benefit of this alternative `dataframe` is that several functions for time aggregation and manipulation are available. We can turn a whole set of daily data for several variables to the weekly frequency in one line of code. In addition, various other functions automatically recognize the time index and adapt accordingly. One example is the creation of a figure with the values of a variable over time. The horizontal axes of the figure are automatically arranged as dates.

See the following example, where we represent the previous stock data as an `xts` object:

```
# load pkg
library(xts)

# set ticker symbols as a vector
tickers <- c('AAP', 'COG', 'BLK', 'CAM')

# set a date vector
dates <- as.Date(c("2010-01-04", "2010-01-05", "2010-01-06",
                   "2010-01-07", "2010-01-08"))

# set prices as  matrix
price_matrix <- matrix(c(40.38,  40.13,  40.49,  40.48,  40.63,
                         46.23,  46.16,  45.97,  45.56,  45.45,
                         238.58, 239.61, 234.66, 237.25, 238.91,
                         43.43,  43.95,  44.25,  44.5,   44.86),
                       nrow = length(dates))

# set xts object
my_xts <- xts(price_matrix, order.by = dates)

# set colnames
colnames(my_xts) <- tickers

# print it
print(my_xts)
```

```
R>               AAP   COG   BLK    CAM
R> 2010-01-04 40.38 46.23 238.58 43.43
```

```
R> 2010-01-05 40.13 46.16 239.61 43.95
R> 2010-01-06 40.49 45.97 234.66 44.25
R> 2010-01-07 40.48 45.56 237.25 44.50
R> 2010-01-08 40.63 45.45 238.91 44.86

# show its class
class(my_xts)
```

```
R> [1] "xts" "zoo"
```

In creating the xts object, notice how the time index is explicitly defined using argument order.by. This is a necessary step in creating every xts object.

The previous code can give the impression that the object my_xts is similar to a native dataframe. However, make no mistake. By having an explicit time index, object my_xts can be used for several privileged procedures. See the following example, where we create a new xts object with two columns and calculate the average of each column on a weekly basis.

```
# set number of time periods
N <- 500

# create matrix with data
my_mat <- matrix(c(seq(1, N), seq(N, 1)), nrow=N)

# set xts object
my_xts <- xts(my_mat, order.by = as.Date('2016-01-01')+1:N)

# apply mean function for each weel
my_xts_weekly_mean <- apply.weekly(my_xts, mean)

# print result
print(head(my_xts_weekly_mean))
```

```
R>              X.1   X.2
R> 2016-01-03   1.5 499.5
R> 2016-01-10   6.0 495.0
R> 2016-01-17  13.0 488.0
R> 2016-01-24  20.0 481.0
R> 2016-01-31  27.0 474.0
R> 2016-02-07  34.0 467.0
```

6.1. DATAFRAMES

In finance and economics, these time aggregations with `xts` objects are useful when working with data at different time frequencies. It is common to aggregate transaction data in the financial market for high-frequency intervals of 5 by 5 minutes. Such a procedure is easily accomplished in R through the correct representation of the data as `xts` objects. There are several other features in this package. Users that work frequently with time-indexed data are encouraged to read the manual[2] and learn more about it.

Package `xts` is not alone as an alternative to `dataframes`. For example, the data structure proposed by package `data.table` (Dowle et al., 2015) prioritizes processing time and uses a compact notation. If you like short notations for writing code and need a quick execution time, `data.table` is an impressive and powerful package. As another example, package `tibbletime` (Vaughan and Dancho, 2019) is, well, a time-oriented version of `tibble`, bringing together the benefits of `tidyverse` and `xts`.

6.1.10 Other Useful Functions for Handling dataframes

head Returns the first n rows of a `dataframe`. This function is mostly used for showing only a small part of a `dataframe` in the prompt.

```
# set df
my_df <- tibble(col1 = 1:5000,
                col2 = rep('a', 5000))

# print its first 5 rows
print(head(my_df, 5))
```

```
R> # A tibble: 5 x 2
R>     col1 col2
R>    <int> <chr>
R> 1      1 a
R> 2      2 a
R> 3      3 a
R> 4      4 a
R> 5      5 a
```

tail - Returns the last n rows of a `dataframe`. Also used to glimpse the last rows of a `dataframe`.

---
[2]https://cran.r-project.org/web/packages/xts/xts.pdf

```r
# print its last 5 rows
print(tail(my_df, 5))
```

```
R> # A tibble: 5 x 2
R>    col1 col2
R>   <int> <chr>
R> 1  4996 a
R> 2  4997 a
R> 3  4998 a
R> 4  4999 a
R> 5  5000 a
```

complete.cases - Returns a logical vector with the same length as the number of rows of the `dataframe`, containing **TRUE** when all columns have non **NA** values and **FALSE** otherwise.

```r
# create df
my_df <- tibble(x = c(1:5, NA, 10),
                y = c(5:10, NA))

# show df
print(my_df)
```

```
R> # A tibble: 7 x 2
R>       x     y
R>   <dbl> <int>
R> 1     1     5
R> 2     2     6
R> 3     3     7
R> 4     4     8
R> 5     5     9
R> 6    NA    10
R> 7    10    NA
```

```r
# print logical test of complete.cases
print(complete.cases(my_df))
```

```
R> [1]  TRUE  TRUE  TRUE  TRUE  TRUE FALSE FALSE
```

6.1. DATAFRAMES

```
# print all rows where there is at least one NA
print(which(!complete.cases(my_df)))
```

```
R> [1] 6 7
```

na.omit - Returns a `dataframe` without the rows where a `NA` in any column is found.

```
print(na.omit(my_df))
```

```
R> # A tibble: 5 x 2
R>       x     y
R>   <dbl> <int>
R> 1     1     5
R> 2     2     6
R> 3     3     7
R> 4     4     8
R> 5     5     9
```

unique - Returns a `dataframe` where all duplicated rows are removed and only the unique cases, row-wise, are kept.

```
# set df with repeating rows
my_df <- data.frame(col1 = c(1, 1, 2, 3, 3, 4, 5),
                    col2 = c('A', 'A', 'A', 'C', 'C', 'B', 'D'))

# print it
print(my_df)
```

```
R>   col1 col2
R> 1    1    A
R> 2    1    A
R> 3    2    A
R> 4    3    C
R> 5    3    C
R> 6    4    B
R> 7    5    D
```

```r
# print unique df
print(unique(my_df))
```

```
R>   col1 col2
R> 1   1    A
R> 3   2    A
R> 4   3    C
R> 6   4    B
R> 7   5    D
```

6.2 Lists

A `list` is a flexible container that can hold many elements. Unlike atomic vectors, a `list` has no restriction on the classes or types of elements – we can group `numeric` objects with `character` objects, `factor` with `Dates` and even `lists` within `lists`. Likewise, each element of a list need not have the same length as the others. We can also name each element within a `list`. These properties make the `list` class the most flexible object in R. It is not by accident that several functions in R return an object of type `list`.

6.2.1 Creating lists

A `list` can be created with the `base::list` command, followed by their comma-separated elements:

```r
# create list
my_l <- list(c(1, 2, 3),
             c('a', 'b'),
             factor('A', 'B', 'C'),
             data.frame(col1 = 1:5))

# use base::print
print(my_l)
```

```
R> [[1]]
R> [1] 1 2 3
R>
R> [[2]]
```

6.2. LISTS

```
R> [1] "a" "b"
R>
R> [[3]]
R> [1] <NA>
R> Levels: C
R>
R> [[4]]
R>   col1
R> 1   1
R> 2   2
R> 3   3
R> 4   4
R> 5   5
```

```r
# use dplyr::glimpse
glimpse(my_l)
```

```
R> List of 4
R>  $ : num [1:3] 1 2 3
R>  $ : chr [1:2] "a" "b"
R>  $ : Factor w/ 1 level "C": NA
R>  $ :'data.frame':    5 obs. of  1 variable:
R>   ..$ col1: int [1:5] 1 2 3 4 5
```

Notice how we gather four objects: a numeric vector, a character vector, a factor and a dataframe/tibble into a single `list`. Also, notice that a `list` type object is printed differently than atomic vectors. The elements of the `list` are separated vertically and the content appears within double brackets (`[[ ]]`). We will soon learn that we can access its elements in the same way by using double brackets.

Following other objects, the elements of a `list` can also be named, making it easier to work with heterogenous data. For example, let's consider a set of data with information about a particular company traded in the NYSE market:

```r
# set named list
my_named_l <- list(tickers = 'CMPY',
                   markets = 'NYSE',
                   df_prices = data.frame(P = c(1,1.5,2,2.3),
                                          ref_date = Sys.Date()+0:3))
```

```
# check content
glimpse(my_named_l)
```

```
R> List of 3
R>  $ tickers  : chr "CMPY"
R>  $ markets  : chr "NYSE"
R>  $ df_prices:'data.frame':   4 obs. of  2 variables:
R>   ..$ P       : num [1:4] 1 1.5 2 2.3
R>   ..$ ref_date: Date[1:4], format:  ...
```

The information is self-contained in a single object. By using a `list` object, we can aggregate and structure all sorts of information about the company CMPY.

6.2.2 Accessing the Elements of a `list`

As mentioned, the individual elements of a `list` can be accessed with double brackets (`[[ ]]`), as in:

```
# accessing elements from list
print(my_named_l[[2]])
```

```
R> [1] "NYSE"
```

```
print(my_named_l[[3]])
```

```
R>     P ref_date
R> 1 1.0 2020-02-08
R> 2 1.5 2020-02-09
R> 3 2.0 2020-02-10
R> 4 2.3 2020-02-11
```

You can also access the elements of a `list` with simple brackets (`[]`), but be careful with this operation as the result will not be the element itself, but another `list`. This is a common mistake. See it below:

6.2. LISTS

```r
# set list
my_l <- list('a',
             c(1, 2, 3),
             factor('a', 'b'))

# check classes
class(my_l[[2]])
```

R> [1] "numeric"

```r
class(my_l[2])
```

R> [1] "list"

If we try to add an element to `my_l[2]`, we will receive an error message.

```r
# adding an element to a list (WRONG)
my_l[2] + 1
```

R> Error in my_l[2] + 1: non-numeric argument to binary operator

An error is returned because a `list` object cannot be summed with a `numeric` object. To fix it, simply use double brackets, as in `my_l[[2]] + 1`. Accessing elements of a list with simple brackets is only useful when looking for a sub-list within a larger list. As an example, if we wanted to obtain the first and second elements of `my_l`, we would write:

```r
# set new list with the first and second element of my_l
my_new_l <- my_l[c(1,2)]

# print result
print(my_new_l)
```

R> [[1]]
R> [1] "a"
R>
R> [[2]]
R> [1] 1 2 3

With the named lists, we can access its elements with operator $ as in `my_named_l$df_prices` or using the element's name. In general, this is a more efficient and advised way of working with `lists`. Avoid using positional access of a `list`. The problem is, if you are working interactively with a `list`, the position of the elements may change as new data arrives. Using names prevents this problem because, by modifying the `list` and adding elements, you can change the order of elements, but not the names.

Next, we provide several examples of how to access the elements of a `list` using operator $ and double brackets.

```
# different ways to access a list
my_named_l$tickers
my_named_l$markets
my_named_l[['tickers']]
my_named_l[['markets']]
```

Another useful trick for working with lists is you can access all inner elements directly – in one line of code – by simply using consecutive brackets or names. See below:

```
my_l <- list(slot1 = c(num1 = 1,
                       num2 = 2,
                       num3 = 3),
             slot2 = c('a', 'b'))

# access the second value of the first element of my_l
print(my_l[[1]][2])
```

```
R> num2
R>    2
```

```
# access the first value of the second element of my_l
print(my_l[[2]][1])
```

```
R> [1] "a"
```

```
# access the value 'num3' in 'slot1'
print(my_l[['slot1']]['num3'])
```

6.2. LISTS

```
R> num3
R>     3
```

This operation is very useful when interested in a few elements within a larger object. It avoids the need for creating intermediate objects.

6.2.3 Adding and Removing Elements from a `list`

To add or replace elements in a `list`, just set the new object in the desired position:

```
# set list
my_l <- list('a', 1, 3)
glimpse(my_l)
```

```
R> List of 3
R>  $ : chr "a"
R>  $ : num 1
R>  $ : num 3
```

```
# add new elements to list
my_l[[4]] <- c(1:5)
my_l[[2]] <- c('b')

# print result
glimpse(my_l)
```

```
R> List of 4
R>  $ : chr "a"
R>  $ : chr "b"
R>  $ : num 3
R>  $ : int [1:5] 1 2 3 4 5
```

This operation is also possible with the use of names and $:

```
# set list
my_l <- list(elem1 = 'a',
             name1=5)
```

```r
# set new element
my_l$name2 <- 10

# check it
glimpse(my_l)
```

```
R> List of 3
R>  $ elem1: chr "a"
R>  $ name1: num 5
R>  $ name2: num 10
```

To remove elements from a list, set the element to the reserved symbol NULL, as in:

```r
# set list
my_l <- list(text = 'b', num1 = 2, num2 = 4)
glimpse(my_l)
```

```
R> List of 3
R>  $ text: chr "b"
R>  $ num1: num 2
R>  $ num2: num 4
```

```r
# remove elements
my_l[[3]] <- NULL
glimpse(my_l)
```

```
R> List of 2
R>  $ text: chr "b"
R>  $ num1: num 2
```

```r
# remove elements
my_l$num1 <- NULL
glimpse(my_l)
```

```
R> List of 1
R>  $ text: chr "b"
```

6.2. LISTS

Another way of removing elements from a `list` is to use a negative index, which will exclude it from the returned object. See the next example, where we remove the second element of a `list` using a negative index.

```
# set list
my_l <- list(a = 1,
             b = 'text')

# remove second element
glimpse(my_l[[-2]])
```

```
R>   num 1
```

As with atomic vectors, removing elements of a `list` can also be accomplished with logical conditions. See next:

```
# set list
my_l <- list(1, 2, 3, 4)

# remove elements by condition
my_l[my_l > 2] <- NULL
glimpse(my_l)
```

```
R> List of 2
R>  $ : num 1
R>  $ : num 2
```

However, note this operation only works because all elements of `my_l` are numeric, and a logical test can be applied to all cases. If that is impossible for a particular element, R will return an `NA` value.

6.2.4 Processing the Elements of a `list`

A very important point about working with `lists` is is that its elements can be iterated in a very simple and direct way. For example, if you have a `list` with twenty dataframes, you can easily apply function `base::summary` to all of them in a single line of code. A real example will clarify it. Consider a list of numeric vectors of different sizes:

```r
# set list with different numerical vectors.
my_l_num <- list(c(1,2,3),
                 seq(1:50),
                 seq(-5,5, by=0.5))
```

Let's assume we need to calculate the average of each vector in `my_l_num` and store the result in an atomic vector. We could do this operation by calling the `mean` function to each element of the `list`, as in:

```r
# calculate means
mean_1 <- mean(my_l_num[[1]])
mean_2 <- mean(my_l_num[[2]])
mean_3 <- mean(my_l_num[[3]])

# print result
print(c(mean_1, mean_2, mean_3))
```

R> [1] 2.0 25.5 0.0

However, the code looks bad and it took three lines of code, not one! An easier, more elegant, and smarter way of doing that would be to use the `sapply` function, which will apply a function to each element of a list. All you need is the name of the list object and the name of the function used to process each element. See its use next:

```r
# using sapply
my_mean <- sapply(my_l_num, mean)

# print result
print(my_mean)
```

R> [1] 2.0 25.5 0.0

As expected, the result is identical to the previous example. Using function `sapply` is preferable, because it is more compact and efficient than the alternative - creating `mean_1`, and `mean_2` and `mean_3`. Notice the first example code only works for a `list` with three elements. If we had a fourth element and we wanted to keep this code structure, we would have to add a new line `mean_4 <- mean(my_l_num[[4]])` and modify the output command to `print <-c(mean_1, mean_2, mean_3, mean_4))`.

6.2. LISTS

Intelligently, function `sapply` works the same way in `lists` of any size. If we had more elements in `my_l_num`, no modification is necessary for `my_mean <- sapply(my_l_num, mean)`, making it easier to extend the code for more information. By combining a flexible object, such as a `list`, with the programming capacity of R, performing extensive operations in many complex objects becomes easy.

Using generic procedures is one premise of good and efficient programming practices. For the case of R, the rule is simple: **always write code flexible to the size of your objects**. The arrival of new data should never require modifications in the code. This is called the *DRY* rule (**don't repeat yourself**). If you are repeating lines of code, as in the previous example, certainly a more elegant and flexible solution could be used. This section only gives a taste of the programming capacity of R. This will be explained in greater detail in chapter 8.

6.2.5 Other Useful Functions

unlist - Returns the elements of a `list` in a single atomic vector.

```
my_named_l <- list(ticker = 'XXXX4',
                   price = c(1,1.5,2,3),
                   market = 'Be')
my_unlisted <- unlist(my_named_l)
print(my_unlisted)
```

```
R>  ticker   price1  price2   price3  price4   market
R>  "XXXX4"    "1"    "1.5"    "2"     "3"      "Be"
```

```
class(my_unlisted)
```

```
R> [1] "character"
```

as.list - Converts an object to the `list` type.

```
my_x <- 10:13
my_x_as_list <- as.list(my_x)
print(my_x_as_list)
```

```
R> [[1]]
R> [1] 10
R>
R> [[2]]
R> [1] 11
R>
R> [[3]]
R> [1] 12
R>
R> [[4]]
R> [1] 13
```

names - Returns or defines the names of the elements of a `list`.

```
my_l <- list(value1 = 1, value2 = 2, value3 = 3)
print(names(my_l))
```

```
R> [1] "value1" "value2" "value3"
```

```
my_l <- list(1,2,3)
names(my_l) <- c('num1', 'num2', 'num3')
print(my_l)
```

```
R> $num1
R> [1] 1
R>
R> $num2
R> [1] 2
R>
R> $num3
R> [1] 3
```

6.3 Matrices

A matrix is a two-dimensional representation of numbers, arranged in rows and columns. Using matrices is a powerful way of representing numerical data in two dimensions and, in certain situations, matrix functions can simplify complex mathematical operations.

6.3. MATRICES

In R, matrices are objects with two dimensions, where all elements must have the same class. You can think of matrices as atomic vectors with one extra dimension. In matrices, lines and columns can be named. When used correctly, `matrix` objects can facilitate the storage and context of the data.

A simple example of using matrices in finance is the representation of stock prices over time. The rows of the matrix represents the different dates, and the columns set each stock apart:

	AAP	COG	BLK	CAM
1	40.38	46.23	238.58	43.43
2	40.14	46.17	239.61	43.96
3	40.49	45.97	234.67	44.26
4	40.48	45.56	237.25	44.50
5	40.64	45.46	238.92	44.86

The above matrix could be created in R with the following code:

```
# set raw data with prices
raw_data <- c(40.38,  40.14,  40.49,  40.48,  40.64,
              46.23,  46.17,  45.97,  45.56,  45.46,
              238.58, 239.61, 234.67, 237.25, 238.92,
              43.43,  43.96,  44.26,  44.5,   44.86)

# create matrix
my_mat <- matrix(raw_data, nrow = 5, ncol = 4)
colnames(my_mat) <- c('AAP', 'COG', 'BLK', 'CAM')
rownames(my_mat) <- c("2010-01-04", "2010-01-05", "2010-01-06",
                      "2010-01-07", "2010-01-08")

# print result
print(my_mat)
```

```
R>              AAP   COG    BLK    CAM
R> 2010-01-04 40.38 46.23 238.58 43.43
R> 2010-01-05 40.14 46.17 239.61 43.96
R> 2010-01-06 40.49 45.97 234.67 44.26
R> 2010-01-07 40.48 45.56 237.25 44.50
R> 2010-01-08 40.64 45.46 238.92 44.86
```

We set the number of rows and columns explicitly with arguments `nrow = 4` and `ncol = 3` in `base::matrix`. The names of rows and columns are defined with functions `colnames` and `rownames`, using a left side notation as in `rownames(my_mat) <- c(...)`. Going further, we can also retrieve the names of rows and columns with the same functions:

```
# print the names of columns
print(colnames(my_mat))
```

R> [1] "AAP" "COG" "BLK" "CAM"

```
# print the names of rows
print(rownames(my_mat))
```

R> [1] "2010-01-04" "2010-01-05" "2010-01-06" "2010-01-07"
R> [5] "2010-01-08"

After matrix `my_mat` is created, we have at our disposal all its numerical properties. A simple example of using matrix operations in finance is the calculation of the value of a portfolio. If an investor has 200 shares of AAP, 300 share of COG, 100 of BLK and 50 of CAM, the value of his portfolio over time can be calculated as follows:

$$V_t = \sum_{i=1}^{4} N_i P_{i,t}$$

In this formula, N_i is the number of shares purchased for each asset, and $P_{i,t}$ is the price of stock i at date t. This is a simple operation to be performed with a matrix multiplication. Translating the procedure to R code, we have:

```
# set vector with shares purchased
my_stocks <- as.matrix(c(200, 300, 100, 50), nrow = 4)

# get value of portfolio with matrix multiplication
my_port <- my_mat %*% my_stocks

# print result
print(my_port)
```

R>   [,1]
R> 2010-01-04 47974.5

6.3. MATRICES

```
R> 2010-01-05 48038.0
R> 2010-01-06 47569.0
R> 2010-01-07 47714.0
R> 2010-01-08 47901.0
```

In this last example, we use symbol %*%, which does a matrix multiplication between two objects of the class `matrix`. The output shows the value of the portfolio over time, resulting in a small loss for the investor on the last date.

A `matrix` object is also flexible with its content, as long as it is a single class. For example, you can create matrices with `character` elements:

```
# create matrix with character
my_mat_char <- matrix(rep(c('a','b','c'), 3),
                      nrow = 3,
                      ncol = 3)

# print it
print(my_mat_char)
```

```
R>      [,1] [,2] [,3]
R> [1,] "a"  "a"  "a"
R> [2,] "b"  "b"  "b"
R> [3,] "c"  "c"  "c"
```

Now with a `logic` type:

```
# create matrix with logical
my_mat_logical <- matrix(sample(c(TRUE,FALSE),
                                size = 3*3,
                                replace = TRUE),
                         nrow = 3,
                         ncol = 3)

# print it
print(my_mat_logical)
```

```
R>       [,1]  [,2]  [,3]
R> [1,]  TRUE  TRUE  FALSE
R> [2,]  FALSE TRUE  FALSE
R> [3,]  FALSE FALSE TRUE
```

This flexibility allows the user to expand the representation of two-dimensional data beyond numerical values.

6.3.1 Selecting Elements from a `matrix`

Following the same notation as the atomic vector, you can select *pieces* of a `matrix` using indexes. A difference here is that matrices are two-dimensional objects, while atomic vectors are one-dimensional.[3] The extra dimension of matrices requires selecting elements not only by lines, but also by columns. The elements of an array can be accessed with the notation [i, j] where i represents the row and j the column. See the following example:

```
# create matrix
my_mat <- matrix(1:9, nrow = 3)

# display it
print(my_mat)
```

```
R>      [,1] [,2] [,3]
R> [1,]   1    4    7
R> [2,]   2    5    8
R> [3,]   3    6    9
```

```
# display element in [1,2]
print(my_mat[1,2])
```

```
R> [1] 4
```

To select an entire row or column, simply leave a blank index, as in the following example:

```
# select all rows from column 2
print(my_mat[, 2])
```

```
R> [1] 4 5 6
```

---

[3]To avoid confusion, atomic vectors in R have no dimension attribute in the strict sense of the function. When using the `dim` function in an atomic vector, such as `dim(c(1,2,4))`, the result is `NULL`. Away from the computing environment, however, atomic vectors can be considered one-dimensional objects as it can only increase its size in one direction.

6.3. MATRICES

```
# select all columns from row 1
print(my_mat[1, ])
```

```
R> [1] 1 4 7
```

Notice the result of indexing is an atomic vector, not a `matrix`. If we wanted the extracted piece to maintain its `matrix` class, with vertical or horizontal orientation, we could force this conversion using functions `as.matrix` and `matrix`:

```
# force matrix conversion and print result
print(as.matrix(my_mat[ ,2]))
```

```
R>      [,1]
R> [1,]   4
R> [2,]   5
R> [3,]   6
```

```
# force matrix conversion for one row and print result
print(matrix(my_mat[1, ], nrow=1))
```

```
R>      [,1] [,2] [,3]
R> [1,]   1    4    7
```

Pieces of the `matrix` can also be selected using vectors. If we wanted a new `matrix` with all elements from the second row and first column to the third row and second column, we could use the following code:

```
# select some elements and print them
print(my_mat[2:3, 1:2])
```

```
R>      [,1] [,2]
R> [1,]   2    5
R> [2,]   3    6
```

Finally, using logical tests to select elements of matrices is also possible:

```
# set matrix
my_mat <- matrix(1:9, nrow = 3)

# print logical matrix where value is higher than 5
print(my_mat >5)
```

```
R>       [,1]  [,2] [,3]
R> [1,] FALSE FALSE TRUE
R> [2,] FALSE FALSE TRUE
R> [3,] FALSE  TRUE TRUE
```

```
# print the result
print(my_mat[my_mat >5])
```

```
R> [1] 6 7 8 9
```

6.3.2 Other Useful Functions

as.matrix - Transforms raw data to a `matrix` object.

```
my_mat <- as.matrix(1:5)
print(my_mat)
```

```
R>      [,1]
R> [1,]  1
R> [2,]  2
R> [3,]  3
R> [4,]  4
R> [5,]  5
```

t - Returns a transposed `matrix`.

```
my_mat <- matrix(seq(10,20,
                 length.out = 6),
                 nrow = 3)
print(my_mat)
```

6.3. MATRICES

```
R>      [,1] [,2]
R> [1,]  10   16
R> [2,]  12   18
R> [3,]  14   20
```

```
print(t(my_mat))
```

```
R>      [,1] [,2] [,3]
R> [1,]  10   12   14
R> [2,]  16   18   20
```

rbind - Returns the merger (bind) of matrices, with row orientation.

```
my_mat_1 <- matrix(1:5, nrow = 1)
print(my_mat_1)
```

```
R>      [,1] [,2] [,3] [,4] [,5]
R> [1,]   1    2    3    4    5
```

```
my_mat_2 <- matrix(10:14, nrow = 1)
print(my_mat_2)
```

```
R>      [,1] [,2] [,3] [,4] [,5]
R> [1,]  10   11   12   13   14
```

```
my_rbind_mat <- rbind(my_mat_1, my_mat_2)
print(my_rbind_mat)
```

```
R>      [,1] [,2] [,3] [,4] [,5]
R> [1,]   1    2    3    4    5
R> [2,]  10   11   12   13   14
```

cbind - Returns the merger (bind) of matrices, with column orientation.

```
my_mat_1 <- matrix(1:4, nrow = 2)
print(my_mat_1)
```

```
R>      [,1] [,2]
R> [1,]   1    3
R> [2,]   2    4
```

```
my_mat_2 <- matrix(10:13, nrow = 2)
print(my_mat_2)
```

```
R>      [,1] [,2]
R> [1,]  10   12
R> [2,]  11   13
```

```
my_cbind_mat <- cbind(my_mat_1, my_mat_2)
print(my_cbind_mat)
```

```
R>      [,1] [,2] [,3] [,4]
R> [1,]  1    3    10   12
R> [2,]  2    4    11   13
```

rowMeans - Returns the mean of a matrix, row wise.

```
my_mat <- matrix(1:9, nrow=3)
print(rowMeans(my_mat))
```

```
R> [1] 4 5 6
```

colMeans - Returns the mean of a matrix, column wise.

```
my_mat <- matrix(1:9, nrow=3)
print(colMeans(my_mat))
```

```
R> [1] 2 5 8
```

6.4 Exercises

1. Use functions from the `tibble` package to create a dataframe called `my_df` with a column named x containing a randomized selection (see function `sample`) of a sequence from 1 to 100 and another column named y with the value of column x plus 5. How many values in column y are greater than 10 and less than 25?

6.4. EXERCISES

2. Using operator $, create a new column named `cumsum_x` in `my_df`, which will contain the cumulative sum of `x` (see `cumsum` function). How many values of the new column `cumsum_x` are greater than 50?

3. Use function `dplyr::filter` and the *pipeline* operator to filter `my_df`, so it only keeps rows where the value of column `x` is greater than 30.

4. If not done yet, repeat exercises 1, 2 and 3 using the `tidyverse` functions and the *pipeline* operator to chain all operations.

5. Use package `BatchGetSymbols` to download Facebook (FB) stock data since '2010-01-01' until today. If an investor bought $1,000 worth of FB stock on the first available day after '2010-01-01', what would be the value of his portfolio today?

6. Use function `afedR::afedR_get_data_file` to find the path of the book file `'grunfeld.csv'`. After reading it with `readr::read_csv`, use functions `dplyr::glimpse` and `base::summary` to better understand the content of the imported dataset.

7. Create a list object with three dataframes in its contents, `df1`,`df2` and `df3`. The content and size of dataframes is your choice. Use `sapply` function to discover the number of rows and columns in each dataframe.

8. Create an identity matrix (value 1 diagonally, zero anywhere else) of size 3 X 3. Tip: Use function `diag` to set the diagonal values in the matrix.

Chapter 7

Basic Object Classes

The basic classes are the most primary elements of data representation in R. Previously, we used the basic classes to translate raw information from files or the internet. The numeric data became a `numeric` column in a `dataframe`, while text data became a `character` object.

In this chapter, we will study R's basic object classes with depth, including the manipulation of their content. This chapter will show you what operations are possible with each object class and how you can use functions and packages to manipulate the information efficiently. It includes the following types of objects:

- Numeric (`numeric`)
- Text (`character`)
- Factors (`factor`)
- Logical Values (`logical`)
- Dates and Time (`Date` and `timedate`)
- Missing Data (`NA`)

7.1 Numeric Objects

The objects of type `numeric` represent quantities and, unsurprisingly, are one of the most used objects in data research. For example, the price of a stock at a given date, the value of inflation in a given period and country, the net profit of a company at the end of the fiscal year, among many other possibilities.

7.1.1 Creating and Manipulating numeric Objects

It is easy to create and manipulate the numeric objects. As expected, we can use the common symbols of mathematical operations, such as sum (+), difference (-), division (/) and multiplication (*). When working with numeric vectors, all mathematical operations are carried out using an **element by element** orientation and using vector notation. For example, this means that we can add the elements from two vectors in a single line of code.

As you can see in the next example, where we have created two vectors and perform various operations.

```
# create numeric vectors
x <- 1:5
y <- 2:6

# print sum
print(x+y)
```

R> [1] 3 5 7 9 11

```
# print multiplication
print(x*y)
```

R> [1] 2 6 12 20 30

```
# print division
print(x/y)
```

R> [1] 0.5000000 0.6666667 0.7500000 0.8000000 0.8333333

```
# print exponentiation
print(x^y)
```

R> [1]   1   8   81 1024 15625

The difference between R and other programming languages is that operations between vectors of different sizes are accepted. That is, we can also add a numeric vector with four elements to another with only two. Whenever that happens, R calls for the **recycling rule**. It states that, if two

7.1. NUMERIC OBJECTS

different sized vectors are interacting, the smaller vector is repeated as often as necessary to obtain the same number of elements as the larger vector. See the following example:

```
# set x with 4 elements and y with 2
x <- 1:4
y <- 2:1

# print multiplication
print(x + y)
```

```
R> [1] 3 3 5 5
```

The result of x + y is equivalent to 1:4 + c(2, 1, 2, 1). If you try to operate with vectors in which the length of the largest vector is not a multiple of the length of the smaller, R performs the same recycling procedure. However, it also sends a **warning** message to inform the user that the recycling procedure did not result in a perfect match.

```
# set x = 4 elements and y with 3
x <- c(1, 2, 3, 4)
y <- c(1, 2, 3)

# print sum (recycling rule)
print(x +y)
```

```
R> Warning in x + y: longer object length is not a
R> multiple of shorter object length
```

```
R> [1] 2 4 6 5
```

The first three elements of x were summed to the first three elements of y, as expected. However, the fourth element of x was summed to the first element of y. In order to complete the operation, R cycled through the values of the vector, restarting with the first element of y.

Elements of a **numeric** vector can also be named. See an example next, where we create a vector with several named items.

```
# create named vector
x <- c(item1 = 10,
       item2 = 14,
       item3 = 9,
       item4 = 2)

# print it
print(x)
```

```
R> item1 item2 item3 item4
R>    10    14     9     2
```

Empty **numeric** vectors can also be created. Sometimes, you need to preallocate an empty vector to be filled with values later. In some situations this simple procedure can make the code faster; and for that, you need to use the **numeric** function:

```
# create empty numeric vector of length 10
my_x <- numeric(length = 10)

# print it
print(my_x)
```

```
R> [1] 0 0 0 0 0 0 0 0 0 0
```

As you can see, when using **numeric(length = 10)**, all values are set to zero.

7.1.2 Creating a numeric Sequence

In R, you have two ways to create a sequence of numerical values. The first with operator : as in `my_seq <- 1:10`. This method is practical because the notation is clear and direct.

However, using the operator : can be restrictive. Did you notice that it only creates sequences where the difference between adjacent elements is +1 or -1? A more powerful version for the creation of sequences is the use of function **seq**. With it, you can set the intervals between each value with the argument **by**. See an example next:

7.1. NUMERIC OBJECTS

```
# create sequence with seq
my_seq <- seq(from = -10,
              to = 10,
              by = 2)

# print it
print(my_seq)
```

```
R> [1] -10 -8 -6 -4 -2 0 2 4 6 8 10
```

Another interesting feature of function `seq` is the possibility of creating equally spaced vectors with an initial value, a final value, and the desired number of elements. This is accomplished using option `length.out`. In the following code, we create a array from 0 to 10 with 20 elements:

```
# create sequence with defined number of elements
desired_len <- 20
my_seq <- seq(from = 0,
              to = 10,
              length.out = desired_len)

# print it
print(my_seq)
```

```
R>  [1] 0.0000000  0.5263158  1.0526316  1.5789474
R>  [5] 2.1052632  2.6315789  3.1578947  3.6842105
R>  [9] 4.2105263  4.7368421  5.2631579  5.7894737
R> [13] 6.3157895  6.8421053  7.3684211  7.8947368
R> [17] 8.4210526  8.9473684  9.4736842 10.0000000
```

The final number of elements in object `my_seq` is exactly 20. Function `seq` automatically calculates and sets the difference of 0.5263 between the adjacent elements. That is, if we calculate the difference from one element to the other, we will always find the same result of 0.5263.

7.1.3 Creating Vectors with Repeated Elements

Another way to create `numeric` vectors is by using repetition. For example, imagine that we are interested in a vector with the value 1 repeated ten times. For that, we use function `rep`:

```
# repeat vector three times
my_x <- rep(x = 1, times = 10)

# print it
print(my_x)
```

```
R> [1] 1 1 1 1 1 1 1 1 1 1
```

It also works with vectors. For example, let's say you need to create a vector with the repeated values of c(1, 2). The result should be equal to c(1, 2, 1, 2, 1, 2). For that, we use rep the same way:

```
# created a vector with repeated elements
my_x <- rep(x = c(1, 2),
            times = 3)

# print it
print(my_x)
```

```
R> [1] 1 2 1 2 1 2
```

7.1.4 Creating Vectors with Random Numbers

Some applications in finance and economics require the use of random numbers to simulate mathematical models. For example, the simulation method of Monte Carlo can generate asset prices based on random numbers from the Normal distribution.

In R, several functions create random numbers for different statistical distributions. The most commonly used, however, are functions stats::rnorm and stats::runif. Remember that package stats is automatically loaded when R starts. So, unless you changed the default settings of R's startup, there is no need to make a call to library(stats).

Function rnorm generates random numbers from the Normal distribution, with options for the mean and standard deviation. The mean will set the point with the highest frequency and sd (standard deviation) will change the dispersion of the histogram.

7.1. NUMERIC OBJECTS

```
# generate 10 random numbers from a Normal distribution
my_rnd_vec <- rnorm(n = 10000,
                    mean = 0,
                    sd = 1)

# print it
glimpse(my_rnd_vec)
```

R>   num [1:10000] 0.5849 -0.753 -0.0504 1.8245 1.6952 ...

We generated ten thousand random numbers from a Normal distribution, with mean zero and standard deviation equal to one. Let's see if its distribution of numbers looks close to the Normal, a bell shaped distribution:

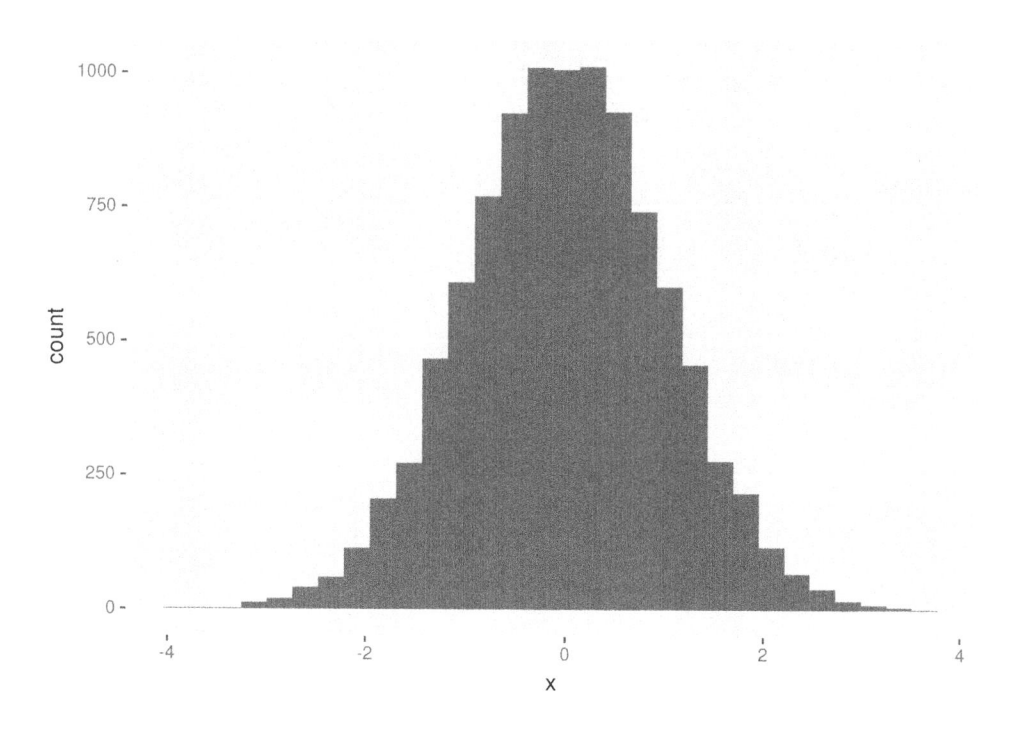

```
p <- ggplot(tibble(x = my_rnd_vec), aes(x = x)) +
  geom_histogram()

print(p)
```

Yes, it is pretty close. You can change the parameters `mean` and `sd` for different shapes of a Normal distribution.

Function **runif** generates random values uniformly distributed between a maximum and a minimum. It is commonly used to simulate probabilities with values between zero and one. The **runif** function has three input parameters: the desired number of random values, the minimum value, and maximum value. See the following example:

```
# create a random vector with minimum and maximum
my_rnd_vec <- runif(n = 10,
                    min = -5,
                    max = 5)

# print it
print(my_rnd_vec)
```

```
R> [1] -2.6399843 -4.7858644 -3.4607132 -4.8254468
R> [5] -1.6945900 -3.2637479 -2.6834573 -1.5368919
R> [9]  0.2138239  2.1499893
```

Note that both functions, **rnorm** and **runif**, are limited to their respective distribution. An alternative and flexible way to generate random values is to use the **sample** function. It accepts any vector as input and returns a scrambled version of its elements. Its flexibility lies in the fact that the input vector can be anything. For example, if we wanted to create a random vector with elements taken from vector c(0, 5, 15, 20, 25), we could do it like this:

```
# create sequence
my_vec <- seq(from = 0, to = 25, by=5)

# sample sequence
my_rnd_vec <- sample(my_vec)

# print it
print(my_rnd_vec)
```

```
R> [1] 20 15 25  0 10  5
```

Function **sample** also allows the random selection of a fixed number of elements. If we wanted to select only one element of **my_vec** randomly, we could write the code as:

7.1. NUMERIC OBJECTS

```r
# sample one element of my_vec
my_rnd_vec <- sample(my_vec, size = 1)

# print it
print(my_rnd_vec)
```

```
R> [1] 20
```

If we wanted two random elements from `my_rnd_vec`:

```r
# sample two elements of my_vec
my_rnd_vec <- sample(my_vec, size = 2)

# print it
print(my_rnd_vec)
```

```
R> [1]  0 25
```

Besides, you can select values from a smaller vector to create a larger vector. Consider the case where you have a vector with numbers `c(5, 10, 15)` and want to create a random vector with ten elements. For that, we use the option `replace = TRUE`.

```r
# create vector
my_vec <- c(5, 10, 15)

# sample
my_rnd_vec <- sample(x = my_vec, size = 10, replace = TRUE)
print(my_rnd_vec)
```

```
R>  [1]  5 15  5 10 10  5 15  5 10 10
```

Another important feature of `sample` is it works for any type of vector, not only for those of the `numeric` class:

```r
# example of sample with characters
print(sample(c('elem 1','elem 2','elem 3'),
             size = 1))
```

```
R> [1] "elem 2"
```

```r
# example of sample with list
print(sample(list(x = c(1,1,1),
                  y = c('a', 'b')),
             size = 1))
```

```
R> $y
R> [1] "a" "b"
```

At this point, it is important to acknowledge that **the generation of random values in R is not entirely random!** Internally, the computer makes selections based on a deterministic queue. Every time that chance-related functions, such as `rnorm`, `runif`, and `sample`, are called in the code, the computer chooses a different place in this queue according to various parameters. The practical effect is that the actual chosen values are unpredictable from the user's viewpoint. However, for the computer, this selection is absolutely predictable and deterministic.

One neat trick is that we can select the starting place in the queue of random values using function `base::set.seed`. In practical terms, the result is that, after a call to `set.seed`, all subsequent numbers and random selections will be the same in every code execution. Using `set.seed` is strongly recommended for the reproducibility of code involving randomness. Anyone can replicate the exact same results, even if it involves the selection of random numbers. See the following example.

```r
# set seed with integer 10
set.seed(seed = 10)

# create and print "random" vectors
my_rnd_vec_1 <- runif(5)
print(my_rnd_vec_1)
```

```
R> [1] 0.50747820 0.30676851 0.42690767 0.69310208
R> [5] 0.08513597
```

```r
my_rnd_vec_2 <- runif(5)
print(my_rnd_vec_2)
```

```
R> [1] 0.2254366 0.2745305 0.2723051 0.6158293 0.4296715
```

7.1. NUMERIC OBJECTS

In the previous code, the value 10 in set.seed(10) is an integer chosen by the user. After the call to set.seed(10), all selections and random numbers will start from the same point in the queue. Therefore, the random vectors are the same. By running that previous chunk of code in your computer, you'll see that the values of my_rnd_vec_1 and my_rnd_vec_2 will be exactly the same as the ones printed in this book.

Function set.seed also works for sample:

```
# fix seed
set.seed(seed = 15)

# print vectors
print(sample(1:10))
```

R> [1] 5 2 1 6 8 10 3 7 9 4

```
print(sample(10:20))
```

R> [1] 13 15 10 17 20 14 19 12 11 18 16

Likewise, if you execute the previous code in your R session, you'll see the exact same selections.

7.1.5 Accessing the Elements of a numeric Vector

All elements of a numerical vector can be accessed with brackets ([]). For example, if we wanted only the first element of x, we can use x[1]:

```
# set vector
x <- c(-1, 4, -9, 2)

# get first element
first_elem_x <- x[1]

# print it
print(first_elem_x)
```

R> [1] -1

The same notation is used to extract parts of a vector. If we wanted to create a sub-vector with the first and second element of x, we can achieve this goal with the next chunk of code:

```
# sub-vector of x
sub_x <- x[1:2]

# print it
print(sub_x)
```

R> [1] -1 4

To access named elements of a numeric array, simply use its name as a `character` value or vector inside the brackets.

```
# set named vector
x <- c(item1 = 10, item2 = 14, item3 = -9, item4 = -2)

# access elements by name
print(x['item2'])
```

R> item2
R>   14

```
print(x[c('item2','item4')])
```

R> item2 item4
R>   14   -2

We can also access the elements of a numerical vector using logical tests. For example, if we were interested in knowing which values of x are larger than *0*, we could use the following code:

```
# find all values of x higher than zero
print(x[x > 0])
```

R> item1 item2
R>   10   14

The selection of elements from a vector, according to some criteria, is called logical indexing. Objects of type `logical` will be treated later in this same chapter.

7.1.6 Modifying and Removing Elements of a `numeric` Vector

The modification of a vector is very simple. Just indicate the changes with the *assign* symbol (<-):

```
# set vector
my_x <- 1:4

# modify first element to 5
my_x[1] <- 5

# print result
print(my_x)
```

R> [1] 5 2 3 4

This modification can also be performed block-wise:

```
# set vector
my_x <- 0:5

# set the first three elements to 5
my_x[1:3] <- 5

# print result
print(my_x)
```

R> [1] 5 5 5 3 4 5

Using conditions to change values in a vector is also possible:

```
# set vector
my_x <- -5:5

# set any value lower than 2 to 0
my_x[my_x<2] <- 0

# print result
print(my_x)
```

```
R> [1] 0 0 0 0 0 0 0 2 3 4 5
```

The removal of elements of a vector is carried out using a negative index:

```
# create vector
my_x <- -5:5

# remove first and second element of my_x
my_x <- my_x[-(1:2)]

# show result
print(my_x)
```

```
R> [1] -3 -2 -1  0  1  2  3  4  5
```

Notice how using negative index simply returns the original vector, without the elements in the brackets.

7.1.7 Creating Groups

A common data task is to create groups based on numerical data. For example, we can calculate how many cases in the sample are located within a certain numerical range. Now, let's imagine that we have a vector of daily returns of a stock, the percentage change in prices from one day to another. A simple way to measure the risk of the investment is to divide the return interval into five parts and verify the percentage of occurrences of returns at each range. This simple calculation will show, for example, how many days the return was negative, with a drop of the stock price.

In R, the function used to create intervals from a numerical vector is `base::cut`. See the following example, where we create a random vector from the Normal distribution and five groups from intervals defined by the data.

```
# set random vector
my_x <- rnorm(10000)

# create groups with 5 breaks
my_cut <- cut(x = my_x, breaks = 5)

# print it!
print(head(my_cut))
```

7.1. NUMERIC OBJECTS

```
R> [1] (-2.18,-0.71] (-0.71,0.759] (-2.18,-0.71]
R> [4] (-0.71,0.759] (-0.71,0.759] (-2.18,-0.71]
R> 5 Levels: (-3.66,-2.18] ... (2.23,3.7]
```

You should take note that the ranges define the names in `my_cut`, and the result is an object, which is a type `factor`. We will cover this object in a future section. For now, it is worthwhile to say `factors` are simply groups within our data. Going forward, we can also check how often we find it in each group:

```
print(table(my_cut))
```

```
R> my_cut
R> (-3.66,-2.18]  (-2.18,-0.71]  (-0.71,0.759]
R>           154           2132            5459
R>  (0.759,2.23]     (2.23,3.7]
R>          2149            106
```

As expected, the distribution of values is balanced, with a higher occurrence of values around zero – the mean.

With the `cut` function, you can also define custom breaks in data and group names. See next, where we use a `tibble` to organize our data:

```
# create random vector in tibble
my_df <- tibble(x = rnorm(10000))

# define breaks and labels manually
my_breaks <- c(min(my_x)-1, -1, 1, max(my_x)+1)
my_labels <- c('Low','Normal', 'High')

# create group from numerical vector
my_df <- my_df %>%
  mutate(cut_x = cut(x = x,
                     breaks = my_breaks,
                     labels = my_labels))

# glimpse it!
glimpse(my_df)
```

```
R> Observations: 10,000
```

```
R> Variables: 2
R> $ x     <dbl> -0.42217453, 1.21510691, -0.48018365...
R> $ cut_x <fct> Normal, High, Normal, Normal, Low, N...
```

Notice that, in this example of creating a group from a numerical vector, the breaks were defined in `my_breaks` and the names in `my_labels`. We can once again check the distribution of groups with function `table`:

```
print(table(my_df$cut_x))
```

```
R>
R>    Low Normal   High
R>   1593   6770   1637
```

7.1.8 Other Useful Functions

as.numeric - Converts an object to the **numeric** class.

```
my_text <- c('1', '2', '3')
class(my_text)
```

```
R> [1] "character"
```

```
my_x <- as.numeric(my_text)
print(my_x)
```

```
R> [1] 1 2 3
```

```
class(my_x)
```

```
R> [1] "numeric"
```

unique - Returns all unique values of a numeric vector.

```
my_x <- c(1, 1, 2, 3, 3, 5)
print(unique(my_x))
```

```
R> [1] 1 2 3 5
```

sum - Sums all elements of a **numeric** vector.

7.1. NUMERIC OBJECTS

```
my_x <- 1:50
my_sum <- sum(my_x)
print(my_sum)
```

R> [1] 1275

max - Returns the maximum value of a **numeric** vector.

```
x <- c(10, 14, 9, 2)
max_x <- max(x)
print(max_x)
```

R> [1] 14

min - Returns the minimum value of a **numeric** vector.

```
x <- c(12, 15, 9, 2)
min_x <- min(x)
print(min_x)
```

R> [1] 2

which.max - Returns the position of the maximum value of a **numeric** object.

```
x <- c(100, 141, 9, 2)
which_max_x <- which.max(x)
cat(paste('The position of the maximum value of x is ',
          which_max_x))
```

R> The position of the maximum value of x is 2

```
cat(' and its value is ', x[which_max_x])
```

R> and its value is 141

which.min - Returns the position of the minimum value of a **numeric** object.

```
x <- c(10, 14, 9, 2)
which_min_x <- which.min(x)
cat(paste('The position of the minimum value of x is ',
          which_min_x, ' and its value is ', x[which_min_x]))
```

```
R> The position of the minimum value of x is  4  and its value is  2
```

sort - Returns a sorted (ascending or descending) version of a **numeric** vector.

```
x <- runif(5)
print(sort(x, decreasing = FALSE))
```

```
R> [1] 0.1032680 0.3004002 0.4337767 0.5133841 0.7782837
```

```
print(sort(x, decreasing = TRUE))
```

```
R> [1] 0.7782837 0.5133841 0.4337767 0.3004002 0.1032680
```

cumsum - Returns the cumulative sum of the elements of a **numerical** vector.

```
my_x <- 1:25
my_cumsum <- cumsum(my_x)
print(my_cumsum)
```

```
R>  [1]   1   3   6  10  15  21  28  36  45  55  66  78
R> [13]  91 105 120 136 153 171 190 210 231 253 276 300
R> [25] 325
```

prod - Returns the product (multiplication) of all the elements of a **numerical** vector.

```
my_x <- 1:10
my_prod <- prod(my_x)
print(my_prod)
```

```
R> [1] 3628800
```

cumprod - Returns the cumulative product of the elements of a **numeric** vector.

7.2. CHARACTER OBJECTS

```
my_x <- 1:10
my_prod <- cumprod(my_x)
print(my_prod)
```

```
R>  [1]       1       2       6      24     120     720
R>  [7]    5040   40320  362880 3628800
```

7.2 Character Objects

The `character` class, or simply text class, is used to store textual information. A practical example in finance would be to extract sentiments from Facebook and Twitter posts and use that to predict future market prices. It is worth knowing that analyzing textual information is an upward trend in research (Gentzkow et al., 2017), with many R packages developed over the last few years.

R has several features that facilitate the creation and manipulation of text type objects. The base functions shipped with the installation of R are comprehensive and suited for most cases. However, package `stringr` (Wickham, 2015) provides many functions that greatly expand the basic functionality.

A positive aspect of `stringr` is that all functions start with the name `str_` and are informative. So, using the auto-completion feature (*tab* key) described in the previous chapter, it is easy to find the names of functions. Following our preference for the packages in the `tidyverse`, we will focus only on the functions of `stringr`. The `base` functions for string manipulation will be presented but in a limited way.

7.2.1 Creating a Simple `character` Object

In R, every `character` object is created by encapsulating a text with double quotation marks (" ") or single (' '). To create an array of characters with stock *tickers*, we can do it with the following code:

```
tickers <- c('MMM', 'FB', 'ICE')
print(tickers)
```

```
R> [1] "MMM" "FB"  "ICE"
```

We can confirm the class of the created object with function `class`:

```
class(tickers)
```

```
R> [1] "character"
```

7.2.2 Creating Structured character Objects

We can also use R to create a text vector with some sort of structure. For example, vector c('ticker 1', 'ticker 2', ..., 'ticker 19', 'ticker 20') has a clear logic. It combines a text `ticker` with values from a vector that starts in 1 and ends in 20.

To create a text vector with the junction of text and numbers, use the `stringr::str_c` or `paste` function. See the following example, where we create the previous structured text in two ways, with space between the characters and numbers, and without it.

```
library(stringr)

# create sequence and tex
my_seq <- 1:20
my_text <- 'text'

# paste objects together (without space)
my_char <- str_c(my_text, my_seq)
print(my_char)
```

```
R>  [1] "text1"  "text2"  "text3"  "text4"  "text5"
R>  [6] "text6"  "text7"  "text8"  "text9"  "text10"
R> [11] "text11" "text12" "text13" "text14" "text15"
R> [16] "text16" "text17" "text18" "text19" "text20"
```

```
# paste objects together (with space)
my_char <- str_c(my_text,
                 my_seq,
                 sep = ' ')
print(my_char)
```

7.2. CHARACTER OBJECTS

```
R>  [1] "text 1"  "text 2"  "text 3"  "text 4"  "text 5"
R>  [6] "text 6"  "text 7"  "text 8"  "text 9"  "text 10"
R> [11] "text 11" "text 12" "text 13" "text 14" "text 15"
R> [16] "text 16" "text 17" "text 18" "text 19" "text 20"
```

We can do the same procedure with text vectors:

```
# set character value
my_x <- 'My name is'

# set character vector
my_names <- c('Marcelo', 'Ricardo', 'Tarcizio')

# paste and print
print(str_c(my_x, my_names, sep = ' '))
```

```
R> [1] "My name is Marcelo"  "My name is Ricardo"
R> [3] "My name is Tarcizio"
```

Another possibility of building structured text is the repetition of the content of another object. With character objects, use function stringr!str_dup or base::strrep for this purpose. Consider the following example:

```
# repeat 'abc' five times
my_char <- str_dup(string = 'abc', times = 5)

# print it
print(my_char)
```

```
R> [1] "abcabcabcabcabc"
```

7.2.3 character Constants

R also allows direct access to all letters of the Roman alphabet. They are stored in the reserved (constant) objects, called letters and LETTERS. See an example next.

```
# print all letters in alphabet (no cap)
print(letters)
```

```
R>  [1] "a" "b" "c" "d" "e" "f" "g" "h" "i" "j" "k" "l"
R> [13] "m" "n" "o" "p" "q" "r" "s" "t" "u" "v" "w" "x"
R> [25] "y" "z"
```

```r
# print all letters in alphabet (WITH CAP)
print(LETTERS)
```

```
R>  [1] "A" "B" "C" "D" "E" "F" "G" "H" "I" "J" "K" "L"
R> [13] "M" "N" "O" "P" "Q" "R" "S" "T" "U" "V" "W" "X"
R> [25] "Y" "Z"
```

Note that, in both cases, letters and LETTERS are not functions. They are character objects automatically embedded as constants in R. Even though they do not appear in the environment, and they are always available for use. You may overwrite their object names, such as in letters <- 'other char', but this is not advised. You never know where it is being used.

Other constant character objects in R are month.abb, which shows an abbreviation of months and month.name. Their content is presented next.

```r
# print abbreviation and full names of months
print(month.abb)
```

```
R> [1] "Jan" "Feb" "Mar" "Apr" "May" "Jun" "Jul" "Aug"
R> [9] "Sep" "Oct" "Nov" "Dec"
```

```r
print(month.name)
```

```
R> [1] "January"   "February" "March"    "April"
R> [5] "May"       "June"     "July"     "August"
R> [9] "September" "October"  "November" "December"
```

7.2.4 Selecting Pieces of a Text Object

A common beginner's mistake is to select characters of a text using brackets, as it is done for selecting elements of a vector. Consider the following code:

7.2. CHARACTER OBJECTS

```
# set char object
my_char <- 'ABCDE'

# print its second element (WRONG - RESULT is NA)
print(my_char[2])
```

```
R> [1] NA
```

The NA value indicates the second element of my_char does not exist. This happens because using square brackets is reserved for accessing the elements of an atomic vector, not characters within a larger text. Watch what happens when we use my_char[1]:

```
print(my_char[1])
```

```
R> [1] "ABCDE"
```

The result is simply the *ABCDE* text, on the first item of my_char. To select pieces of text, we need to use function stringr::str_sub or base::substr:

```
# print third and fourth characters
my_substr <- str_sub(string = my_char,
                     start = 2,
                     end = 2)
print(my_substr)
```

```
R> [1] "B"
```

These functions also work for atomic vectors. Let's assume you imported text data, and the raw dataset contains a 3-letter identifier of a company, always in the same location of the string. Let's simulate the situation in R:

```
# build char vec
my_char_vec <- paste0(c('ABC','VBC','ZMN'),
                      ' - other ignorable text')
print(my_char_vec)
```

```
R> [1] "ABC - other ignorable text"
R> [2] "VBC - other ignorable text"
R> [3] "ZMN - other ignorable text"
```

Here, we want the information in the first three characters of each element only in `my_char_vec`. To select them, we can use the same functions as before.

```
# get ids with stringr::str_sub
ids_vec <- str_sub(my_char_vec, 1, 3)
print(ids_vec)
```

```
R> [1] "ABC" "VBC" "ZMN"
```

Vector operations in character objects are very common in R. Almost anything you can do to a single element can be expanded to vectors. This facilitates the development of research scripts as you can easily perform complicated tasks to a series of elements in a single line of code.

7.2.5 Finding and Replacing Characters of a Text

A useful operation in handling texts is to locate specific patterns of text within a `character` object with functions `stringr::str_locate/base::regexpr` and `stringr::str_locate_all/base::gregexpr`. However, before we move on to the examples, it is important to point out that, by default, these functions use expressions of the type `regex` – regular expressions (Thompson, 1968). This is a specific format for the identification of patterns in text. When `regex` is used correctly, it can make your life a lot easier. You'll be able to find complex string patterns effortlessly.

The most common case of string search is to verify the position or the existence of a smaller text within a larger text. For these cases, however, using language `regex` is unnecessary. Therefore, the location and replacement of characters in the next example is of the fixed type, i.e., without using `regex`. Such information is passed to the `stringr` function by setting the `pattern` input with `stringr::fixed`, as in `str_locate(str_in, pattern = fixed('pattern to match'))`.

The following example shows how to find the *D* character from a range of characters.

7.2. CHARACTER OBJECTS

```r
# set character object
my_char <- 'ABCDEF-ABCDEF-ABC'

# find position of 'D' using str_locate
pos <- str_locate(my_char, fixed('D'))
print(pos)
```

```
R>      start end
R> [1,]    4   4
```

Note the str_locate function returns only the **first occurrence** of D. To locate all instances, we use function str_locate_all.

```r
# set object
my_char <- 'ABCDEF-ABCDEF-ABC'

# find position of ALL 'D' using str_locate_all
pos <- str_locate_all(my_char, fixed('D'))
print(pos)
```

```
R> [[1]]
R>      start end
R> [1,]    4   4
R> [2,]   11  11
```

To replace characters in a text, use functions str_replace and str_replace_all from stringr or sub and gsub from the base package. As with previous example, stringr::str_replace replaces the first occurrence of the character, while stringr::str_replace_all performs a global substitution; applies to all matches. Here are the differences:

```r
# set char object
my_char <- 'ABCDEF-ABCDEF-ABC'

# substitute the FIRST 'ABC' for 'XXX' with str_replace
my_char <- str_replace(string = my_char,
                       pattern = 'ABC',
                       replacement = 'XXX')
print(my_char)
```

```
R> [1] "XXXDEF-ABCDEF-ABC"
```

And now, we globally substitute characters.

```
# set char object
my_char <- 'ABCDEF-ABCDEF-ABC'

# substitute ALL 'ABC' for 'XXX' with str_replace_all
my_char <- str_replace_all(string = my_char,
                           pattern = 'ABC',
                           replacement = 'XXX')

# print result
print(my_char)
```

```
R> [1] "XXXDEF-XXXDEF-XXX"
```

Again, it is worth pointing out that the operations of replacements of strings also work for vectors. Have a look at the next example.

```
# set char object
my_char <- c('ABCDEF','DBCFE','ABC')

# create an example of vector
my_char_vec <- paste(sample(my_char, 5, replace = T),
                     sample(my_char, 5, replace = T),
                     sep = ' - ')

# show it
print(my_char_vec)
```

```
R> [1] "ABC - DBCFE"      "ABCDEF - ABCDEF"
R> [3] "DBCFE - DBCFE"    "ABCDEF - ABC"
R> [5] "ABCDEF - ABCDEF"
```

```
# substitute all occurrences of 'ABC'
my_char_vec <- str_replace_all(string = my_char_vec,
                               pattern = 'ABC',
                               replacement = 'XXX')

# print result
print(my_char_vec)
```

7.2. CHARACTER OBJECTS

```
R> [1] "XXX - DBCFE"     "XXXDEF - XXXDEF"
R> [3] "DBCFE - DBCFE"   "XXXDEF - XXX"
R> [5] "XXXDEF - XXXDEF"
```

7.2.6 Splitting Text

Eventually, you will need to break a text into different parts. Most of the time, you want to isolate a piece of particular information in the full string by using a delimiter in the text. For example, the text `'ABC;DEF;GHI'` has three sub-characters divided by the symbol `;`. To separate a text into several parts, use `stringr::str_split` or `base::strsplit`. Both functions break the original text into several fractions, according to a chosen delimiter character:

```
# set char
my_char <- 'ABC;ABC;BCD'

# split it based on ';' and using stringr::str_split
splitted_char <- str_split(my_char, ';')

# print result
print(splitted_char)
```

```
R> [[1]]
R> [1] "ABC" "ABC" "BCD"
```

The output of this function is an object of type `list`. To access the text BCD in object `splitted_char`, we can use the following code:

```
print(splitted_char[[1]][3])
```

```
R> [1] "BCD"
```

For an example of a split in character vectors, see the next code.

```
# set char
my_char_vec <- c('ABCDEF','DBCFE','ABFC','ACD')

# split it based on 'B' and using stringr::strsplit
```

```r
splitted_char <- str_split(my_char_vec, 'B')

# print result
print(splitted_char)
```

```
R> [[1]]
R> [1] "A"     "CDEF"
R>
R> [[2]]
R> [1] "D"     "CFE"
R>
R> [[3]]
R> [1] "A"     "FC"
R>
R> [[4]]
R> [1] "ACD"
```

Notice how, again, an object of type `list` is returned, where each element is the split text from the input vector.

7.2.7 Finding the Number of Characters in a Text

If we want to discover the number of characters in a `character` object, you can use functions `stringr::str_length` and `base::nchar`. Both functions also work for atomic vectors. See the examples below:

```r
# set char
my_char <- 'abcdef'

# print number of characters using stringr::str_length
print(str_length(my_char))
```

```
R> [1] 6
```

And now an example with vectors.

```r
#set char
my_char <- c('a', 'ab', 'abc')

# print number of characters using stringr::str_length
print(str_length(my_char))
```

7.2. CHARACTER OBJECTS

```
R> [1] 1 2 3
```

7.2.8 Generating Combinations of Text

One useful trick in R is to use functions `outer` and `expand.grid` to create all possible combinations of elements in different objects. This is useful when you want to create a `character` vector by combining all possible elements from different vectors. For example, if we wanted to create a vector with all combinations between c('a', 'b') and 'c('A','A') as c('a-A', 'a-B',...), we could write:

```
# set char vecs
my_vec_1 <- c('a','b')
my_vec_2 <- c('A','B')

# combine in matrix
comb_mat <- outer(my_vec_1, my_vec_2, paste, sep='-')

# print it!
print(comb_mat)
```

```
R>      [,1]  [,2]
R> [1,] "a-A" "a-B"
R> [2,] "b-A" "b-B"
```

The output of `outer` is a `matrix` type of object. If we wanted to change `comb_mat` to an atomic vector, we can use function `as.character`:

```
print(as.character(comb_mat))
```

```
R> [1] "a-A" "b-A" "a-B" "b-B"
```

Another way to reach the same objective is by using function `expand.grid`. Look at the next example, where we create different phrases based on all combinations of character vectors.

```r
library(tidyverse)

# set vectors
my_vec_1 <- c('John ', 'Claire ', 'Adam ')
my_vec_2 <- c('is fishing.', 'is working.')

# create df with all combinations
my_df <- expand.grid(name = my_vec_1,
                     verb = my_vec_2)

# print df
print(my_df)
```

```
R>     name       verb
R> 1   John    is fishing.
R> 2   Claire  is fishing.
R> 3   Adam    is fishing.
R> 4   John    is working.
R> 5   Claire  is working.
R> 6   Adam    is working.
```

```r
# paste columns together in tibble
my_df <- my_df %>%
  mutate(phrase = paste0(name, verb) )

# print result
print(my_df)
```

```
R>     name       verb            phrase
R> 1   John    is fishing.    John is fishing.
R> 2   Claire  is fishing.    Claire is fishing.
R> 3   Adam    is fishing.    Adam is fishing.
R> 4   John    is working.    John is working.
R> 5   Claire  is working.    Claire is working.
R> 6   Adam    is working.    Adam is working.
```

Here, we used the function `expand.grid` to create a `dataframe` containing all possible combinations of `my_vec_1` and `my_vec_2`. We pasted the contents of these columns using `paste0`.

7.2.9 Encoding of `character` Objects

For R, a text string is just a sequence of *bytes*. The translation of *bytes* to actual characters is achieved using a particular encoding structure. Most of the time, and especially in English speaking countries, the character encoding is not an issue. However, when dealing with text data from different spoken languages, such as Portuguese or German, the character encoding is something that you must learn and understand.

Let's explore an example to understand the problem better. Here, we will import data from a text file with the `'ISO-8859-9'` encoding and check the result.

```
# read text file
my_char <- readLines('data/FileWithLatinChar_ISO-8859-9.txt')

# print it
print(my_char)
```

```
R> [1] "A casa \xe9 bonita e tem muito espa\xe7o"
```

The original content of the file is a text in Portuguese. As you can see, the output of `readLines` shows all Latin characters as ugly, unreadable symbols. It happens that the encoding of the file has been manually changed to `'ISO-8859-9'`, while the `readLines` function uses `'UTF-8'` as *default*.

The easiest solution is to modify the encoding of the text file before reading it in R. This change can be made by external programs in Windows, such as Notepad++[1]. Next, we import another file with the same content, but correct encoding (`'UTF-8'`):

```
# read a text file with utf-8
my_char <- readLines('data/FileWithLatinChar_UTF-8.txt')

# print it
print(my_char)
```

```
R> [1] "A casa é bonita e tem muito espaço"
```

---

[1] https://notepad-plus-plus.org/

The Latin characters are now correct because the *default* encoding in `readLines` is the same as the file, `'UTF-8'`. A good policy in this topic is always to check the encoding of imported text files and combine it into R. Most import functions have an option to do so. When possible, always give preference to `'UTF-8'` encoding.

As for the text objects available in the environment, you can use the `Encoding` function to check and set encoding:

```
# read text file
my_char <- readLines('data/FileWithLatinChar_ISO-8859-9.txt')

# change encoding
Encoding(my_char) <- 'UTF-8'

# show its encoding
print(Encoding(my_char))
```

```
R> [1] "UTF-8"
```

After reading the contents of `"FileWithLatinChar_ISO-8859-9.txt"`, we changed the encoding of the output by using function `Encoding`. This function also works on vectors, making it easy to change the encoding of large `character` objects.

7.2.10 Other Useful Functions

stringr::str_to_lower/base::tolower - Converts a string to small caps.

```
print(stringr::str_to_lower('ABC'))
```

```
R> [1] "abc"
```

stringr::str_to_upper/base::toupper - Converts a string to upper caps.

```
print(stringr::str_to_upper('abc'))
```

```
R> [1] "ABC"
```

7.3 Factor Objects

Object class `factor` is used to represent groups (categories) in a database. Imagine a dataset containing the financial expenses of different people over a whole year. In this database, you find a column that defines the gender of the individual – male or female. This information can be imported in R as a `character` object; however, the best way to represent it is by mutating it to class `factor`.

The `factor` class offers a special object to denote groups within the data. It integrates nicely with statistical procedures and packages, so the work of dealing with groups becomes easier. For example, if we wanted to create a chart for each group within our database, we could do it by simply telling the graphing function, we have a grouping variable of type `factor`. If we wanted to check whether the medians of different groups are statistically different from each other, all we need to do is to pass the numerical values and the grouping factor to the function that performs the statistical test. When the categories of data are appropriately represented in R, working with them becomes easier and more efficient.

7.3.1 Creating factors

The creation of factors is accomplished with function `factor`:

```
# create factor
my_factor <- factor(c('M', 'F', 'M',
                      'M', 'F', 'F'))

# print it
print(my_factor)
```

```
R> [1] M F M M F F
R> Levels: F M
```

Notice that, in the previous example, the presentation of factors with function `print` shows its content and an extra item called `Levels`, which identifies the possible groups in the object, in this case, only `M` and `F`. If we had a larger number of groups, the item `Levels` increases. See next:

```r
# create factor with 3 levels
my_factor <- factor(c('M', 'F', 'M',
                      'M', 'F', 'F',
                      'ND'))

# print factor
print(my_factor)
```

```
R> [1] M  F  M  M  F  F  ND
R> Levels: F M ND
```

Here, we also have the ND (not defined) group.

An important point about creating factors is that the Levels are inferred from the data, and that may not correspond to reality. Consider the following example:

```r
# set factors with 1 level
my_status <- factor(c('Single', 'Single', 'Single'))

# print it
print(my_status)
```

```
R> [1] Single Single Single
R> Levels: Single
```

Accidentally, the data in my_status only shows one category: Single. However, it is well-known that another category, Married, is expected. If we used my_status as it is, we might omit important information, and that may cause problems in future parts of the code. The correct procedure is to define the Levels, as follows manually:

```r
my_status <- factor(c('Single', 'Single', 'Single'),
                    levels = c('Single', 'Married'))

print(my_status)
```

```
R> [1] Single Single Single
R> Levels: Single Married
```

7.3.2 Modifying factors

An important point about the `factor` type of objects is their `Levels` are immutable and will not update with the input of new data. You cannot modify the `Levels` after the creation of a `factor`. All new groups not in the `Levels` will be transformed into `NA` (*not available*) and a `warning` message will appear on the screen. This behavior may seem strange, at first, but it avoids possible errors in the code. See the following example:

```
# set factor
my_factor <- factor(c('a', 'b', 'a', 'b'))

# change first element of a factor to 'c'
my_factor[1] <- 'c'
```

```
R> Warning in `[<-.factor`(`*tmp*`, 1, value = "c"):
R> invalid factor level, NA generated
```

```
# print result
print(my_factor)
```

```
R> [1] <NA> b    a    b
R> Levels: a b
```

As we expected, the first element of `my_factor` becomes an `NA`. Here, the proper way to add a new factor is to first transform the `factor` object to a `character` object, change the content and, finally, change the class back from `character` to `factor`.

```
# set factor
my_factor <- factor(c('a', 'b', 'a', 'b'))

# change factor to character
my_char <- as.character(my_factor)

# change first element
my_char[1] <- 'c'

# mutate it back to class factor
my_factor <- factor(my_char)
```

```
# show result
print(my_factor)
```

```
R> [1] c b a b
R> Levels: a b c
```

Using these steps, we have the desired result in vector `my_factor`, with three Levels: a, b and c.

The `tidyverse` universe also has its own package for handling factors: `forcats`. For the current factor modification problem, we can use `forcats::fct_recode` function. Here's an example where we change the values of factors and levels:

```
library(forcats)
```

```
# set factor
my_factor <- factor(c('A', 'B', 'C',
                      'A', 'C', 'M',
                      'N'))
```

```
# modify factors
my_factor <- fct_recode(my_factor,
                        'D' = 'A',
                        'E' = 'B',
                        'F' = 'C')
```

```
# print result
print(my_factor)
```

```
R> [1] D E F D F M N
R> Levels: D E F M N
```

Using `forcats::fct_recode` is intuitive. All we need to do is to set the new names with the equality symbol.

7.3.3 Converting factors to Other Classes

Attention is required when converting a `factor` to another class. When converting a `factor` to the `character` class, the result is as expected:

7.3. FACTOR OBJECTS

```
# create factor
my_char <-factor(c('a', 'b', 'c'))

# convert and print
print(as.character(my_char))
```

R> [1] "a" "b" "c"

However, when the same procedure is performed for conversion from factor to the numeric class, the result is far from expected:

```
# set factor
my_values <- factor(5:10)

# convert to numeric (WRONG)
print(as.numeric(my_values))
```

R> [1] 1 2 3 4 5 6

As you can see, all elements in my_values were converted to c(1, 2, 3, 4, 5), which are obviously wrong. It happens that, internally, factors are stored as numerical counters, ranging from 1 to the total number of Levels. This simple transformation minimizes the use of computer memory. When we asked R to transform the factor object into numbers, it returns the values of the counters, not the actual numbers stored as factors. Solving this problem and getting the result we want is easy; just turn the factor object into a character and then to numeric, as shown next:

```
# converting factors to character and then to numeric
print(as.numeric(as.character(my_values)))
```

R> [1] 5 6 7 8 9 10

As we can see, now we got the result we expected. As a rule of thumb, **always be careful when transforming factors into numbers**. This bug is hard to catch and may go unnoticed until it breaks your code or jeopardizes your analysis.

7.3.4 Creating Contingency Tables

After creating a factor, we can find the number of times that each group, or combination of groups, is found with function `table`. This is also called a contingency table. In a simple case, with only one factor, function `table` counts the number of occurrences of each category:

```
# create factor
my_factor <- factor(sample(c('Pref', 'Ord'),
                           size = 20,
                           replace = TRUE))

# print contingency table
print(table(my_factor))
```

```
R> my_factor
R>  Ord Pref
R>   10   10
```

A more advanced usage of function `table` is to consider more than one factor:

```
# set factors
my_factor_1 <- factor(sample(c('Pref', 'Ord'),
                             size = 20,
                             replace = TRUE))

my_factor_2 <- factor(sample(paste('Grupo', 1:3),
                             size = 20,
                             replace = TRUE))

# print contingency table with two factors
print(table(my_factor_1,
            my_factor_2))
```

```
R>            my_factor_2
R> my_factor_1 Grupo 1 Grupo 2 Grupo 3
R>        Ord       4       2       8
R>        Pref      1       1       4
```

The table that we created previously demonstrates the number of occurrences for each combination of groups. Therefore, it is worth knowing you can also use it with more than two factors.

7.3.5 Other Useful Functions

levels - Returns the `Levels` an object of class `factor`.

```
my_factor <- factor(c('A', 'A', 'B', 'C', 'B'))
print(levels(my_factor))
```

```
R> [1] "A" "B" "C"
```

as.factor - Transforms an object to the class `factor`.

```
my_y <- c('a','b','c','c','a')
my_factor <- as.factor(my_y)

print(my_factor)
```

```
R> [1] a b c c a
R> Levels: a b c
```

split - Based on a grouping variable and another vector, creates a list with subsets of groups of the target object. This function is best used to separate different samples according to groups.

```
my_factor <- factor(c('A','B','C','C','C','B'))
my_x <- 1:length(my_factor)

my_l <- split(x = my_x, f = my_factor)

print(my_l)
```

```
R> $A
R> [1] 1
R>
R> $B
R> [1] 2 6
R>
R> $C
R> [1] 3 4 5
```

7.4 Logical Objects

Logical tests are at the heart of R. In one line of code, and we can test a condition for a large vector of data. This procedure is commonly used to find outliers in a dataset or to split the sample according to some condition, such as a particular period.

7.4.1 Creating logical Objects

Objects of class `logical` are created based on the use of condition tests on other objects. For example, in a sequence from 1 to 10, we can check what elements are higher than five with the following code:

```
# set numerical
my_x <- 1:10

# print a logical test
print(my_x > 5)
```

```
R>  [1] FALSE FALSE FALSE FALSE FALSE  TRUE  TRUE  TRUE
R>  [9]  TRUE  TRUE
```

```
# print position of elements from logical test
print(which(my_x > 5))
```

```
R> [1]  6  7  8  9 10
```

In the previous example, function `which` returned the index (position) where the condition is true (`TRUE`).

To perform equality tests, simply use the equality symbol twice (`==`):

```
# create char
my_char <- rep(c('abc', 'bcd'),
               times = 5)

# print its contents
print(my_char)
```

7.4. LOGICAL OBJECTS

```
R> [1] "abc" "bcd" "abc" "bcd" "abc" "bcd" "abc" "bcd"
R> [9] "abc" "bcd"
```

```
# print logical test
print(my_char == 'abc')
```

```
R> [1]  TRUE FALSE  TRUE FALSE  TRUE FALSE  TRUE FALSE
R> [9]  TRUE FALSE
```

For an inequality test, use symbol !=, as shown in the next code:

```
# print inequality test
print(my_char != 'abc')
```

```
R> [1] FALSE  TRUE FALSE  TRUE FALSE  TRUE FALSE  TRUE
R> [9] FALSE  TRUE
```

It is also possible to test multiple logical conditions. For simultaneous occurrences of events, use operator &. For example, if we wanted to check the values from a sequence between 1 and 10 that are larger than 4 **and** smaller than 7, we write:

```
my_x <- 1:10
```

```
# print logical for values higher than 4 and lower than 7
print((my_x > 4)&(my_x < 7) )
```

```
R> [1] FALSE FALSE FALSE FALSE  TRUE  TRUE FALSE FALSE
R> [9] FALSE FALSE
```

```
# print the actual values
idx <- which( (my_x > 4)&(my_x < 7) )
print(my_x[idx])
```

```
R> [1] 5 6
```

For non-simultaneous conditions, i.e., the occurrence of one event or other, use the operator |. For instance, considering the previous sequence, we can find the values greater than 7 **or** lower than four by writing:

```
# location of elements higher than 7 or lower than 4
idx <- which( (my_x > 7)|(my_x < 4) )

# print elements from previous condition
print(my_x[idx])
```

```
R> [1]  1  2  3  8  9 10
```

Besides, you should be aware that we used parentheses to encapsulate the logical conditions for both cases. Although it is not strictly necessary, it is a good coding practice. We could have used idx <- which(my_x > 7 | my_x < 4) for the same result, but using parentheses makes the code cleaner by isolating the logical tests.

Another interesting use of logical objects is to test whether an item or more is found or not in another vector. For this, we use the operator %in%. For example, suppose you have the names of two countries, c('Country 1', 'Country 2'), and you want to know if you can find the same countries in another vector. This is an operation similar to using the equality test but in vector notation. Here's an example:

```
library(dplyr)
# location of elements higher than 7 or lower than 4
my_contries <- c('Country 1', 'Country 2')

# set df
n_obs <- 100
df_temp <- tibble(country = str_c('Country ',
                                  sample(1:10,
                                         size = n_obs,
                                         replace = TRUE)),
                  inflation.rate = rnorm(n_obs, sd = 0.05) ) %>%
  glimpse()
```

```
R> Observations: 100
R> Variables: 2
R> $ country        <chr> "Country 3", "Country 1", "...
R> $ inflation.rate <dbl> -0.037301808, -0.060783522,...
```

7.5. DATE AND TIME

```
# filter rows of df with selected tickers
df_temp <- df_temp %>%
  filter(country %in% my_contries) %>%
  glimpse()
```

```
R> Observations: 18
R> Variables: 2
R> $ country        <chr> "Country 1", "Country 2", "...
R> $ inflation.rate <dbl> -0.060783522, -0.002706447,...
```

The resulting dataframe only has rows for 'Country 1' and 'Country 2'. With operator %in%, we filtered our table so it only keeps the desired rows.

7.5 Date and Time

The representation and manipulation of dates is an important aspect of research. When you have dates in your dataset, you must be certain they are correctly represented in R with the correct timezone. In this section, we will give priority to package lubridate (Grolemund and Wickham, 2011), which offers efficient and diverse functions for time manipulation. There are, however, many packages that can also help the user. If the reader must perform a date operation not covered here, I suggest looking into packages chron (James and Hornik, 2017), timeDate (Team et al., 2015), lubridate (Grolemund and Wickham, 2011) and bizdays (Freitas, 2016).

7.5.1 Creating Simple Dates

In R, several classes can represent dates. The choice between one to another depends on the required precision of time representation. Some situations only require the knowledge of the day (and not time), while in others, the clock time can be very important as the data is collected over a day and knowing the time of day of each data point can affect the research.

The most basic class, indicating the day, month, and year, is Date. Using package lubridate, we create a date class object with functions ymd (year-month-date), dmy (day-month-year) e mdy (month-day-year). The order of components, and choice of function, is set according to the input character. Have a look:

```
library(lubridate)

# set Date object (YMD)
print(ymd('2020-06-24'))
```

R> [1] "2020-06-24"

```
# set Date object (DMY)
print(dmy('24-06-2020'))
```

R> [1] "2020-06-24"

```
# set Date object (MDY)
print(mdy('06-24-2020'))
```

R> [1] "2020-06-24"

Note that the functions return the exact same object. The difference in usage is only by the way the input string is structured with the position of the day, month, and year.

One benefit of using the `lubridate` package is that its functions are smart when dealing with different formats. You should note that we defined the data elements using the dash (-) separator and numeric values, as in '2020-06-24' in the previous case. Other formats are also automatically recognized:

```
# set Date object
print(ymd('2020/06/24'))
```

R> [1] "2020-06-24"

```
# set Date object
print(ymd('2020&06&24'))
```

R> [1] "2020-06-24"

7.5. DATE AND TIME

```
# set Date object
print(ymd('2020 june 24'))
```

R> [1] "2020-06-24"

```
# set Date object
print(dmy('24 of june 2020'))
```

R> [1] "2020-06-24"

This is a very useful property of **lubridate**, making it easy to import date information in different formats.

Now, using the **base** package, we can create a date with function as.Date:

```
# set Date from dd/mm/yyyy with the definition of format
my_date <- as.Date('24/06/2020', format = '%d/%m/%Y')

# print result
print(my_date)
```

R> [1] "2020-06-24"

The symbols used in *input* format, such as %d, %m, and %Y, indicate how the character object should be converted and where the day, month and year are in the text. Likewise, many other symbols may be used for processing dates in specific formats. An overview of the main symbols is given next.

Symbol	Description	Example
%d	day of month (decimal)	0
%m	month (decimal)	12
%b	month (abbreviation)	Apr
%B	month (complete name)	April
%y	year (2 digits)	16
%Y	month (4 digits)	2020

By using the previous table, you'll be able to create and represent dates in a vast number of ways. Notice how the **lubridate** functions, regarding **base**, are simpler and easier to use.

7.5.2 Creating a Sequence of Dates

An interesting aspect of objects `Date` is they interact with `numeric` objects and can be used for logical tests. If we wanted to add a day after a particular date, all we need to do is to add value 1 to the object, as shown next:

```r
# create date
my_date <- ymd('2020-06-01')

# find next day
my_date_2 <- my_date + 1

# print result
print(my_date_2)
```

```
R> [1] "2020-06-02"
```

This property also works with vectors, facilitating the creation of `Date` sequences. See an example next.

```r
# create a sequence of Dates
my_date_vec <- my_date + 0:15

# print it
print(my_date_vec)
```

```
R>  [1] "2020-06-01" "2020-06-02" "2020-06-03"
R>  [4] "2020-06-04" "2020-06-05" "2020-06-06"
R>  [7] "2020-06-07" "2020-06-08" "2020-06-09"
R> [10] "2020-06-10" "2020-06-11" "2020-06-12"
R> [13] "2020-06-13" "2020-06-14" "2020-06-15"
R> [16] "2020-06-16"
```

A more customizable way for creating `Date` sequences is using function `seq`. In the same way, it worked for a numerical object. Moreover, we can use the function `seq` to create sequences of dates with custom time intervals or use it to create a `Date` sequence with a fixed size. If we wanted a `Date` sequence, where the elements are set every two days, we could use the following code:

7.5. DATE AND TIME

```
# set first and last Date
my_date_1 <- ymd('2017-03-07')
my_date_2 <- ymd('2017-03-20')

# set sequence
my_vec_date <- seq(from = my_date_1,
                   to = my_date_2,
                   by = '2 days')

# print result
print(my_vec_date)
```

```
R> [1] "2017-03-07" "2017-03-09" "2017-03-11" "2017-03-13"
R> [5] "2017-03-15" "2017-03-17" "2017-03-19"
```

Likewise, if we wanted a sequence of dates for every two weeks, we can simply change input `by` to `'2 weeks'`:

```
# set first and last Date
my_date_1 <- ymd('2017-03-07')
my_date_2 <- ymd('2017-04-20')

# set sequence
my_vec_date <- seq(from = my_date_1,
                   to = my_date_2,
                   by = '2 weeks')

# print result
print(my_vec_date)
```

```
R> [1] "2017-03-07" "2017-03-21" "2017-04-04" "2017-04-18"
```

Another way to use function `seq` is by setting the desired length of the sequence of dates. For example, if we wanted an array of dates with 10 elements, we would use:

```
# set dates
my_date_1 <- as.Date('2020-06-27')
my_date_2 <- as.Date('2020-07-27')
```

```
# set sequence with 10 elements
my_vec_date <- seq(from = my_date_1,
                   to = my_date_2,
                   length.out = 10)

# print result
print(my_vec_date)
```

```
R>  [1] "2020-06-27" "2020-06-30" "2020-07-03"
R>  [4] "2020-07-07" "2020-07-10" "2020-07-13"
R>  [7] "2020-07-17" "2020-07-20" "2020-07-23"
R> [10] "2020-07-27"
```

Once again, the interval between the dates is automatically defined by the function.

7.5.3 Operations with Dates

We can calculate difference of days between two dates by simply subtracting one from the other. Have a look:

```
# set dates
my_date_1 <- ymd('2015-06-24')
my_date_2 <- ymd('2020-06-24')

# calculate difference
diff_date <- my_date_2 - my_date_1

# print result
print(diff_date)
```

```
R> Time difference of 1827 days
```

The output of the subtraction operation is an object of class `diffdate`, based on the `list` class. In the previous chapter, we mentioned that we could access the elements of a `list` using double brackets. The numerical value of the difference of days is contained in the first element of `diff_date`:

7.5. DATE AND TIME

```
# print difference of days as numerical value
print(diff_date[[1]])
```

R> [1] 1827

Going further, we can also use mathematical operators to test whether a date is more recent or not than another:

```
# set date and vector
my_date_1 <- ymd('2020-06-20')
my_date_vec <- ymd('2020-06-20') + seq(-5,5)

# test which elements of my_date_vec are older than my_date_1
my.test <- (my_date_vec > my_date_1)

# print result
print(my.test)
```

R> [1] FALSE FALSE FALSE FALSE FALSE FALSE TRUE TRUE
R> [9] TRUE TRUE TRUE

The previous operation is useful when selecting a certain period of time in your dataset. This is a common practice in research. We set the first and last dates of the period we are interested in and use a logical test to find all dates between:

```
library(dplyr)
library(lubridate)

# set first and last dates
first_date <- ymd('2020-06-01')
last_date <- ymd('2020-06-15')

# create dataframe and glimpse it
my_temp_df <- tibble(date.vec = ymd('2020-05-25') + seq(0,30),
                     prices=seq(1,10,
                                length.out = length(date.vec)))

# find dates that are between the first and last date
my_idx <- (my_temp_df$date.vec >= first_date) &
```

```r
(my_temp_df$date.vec <= last_date)

# use index to filter dataframe
my_temp_df_filtered <- my_temp_df %>%
  filter(my_idx) %>%
  glimpse()
```

```
R> Observations: 15
R> Variables: 2
R> $ date.vec <date> 2020-06-01, 2020-06-02, 2020-06-...
R> $ prices   <dbl> 3.1, 3.4, 3.7, 4.0, 4.3, 4.6, 4.9...
```

In the previous code, the object `my_temp_df_filtered` will only contain rows for the time period between 2020-06-01 and 2020-06-15.

7.5.4 Dealing with Time

Using the `Date` class is sufficient when dealing only with days, and the hours are irrelevant. When it is necessary to consider time, we have to use an object of type `datetime`.

In the `base` package, one class used for this purpose is `POSIXlt`, which stores the contents of a date as a list. Another class is `POSIXct`, which stores dates as seconds counted from `1970-01-01`. Due to its storage format, the `POSIXct` class takes up less computer memory and is the one used in package `lubridate`. Given that, we will prioritize it in these sections. Worth knowing that all examples presented here can also be replicated with the `POSIXlt` class.

In R, the time/date format also follows the ISO 8601 standard[2] and is represented as "year-month-day hours:minutes:seconds timezone" (YYYY-MM-DD HH:mm:SS TMZ). See the following example:

```r
# creating a POSIXct object
my_timedate <- as.POSIXct('2020-01-01 16:00:00')

# print result
print(my_timedate)
```

```
R> [1] "2020-01-01 16:00:00 -03"
```

---

[2]https://www.iso.org/iso-8601-date-and-time-format.html

7.5. DATE AND TIME

The `lubridate` package also offers intelligent functions for creating date-time objects. These follow the same structural intuition as the date creation functions.

```
library(lubridate)

# creating a POSIXlt object
my_timedate <- ymd_hms('2020-01-01 16:00:00')

# print it
print(my_timedate)
```

R> [1] "2020-01-01 16:00:00 UTC"

You should note that this class automatically adds the time zone. If you need to represent a different time zone, you can do so with the `tz` argument:

```
# creating a POSIXlt object with custom timezone
my_timedate_tz <- ymd_hms('2020-01-01 16:00:00',
                          tz = 'GMT')

# print it
print(my_timedate_tz)
```

R> [1] "2020-01-01 16:00:00 GMT"

An important note in the case of `POSIXlt` and `POSIXct` objects, **the operations of sum and subtraction refer to seconds**, not days, as with objects from the `Date` class:

```
# Adding values (seconds) to a POSIXlt object and printing it
print(my_timedate_tz + 30)
```

R> [1] "2020-01-01 16:00:30 GMT"

7.5.5 Customizing the Format of Dates and Times

The ISO format for representing dates and `datetime` object in R may not be what we need. When writing reports, using a date-time format different than the local one can unnecessarily generate confusion in your audience.

In the same way as objects of class `Date`, there are specific symbols for dealing with components of a `POSIX1t` object. These symbols allow for custom formatting. Next, we have a table with the main symbols and their meanings.

Symbol	Description	Example
%H	Hour (decimal, 24 hours)	23
%I	Hour (decimal, 12 hours)	11
%M	Minutes (decimal, 0-59)	12
%p	AM/PM indicator	AM
%S	Seconds (decimal, 0-59)	50

To format a date, use the `format` function. Using the symbols presented in the previous table, the user can create any desired customization. See the following example, where we change a date vector to the American format (MM/DD/YYYY):

```
# create vector of dates
my_dates <- seq(from = as.Date('2020-01-01'),
                to = as.Date('2020-01-15'),
                by = '1 day')

# change format
my_dates_US_format <- format(my_dates, '%m/%d/%Y')

# print result
print(my_dates_US_format)
```

```
R>  [1] "01/01/2020" "01/02/2020" "01/03/2020"
R>  [4] "01/04/2020" "01/05/2020" "01/06/2020"
R>  [7] "01/07/2020" "01/08/2020" "01/09/2020"
R> [10] "01/10/2020" "01/11/2020" "01/12/2020"
R> [13] "01/13/2020" "01/14/2020" "01/15/2020"
```

The same procedure can be used for `POSIX1t` objects:

7.5. DATE AND TIME

```r
# create vector of date-time
my_datetime <- as.POSIX1t('2020-02-01 12:00:00') + seq(0,560,60)

# change to US format
my_dates_US_format <- format(my_datetime, '%m/%d/%Y %H:%M:%S')

# print result
print(my_dates_US_format)
```

```
R> [1] "02/01/2020 12:00:00" "02/01/2020 12:01:00"
R> [3] "02/01/2020 12:02:00" "02/01/2020 12:03:00"
R> [5] "02/01/2020 12:04:00" "02/01/2020 12:05:00"
R> [7] "02/01/2020 12:06:00" "02/01/2020 12:07:00"
R> [9] "02/01/2020 12:08:00" "02/01/2020 12:09:00"
```

Likewise, we can customize our dates for very specific formats:

```r
# set custom format
my_dates_my_format <- format(my_dates,
                             'Year=%Y | Month=%m | Day=%d')

# print result
print(my_dates_my_format)
```

```
R>  [1] "Year=2020 | Month=01 | Day=01"
R>  [2] "Year=2020 | Month=01 | Day=02"
R>  [3] "Year=2020 | Month=01 | Day=03"
R>  [4] "Year=2020 | Month=01 | Day=04"
R>  [5] "Year=2020 | Month=01 | Day=05"
R>  [6] "Year=2020 | Month=01 | Day=06"
R>  [7] "Year=2020 | Month=01 | Day=07"
R>  [8] "Year=2020 | Month=01 | Day=08"
R>  [9] "Year=2020 | Month=01 | Day=09"
R> [10] "Year=2020 | Month=01 | Day=10"
R> [11] "Year=2020 | Month=01 | Day=11"
R> [12] "Year=2020 | Month=01 | Day=12"
R> [13] "Year=2020 | Month=01 | Day=13"
R> [14] "Year=2020 | Month=01 | Day=14"
R> [15] "Year=2020 | Month=01 | Day=15"
```

7.5.6 Extracting Elements of a Date

We can use function `format` to extract data elements such as the year, month, day, hour, minute and second. Look at the next example, where we retrieve only the hours of a `POSIXct` object:

```r
library(lubridate)

# create vector of date-time
my_datetime <- seq(from = ymd_hms('2020-01-01 12:00:00'),
                   to = ymd_hms('2020-01-01 18:00:00'),
                   by = '1 hour')

# get hours from POSIXlt
my_hours <- format(my_datetime, '%H')

# print result
print(my_hours)
```

```
R> [1] "12" "13" "14" "15" "16" "17" "18"
```

Likewise, we can use symbols `%M` and `%S` to extract the hours, minutes and seconds of a `POSIXct` object:

```r
# create vector of date-time
n_dates <- 10
my_datetime <- seq(from = ymd_hms('2020-01-01 12:00:00'),
                   to = ymd_hms('2020-01-01 18:00:00'),
                   length.out = n_dates) + sample(1:59,
                                                  size = n_dates)

# get minutes from POSIXlt
my_minutes <- format(my_datetime, '%H:%M:%S')

# print result
print(my_minutes)
```

```
R> [1] "12:00:45" "12:40:44" "13:20:58" "14:00:22"
R> [5] "14:40:03" "15:20:34" "16:00:14" "16:40:24"
R> [9] "17:20:54" "18:00:08"
```

7.5. DATE AND TIME

Alternatively, we can use `lubridate` functions such as `hour` and `minute`:

```
# get hours with lubridate
print(hour(my_datetime))
```

```
R> [1] 12 12 13 14 14 15 16 16 17 18
```

```
# get minutes with lubridate
print(minute(my_datetime))
```

```
R> [1]  0 40 20  0 40 20  0 40 20  0
```

Functions for extracting other components of a date, such as `lubridate::year` and `lubridate::second`, are also available.

7.5.7 Find the Current Date and Time

R's specific functions allow the user to find the current date and time from the operating system. Therefore, this is useful when it is important for the user (us) to know the time when the code was executed.

If you want to find the present day, use function `base::Sys.Date` or `lubridate::today`

```
library(lubridate)

# get today
print(Sys.Date())
```

```
R> [1] "2020-02-08"
```

```
# print it
print(today())
```

```
R> [1] "2020-02-08"
```

If you want to find the current date and time, we use function `base::Sys.time` or `lubridate::now`:

```r
# get time!
print(Sys.time())
```

```
R> [1] "2020-02-08 17:47:20 -03"
```

```r
# get time!
print(now())
```

```
R> [1] "2020-02-08 17:47:20 -03"
```

Going further, based on these functions, we can write:

```r
# example of log message
my_sys_info <- Sys.info()
my_str <- str_c('Log of execution\n',
                'Time of execution: ', now(), '\n',
                'User: ', my_sys_info['user'], '\n',
                'Computer: ', my_sys_info['nodename'])

# print it
cat(my_str)
```

```
R> Log of execution
R> Time of execution: 2020-02-08 17:47:20
R> User: msperlin
R> Computer: Dell-Desktop
```

This is the exact time when this book was compiled in its final version. Notice we also got some details regarding username and computer with function Sys.info.

7.5.8 Other Useful Functions

weekdays - Returns the day of the week from one or more dates.

7.5. DATE AND TIME

```r
# set date vector
my_dates <- seq(from = ymd('2020-01-01'),
                to = ymd('2020-01-5'),
                by = '1 day')

# find corresponding weekdays
my_weekdays <- weekdays(my_dates)

# print it
print(my_weekdays)
```

```
R> [1] "Wednesday" "Thursday"  "Friday"    "Saturday"
R> [5] "Sunday"
```

months - Returns the month of one or more dates.

```r
# create date vector
my_dates <- seq(from = ymd('2020-01-01'),
                to = ymd('2020-12-31'),
                by = '1 month')

# find months
my_months <- months(my_dates)

# print result
print(my_months)
```

```
R> [1] "January"   "February" "March"    "April"
R> [5] "May"       "June"     "July"     "August"
R> [9] "September" "October"  "November" "December"
```

quarters - Returns the location of one or more dates within the year quartiles.

```r
# get quartiles of the year
my_quarters <- quarters(my_dates)
print(my_quarters)
```

```
R>  [1] "Q1" "Q1" "Q1" "Q2" "Q2" "Q2" "Q3" "Q3" "Q3" "Q4"
R> [11] "Q4" "Q4"
```

OlsonNames - Returns an array with the time zones available in R. In total, there are over 500 items. Here, we present only the first five elements.

```
# get possible timezones
possible_tz <- OlsonNames()

# print it
print(possible_tz[1:5])
```

```
R> [1] "Africa/Abidjan"     "Africa/Accra"
R> [3] "Africa/Addis_Ababa" "Africa/Algiers"
R> [5] "Africa/Asmara"
```

Sys.timezone - Returns the current timezone of the operating system.

```
print(Sys.timezone())
```

```
R> [1] "America/Sao_Paulo"
```

cut - Returns a factor by grouping dates and time.

```
# set example date vector
my_dates <- seq(from = as.Date('2020-01-01'),
                to = as.Date('2020-03-01'),
                by = '5 days')

# group vector based on monthly breaks
my_month_cut <- cut(x = my_dates,
                    breaks = 'month',
                    labels = c('Jan', 'Fev', 'Mar'))

# print result
print(my_month_cut)
```

```
R>  [1] Jan Jan Jan Jan Jan Jan Jan Fev Fev Fev Fev Fev
R> [13] Mar
R> Levels: Jan Fev Mar
```

7.6. MISSING DATA - NA (NOT AVAILABLE)

```
# set example datetime vector
my_datetime <- as.POSIXlt('2020-01-01 12:00:00') + seq(0,250,15)

# set groups for each 30 seconds
my_cut <- cut(x = my_datetime, breaks = '30 secs')

# print result
print(my_cut)
```

```
R>  [1] 2020-01-01 12:00:00 2020-01-01 12:00:00
R>  [3] 2020-01-01 12:00:30 2020-01-01 12:00:30
R>  [5] 2020-01-01 12:01:00 2020-01-01 12:01:00
R>  [7] 2020-01-01 12:01:30 2020-01-01 12:01:30
R>  [9] 2020-01-01 12:02:00 2020-01-01 12:02:00
R> [11] 2020-01-01 12:02:30 2020-01-01 12:02:30
R> [13] 2020-01-01 12:03:00 2020-01-01 12:03:00
R> [15] 2020-01-01 12:03:30 2020-01-01 12:03:30
R> [17] 2020-01-01 12:04:00
R> 9 Levels: 2020-01-01 12:00:00 ... 2020-01-01 12:04:00
```

7.6 Missing Data - NA (*Not available*)

One of the main innovations of R is the representation of missing data with objects of class NA (*Not Available*). The lack of data can have many reasons, such as failure to collect information or simply the absence of it. These cases are generally treated by removing or replacing the missing information before analyzing the data. The identification of these cases, therefore, is imperative.

7.6.1 Defining NA Values

To define omissions in the dataset, use symbol NA without quotes:

```
# a vector with NA
my_x <- c(1, 2, NA, 4, 5)

# print it
print(my_x)
```

```
R> [1] 1 2 NA 4 5
```

An important information that you must remember from previous chapters is that an NA object is contagious. Any object that interacts with an NA will turn into the same class of missing data:

```
# a vector
my_y <- c(2, 3, 5, 4, 1)

# example of NA interacting with other objects
print(my_x + my_y)
```

```
R> [1] 3 5 NA 8 6
```

This property demands special attention if you are calculating a value recursively, such as when using functions cumsum and cumprod. In these cases, any value after NA will turn into NA:

```
# set vector with NA
my_x <- c(1:5, NA, 5:10)

# print cumsum (NA after sixth element)
print(cumsum(my_x))
```

```
R>  [1]  1  3  6 10 15 NA NA NA NA NA NA NA
```

```
# print cumprod (NA after sixth element)
print(cumprod(my_x))
```

```
R>  [1]   1   2   6  24 120  NA  NA  NA  NA  NA  NA  NA
```

Therefore, when using functions cumsum and cumprod, make sure no NA value is found in the input vector.

7.6.2 Finding and Replacing NA

To find NA values, use function is.na:

7.6. MISSING DATA - NA (NOT AVAILABLE)

```r
# set vector with NA
my_x <- c(1:2, NA, 4:10)

# Test and find location of NA
print(is.na(my_x))
```

```
R> [1] FALSE FALSE  TRUE FALSE FALSE FALSE FALSE FALSE
R> [9] FALSE FALSE
```

```r
print(which(is.na(my_x)))
```

```
R> [1] 3
```

To replace it, use indexing with the output of is.na:

```r
# set vector
my_x <- c(1, NA, 3:4, NA)

# replace NA for 2
my_x[is.na(my_x)] <- 2

# print result
print(my_x)
```

```
R> [1] 1 2 3 4 2
```

Another way to remove NA values is to use the function na.omit, which returns the same object, but without the NA values. Note, however, the vector size will change and the output will be an object of class omit. Have a look:

```r
# set vector
my_char <- c(letters[1:3], NA, letters[5:8])

# print it
print(my_char)
```

```
R> [1] "a" "b" "c" NA  "e" "f" "g" "h"
```

```r
# use na.omit to remove NA
my_char <- na.omit(my_char)

# print result
print(my_char)
```

```
R> [1] "a" "b" "c" "e" "f" "g" "h"
R> attr(,"na.action")
R> [1] 4
R> attr(,"class")
R> [1] "omit"
```

Although the type of object has been changed due to the use of `na.omit`, the basic properties of the initial vector remain. For example, using the function `nchar` in the resulting object is still possible.

```r
# trying nchar on a na.omit object
print(nchar(my_char))
```

```
R> [1] 1 1 1 1 1 1 1
```

For other objects, however, this property may not hold. Some caution is advised when using `na.omit`. If needed, you can return to the basic class with the `as.*` functions, such as in `as.numeric` or `as.tibble`.

7.6.3 Other Useful Functions

complete.cases - Returns a logical vector indicating whether the lines of a bi-dimensional object are complete (without `NA`). This function is used exclusively for `dataframes` and matrices.

```r
# create matrix
my_mat <- matrix(1:15, nrow = 5)

# set an NA value
my_mat[2,2] <- NA

# print index with rows without NA
print(complete.cases(my_mat))
```

```
R> [1]  TRUE FALSE  TRUE  TRUE  TRUE
```

7.7 Exercises

1. Let's assume that, on a certain date, you bought 100 shares of a company, 15 dollars per share. After some time, you sold 30 shares for 18 dollars each and the remaining shares were sold for 22 dollars in a later day. Using a *script* in R, structure this financial problem by creating numeric objects. What is the gross profit of this stock market transaction?

2. Consider these numeric vectors x and y:

```
set.seed(7)
x <- sample (1:3, size = 5, replace = T)
y <- sample (1:3, size = 5, replace = T)
```

What is the sum of the elements of a new vector resulting from the multiplication between the elements of x and y?

3. Create a sequence called `seq_1`, with values between -10 and 10, where the interval between elements is equal to 2.

4. Define another object named `seq_2`, which contains a sequence of length 1000, with values between 0 and 100.

5. Calculate the sum between `seq_1` and `seq_2`. Did this operation work despite the different sizes of the vectors? Explain your answer.

6. If we create an object with the cumulative sum of a sequence from 1 to 100, what is the position of the first element that exceeds the value of 50?

7. Create a vector according to the following formula, where $i = 1...100$. What is the value of the sum of the elements of x?

$$x_i = \frac{(-1^{i+1})}{2i - 1}$$

8. **CHALLENGE** - Create a z_i vector according to the following formula, where $x_i = 1...50$ and $y_i = 50...1$. What is the value of the sum of z_i elements? (TIP: see function `dplyr::lag`)

$$z_i = \frac{y_i - x_{i-1}}{y_{i-2}}$$

9. Create an object named x with 1000 random values taken from a Normal distribution with average and standard deviation equal to 10. Using the cut function, create another object that defines two groups based on values of x, one for values higher than 10, and another for values under -5. How many observations do we find in each group?

10. Execute the following code and create object my_char:

```
set.seed(10)
my_char <- paste(sample(letters,
                        size = 500,
                        replace = T),
                 collapse = '')
```

How often is the letter 'x' found in the resulting text object?

11. If we split the my_char object from the previous exercise into several smaller pieces of text using the letter "b," what is the number of characters in the largest piece?

12. At link https://www.gutenberg.org/ebooks/2264.txt.utf-8, you can find a file containing the full text of William Shakespeare's "Macbeth" book. Use the link directly with function readr::read_lines to import the entire book as a vector of characters called my_book. How many lines does the resulting object have?

13. Aggregate the vector of characters in my_book to a single text object named full_text using function paste0(my_book, collapse = '\n'). With functions from package stringr, check how often the word 'lord' repeats itself throughout the text.

14. **CHALLENGE** - Use function stringr::str_split in object full_text to break the whole text as a function of whitespace (' '). Use this information with the function base::table and create a frequency table, showing the number of occurrences of each word. What are the five most used words in the text?

15. Assuming you'll live for 100 years, what is the proportion of your birthdays that will land on a weekend day (Sunday/Saturday)? Tip: Use operator %in% to check a multiple equality condition.

Chapter 8

Programming and Data Analysis

In previous chapters, we have learned what the most important object classes are in R. Besides, we have learned how to import tables from local files and the web. Here we will learn how to use programming tools to analyze our data, including the creation of custom functions, structured repetition of code (*loops*), and conditional execution. The concepts presented here are valuable. R offers a complete programming environment. So, based on it, you will be able to solve any computational problem from the real world.

8.1 R Functions

The use of functions is in the heart of R. Using functions organizes the code and its applicability. It also makes it easy to fix bugs and errors. If you are using a function in different places of a script, you only need to change its source to affect the whole code. For example, consider creating a procedure that cleans a database by removing outliers and NA cases. This set of instructions can be written as a function and used in different `dataframes`, forever.

Moreover, the usability of the function only gets better as it can be developed further and extended over time. Therefore, if we need to use it in a slightly different way, we can add options using arguments. Also, if you use the functions in your work, you'll invest less time in rewriting repetitive tasks and more in writing new procedures. With time and experience, a set of custom functions will be available, allowing you to write complex data operations in minutes.

A function always has three parts: input, processing stage, and output. The inputs are the R objects you need to find the solution to the problem. Processing is the actual code that will manipulate the inputs and produce a result. In R, the definition of a function is structured as follows:

```r
example_fct <- function(arg1 = 1, arg2 = 'abc'){

  msg1 <- paste0('\nValue of arg1: ', arg1)
  cat(msg1)

  msg2 <- paste0('\nValue of arg2: ', arg2)
  cat(msg2)

  cat('\n')

  out <- c(msg1, msg2)

  return(out)
}
```

The definition of a function is similar to the definition of an object in R. The main difference is its content is encapsulated by curly braces ({ }). Objects *arg1* and *arg2* are the inputs of the function, that is, the information required to perform some procedure.

Using the equality symbol in this setting, as in `arg1 = 1`, defines the *default* case for each input. Using default values is useful to define the most likely choice of the inputs of a function. It speeds up the work, as the user do not need to know and enter values for all possible options.

After registering the function in the environment (instructions will soon be given), we can change its input as necessary. For example, we can call `example_fct` with other arguments:

```r
# first call
out1 <- example_fct(arg1 = 2, arg2 = 'bcd')
```

```
R>
R> Value of arg1: 2
R> Value of arg2: bcd
```

8.1. R FUNCTIONS

```
# second call
out2 <- example_fct(arg1 = 10, arg2 = 'dab')


R>
R> Value of arg1: 10
R> Value of arg2: dab
```

Every function will return an object with the `return` command. This is usually placed at the end of the function definition. There is no restriction on the object returned: it can be a `list`, a `numeric` vector, or an object of any other class. This flexibility allows the user to return various information. Just organize it into a `list`, `vector`, or `dataframe`. The command `return` defines the end of the function execution.

As for using the function, you'll first need to register it in the environment by executing its definition like any other R code. A simple way of doing that is to place the cursor in the second curly brace at the end of the function scope and press *control + enter*. The *autocomplete* feature of RStudio also works for arguments of custom functions. To test it, first, register your function, type its name in the prompt or script and, between the two parentheses, press *tab*. At this point, you should now see a small screen with a list of inputs.

The arguments of the function can be set by position or name. So, if you called function `example_fct` as `example_fct(1, 2)`, it will recognize its input as `arg1 = 1` and `arg2 = 2`. When you use names, the position of arguments is irrelevant, i.e., the previous function call is equivalent to `example_fct(arg2 = 2, arg1 = 1)`.

Now, let's create a function that does something more useful: it takes as input a numeric vector and outputs its mean. We know that there is already a function called `mean` that does this procedure from previous chapters. However, we will write a new one as an example.

```
my_mean_fct <- function(x = c(1, 1, 1, 1)){
  # Calculates the average of input x
  #
  # Args:
  #   x: a numerical vector
  #
  # Returns:
  #   The mean of x
```

```
out <- sum(x)/length(x)

return(out)
```

}

Notice how we've set a comment section after the first curly brace to describe the written function, including its arguments and the returned value. By giving this quick summary, the user can quickly grasp what the function does and what to expect from it. From the Google's R style manual[1]:

> "Functions should contain a comments section immediately below the function definition line. These comments should consist of a one-sentence description of the function, a list of the function's arguments, denoted by Args:, with a description of each (including the data type); and a description of the return value, denoted by Returns:. The comments should be descriptive enough that a caller can use the function without reading any of the function's code."
>
> — Google's R style manual

After writing the function down, register it by executing the code. Let's test it:

```
# testing function my_mean_fct
my_mean <- my_mean_fct(x = 1:100)

# print result
print(my_mean)
```

R> [1] 50.5

The mean of a sequence from 1 to 100 is 50.5, as expected.

If function my_mean_fct is called without any input, it will use the *default* value of x = c(1, 1, 1, 1), with a mean equal to 1. Let's try it:

---

[1]https://google.github.io/styleguide/Rguide.xml#functionlanguage

8.1. R FUNCTIONS

```
# calling my_mean_fct without input
my_mean <- my_mean_fct()

# print result
print(my_mean)
```

R> [1] 1

Again, as expected, the returned value is correct.

A note here. A simple strategy for setting default values in functions is to choose the most obvious or simplest case. Moreover, the user does not need to know every aspect of a complex function and the consequences of changing its arguments. Most of the time, he/she only wants to use a simple functionality of a function and move on to the next part of the code. You can make it easier for the user by setting default values that are intuitive and likely to be chosen.

Although simple, the previous example can be further refined by introducing tests for the inputs. Notice how `my_mean_fct` accepts any input we give. If we define input x as a **character** object, the function would still accept it and try to execute the command in `out <- sum(x)/length(x)`. The problem is the function **sum** does not accept a **character** object and it would return an error. **By not testing the types of inputs in the function, we allow for errors that can lead to problems difficult to identify**. This is especially true for complex functions with many lines of code.

Correcting this problem is simple: you just need to conduct a logical test for the class of x and throw a custom error with function **stop** if the class is not **numeric** or **integer**:

```
my_mean_fct <- function(x = c(1, 1, 1, 1)){
  # Calculates the average of input x
  #
  # Args:
  #   x - a numerical vector
  #
  # Returns:
  #   The mean of x, as numeric

  if (!(class(x) %in% c('numeric', 'integer'))){
    stop('x is not a numeric class.')
  }
```

```
out <- sum(x)/length(x)

return(out)
}
```

In the previous code, we use the `class` function to test the input type and `stop` to issue an error. If we tried to set `x` as something different than a `numeric` or `integer` object, the execution stops and an error with the message `Input error: x is not numeric or integer` appears on the prompt. This message helps the user to understand the reason the function was not executed and give a hint on how to fix it. See an example next:

```
# using wrong inputs (ERROR)
my_mean_fct(x = c('a', 'b'))
```

R> Error in my_mean_fct: x is not a numeric vector

Another problem with our custom function is that it is does not handles `NA` values. Once again, remember that an `NA` object is contagious and will turn everything it touches into an `NA`!

To handle `NA` values in function `my_mean_fct`, a possible solution is to issue a warning message informing the user that input `x` contains a `NA`, remove the `NA` values from the input, and proceed with the calculation. The new definition of `my_mean_fct` will look like:

```
my_mean_fct <- function(x = c(1, 1, 1, 1)){
  # Calculates the average of input x
  #
  # Args:
  #   x: a numerical vector
  #
  # Returns:
  #   The mean of x, as numeric

  if (!(class(x) %in% c('numeric', 'integer'))){
    stop('Input error: x is not numeric or integer')
  }

  if (any(is.na(x))){
```

8.1. R FUNCTIONS

```
    warning('Warning: Found NA in x. Removing it.')
    x <- na.omit(x)
  }

  out <- sum(x)/length(x)

  return(out)
}
```

We used function `warning` to issue a message in the prompt, command `any(is.na(x))` to test if any element of x has a NA value, and `na.omit` to remove it from the atomic vector. Let's test it:

```
# set vector with NA
y <- c(1, 2, 3, NA, 1)

# test function
print(my_mean_fct(y))
```

```
R> Warning in my_mean_fct(y): Warning: Found NA in x.
R> Removing it.

R> [1] 1.75
```

As we can see, the function acknowledged the existence of an NA value, issued a warning message, and calculated the mean of x without the NA.

Using comments and input testing is a good programming policy. **Writing R functions does require lot of work. It also demands a great deal of knowledge about R and the underlying operation**. However, the great thing about R is you only need to do it once! The function can be used repeatedly in different scenarios. With time, you'll build a set of functions that will help you do your work more efficiently, and this collection of code will be your greatest asset. If you have written something that might interest other people, package the code and send it to CRAN[2]. The community will certainly appreciate it.

Now, let's move to a more complete example of using functions. A very common task in financial research is to calculate the returns of one or more stocks. This is equivalent to calculating the percentage change of a stock

---
[2]http://r-pkgs.had.co.nz/

price from one period of time to the next. Formally, we define the return of stock i for time t as:

$$R_{i,t} = \frac{P_{i,t}}{P_{i,t-1}} - 1$$

In R, this procedure takes as input a price vector and outputs a return vector. Please note we always miss the first return because, at time t=1, there is no previous day. This creates an issue as we will need to save the returns in a **dataframe** in the long format – stock data piled in top of each other. We will need to handle this problem within the code.

First, let's register a function for calculating returns from a vector of prices.

```
calc_ret <- function(P) {
  # Calculates arithmetic returns from a vector of prices
  #
  # Args:
  #   P - vector of prices (numeric)
  #
  # Returns:
  #   A vector of returns

  # ret = p_{t}/p_{t-1} - 1
  my_length <- length(P)
  ret <- c(NA, P[2:my_length]/P[1:(my_length - 1)] - 1)
  return(ret)
}
```

The function is simple and direct. Notice how we've set an **NA** value in the first element of the return series. We do that because it is important the return object has the same length as the input, and we always lose the first observation when calculating returns. So, we need to replace it with something. We could have simply set a zero value or the mean of the returns, but a **NA** value seems more appropriate.

Although intuitive, note that the **calc_ret** function would not work for stacked data, our long table of prices. The problem is that it was created to calculate returns for a single asset. Remember that in multiple asset **dataframes**, the price column is not unique to a single ticker. So if we used **calc_ret**, we would be mixing prices of different stocks in the calculation. The first observation of every asset's returns would be wrong!

8.1. R FUNCTIONS

To solve this issue is straightforward: we need to know the rows in which a stock ticker's change and, for these cases, add a `NA`. See next:

```r
calc_ret <- function(P,
                     tickers = rep('ticker', length(P))) {
  # Calculates arithmetic returns from a vector of prices
  #
  # Args:
  #   P - vector of prices (numeric)
  #   tickers - vector of tickers (optional)
  #
  # Returns:
  #   A vector of returns

  # ret_t = p_{t}/p_{t-1} - 1

  # error checking
  if ( !(class(P) %in% c('numeric', 'integer'))) {
    stop('P should be a numeric object.')
  }

  if ( !(class(tickers) %in% c('character', 'factor'))) {
    stop('tickers should be a character or factor object.')
  }

  if (length(P) != length(tickers)) {
    stop('The length of P and tickers does not match.')
  }

  if ( length(P) < 2) {
    stop('input P should have at least 2 elements.')
  }

  my_length <- length(P)
  ret <- c(NA, P[2:my_length]/P[1:(my_length - 1)] - 1)

  idx <- (tickers != c(NA, tickers[1:(my_length-1)]))
  ret[idx] <- NA

  return(ret)
}
```

That's a lengthy code! But remember, you only need to do it one time.

The function has many error checking procedures that ensure the inputs are correctly specified. The work pays off in the long run. You can reuse it whenever you need it, for the rest of your life!

Now, let's use the function with the data for the stocks in the SP500 index:

```
library(tidyverse)

my_f <- afedR::afedR_get_data_file('SP500-Stocks_long.csv')

# import data
df_sp500 <- read_csv(my_f, col_types = cols())

# calculate return column
df_sp500 <- df_sp500 %>%
  mutate(ret = calc_ret(P = price.adjusted,
                        tickers = ticker))
```

Let's look at the result:

```
glimpse(df_sp500)
```

```
R> Observations: 829,710
R> Variables: 4
R> $ price.adjusted <dbl> 69.15826, 68.72509, 69.6997...
R> $ ref.date       <date> 2010-01-04, 2010-01-05, 20...
R> $ ticker         <chr> "MMM", "MMM", "MMM", "MMM",...
R> $ ret            <dbl> NA, -0.006263503, 0.0141817...
```

```
summary(df_sp500)
```

```
R>  price.adjusted         ref.date
R>  Min.   :   1.59    Min.   :2010-01-04
R>  1st Qu.:  28.35    1st Qu.:2011-09-30
R>  Median :  44.89    Median :2013-07-05
R>  Mean   :  62.00    Mean   :2013-07-03
R>  3rd Qu.:  71.20    3rd Qu.:2015-04-06
R>  Max.   :1578.13    Max.   :2016-12-30
R>
R>     ticker                 ret
R>  Length:829710      Min.   :-0.3919
```

8.1. R FUNCTIONS

```
R>   Class  :character    1st Qu.:-0.0077
R>   Mode   :character    Median : 0.0006
R>                        Mean   : 0.0007
R>                        3rd Qu.: 0.0091
R>                        Max.   : 0.6191
R>                        NA's   :471
```

It looks great! The return vector is available in column `ret`. We also see from the call to `summary` that the return vector has 471 `NA` values, the same number of unique tickers in the database.

Going further, let's remove all `NA` rows with function `complete.cases`, so we only keep the rows with actual values in all columns.

```
df_sp500 <- df_sp500 %>%
  filter(complete.cases(.))

# check result
glimpse(df_sp500)
```

```
R> Observations: 829,239
R> Variables: 4
R> $ price.adjusted <dbl> 68.72509, 69.69973, 69.7497...
R> $ ref.date       <date> 2010-01-05, 2010-01-06, 20...
R> $ ticker         <chr> "MMM", "MMM", "MMM", "MMM",...
R> $ ret            <dbl> -0.006263503, 0.014181794, ...
```

```
summary(df_sp500)
```

```
R>  price.adjusted       ref.date
R>  Min.   :   1.59   Min.   :2010-01-05
R>  1st Qu.:  28.36   1st Qu.:2011-10-03
R>  Median :  44.90   Median :2013-07-05
R>  Mean   :  62.02   Mean   :2013-07-03
R>  3rd Qu.:  71.21   3rd Qu.:2015-04-06
R>  Max.   :1578.13   Max.   :2016-12-30
R>     ticker               ret
R>  Length:829239     Min.   :-0.3918766
R>  Class :character  1st Qu.:-0.0077069
R>  Mode  :character  Median : 0.0006451
R>                    Mean   : 0.0006771
R>                    3rd Qu.: 0.0090999
R>                    Max.   : 0.6190656
```

Finally, we save the resulting dataset as a *.rds* file.

```
write_rds(x = df_sp500,
          path = 'data/SP500-Stocks-WithRet.rds')
```

As a final word on using functions, don't hesitate to write them down whenever you are using the same data procedure across R code. By pursuing a modular and functional approach in your code, it will be much easier to fix bugs and maintain your code. Good functions will help you do your work more efficiently.

8.2 Using for Loops

A *loop* command is the most basic computer instruction in any programming language. Briefly, loops allow a structured repetition of code for processing individual items, whatever they are. As an example, consider a scenario where we have a database composed of 1,000 *.csv* files in the same folder. Here, we can create a *loop* to read the data individually from each file, clean up the resulting `dataframe`, and finally, aggregate all clean `dataframes` into a single object.

The great thing about *loops* is its length. The number of repetitions is dynamically set. Using the previous example, if we had 5,000 files, the loop would process all 5,000 files. If we had just 500, the *loop* would run 500 times. That means we can encapsulate a generic procedure for processing all found files in a particular folder. With it, you have at your reach a tool for the execution of **any** complex sequential process.

Back to the code, the structure of a *loop* in R follows:

```
for (i in i_vec) {
  ...
}
```

Command `for` indicates the beginning of a *loop*. Object `i`, as in (`i in i_vec`), is the iterator – it will change its value according to each element contained in `i_vec`. Note the *loop* is encapsulated by curly braces (`{}`). These are important as they define where the *loop* starts and where it ends. The code indentation – the use of larger margins – is also important for visual cues, but it is not necessary. Consider the information below as a practical example:

8.2. USING FOR LOOPS

```r
# set seq
my_seq <- seq(-5, 5)

# do loop
for (i in my_seq){
  cat(paste('\nThe value of i is', i))
}
```

```
R>
R> The value of i is -5
R> The value of i is -4
R> The value of i is -3
R> The value of i is -2
R> The value of i is -1
R> The value of i is 0
R> The value of i is 1
R> The value of i is 2
R> The value of i is 3
R> The value of i is 4
R> The value of i is 5
```

We created a sequence from -5 to 5 and presented a text for each element with the `cat` function. Notice how we also broke the prompt line with `'\n'`. The *loop* starts with `i = -5`, execute command `cat(paste('\nThe value of i is', -5))`, proceed to the next iteration by setting `i = -4`, rerun the `cat` command, and so on. At its final iteration, the value of `i` is 5.

The iterated sequence in the *loop* is not exclusive to numerical vectors. Any object can be used within the *loop*, including a `character` class:

```r
# set char vec
my_char_vec <- letters[1:5]

# loop it!
for (i_char in my_char_vec){
  cat(paste('\nThe value of i_char is',
            i_char))
}
```

```
R>
R> The value of i_char is a
```

```
R> The value of i_char is b
R> The value of i_char is c
R> The value of i_char is d
R> The value of i_char is e
```

The same goes for `lists`:

```
# set list
my_l <- list(x = 1:5,
             y = c('abc', 'dfg'),
             z = factor('A', 'B', 'C', 'D'))

# loop list
for (i_l in my_l){

  cat(paste0('\nThe class of i_l is ', class(i_l), '. '))
  cat(paste0('The number of elements is ', length(i_l), '.'))

}
```

```
R>
R> The class of i_l is integer. The number of elements is 5.
R> The class of i_l is character. The number of elements is 2.
R> The class of i_l is factor. The number of elements is 1.
```

In the definition of *loops*, the iterator does not have to be the only object incremented in each iteration. We can create other objects and increment them manually:

```
# set vec and iterators
my_vec <- seq(1:5)
my_x <- 5
my_z <- 10

for (i in my_vec){
  # increment "manually"
  my_x <- my_x + 1
  my_z <- my_z + 2

  cat('\nValue of i = ', i,
      ' | Value of my_x = ', my_x,
      ' | Value of my_z = ', my_z)
}
```

8.2. USING FOR LOOPS

```
R>
R> Value of i = 1  | Value of my_x = 6   | Value of my_z = 12
R> Value of i = 2  | Value of my_x = 7   | Value of my_z = 14
R> Value of i = 3  | Value of my_x = 8   | Value of my_z = 16
R> Value of i = 4  | Value of my_x = 9   | Value of my_z = 18
R> Value of i = 5  | Value of my_x = 10  | Value of my_z = 20
```

Using nested *loops*, that is, a *loop* inside of another *loop* is also possible. See the following example, where we present all the elements of a matrix:

```r
# set matrix
my_mat <- matrix(1:9, nrow = 3)

# loop all values of matrix
for (i in seq(1, nrow(my_mat))){
  for (j in seq(1,ncol(my_mat))){
    cat(paste0('\nElement [', i, ', ', j, '] = ',
               my_mat[i, j]))
  }
}
```

```
R>
R> Element [1, 1] = 1
R> Element [1, 2] = 4
R> Element [1, 3] = 7
R> Element [2, 1] = 2
R> Element [2, 2] = 5
R> Element [2, 3] = 8
R> Element [3, 1] = 3
R> Element [3, 2] = 6
R> Element [3, 3] = 9
```

Let's do a more complex example using data files. We will create several files with random data in our computer and save them in a folder named `many_datafiles`. This is accomplished with the following script:

```r
library(tidyverse)

# set number of files to create
n_files <- 10
```

```r
# set the first part of saved files
pattern_name <- 'myfiles_'

# set dir
out_dir <- 'many_datafiles/'

# test if out.dir exists -- if not, create it
if (!dir.exists(out_dir)) {
  dir.create(out_dir)
} else {
  # clean up folder before creating new files
  file.remove(list.files(out_dir,
                         full.names = TRUE))
}
```

```
R> logical(0)
```

```r
# set vec with filenames
file_names <- paste0(out_dir,
                     pattern_name,
                     seq(1, n_files), '.csv')

# loop it!
for (i_file in file_names){
  # create temp df
  temp_df <- tibble(x = runif(100))

  # write it!
  write_csv(x = temp_df, path = i_file)
}
```

In the previous example, we used function if in if(!dir.exists(out_dir)) to test if folder many_datafiles existed. If it did not, we create it in the current working directory. Before running the loop, we remove all files in out_dir with command file.remove(list.files(out_dir, full.names = TRUE)). In the *loop*, we used function runif to create 100 random numbers between *0* and *1*, so each *dataframe* created in temp_df is unique. Notice how the *loop* size is set by object n_files. If we wanted to create *10,000* files, we need only to set n_files = 10000 and the rest of the code will adjust accordingly.

Now, let's check if the files are in the folder:

8.2. USING FOR LOOPS

```r
# check files
print(list.files(out_dir))
```

```
R> [1] "myfiles_1.csv"  "myfiles_10.csv" "myfiles_2.csv"
R> [4] "myfiles_3.csv"  "myfiles_4.csv"  "myfiles_5.csv"
R> [7] "myfiles_6.csv"  "myfiles_7.csv"  "myfiles_8.csv"
R> [10] "myfiles_9.csv"
```

As expected, the files are there. To complete the example, we will import the contents of these files and aggregate all information into a single `dataframe` by using another *loop* and functions `readr::read_csv` and `readr::bind_rows`.

```r
# set empty df
df_agg <- tibble()
for (i_file in file_names){
  # read file
  temp_df <- read_csv(i_file, col_types = cols())

  # row bind
  df_agg <- bind_rows(df_agg, temp_df)
}

glimpse(df_agg)
```

```
R> Observations: 1,000
R> Variables: 1
R> $ x <dbl> 0.83761088, 0.10966012, 0.95800782, 0.99...
```

Notice how we bind all `dataframes` within the loop with line `df_agg <- bind_rows(df_agg, temp_df)`. The size of `df_agg` increases with each iteration of the *loop*. This chunk of code is not speed-wise efficient, but we write it this way for clarity. Looking at the contents of `df_agg`, we can see the code performed as expected: column x contains numerical values between *0* and *1*, result from the bind operation of several `dataframes`.

Another practical example of using *loops* is processing data according to groups. If we have a price dataset for several tickers and we want to calculate the average price of each stock, we can use a *loop* for that. In this example, we will again use the data from file `SP500-Stocks_long.csv`.

```r
library(tidyverse)

# read data
my_f <- afedR::afedR_get_data_file('SP500-Stocks_long.csv')
df_SP500 <- read_csv(my_f,
                     col_types = cols())

# find unique tickers in column ticker
unique_tickers <- unique(df_SP500$ticker)

# create empty df for saving results
tab_out <- tibble()

# loop tickers
for (i_ticker in unique_tickers){

  # create temp df with ticker i.ticker
  temp <- df_SP500 %>%
    filter(ticker == i_ticker)

  # row bind i.ticker and mean_price
  temp_mean_price <- mean(temp$price.adjusted)
  tab_out <- bind_rows(tab_out,
                       tibble(ticker = i_ticker,
                              mean_price = temp_mean_price))

}

# print result
print(head(tab_out))
```

```
R> # A tibble: 6 x 2
R>   ticker mean_price
R>   <chr>       <dbl>
R> 1 MMM         111.
R> 2 ABT          32.1
R> 3 ACN          70.6
R> 4 ATVI         19.0
R> 5 AYI         113.
R> 6 ADBE         55.2
```

We used the function **unique** to discover the names of all the tickers in the

8.3. CONDITIONAL STATEMENTS (IF, ELSE, SWITCH)

dataset. Soon after, we create an empty *dataframe* to save the results and a loop for filtering the data of each stock sequentially and averaging its prices. At the end of the *loop*, we use function `dplyr::bind_rows` to paste the results of each stock with the results of the main table. As you can see, we can use a *loop* to perform group calculations. There are, however, better ways of doing this procedure, as we will soon learn.

8.3 Conditional Statements (`if`, `else`, `switch`)

Making binary decisions of type *yes* or *no* is common programming practice. Whenever a condition is found true, a specific code is executed. Otherwise, other command lines are executed. It is these decisions that define the conditional statements. In R, we can write them down by using the following structure:

```
# skeleton for if statement
if (cond){

  CodeIfTRUE...

} else {

  CodeIfFALSE...

}
```

The placeholder `cond` is the condition to be evaluated, taking only two values: `TRUE` or `FALSE`. The result of the condition must be a single logical element. With finding a `TRUE` value to `cond`, the code in `CodeIfTRUE` will run. Otherwise, where we find a `FALSE` value in `cond`, the code in `CodeIfFALSE` will be executed. A practical example based on a *loop* is presented next:

```
# set vec and threshold
my_x <- 1:10
my_thresh <- 5

for (i in my_x) {
  if (i > my_thresh){
    cat('\nValue of ', i,
```

```
                ' is higher than ',
          my_thresh)
  } else {
    cat('\nValue of ',
        i,
        ' is lower or equal than ',
        my_thresh)
  }
}
```

```
R>
R> Value of  1  is lower or equal than  5
R> Value of  2  is lower or equal than  5
R> Value of  3  is lower or equal than  5
R> Value of  4  is lower or equal than  5
R> Value of  5  is lower or equal than  5
R> Value of  6  is higher than  5
R> Value of  7  is higher than  5
R> Value of  8  is higher than  5
R> Value of  9  is higher than  5
R> Value of  10  is higher than  5
```

If we want to apply more than one logical condition, we can use the `else if` command as well as `else`:

```
for (i in my_x){
  if (i > my_thresh){
    cat('\nValue of ', i, ' is higher than ', my_thresh)
  } else if (i==my_thresh) {
    cat('\nValue of ', i, ' is equal to ', my_thresh)
  } else {
    cat('\nValue of ', i, ' is lower than ', my_thresh)
  }
}
```

```
R>
R> Value of  1  is lower than  5
R> Value of  2  is lower than  5
R> Value of  3  is lower than  5
R> Value of  4  is lower than  5
R> Value of  5  is equal to  5
```

8.3. CONDITIONAL STATEMENTS (IF, ELSE, SWITCH)

```
R> Value of 6 is higher than 5
R> Value of 7 is higher than 5
R> Value of 8 is higher than 5
R> Value of 9 is higher than 5
R> Value of 10 is higher than 5
```

Another possibility of using conditional executions is function `switch`, designed to give a better structure for a decision based on more than two choices. Let's say you want a conditional execution based on five conditions, A, B, C, and D. For each condition, and you want the code to show a different message. Using `if` function, you could do that using this chunk of code:

```
# set vec
my_vec <- c('A', 'D', 'B', 'A', 'C', 'B')

for (i_vec in my_vec){
  if (i_vec == 'A'){
    cat('\nGot an A!')
  } else if (i_vec == 'B') {
    cat('\nGot a B!')
  } else if (i_vec == 'C') {
    cat('\nGot a C!')
  } else if (i_vec == 'D') {
    cat('\nGot a D!')
  }
}
```

```
R>
R> Got an A!
R> Got a D!
R> Got a B!
R> Got an A!
R> Got a C!
R> Got a B!
```

While the previous code works, using several `else if` conditions is not visually elegant. A better way of doing it is using function `switch`. See next:

```
# set vec
my.vec <- c('A', 'D', 'B', 'A', 'C', 'B')

for (i_vec in my.vec){
  msg.out <- switch(i_vec,
                    'A' = '\nGot an A!',
                    'B' = '\nGot a B!',
                    'C' = '\nGot a C!',
                    'D' = '\nGot a D!')

  cat(msg.out)

}
```

```
R>
R> Got an A!
R> Got a D!
R> Got a B!
R> Got an A!
R> Got a C!
R> Got a B!
```

The main benefit of using `switch` is the code becomes clear and easier to understand.

8.4 Using apply Functions

An alternative way of using *loops* in R is to call functions from the `base::apply` and `purrr::map` family. These are part of the **functional programming** philosophy of R as they require the explicit definition of functions to be used for many items of a vector or `list`.

It is worth pointing out that all procedures using *loops* can be restructured using `apply` and `map` functions and vice versa. The difference in processing speed from one to the other is negligible. The choice between *loops* and `apply` type of functions is determined by the complexity of the operation and personal taste.

Whenever it is possible, give preference to a functional approach of the `apply` and `purr::map` family. These require a function as input and force the author to think of procedures as modules and write good functions.

8.4. USING APPLY FUNCTIONS

In the long term, the benefits are obvious; you will write better and more maintainable code.

8.4.1 Using `lapply`

Function `base::lapply` takes as input a `list` and a function. It works by passing each element of the input `list` to the function. The output of each call is aggregated and returned as an object of class `list`. Notice how the use of `lists` in the input and output of `lapply` provides flexibility. You can use it for any object, with no restriction on its output. See the following example, where we calculate the average of a series of vectors with different sizes:

```
# set list
my_l <- list(c(1, 2, 2),
             c(2:5, NA),
             c(10:-20))

# use lapply with mean
my_mean_vec <- lapply(X = my_l,
                     FUN = mean)

# print result
print(my_mean_vec)
```

```
R> [[1]]
R> [1] 1.666667
R>
R> [[2]]
R> [1] NA
R>
R> [[3]]
R> [1] -5
```

The result shows the means of each vector in `my_l`, as expected. We could also pass other options to `mean` with `lapply`. See next, where we use `na.rm = TRUE`.

```
# set list
my_l <- list(c(1, 2, 2), c(2:5, NA), 10:-20)
```

```r
# use lapply with mean
my_mean_vec <- lapply(X = my_l, 
                     FUN = mean, 
                     na.rm=TRUE)

# print result
print(my_mean_vec)
```

```
R> [[1]]
R> [1] 1.666667
R> 
R> [[2]]
R> [1] 3.5
R> 
R> [[3]]
R> [1] -5
```

As we can see, the extra argument `na.rm = TRUE` is passed to every call to function `mean`.

In particular, using `lapply` is useful when using a custom function. So, now we'll redo the previous example of creating several *.csv* files. The first step is to create a function that generates these files as we did with the *loop*.

```r
# function to generate files
create_rnd_file <- function(name_file, N = 100){
  # Generates a csv file with random content
  #
  # Args:
  #     name.file - name of csv file (character)
  #   N - number of rows in random dataframe (integer)
  #
  # Returns:
  #     TRUE, if successful
  
  require(tidyverse)
  
  if (class(name_file) != 'character'){
    stop('ERROR: input name.file is not a character')
  }
```

8.4. USING APPLY FUNCTIONS

```r
  if ( !(class(N) %in% c('numeric', 'integer')) ){
    stop('ERROR: input N is not an integer or numeric!')
  }
  
  # create random df
  temp_df <- tibble(x = runif(N))
  
  # write it!
  write_csv(x = temp_df,
            path = name_file)
  
  # return TRUE
  return(TRUE)
}
```

Now, we use the function with `lapply`:

```r
# set options
n_files <- 5
pattern_name <- 'myfiles_with_lapply_'
out_dir <- 'many_datafiles/'

# set file names
file_names <- paste0(out_dir,
                     pattern_name,
                     seq(1, n_files), '.csv')

# test if out.dir exists, if not, create it
if (!dir.exists(out_dir)){
  dir.create(out_dir)
}

# clean up folder before creating new files
file.remove(list.files(out_dir,
                       full.names = TRUE))
```

```
R>  [1] TRUE TRUE TRUE TRUE TRUE TRUE TRUE TRUE TRUE TRUE
```

```r
# use lapply
out_l <- lapply(X = file_names,
                FUN = create_rnd_file,
```

```
                        N = 100)

# print result
print(out_1)


R> [[1]]
R> [1] TRUE
R>
R> [[2]]
R> [1] TRUE
R>
R> [[3]]
R> [1] TRUE
R>
R> [[4]]
R> [1] TRUE
R>
R> [[5]]
R> [1] TRUE
```

As you can see, everything worked well, as expected. The creation of the random files was a success.

Notice the returned object of function `lapply` is always a `list`. Such property is useful whenever you need to apply a function that returns a complex object, such as the estimation of a model, and not a single value.

8.4.2 Using `sapply`

Function `base::sapply` works similarly to `lapply`. The main difference is in the type of output. While `lapply` returns a list, `sapply` returns an atomic matrix or vector. See the following example:

```
# create list
my_l <- list(1:10, 2:5, 10:-20)

# use sapply
my_mean_vec <- sapply(my_l, mean)

# print result
print(my_mean_vec)
```

8.4. USING APPLY FUNCTIONS

```
R> [1]  5.5  3.5 -5.0
```

Using `sapply` is recommended when the output of the underlying function is an atomic vector. In such cases, it is unnecessary to return a flexible object, such as a `list`.

An important aspect of using `sapply` is the underlying function can return more than one value. The result comes from the aggregation of the individual vectors into a `matrix`. See the following example, where we create a function that returns the mean and standard deviation of a numeric vector:

```
# set list
my_l <- list(x1 = runif(10),
             x2 = runif(15),
             x3 = rnorm(1000))

my_mean_fct <- function(x){
  # Returns mean and standard deviation of a vector
  #
  # Args:
  #   x - numerical vector
  #
  # Returns:
  #   Vector as c(mean(x), sd(x))

  if (!(class(x) %in% c('numeric','integer'))){
    stop('ERROR: Class of x is not numeric or integer.')
  }

  x <- na.omit(x)

  out <- c(Mean = mean(x),
           StDev = sd(x))
  return(out)

}

# use sapply
my_vec <- sapply(my_l, my_mean_fct)

# check result
print(my_vec)
```

```
R>                    x1          x2          x3
R> Mean       0.6175602   0.4481678   0.01191433
R> StDev      0.3310349   0.2563504   1.04510585
```

When there is more than one output in the underlying function, each row in the returned object represents a different output of the function used with `sapply`, in this case, the mean and standard deviation of `x`. The columns indicate the different processed items in `my_l`.

A practical use of function `sapply` in data analysis is the creation of descriptive tables. Let's use the SP500 data and create a descriptive analysis of the prices of the different stocks. First, let's write the function.

```
describe_vec <- function(x){
  # Describe numerical vector with mean and other stats
  #
  # Args:
  #   x - numerical vector
  #
  # Returns:
  #   A vector with mean, maximum and minimum

  # error checking
  if (!(class(x) %in% c('numeric','integer'))){
    stop('ERROR: Class of x is not numeric or integer.')
  }

  x <- na.omit(x)

  # calc vec
  out <- c(mean_price = mean(x),
           max_price = max(x),
           min_price = min(x))

  return(out)
}
```

Now, let's load the data and apply the function `describe_vec` to the different stocks.

8.4. USING APPLY FUNCTIONS

```
library(tidyverse)

# set file and read it
my_f <- afedR::afedR_get_data_file('SP500-Stocks_long.csv')
df_sp500 <- read_csv(my_f,
                     col_types = cols())

# use split to split prices by ticker
my_l <- split(x = df_sp500$price.adjusted,
              f = df_sp500$ticker)

# use sapply
my_tab <- sapply(X = my_l, FUN = describe_vec)

# check result
print(head(t(my_tab)))
```

```
R>       mean_price max_price min_price
R> A       33.04629  48.18046 18.329764
R> AAL     23.41365  54.66265  3.893684
R> AAP    103.19876 199.99451 38.418693
R> AAPL    75.00174 127.96609 24.881912
R> ABC     58.38558 112.10088 23.307129
R> ABT     32.11558  49.33589 18.430625
```

We used function `split` in `split(x = df_sp500$price.adjusted, f = df_sp500$ticker)` to separate the prices of the different stocks into the different elements of a `list`. We later use this object with `sapply`. We transposed the resulting matrix with function `t`, resulting in a matrix where the rows represent the assets and the columns indicate the different statistics. If necessary, we could easily expand function `describe_vec` by adding other statistics.

8.4.3 Using `tapply`

Function `tapply` is designed to perform group operations. See the following example, where we create a `numeric` vector with a sequence of 1 to 150 and a `factor` with groups A, B, and C. Using `tapply`, we can calculate the average of the numerical vector for each group.

```r
# set numeric vec and factor
my_x <- 1:150
my_factor <- factor(c(rep('C',50),
                      rep('B',50),
                      rep('A',50)))

# use tapply
my_mean_vec <- tapply(X = my_x, INDEX = my_factor, FUN = mean)

# print result
print(my_mean_vec)
```

```
R>    A    B    C
R> 125.5 75.5 25.5
```

A very important point about using `tapply` is the order of groups in the output is set **alphabetically**, and it ignores the order found in `my_factor`. If keeping the same order of groups is important, you must reorder the resulting `list`.

Going back to the previous example using stock prices, we can also use `tapply` to reach the same objective of calculating several descriptive statistics for different tickers. Have a look.

```r
# use tapply for descriptive stats
my_l_out <- tapply(X = df_sp500$price.adjusted,
                   INDEX = df_sp500$ticker,
                   FUN = describe_vec)

# print result
print(my_l_out[1:5])
```

```
R> $A
R> mean_price   max_price   min_price
R>   33.04629    48.18046    18.32976
R>
R> $AAL
R> mean_price   max_price   min_price
R>  23.413651   54.662650    3.893684
R>
R> $AAP
```

8.4. USING APPLY FUNCTIONS

```
R> mean_price  max_price  min_price
R>   103.19876  199.99451   38.41869
R>
R> $AAPL
R> mean_price  max_price  min_price
R>    75.00174  127.96609   24.88191
R>
R> $ABC
R> mean_price  max_price  min_price
R>    58.38558  112.10088   23.30713
```

The output of `tapply` is a `list` of values. Each element contains a vector from `describe_vec`. Despite showing the same results we've found in the previous example, a `list` is not the recommended type of object for tables. Therefore, we should transform the `list` to a `dataframe`, so we can later export it:

```
# convert list to the dataframe
my_tab <- do.call(what = bind_rows,
                  args = my_l_out)

# set ticker column
my_tab <- my_tab %>%
  mutate(ticker = names(my_l_out))

# print result
print(head(my_tab))
```

```
R> # A tibble: 6 x 4
R>   mean_price max_price min_price ticker
R>        <dbl>     <dbl>     <dbl> <chr>
R> 1       33.0      48.2     18.3  A
R> 2       23.4      54.7      3.89 AAL
R> 3      103.      200.      38.4  AAP
R> 4       75.0     128.      24.9  AAPL
R> 5       58.4     112.      23.3  ABC
R> 6       32.1      49.3     18.4  ABT
```

It is the first time that command `do.call` is used. It is a complex function that recursively calls another function (see argument `what`) using a sequence of pair of elements from input `args`. In our case, `do.call` will first use elements one and two of `my_l_out` as inputs in `bind_rows`. This is equal to `bind_rows(my_l_out[[1]], my_l_out[[2]])`. After that, it will use the result of the previous step and feed it to `bind_rows` again, using the third element of `my_l_out`. Function `do.call` will continue this operation until the end of `my_l_out` is reached. As you can see, it is a recursive calculation. For our case, it is simply binding all elements of `my_l_out` into a single `dataframe`. Further details about this function can be obtained with command `help(do.call)`.

Reverting to the example, we can see the result in `my_tab` is exactly as expected, with each stock showing its average, minimum, and maximum price.

8.4.4 Using mapply

Function `mapply` is a multivariate version of `sapply` and `lapply`. It allows the use of more than one argument to a function, so each element in the output is a combination of the inputs in `mapply`. Sounds confusing? Don't worry; an example will make this clear.

Assume we are interested in creating a `list` with the content as in `my_l <- list(1, 1:2, 1:3, 1:4,.., 1:10)`. One possible solution is to use a loop:

```
# set size
N <- 10

# preallocate list
my_l <- list()

for (i in seq(1, N)){
  my_l[[i]] <- seq(1, i)
}

# print result
print(my_l)
```

```
R> [[1]]
R> [1] 1
R>
R> [[2]]
R> [1] 1 2
```

8.4. USING APPLY FUNCTIONS

```
R>
R> [[3]]
R> [1] 1 2 3
R>
R> [[4]]
R> [1] 1 2 3 4
R>
R> [[5]]
R> [1] 1 2 3 4 5
R>
R> [[6]]
R> [1] 1 2 3 4 5 6
R>
R> [[7]]
R> [1] 1 2 3 4 5 6 7
R>
R> [[8]]
R> [1] 1 2 3 4 5 6 7 8
R>
R> [[9]]
R> [1] 1 2 3 4 5 6 7 8 9
R>
R> [[10]]
R>  [1]  1  2  3  4  5  6  7  8  9 10
```

Another, less verbose and more elegant solution, is to use mapply:

```
# use mapply for creating list
my_l <- mapply(FUN = seq,
               rep(1, N),
               seq(1, N))

print(my_l)
```

```
R> [[1]]
R> [1] 1
R>
R> [[2]]
R> [1] 1 2
R>
R> [[3]]
```

```
R> [1] 1 2 3
R> 
R> [[4]]
R> [1] 1 2 3 4
R> 
R> [[5]]
R> [1] 1 2 3 4 5
R> 
R> [[6]]
R> [1] 1 2 3 4 5 6
R> 
R> [[7]]
R> [1] 1 2 3 4 5 6 7
R> 
R> [[8]]
R> [1] 1 2 3 4 5 6 7 8
R> 
R> [[9]]
R> [1] 1 2 3 4 5 6 7 8 9
R> 
R> [[10]]
R>    [1]  1  2  3  4  5  6  7  8  9 10
```

Explaining the result, function `mapply` is calling `seq` for each pair of elements in `rep(1,N)` and `seq(1,N)`. So, the first element of `my_l` is simply `seq(1, 1)`. The second element is `seq(1, 2)`, and its final element is `seq(1, 10)`. As you can see, function `mapply` is a more elaborate use of functions `lapply` and `sapply`, and it is useful when you have more than one argument you want to change in a call to a function.

8.4.5 Using apply

The `apply` function follows the same logic as the others, with the main difference being its use in objects with two dimensions. Here, the user can process the object by rows or columns. Look in the following example where, based on a matrix object, we will need to calculate the sum of the row and column values.

```
# set matrix and print it
my_mat <- matrix(1:15, nrow = 5)
print(my_mat)
```

8.4. USING APPLY FUNCTIONS

```
R>      [,1] [,2] [,3]
R> [1,]   1    6   11
R> [2,]   2    7   12
R> [3,]   3    8   13
R> [4,]   4    9   14
R> [5,]   5   10   15
```

```r
# sum rows with apply and print it
sum_rows <- apply(X = my_mat, MARGIN = 1, FUN = sum)
print(sum_rows)
```

```
R> [1] 18 21 24 27 30
```

```r
# sum columns with apply and print it
sum_cols <- apply(X = my_mat, MARGIN = 2, FUN = sum)
print(sum_cols)
```

```
R> [1] 15 40 65
```

In the previous example, the MARGIN argument sets the orientation of the calculation. With MARGIN = 1, function apply separates each row as a vector and uses function sum in each. With MARGIN = 2, the calculation is column-oriented.

Expanding the example, we can use apply to find the maximum values of my_mat per row and per column. Have a look at the next example:

```r
# print max by row
print(apply(X = my_mat, MARGIN = 1, FUN = max))
```

```
R> [1] 11 12 13 14 15
```

```r
# print max by column
print(apply(X = my_mat, MARGIN = 2, FUN = max))
```

```
R> [1]  5 10 15
```

8.4.6 Using by

The by function differentiates itself because of its **dataframe** orientation: it splits a **dataframe** into smaller pieces according to a **factor**. The main advantage is it allows the user to access any column available in the data. Whenever you need to process the data by groups and use information from several columns of a **dataframe**, the by function should be used.

Look at the next example, where we create a more complex descriptive table using the information on prices and returns.

```
# load data
df_sp500 <- read_rds(afedR::afedR_get_data_file(
  'SP500-Stocks-WithRet.rds')
)

# set function for processing df
describe_vec_with_ret <- function(df_in){
  
  P <- df_in$price.adjusted
  ret <- df_in$ret
  
  out <- c(ticker = df_in$ticker[1],
           MeanPrice= mean(P),
           MaxPrice = max(P),
           MinPrice = min(P),
           MeanRet = mean(ret),
           MaxRet = max(ret),
           MinRet = min(ret))
  
  return(out)
  
}

# apply example_fct for each ticker in df_sp500
my_l <- by(data = df_sp500,
           INDICES = df_sp500$ticker,
           FUN = describe_vec_with_ret)

# convert list to dataframe
my_tab <- do.call(what = bind_rows, args = my_l)

# print result
```

8.5 Using package purrr

```
print(head(my_tab))
```

```
R> # A tibble: 6 x 7
R>   ticker MeanPrice MaxPrice MinPrice MeanRet MaxRet
R>   <chr>  <chr>     <chr>    <chr>    <chr>   <chr>
R> 1 A      33.05298~ 48.1804~ 18.3297~ 0.0006~ 0.117~
R> 2 AAL    23.42431~ 54.66265 3.893684 0.0017~ 0.173~
R> 3 AAP    103.2348~ 199.994~ 38.4186~ 0.0009~ 0.165~
R> 4 AAPL   75.02858~ 127.966~ 24.8819~ 0.0009~ 0.088~
R> 5 ABC    58.40505~ 112.100~ 23.3071~ 0.0007~ 0.095~
R> 6 ABT    32.12158~ 49.3358~ 18.4306~ 0.0003~ 0.064~
R> # ... with 1 more variable: MinRet <chr>
```

Function `describe_vec_with_ret` was a requirement for using by. Notice how its input is a `dataframe` and columns `ret`, and `price.adjusted` is used in its scope. As explained, the by function is passing each smaller `dataframe` related to a particular ticker to function `describe_vec_with_ret` and directing the result to a `list` object.

8.5 Using package purrr

The `tidyverse` universe also offers functions for programming in package `purrr` (Henry and Wickham, 2019). The main functions of this package are `map`, `map_dbl`, `map_chr`, `map_int`, `map_lgl`. Their use is similar to what we learned from the `apply` family functions, but with some advantages. First, the syntax of `purrr` functions is consistent and allows the use of the pipeline operator. Secondly, at this stage, we have more control when it comes to the class of the returned object. For example, `map_dbl` always returns numeric values, while `map_chr` always returns characters. Third, it can handle execute errors elegantly. Here's a simple example:

```
library(purrr)

# set list
my_l <- list(vec1 = 1:10,
             vec2 = 1:50,
             vec3 = 1:5,
             char1 = letters[1:10])
```

```
# get length of objects
res_out <- my_l %>%
  map_int(length) %>%
  print()
```

```
R>   vec1 vec2 vec3 char1
R>     10   50    5    10
```

```
# find character objects
res_out <- my_l %>%
  map_lgl(is.character) %>%
  print()
```

```
R>   vec1  vec2  vec3 char1
R>  FALSE FALSE FALSE  TRUE
```

Another interesting point about the `purrr` functions is they allow simple access to elements of a `list`. For that, simply enter a position or name in the `map` function:

```
# set list
my_l <- list(vec1 = c(elem1 = 10, elem2 = 20, elem3 = 5),
             char1 = c(elem1 = 40, elem2 = 50, elem3 = 15))

# get second element of each element in list, by position
res_out <- my_l %>% map(2)
print(res_out)
```

```
R> $vec1
R> [1] 20
R>
R> $char1
R> [1] 50
```

```
# get third element of each element in list, by name
res_out <- my_l %>% map('elem3')
print(res_out)
```

8.5. USING PACKAGE PURRR

```
R> $vec1
R> [1] 5
R>
R> $char1
R> [1] 15
```

This functionality is very useful because in many data analysis situations, we are only interested in one element of each object in an extensive `list`.

The great innovation of `purrr` over `base` is the way it can handle errors in the code execution. When using the `apply` family of functions, there is no direct way of handling execution errors. Say you have a vector of size 500, and, at some element, there is a runtime error. It can be frustrating because the information on which element resulted in the error has to be manually investigated, adding time to code development. For that, functions `purrr::safely` and `purrr::possibly` provide a clever way to observe and manage runtime errors with the `purrr::map` family functions.

Using function `safely` is simple. It encapsulates (encloses) another function and always returns two elements, the result of the call and the error message (if it exists). Here's a simple example, where we force an error with a direct function call:

```
library(purrr)

example_fct <- function(x) {
  return(x+1)
}

# ERROR
example_fct('a')
```

```
R> Error in x + 1: non-numeric argument to binary operator
```

Now, let's use `safely` to enclose `example_fct` into another function called `example_fct_safely`:

```
# with safely
example_fct_safely <- safely(example_fct)

class(example_fct_safely('a'))
```

```
R> [1] "list"
```

The code `print(example_fct_safely('a'))` resulted in a `list`, not an error. Therefore, when using `safely` with `map`, the return object is the result of calling the function for all cases. See the following example:

```
my_l <- list(1:5,
             'a',
             1:4)

res_out <- my_l %>%
  map(safely(example_fct))

print(res_out)
```

```
R> [[1]]
R> [[1]]$result
R> [1] 2 3 4 5 6
R>
R> [[1]]$error
R> NULL
R>
R>
R> [[2]]
R> [[2]]$result
R> NULL
R>
R> [[2]]$error
R> <simpleError in x + 1: non-numeric argument to binary operator>
R>
R>
R> [[3]]
R> [[3]]$result
R> [1] 2 3 4 5
R>
R> [[3]]$error
R> NULL
```

We can easily see that the function had an error in the second element of `my_l`. Going further, if we just wanted the results, without the error, we can write:

8.5. USING PACKAGE PURRR

```
# only print results without errors
print(res_out %>% map('result'))

R> [[1]]
R> [1] 2 3 4 5 6
R>
R> [[2]]
R> NULL
R>
R> [[3]]
R> [1] 2 3 4 5
```

Or just the error messages:

```
# only print error messages
print(res_out %>% map('error'))

R> [[1]]
R> NULL
R>
R> [[2]]
R> <simpleError in x + 1: non-numeric argument to binary operator>
R>
R> [[3]]
R> NULL
```

An interesting option of `safely` is the choice of output whenever an error occurs. See the next example, where we set an `NA` value every time function `example_fct` results in an error:

```
my_l <- list(1,
             'a',
             4)

# NA for errors
res_out <- my_l %>%
  map(safely(example_fct,
             otherwise = NA)) %>%
  map_dbl('result')

# print result
print(res_out)
```

```
R> [1]  2 NA  5
```

Other functions for controlling errors in `purrr` are `possibly` and `quietly`. These functions behave similarly to `safely` and will not be demonstrated here.

8.5.1 The `purrr::pmap` function

The `purrr::pmap` is one of the best functional alternatives to loops. Whenever we need to call a function with many different varying arguments (and not just one), `pmap` is the solution. Unlike other `purrr` functions, it allows us to pass any number of arguments for a target function. In other words, the `purrr::pmap` is a functional alternative to nested loops.

As an example, let's consider a function that builds a phrase:

```
build_phrase <- function(name_in, fruit_in, verb_in) {
  my_msg <- paste0('My name is ', name_in,
                  ' and I like to eat ', fruit_in,
                  ' while ', verb_in, '.')

  return(my_msg)
}

build_phrase('Joe', 'apple', 'studying')
```

```
R> [1] "My name is Joe and I like to eat apple while studying."
```

Function `build_phrase` has three text inputs: a name, a fruit and a verb. Suppose we need to create phrases for all combinations of several names, fruits and verbs. When using nested loops, we can do so with the following code:

```
names_vec <- c('Joe', 'Kate')
fruits_vec <- c('kiwi', 'apple')
verb_vec <- c('rowing', 'studying')

my_phrases <- character()
for (i_name in names_vec) {
  for (i_fruit in fruits_vec) {
```

8.5. USING PACKAGE PURRR

```
    for (i_verb in verb_vec) {
      my_phrases <- c(my_phrases,
                      build_phrase(i_name, i_fruit, i_verb))
    }
  }
}

print(my_phrases)
```

```
R> [1] "My name is Joe and I like to eat kiwi while rowing."
R> [2] "My name is Joe and I like to eat kiwi while studying."
R> [3] "My name is Joe and I like to eat apple while rowing."
R> [4] "My name is Joe and I like to eat apple while studying."
R> [5] "My name is Kate and I like to eat kiwi while rowing."
R> [6] "My name is Kate and I like to eat kiwi while studying."
R> [7] "My name is Kate and I like to eat apple while rowing."
R> [8] "My name is Kate and I like to eat apple while studying."
```

While the code works as expected, a better approach is using purrr::pmap. All we need to do is to pass all combinations of arguments to the function:

```
df_grid <- expand.grid(names_vec = names_vec,
                       fruits_vec = fruits_vec,
                       verb_vec = verb_vec)

l_args <- list(name_in = df_grid$names_vec,
               fruit_in = df_grid$fruits_vec,
               verb_in = df_grid$verb_vec)

my_phrases <- purrr::pmap(.l = l_args,
                          .f = build_phrase)

print(my_phrases)
```

```
R> [[1]]
R> [1] "My name is Joe and I like to eat kiwi while rowing."
R>
R> [[2]]
R> [1] "My name is Kate and I like to eat kiwi while rowing."
R>
```

```
R> [[3]]
R> [1] "My name is Joe and I like to eat apple while rowing."
R>
R> [[4]]
R> [1] "My name is Kate and I like to eat apple while rowing."
R>
R> [[5]]
R> [1] "My name is Joe and I like to eat kiwi while studying."
R>
R> [[6]]
R> [1] "My name is Kate and I like to eat kiwi while studying."
R>
R> [[7]]
R> [1] "My name is Joe and I like to eat apple while studying."
R>
R> [[8]]
R> [1] "My name is Kate and I like to eat apple while studying."
```

Do notice that the names in l_args match the input names in build_phrase. The output of purrr::pmap is a list, but we could easily transform it into a vector using as.character:

```
print(as.character(my_phrases))
```

```
R> [1] "My name is Joe and I like to eat kiwi while rowing."
R> [2] "My name is Kate and I like to eat kiwi while rowing."
R> [3] "My name is Joe and I like to eat apple while rowing."
R> [4] "My name is Kate and I like to eat apple while rowing."
R> [5] "My name is Joe and I like to eat kiwi while studying."
R> [6] "My name is Kate and I like to eat kiwi while studying."
R> [7] "My name is Joe and I like to eat apple while studying."
R> [8] "My name is Kate and I like to eat apple while studying."
```

If necessary, we can also set fixed arguments in l_args:

```
l_args <- list(name_in = names_vec,
               fruit_in = 'orange',
               verb_in = 'studying')

my_phrases <- purrr::pmap(.l = l_args,
                          .f = build_phrase)
```

8.6. DATA MANIPULATION WITH PACKAGE DPLYR

```
print(my_phrases)
```

```
R> [[1]]
R> [1] "My name is Joe and I like to eat orange while studying."
R>
R> [[2]]
R> [1] "My name is Kate and I like to eat orange while studying."
```

Whenever you have a situtation where a nested loop is need, using `purrr:pmap` is highly recommended. We will use it whenever necessary throughout the rest of the book.

8.6 Data Manipulation with Package `dplyr`

Package `dplyr` (Wickham and Francois, 2016) is very handy for data processing operations. Many loop operations can be replaced with a simpler code structure using `dplyr` functions. The package allows complex data operations to be carried out with its own intuitive and customizable syntax. Not only that, but it also decreases computational time.

In its current version, 0.8.4, `dplyr` has 267 functions. Describing each functionality would be too exhaustive for this book. Therefore, we will focus on the main functions of the package.

8.6.1 Group Operations with `dplyr`

The greatest functionality of `dplyr` is in performing group calculation – commonly called **split-apply-combine**–, that is, we separate the data into groups, apply some function, and finally combine all the results into a new table. Note this is exactly what we did with *loops* in the previous section: we separate financial data by a ticker, calculate the average, maximum and minimum price, and finally aggregate all results into a single `dataframe`.

To illustrate the use of the functions `group_by` and `summarise`, we will execute the same example of describing stock prices from the previous section. This time, however, we will use the structure of package `dplyr` to perform these calculations using the pipeline operator. Consider the following code:

```
library(tidyverse)

# load data
my_f <- 'data/SP500-Stocks-WithRet.rds'
df_sp500 <- readRDS(my_f)

# group data and calculate stats
my_tab <- df_sp500 %>%
  group_by(ticker) %>%
  summarise(mean_price = mean(price.adjusted),
            max_price = max(price.adjusted),
            min_price = min(price.adjusted),
            max_ret = max(ret),
            min_ret = min(ret))

# check result
print(my_tab)
```

```
R> # A tibble: 471 x 6
R>    ticker mean_price max_price min_price max_ret
R>    <chr>       <dbl>     <dbl>     <dbl>   <dbl>
R>  1 A            33.1      48.2      18.3   0.118
R>  2 AAL          23.4      54.7       3.89  0.173
R>  3 AAP         103.      200.       38.4   0.166
R>  4 AAPL         75.0     128.       24.9   0.0887
R>  5 ABC          58.4     112.       23.3   0.0953
R>  6 ABT          32.1      49.3      18.4   0.0650
R>  7 ACN          70.6     125.       31.6   0.0799
R>  8 ADBE         55.3     111.       22.7   0.128
R>  9 ADI          42.4      73.9      21.6   0.101
R> 10 ADM          33.8      50.5      20.9   0.0730
R> # ... with 461 more rows, and 1 more variable:
R> #   min_ret <dbl>
```

The first step in using dplyr is to group the data with function group_by. Here, we are grouping based on column ticker. Thus, it means that we intend to perform a certain calculation for each stock in our database. As we will soon learn, group_by is a flexible function, allowing group operations with multiple columns, e.g., more than one factor.

After we group the data in line group_by(ticker) %>%, we pass the object to the next stage, function summarise. It processes the data in blocks defined by the formation of groups in function group_by. Note each argument

8.6. DATA MANIPULATION WITH PACKAGE DPLYR

in `summarise` turns into a column in the output: `mean_price`, `max_price`, `min_price`, `max_ret`, `min_ret`. Each of the previous arguments is doing a different calculation based on the columns of `df_sp500`. We could add several other calculations with different columns by simply expanding the input arguments in `summarise`.

Using `dplyr` is highly recommended when you have to group the data based on more than one factor. Let's consider grouping stock data by ticker and the day of the week (Monday, Tuesday...). First, let's use function `weekday` to create a column called `week_day` in `df_sp500`.

```
# set new col week.day
df_sp500 <- df_sp500 %>%
  mutate(week_day = weekdays(ref.date))

# check result
glimpse(df_sp500)
```

```
R> Observations: 829,239
R> Variables: 5
R> $ price.adjusted <dbl> 68.72509, 69.69973, 69.7497...
R> $ ref.date       <date> 2010-01-05, 2010-01-06, 20...
R> $ ticker         <chr> "MMM", "MMM", "MMM", "MMM",...
R> $ ret            <dbl> -0.006263503, 0.014181794, ...
R> $ week_day       <chr> "Tuesday", "Wednesday", "Th...
```

Now, we proceed by adding column `week_day` in `group_by`.

```
# group by ticker and weekday, calculate stats
my_tab <- df_sp500 %>%
  group_by(ticker, week_day) %>%
  summarise(mean_price = mean(price.adjusted),
            max_price = max(price.adjusted),
            min_price = min(price.adjusted),
            max.ret = max(ret),
            min.ret = min(ret))

# print result
print(my_tab)
```

```
R> # A tibble: 2,355 x 7
```

```
R> # Groups:   ticker [471]
R>    ticker week_day mean_price max_price min_price
R>    <chr>  <chr>        <dbl>     <dbl>     <dbl>
R>  1 A      Friday        33.0      47.9      18.4
R>  2 A      Monday        33.1      48.2      18.5
R>  3 A      Thursday      33.0      47.9      18.7
R>  4 A      Tuesday       33.1      48.0      18.3
R>  5 A      Wednesd~      33.0      48.2      18.7
R>  6 AAL    Friday        23.3      54.7       3.91
R>  7 AAL    Monday        23.6      54.2       4.14
R>  8 AAL    Thursday      23.3      54.4       4.28
R>  9 AAL    Tuesday       23.5      52.9       3.94
R> 10 AAL    Wednesd~      23.4      53.1       3.89
R> # ... with 2,345 more rows, and 2 more variables:
R> #   max.ret <dbl>, min.ret <dbl>
```

And that's it! To group the data to a new `factor`, all we need to do is add it in `group_by`. Using `dplyr` to do simple group calculations is straightforward. The resulting code is efficient, self-contained, and elegant.

8.6.2 Complex Group Operations with `dplyr`

The previous example shows a simple case of group calculations. We can say it was simple because all of the argument operations in `summarise` had one value as a result. We had a mean for ticker XYZ in weekday `'Monday'`, another means for ticker ZYX in weekday `'Tuesday'`, and so on.

Package `dplyr` also supports more complex operations, where the output is not a single value, but a complex object. The benefit is in manipulating the data in the same tabular structure we usually think. Since we can estimate a different model for each ticker in our sample of financial data and store the whole result as a more complex table, where an element may not be a single value. Instead, it is a full econometric model with several parameters.

Let's look at the following example, where we use stock returns to calculate their accumulated value over time and store it in a `tibble`. In this case, the output we need is not a single value but a whole vector. See an example with code:

```
# simulated vector of returns
ret <- c(0, rnorm(4, sd= 0.05))
```

8.6. DATA MANIPULATION WITH PACKAGE DPLYR

```r
# vector of accumulated returns
acum_ret <- cumprod(1+ret)
print(acum_ret)
```

```
R> [1] 1.000000 1.019577 1.056253 1.132011 1.060950
```

Vector `acum_ret` represents a multiplier of an investor's portfolio. Based on it, we could track how much the investment is worth each day. Now, let's do the same for all stocks in the SP500, also saving the maximum and minimum value.

```r
library(dplyr)

# get acum ret of stocks
my_tab <- df_sp500 %>%
  group_by(ticker) %>%
  do(acum_ret = cumprod(1+.$ret)) %>%
  mutate(last_cumret = acum_ret[length(acum_ret)],
         min_cumret = min(acum_ret))

print(head(my_tab))
```

```
R> Source: local data frame [6 x 4]
R> Groups: <by row>
R>
R> # A tibble: 6 x 4
R>    ticker acum_ret          last_cumret min_cumret
R>    <chr>  <list>            <dbl>       <dbl>
R> 1  A      <dbl [1,761]>     2.14        0.862
R> 2  AAL    <dbl [1,761]>     10.0        0.839
R> 3  AAP    <dbl [1,761]>     4.27        0.970
R> 4  AAPL   <dbl [1,761]>     4.16        0.897
R> 5  ABC    <dbl [1,761]>     3.23        0.968
R> 6  ABT    <dbl [1,761]>     1.77        0.855
```

Notice how column `acum_ret` is not a single value but an atomic vector. Formally, `acum_ret` is a list-column, meaning it can store any kind of object. We achieved this result by using function `dplyr::do` in the pipeline. As for the other columns, `last_cumret` and `min_cumret` are simple manipulations of `acum_ret` and, therefore, can be created with `dply::mutate`. An important observation is we used symbol `.$` to access the columns of `df_sp500` in the call to function `do`. Whenever you use the `dplyr::do` function, you must use this notation.

The greatest advantage of using complex group operations with `dplyr` is you can keep the same tabular representation. We can read the object `my_tab` as "for each stock, define a vector of accumulated returns." Using function `dplyr::do` is particularly interesting in the estimation of several models from the data. We will cover this topic in chapter 11.

In sum, the `dplyr` package was a very significant innovation for the R community. No wonder this is one of the most installed packages, according to CRAN statistics. Therefore, you should ensure that you use it in your R code, whenever it is possible or necessary.

8.7 Exercises

1. Create a function called `say_my_name` that uses a person's name as input and displays the text *Your name is ...* in the prompt. It should return `TRUE` at the end of its execution. Within the scope of the function, use comments to describe the purpose of the function, its inputs, and outputs.

2. Considering the previous `say_my_name` function, implement a test code for the input. If its class is not `character,` an error is returned to the user. Likewise, make sure the input object has a length equal to one, and not a vector. Test your new function with the wrong inputs to make sure it catches it, as expected.

3. Download a database of popular Canadian baby names from CHHS Data[3]. Import the data into R and, using a *loop*, apply the `say_my_name` function to 15 random names from the database. Tip: In this case, you must manually download the data from the website.

4. Redo the previous exercise 3 using `sapply` and `purrr::map` commands.

5. Use package `BatchGetSymbols` to download values for the SP500 index (`^GSPC`), Ibovespa (`'^BVSP'`), FTSE (`'^FSTE'`) and Nikkei 225 (`'^N225'`) from `'2010-01-01'` to the current date. With the imported data, use a *loop* to calculate average, maximum, and minimum return of each index over the analyzed period.

---

[3]https://data.chhs.ca.gov/dataset/most-popular-baby-names-2005-current

8.7. EXERCISES

6. Redo the previous exercise using the `dplyr` package functions `group_by` and `summarise`.

7. With the dataset of names from exercise 3, use functions `dplyr::group_by` and `dplyr::summarise` to build a table with the most popular names by year.

8. CHALLENGE - In Rstudio CRAN logs[4] you can find data regarding the download statistics for the base distribution of R in section *Daily R downloads*. Using your programming skills, import all available data for the current month, and aggregate it into a single file. Which country presents the highest download count for R?

---

[4]http://cran-logs.rstudio.com/

Chapter 9

Cleaning and Structuring Data

So, now that we learned the basics of programming in R, it is time to get our hands dirty with practical problems. When working with raw data, a great deal of time will be spent in structuring and cleaning it. In this chapter, we will cover basic financial and economic data cleansing and restructuring operations. This includes:

- Changing the format of a dataframe (long/wide);
- Converting a `list` of `dataframes` into a single table;
- Identifying and treating extreme values (*outliers*);
- Price data deflation;
- Data aggregation based on a change of time-frequency (e.g. from daily to monthly).

9.1 The Format of a `dataframe`

The `dataframe` format discussion arose due to the introduction of `tidyverse`. At the heart of the debate, we discuss whether the data should be guided by columns (*wide* format) or lines (*long* format).

In the wide format, the rows of the table are usually indexed by a single factor, such as a date, and the columns indicate the different variables. As new information is added to the database, it usually grows in the number of columns. An example:

refdate	STOCK1	STOCK2	STOCK3
2020-02-09	10.02	3.15	5.19
2020-02-10	9.79	3.34	5.06
2020-02-11	8.08	2.74	5.61
2020-02-12	7.33	2.56	5.99

The above table has three distinct pieces of information for each data point: ticker, price, and date. If we added one more stock, the table would be incremented by one column.

In the long format, each row of the `dataframe` represents a slice of the database and each column is a variable. When new data arrives, the table usually grows in the number of rows. Example:

refdate	ticker	price
2020-02-09	STOCK1	10.02
2020-02-10	STOCK1	9.79
2020-02-11	STOCK1	8.08
2020-02-12	STOCK1	7.33
2020-02-09	STOCK2	3.15
2020-02-10	STOCK2	3.34
2020-02-11	STOCK2	2.74
2020-02-12	STOCK2	2.56
2020-02-09	STOCK3	5.19
2020-02-10	STOCK3	5.06
2020-02-11	STOCK3	5.61
2020-02-12	STOCK3	5.99

In comparison, the wide format is more intuitive because the data of each stock is easily separable by columns. Anyone with experience using spreadsheets can easily recognize this format. The problem here is the difficulty of expanding the data as each variable is contained in a single table. For example, if we were also interested in the trading volume of each stock, we would have to create another table to allocate this information. As the number of variables grows, so does the number of tables. The long format does not have this problem because entering new variables only increments the columns in a single `dataframe`.

This argument may seem trivial since the information is the same in both formats. But, make no mistake: **the format of the data is very important as it can facilitate the analysis of the data**. Specialized packages, such as `dplyr` (Wickham and Francois, 2016) and `ggplot2` (Wickham, 2009), expect a `dataframe` in the *long* format; therefore, this structure must be prioritized if one is using these packages.

It is worth noting that, in finance, the wide format is popular in the manip-

9.1. THE FORMAT OF A DATAFRAME

ulation of investment portfolios with the creation of a matrix of returns or prices, where the rows are the dates and the columns represents the stocks. Each value in the matrix is the return (percent change) of a particular asset from one period to the other. The wide format is justified as the matrix notation facilitates matrix calculations. I emphasize, however, these same calculations could also be performed with the *long* format. Conversion between formats is also possible, as we will see next.

9.1.1 Converting a dataframe Structure (long and wide)

The conversion from one format to the other is possible with the tidyr package (Wickham, 2016c). See the following example, where we change the *wide* format of the previous table for the *long* format using the function gather. Here, it is necessary to know the variable id that will index the lines (in this case, the dates) and the names of the new columns.

```
library(tidyr)
library(tidyverse)

# set dates and stock vectors
refdate <- as.Date('2015-01-01') + 0:3
STOCK1 <- c(10, 11, 10.5, 12)
STOCK2 <- c(3, 3.1, 3.2, 3.5)
STOCK3 <- c(6, 7, 7.5, 6)

# create wide dataframe
my_df_wide <- tibble(refdate, STOCK1, STOCK2, STOCK3)

# print it
print(my_df_wide)
```

```
R> # A tibble: 4 x 4
R>   refdate     STOCK1 STOCK2 STOCK3
R>   <date>       <dbl>  <dbl>  <dbl>
R> 1 2015-01-01    10     3      6
R> 2 2015-01-02    11     3.1    7
R> 3 2015-01-03    10.5   3.2    7.5
R> 4 2015-01-04    12     3.5    6
```

```r
# convert wide to long
my_df_long <- gather(data = my_df_wide,
                     key = 'ticker',
                     value = 'price',
                     - refdate)

# print result
print(my_df_long)
```

```
R> # A tibble: 12 x 3
R>    refdate    ticker price
R>    <date>     <chr>  <dbl>
R>  1 2015-01-01 STOCK1  10
R>  2 2015-01-02 STOCK1  11
R>  3 2015-01-03 STOCK1  10.5
R>  4 2015-01-04 STOCK1  12
R>  5 2015-01-01 STOCK2   3
R>  6 2015-01-02 STOCK2   3.1
R>  7 2015-01-03 STOCK2   3.2
R>  8 2015-01-04 STOCK2   3.5
R>  9 2015-01-01 STOCK3   6
R> 10 2015-01-02 STOCK3   7
R> 11 2015-01-03 STOCK3   7.5
R> 12 2015-01-04 STOCK3   6
```

To perform the reverse conversion, *long* to *wide*, we can use the `spread` function from the same package:

```r
# convert from long to wide
my_df_wide_converted <- spread(data = my_df_long,
                               key = 'ticker',
                               value = 'price')

# print result
print(my_df_wide_converted)
```

```
R> # A tibble: 4 x 4
R>   refdate    STOCK1 STOCK2 STOCK3
R>   <date>     <dbl>  <dbl>  <dbl>
R> 1 2015-01-01   10      3      6
```

9.1. THE FORMAT OF A DATAFRAME 321

```
R> 2 2015-01-02    11      3.1     7
R> 3 2015-01-03    10.5    3.2     7.5
R> 4 2015-01-04    12      3.5     6
```

With more complex conversions, where it is necessary to aggregate some variables, I recommend package `reshape2` (Wickham, 2007), which offers more features than `tidyr`. The syntax, however, is different. See the following code, where we use functions from package `reshape2` for the same conversion.

```
library(reshape2)

# use melt to change from wide to long
my_df_long <- melt(data = my_df_wide,
                   id.vars = 'refdate',
                   variable.name = 'ticker',
                   value.name = 'price')

# print result
print(my_df_long)
```

```
R>        refdate ticker price
R> 1  2015-01-01 STOCK1  10.0
R> 2  2015-01-02 STOCK1  11.0
R> 3  2015-01-03 STOCK1  10.5
R> 4  2015-01-04 STOCK1  12.0
R> 5  2015-01-01 STOCK2   3.0
R> 6  2015-01-02 STOCK2   3.1
R> 7  2015-01-03 STOCK2   3.2
R> 8  2015-01-04 STOCK2   3.5
R> 9  2015-01-01 STOCK3   6.0
R> 10 2015-01-02 STOCK3   7.0
R> 11 2015-01-03 STOCK3   7.5
R> 12 2015-01-04 STOCK3   6.0
```

```
# use melt to change from long to wide
my_df_wide_converted <- dcast(data = my_df_long,
                              formula = refdate ~ ticker,
                              value.var = 'price')
print(my_df_wide_converted)
```

```
R>         refdate STOCK1 STOCK2 STOCK3
R> 1    2015-01-01   10.0    3.0    6.0
R> 2    2015-01-02   11.0    3.1    7.0
R> 3    2015-01-03   10.5    3.2    7.5
R> 4    2015-01-04   12.0    3.5    6.0
```

Although, it is worth noting that it is important to know these functions when working with R because the analyst often has no control over the format of the imported data. Then, when it is necessary, you need to convert the data to the *long* format right after importing it. This will facilitate the future analysis of the table.

9.2 Converting lists into dataframes

Another important case in data structuring is the situation where multiple `dataframes` are allocated into a single or multiple `list` object. Such an occurrence is common in two cases: 1) when we are importing data from many local files and 2) when using particular packages for importing multiple series from the internet. Here we will look at an example for each.

For the first, let's use the `purrr` package as well as a custom defined function to create some files with random data. Here we will take the data generating process one step further when using `wakefield`, an excellent package for creating artificial data.

```
create_rnd_data <- function(n_obs = 100,
                            folder_out) {
  # function for creating random datasets
  #
  # ARGS: n_obs - number of observations
  #       folder_out - folder where to save files
  #
  # RETURN: TRUE, if sucessfull

  require(tidyverse)
  require(wakefield)

  # check if folder exists
  if (!dir.exists(folder_out)) dir.create(folder_out)

  # create extensive random data
```

9.2. CONVERTING LISTS INTO DATAFRAMES 323

```r
  rnd_df <- r_data_frame(n = n_obs,
                         id,
                         race,
                         age,
                         sex) %>%
    r_na(prob = 0.1)

  # for 15% of the time, create a new column
  if (runif(1) < 0.15 ) {
    rnd_df$bad_column <- 'BAD COLUMN!'
  }

  # set file name
  f_out <- tempfile(fileext = '.csv',
                    pattern = 'file_',
                    tmpdir = folder_out)

  write_csv(x = rnd_df,
            path = f_out)

  return(TRUE)
}
```

Function `create_rnd_data` will create and write a dataframe with n_obs observations and four columns: id, race, age and sex. For 15% of the time, whenever `runif(1)` is lower than 0.15, a new column will be added to the dataframe. Finally, we write the table to a CSV file at folder `folder_out`.

Going forward, let's use `purrr::pmap` to create several files.

```r
n_files <- 50
n_obs <- 100
folder_out <- 'many_datafiles_2'

# create random datasets
l_out <- pmap(.l = list(n_obs = rep(n_obs, n_files),
                        folder_out = rep(folder_out, n_files)),
              .f = create_rnd_data)

# check if files are there
print(head(list.files(folder_out)))
```

```
R> [1] "file_17ed10ac878d.csv" "file_17ed10aeb2a3.csv"
```

```
R> [3] "file_17ed11806152.csv" "file_17ed150db2ed.csv"
R> [5] "file_17ed1629e9c9.csv" "file_17ed16321d21.csv"
```

The files are available, as expected. Now, let's create a function that will read each file and output a dataframe:

```
read_single_file <- function(f_in) {
  # Function for reading single csv file with random data
  #
  # ARGS: f_in - path of file
  #
  # RETURN: A dataframe with the data

  require(tidyverse)

  df <- read_csv(f_in, col_types = cols())

  return(df)
}

library(purrr)

files_to_read <- list.files('many_datafiles_2/',
                            full.names = TRUE)

l_out <- map(files_to_read, read_single_file)
```

And now we bind them all together with a simple call to `dplyr::bind_rows`:

```
compiled_df <- bind_rows(l_out)

glimpse(compiled_df)


R> Observations: 5,000
R> Variables: 5
R> $ ID          <chr> "001", "002", "003", "004", "00...
R> $ Race        <chr> "White", "White", NA, "White", ...
R> $ Age         <dbl> 57, 71, 26, 28, NA, 57, 55, 34,...
R> $ Sex         <chr> NA, "Male", "Female", "Male", "...
R> $ bad_column  <chr> NA, NA, NA, NA, NA, NA, NA, NA,...
```

9.2. CONVERTING LISTS INTO DATAFRAMES

It worked, as expected. We have 5000 rows and 5 columns in the compiled dataframe. Also notice that column bad_column, which was only created in a proportion of the files, was still imported. One advantage of function dplyr::bind_rows is that it can merge dataframes with different columns by setting NAs where the data is not available.

For the second example, let's take a case of data structuring using BETS, a package for downloading economic series. We did not cover BETS in chapter 5 given that most of its series is available in Quandl. We will use it here because whenever we request multiple tables, it returns it as a list:

```
library(BETS)

my_id <- 3785:3791

# set dates
first_date = '2010-01-01'
last_date  = as.character(Sys.Date())

# get data
l_out <- BETSget(code = my_id, data.frame = TRUE,
                 from = first_date, to = last_date)

# check data in first dataframe
glimpse(l_out[[1]])
```

```
R> Observations: 79
R> Variables: 2
R> $ date  <date> 2010-01-01, 2010-02-01, 2010-03-01,...
R> $ value <dbl> 7.4, 7.4, 7.3, 7.2, 7.0, 6.9, 6.8, 6...
```

In this example we gather data for unemployment rates for 7 countries. Each dataset is an element in l_out. Looking at the data itself, we have two columns: date and value. One issue with the raw data is that we will need to know where the data is coming from when binding all tables together. The final table will have a column for the unemployment values, another for dates and another for the country.

Now, if we want to structure all imported tables, we will first create another column, country, which will store the information of where the unemployment rate was registered. The first step is registering the actual names (and not code) of the countries. These are available in the description of the time series from BETS.

```
my_countries <- c("Germany", "Canada", "United States",
                  "France", "Italy", "Japan",
                  "United Kingdom")
```

The order of elements in vector `my_countries` follows the order of countries in `l_out`. This is important as we will use it later for matching the information.

Going further, we now create a function that will organize the tables. It will take two inputs, a `dataframe` and the name of the country:

```
clean_bets <- function(df_in, country_in) {
  # function for cleaning data from BETS
  #
  # ARGS: df_in - dataframe within a list
  #       country_in - name of country
  #
  # VALUE: a new dataframe with new column type

  #set column
  df_in$country <- country_in

  # return df
  return(df_in)
}
```

The next step is to use the previous function to create another list with the organized dataframes. We need to call `clean_bets` for each element of `l_out`, together with its country name. For that, we again use `purrr::pmap` (see chapter 8).

```
library(purrr)

# set args
l_args <- list(df_in = l_out,
               country_in = my_countries)
# format dfs
l_out_formatted <- pmap(.l = l_args,
                        .f = clean_bets)

# check first element (all are the same structure)
glimpse(l_out_formatted[[1]])
```

9.3. REMOVING OUTLIERS

```
R> Observations: 79
R> Variables: 3
R> $ date    <date> 2010-01-01, 2010-02-01, 2010-03-0...
R> $ value   <dbl> 7.4, 7.4, 7.3, 7.2, 7.0, 6.9, 6.8,...
R> $ country <chr> "Germany", "Germany", "Germany", "...
```

From the output of `glimpse` we see that the column `country` was added to each dataframe. The next and final step is to bind all elements of `l_out_formatted` into a single dataframe with `dplyr::bind_rows`:

```
# bind all rows of dataframes in list
df_unemp <- bind_rows(l_out_formatted)

# check it
glimpse(df_unemp)
```

```
R> Observations: 553
R> Variables: 3
R> $ date    <date> 2010-01-01, 2010-02-01, 2010-03-0...
R> $ value   <dbl> 7.4, 7.4, 7.3, 7.2, 7.0, 6.9, 6.8,...
R> $ country <chr> "Germany", "Germany", "Germany", "...
```

Done! The result is an organized `dataframe` in the long format, ready be to analyzed.

9.3 Removing Outliers

A recurrent issue in data analysis is handling extreme data points, the so-called *outliers*. In short, these are cases that do not fit well with the overall distribution of the rest of the database. For example, assume you have a vector that, for 99% of the time, ranges from 1 to 10. In a specific element, however, we find a value of 100. Clearly, this is an odd and extreme value when comparing to the other elements. Undoubtedly, this single data point will compromise the statistical analysis.

So, because we want to visualize the destructive effect of an *outlier* in data analysis, let's use R to simulate a linear process and add an extreme case to the independent variable. Our concern here is to understand how this variable can, in isolation, completely modify our statistical results.

The next example might be challenging if it is the first time you read about the simulation and estimation of linear models. Unfortunately, this is the best way to show how an outlier can completely change a statistical result. However, you should be aware that in section 11.1 of chapter 11 we describe the simulation and estimation of linear models.

```
# set seed for reproducibility
set.seed(100)

# set options
nT <- 100
sim_x <- rnorm(nT)
my_beta <- 0.5

# simulate x and y
sim_y <- sim_x*my_beta + rnorm(nT)
sim_y_with_outlier <- sim_y

# simulate y with outlier
sim_y_with_outlier[10] <- 50
```

Objects `sim_y` and `sim_y_with_outlier` are exactly the same, except for the tenth observation. Let's check its effect in the estimation of a simple regression model:

```
library(texreg)

# estimate models
model_no_outlier <- lm(formula = sim_y ~ sim_x)
model_with_outlier <- lm(formula = sim_y_with_outlier ~ sim_x)

# report them
screenreg(list(model_no_outlier,
               model_with_outlier),
          custom.model.names = c('No Outlier', 'With Outlier'))
```

```
R>
R> ================================
R>              No Outlier  With Outlier
R> --------------------------------
R> (Intercept)    0.01        0.51
```

9.3. REMOVING OUTLIERS

```
R>                      (0.08)         (0.51)
R> sim_x                0.39 ***       0.22
R>                      (0.08)         (0.50)
R> -----------------------------------------
R> R^2                  0.21           0.00
R> Adj. R^2             0.20          -0.01
R> Num. obs.            100            100
R> RMSE                 0.79           5.10
R> =========================================
R> *** p < 0.001, ** p < 0.01, * p < 0.05
```

Here we report the models with the `texreg` package. Don't worry about its use, for now, we'll study model reporting in chapter 12.

Notice from the estimation table that the slope (beta) of the model changed from 0.3946 to 0.2178 in the case with *outlier*. So, that is to say, that the single observation (out of 100) completely modified the model output. The reason is simple, the linear model prioritized the minimization of the large error in the extreme observation by pushing the beta coefficient upwards. It should be clear by now that if we are interested in creating a model, or analysis, that can reasonably explain the vast majority of the data and not just a single data point, we should identify and handle *outliers* properly.

One way to accomplish this is to identify potential extreme values with function `quantile`, which returns the value that sets the limit of a cumulative probability. For example, if we want to know which value from `sim_y_with_outlier` that sets the cumulative distribution limit at 95%, we use the following code:

```
# find the value of vector that sets the 95% quantile
quantile95 <- quantile(x = abs(sim_y_with_outlier),
                      probs = 0.95)

print(quantile95)


R>      95%
R> 1.781531
```

Here, the value of 1.7815306 is higher than 95% of all other values available in `sim_y_with_outlier`. Now, we can use this information to find the extreme cases at the tail of the distribution:

```r
# find cases higher than 95% quantile
idx <- which(sim_y_with_outlier > quantile95)
print(sim_y_with_outlier[idx])
```

```
R> [1] 50.000000  2.770339  2.085660
```

We find the "artificial" outlier we've set in previous code, plus two more cases. We can set how rigorous we are in finding outliers by changing the argument `probs` in `quantile`.

Finally, we need to treat outliers. We can either set it as `NA` or remove it from the vector:

```r
# copy content
sim_y_without_outlier <- sim_y_with_outlier

# set NA in outlier
sim_y_without_outlier[idx] <- NA

# or remove it
sim_y_without_outlier <- sim_y_without_outlier[-idx]
```

An alternative for identifying extreme values is the use of statistical tests. For that, the package `outlier` provides functions to identify and remove these cases based on the average distance of each element. See an example next:

```r
library(outliers)

# find outlier
my_outlier <- outlier(sim_y_with_outlier)

# print it
print(my_outlier)
```

As expected, it correctly identified the outlier.

9.3.1 Treating Outliers in `dataframes`

Let's go a bit deeper. In a real data analysis situation, often we need to treat outliers in several columns of a `dataframe`, and not a single vector. For that,

9.3. REMOVING OUTLIERS

we can use the programming tools presented in chapter 8. One important property to remember here is that every `dataframe` is internally represented as a `list`, where each element/column is an atomic vector. Therefore, we can process each column separately and then combine it later to form a new and outlier-free `dataframe`.

The first step is to define a function that accepts a numeric column and a probability as input, returning the original vector with the extreme cases replaced by `NA`. Probability, similar to the other cases, serves as a parameter to identify extreme values in the cumulative distribution of the data. We will also need to handle cases of non-numeric columns. For example, for a text column, it makes no sense to search and delete *outliers*. Thus, we must test each class and return the original object if it is not of the `numeric` or `integer` class. Here's the definition of the function:

```
replace_outliers <- function(col_in, my_prob = 0.05) {
  # Replaces outliers from a vector and returns a new
  # vector
  #
  # INPUTS: col_in The vector
  #         my_prob Probability of quantiles
  #                 (will remove quantiles at p and 1-p)
  #
  # OUTPUT: A vector without the outliers

  # return if class is other than numeric
  if (!(class(col_in) %in%
        c('numeric', 'integer'))) return(col_in)

  my_outliers <- stats::quantile(x = col_in,
                                 probs = c(my_prob, 1-my_prob),
                                 na.rm = TRUE)

  idx <- (col_in <= my_outliers[1])|(col_in >= my_outliers[2])
  col_in[idx] <- NA

  return(col_in)

}
```

Let's test it:

```r
# set test vector
my_x <- runif(25)

# find and replace outliers
print(replace_outliers(my_x, my_prob = 0.05))
```

```
R>  [1] 0.5112374 0.2777107 0.3606569 0.4375279 0.8030667
R>  [6] 0.5206097 0.6961521 0.8478369 0.8457093 0.3918757
R> [11] 0.1535138 0.6394258 0.2871710        NA 0.1556361
R> [16]        NA        NA 0.7075262 0.6301876 0.7730780
R> [21] 0.8926069 0.5112041 0.7490011 0.9263798        NA
```

As we can see, it performed correctly. The output vector has some `NA` elements, which were *outliers* in the original vector. Now, let's use this function in a dataframe. First, we will again use package `wakefield` to create a `dataframe` with columns of different classes:

```r
library(wakefield)
library(tidyverse)

# options
n_obs <- 100

# create extensive random data
my_df <- r_data_frame(n = n_obs,
                      race,
                      age,
                      birth,
                      height_cm,
                      sex)

# check it
glimpse(my_df)
```

```
R> Observations: 100
R> Variables: 5
R> $ Race       <fct> White, White, Native, White, ...
R> $ Age        <int> 37, 62, 76, 64, 21, 28, 75, 3...
R> $ Birth      <date> 2006-05-17, 2006-08-30, 2006...
R> $ `Height(cm)` <dbl> 177.9, 183.0, 171.2, 180.7, 1...
R> $ Sex        <fct> Female, Female, Female, Femal...
```

9.3. REMOVING OUTLIERS

Now, let's use `purrr::map` to iterate all elements (columns) of `my_df`, recreating all vectors without outliers:

```
library(purrr)

# remove outlivers from vectors
l_out <- map(my_df, replace_outliers)
```

Next, we regroup all vectors into a single dataframe with `dplyr::as_tibble`:

```
# rebuild dataframe
my_df_no_outlier <- as_tibble(l_out)

# check it
glimpse(my_df_no_outlier)
```

```
R> Observations: 100
R> Variables: 5
R> $ Race        <fct> White, White, Native, White, ...
R> $ Age         <int> 37, 62, 76, 64, NA, 28, 75, 3...
R> $ Birth       <date> 2006-05-17, 2006-08-30, 2006...
R> $ `Height(cm)` <dbl> 177.9, 183.0, 171.2, 180.7, 1...
R> $ Sex         <fct> Female, Female, Female, Femal...
```

```
# summary of my_df_no_outlier
summary(my_df_no_outlier)
```

```
R>         Race          Age              Birth
R>  White     :68   Min.   :23.00   Min.   :2005-02-16
R>  Hispanic  :15   1st Qu.:37.00   1st Qu.:2005-09-04
R>  Black     : 7   Median :55.00   Median :2006-01-14
R>  Native    : 4   Mean   :53.49   Mean   :2006-02-05
R>  Asian     : 3   3rd Qu.:69.25   3rd Qu.:2006-08-03
R>  Bi-Racial : 2   Max.   :85.00   Max.   :2007-02-02
R>  (Other)   : 1   NA's   :10
R>    Height(cm)         Sex
R>  Min.   :156.9    Male  :41
R>  1st Qu.:169.7    Female:59
R>  Median :175.0
```

```
R>   Mean     :174.5
R>   3rd Qu. :180.7
R>   Max.     :188.2
R>   NA's     : 10
```

Note that, as expected, we find `NA` values for the numeric columns `Age` and `Height(cm)`.

For last, we remove all rows with outliers using `base::na.omit`:

```
# remove outliers
my_df_no_outlier <- na.omit(my_df_no_outlier)

glimpse(my_df_no_outlier)
```

```
R> Observations: 81
R> Variables: 5
R> $ Race        <fct> White, White, Native, White, ...
R> $ Age         <int> 37, 62, 76, 64, 28, 75, 37, 5...
R> $ Birth       <date> 2006-05-17, 2006-08-30, 2006...
R> $ `Height(cm)` <dbl> 177.9, 183.0, 171.2, 180.7, 1...
R> $ Sex         <fct> Female, Female, Female, Femal...
```

Notice, however, that some rows were lost. The final `dataframe` has 81 rows, while the original had 100 rows. This is the price paid for removing extreme cases from our original table. Nonetheless, the resulting set of data will be robust to outliers and likely to provide more accurate information in our analysis. The previous procedure for removing outliers from a dataframe is available at function `afedR::afedR_replace_outliers_df`. So, please feel free to use it in or for your own analysis.

9.4 Inflation and Price Data

A common effect in economic and financial data is inflation. In summary, inflation is the decrease in the purchasing power of monetary units. The necessity of considering inflation in data analysis is directly related to the time frame. The longer the time period, the greater is the impact of inflation on the prices. Case in point, one hundred dollars in 1950 differs from one hundred dollars in 2020, i.e., we cannot buy the same amount of goods and, therefore, the purchasing power of one dollar today is much lower than what it was in the 1950s.

9.4. INFLATION AND PRICE DATA

To offset the effect of inflation on price data, the first step is to import a benchmark for inflation rates. Each country will have its own benchmark so you need to do some digging to discover which one is most used. Here we will use the case of the USA, where the most popular inflation index is CPI (consumer price index), reported by the U.S. Bureau of Labor Statistics (BLS) on a monthly basis. Here we will use `Quandl` to download CPI data since 2000:

```
library(GetQuandlData)
library(tidyverse)

# set api (you need your OWN from www.quandl.com)
my_api_key <- readLines(
  '~/Dropbox/98-pass_and_bash/.quandl_api.txt'
  )

# set symbol and dates
my_symbol <- 'RATEINF/INFLATION_USA'
first_date <- as.Date('2000-01-01')
last_date <- Sys.Date()

# get data!
df_inflation <- get_Quandl_series(id_in = my_symbol,
                                  api_key = my_api_key,
                                  first_date = first_date,
                                  last_date = last_date)

# sort by date
df_inflation <- df_inflation %>%
  arrange(ref_date)

# check content
glimpse(df_inflation)


R> Observations: 240
R> Variables: 4
R> $ series_name <chr> "RATEINF/INFLATION_USA", "RATE...
R> $ ref_date    <date> 2000-01-31, 2000-02-29, 2000-...
R> $ value       <dbl> 2.739, 3.222, 3.758, 3.069, 3....
R> $ id_quandl   <chr> "RATEINF/INFLATION_USA", "RATE...
```

Now, let's create a random dataframe with random prices:

```
n_T <- nrow(df_inflation)

# create df with prices
my_df <- tibble(Date = df_inflation$ref_date,
                x = 100 + cumsum(rnorm(n_T)),
                y = 100 + cumsum(rnorm(n_T)))

# check it
glimpse(my_df)
```

```
R> Observations: 240
R> Variables: 3
R> $ Date  <date> 2000-01-31, 2000-02-29, 2000-03-31, ...
R> $ x     <dbl> 99.33629, 99.20978, 100.85216, 100.34...
R> $ y     <dbl> 99.54655, 100.90406, 99.43098, 99.533...
```

The first step is to create a deflator index based on the last period. Since the CPI data is already in percentage format, we can just accumulate it assuming an initial value of 1 and dividing the result by the value found on the base date:

```
# accumulate: R_a = cumprod(r_t + 1)
my_df$infl_idx <- cumprod(df_inflation$value/100 +1)

# set inflation index
my_df$infl_idx <- my_df$infl_idx/my_df$infl_idx[nrow(my_df)]
```

And now we create the new variables:

```
my_df$x_desinflated <- my_df$x*my_df$infl_idx
my_df$y_desinflated <- my_df$y*my_df$infl_idx

glimpse(my_df)
```

```
R> Observations: 240
R> Variables: 6
R> $ Date           <date> 2000-01-31, 2000-02-29, 200...
R> $ x              <dbl> 99.33629, 99.20978, 100.8521...
R> $ y              <dbl> 99.54655, 100.90406, 99.4309...
R> $ infl_idx       <dbl> 0.006013139, 0.006206883, 0....
R> $ x_desinflated  <dbl> 0.5973229, 0.6157835, 0.6495...
R> $ y_desinflated  <dbl> 0.5985873, 0.6262997, 0.6403...
```

Done. Following the previous example, we could apply `purrr::map` for all numeric columns of a dataframe.

9.5 Modifying Time Frequency and Aggregating Data

Sometimes we receive data with a mismatch of time frequency, i.e., daily instead of monthly. Here we will show how to change the time frequency of the data, from low to high: daily to weekly, monthly to annual data or the opposite. Here, a choice must be made about how to aggregate the data. So, that is how we will transform a daily data vector into a single monthly value? We can use the mean of the numeric vector to represent a single value for the month, median, last available value, and other choices.

Let's start with an example with the SP500 index, which is available on the daily frequency and will be transformed into an annual table. The first step is to download the daily data with `BatchGetSymbols`.

```
library(BatchGetSymbols)

df_SP500 <- BatchGetSymbols(tickers = '^GSPC',
                            first.date = '2010-01-01',
                            freq.data = 'daily',
                            last.date = '2018-01-01')[[2]]
```

Every time-frequency operation from higher to lower is a simple split-apply-combine type of calculation. For that, we can use the `dplyr` package and `group_by` and `summarise` functions. See the following steps:

```
# from daily to annual
df_SP500_annual <- df_SP500 %>%
  mutate(ref_year = lubridate::year(ref.date)) %>%
  group_by(ref_year) %>%
  summarise(last_value = last(price.adjusted))

# glimpse it
glimpse(df_SP500_annual)
```

```
R> Observations: 8
R> Variables: 2
```

```
R> $ ref_year   <dbl> 2010, 2011, 2012, 2013, 2014, 2...
R> $ last_value <dbl> 1257.64, 1257.60, 1426.19, 1848...
```

We will create a new column with the years, group the data according to it and, finally, we searched for the latest available SP500 value. One of the great benefits of using `dplyr` for time operations is full control of the aggregation process. Anyone reading the code can easily understand how the data was aggregated. If we wanted to use another aggregate measure such as average or median, we could simply add more columns at `summarise`.

9.6 Exercises

1. Consider the following `dataframe`:

```
library(tidyverse)

my_N <- 100

df <- bind_rows(tibble(ticker = rep('STOCK 1', my_N),
                       ref_date = Sys.Date() + 1:my_N,
                       price = 100 + cumsum(rnorm(my_N))),
                tibble(ticker = rep('STOCK 2', my_N),
                       ref_date = Sys.Date() + 1:my_N,
                       price = 100 + cumsum(rnorm(my_N))) )

print(df)
```

```
R> # A tibble: 200 x 3
R>    ticker  ref_date    price
R>    <chr>   <date>      <dbl>
R>  1 STOCK 1 2020-02-09   99.2
R>  2 STOCK 1 2020-02-10  100.
R>  3 STOCK 1 2020-02-11   99.3
R>  4 STOCK 1 2020-02-12  100.
R>  5 STOCK 1 2020-02-13  100.
R>  6 STOCK 1 2020-02-14   99.8
R>  7 STOCK 1 2020-02-15  100.
R>  8 STOCK 1 2020-02-16   98.5
R>  9 STOCK 1 2020-02-17   98.6
R> 10 STOCK 1 2020-02-18   97.5
R> # ... with 190 more rows
```

9.6. EXERCISES

The format is long or wide? Explain your answer.

2. Modify the format of the previous dataframe, from long to wide or vice-versa.

3. Consider the following `list`:

```
my_l <- list(df1 = tibble(x = 1:100,
                          y = runif(100)),
             df2 = tibble(x = 1:100,
                          y = runif(100),
                          v = runif(100)),
             df3 = tibble(x = 1:100,
                          y = runif(100),
                          z = runif(100)) )
```

Aggregate all elements of `my_l` into a single dataframe. So, the question is, what happened to the data points in `df1` for columns `v` and `z`?

4. Use package `BatchGetSymbols` to download SP500 index data (`'^GSPC'`) from 1950-01-01 to today. What are the top 5 absolute returns (positive or negative) of the index? Create and present on screen a `dataframe` with the values and dates of these extreme returns.

5. Use the function created in this chapter for removing outliers from the SP500 data with `p = 0.025`. How many rows were lost in this process?

6. Use function `BatchGetSymbols::BatchGetSymbols` to download FTSE index prices (`'^FTSE'`) from `'2010-01-01'` to the present day. Next, build a dataset of index values in the annual frequency by looking at the latest available index value for each year. Tip: see function `dplyr::summarise_all` for a functional way of aggregating all columns.

7. Use the same daily data from the previous exercise and build a new dataset in the monthly frequency.

8. CHALLENGE - For the previously downloaded FTSE daily data, check the dates and prices of the 20 biggest price drops. If an investor bought the index at the prices of the biggest drops and maintained it for 30 days, what would be his average nominal return per transaction?

Chapter 10

Creating and Saving Figures with ggplot2

It is a well-known fact that communication is one of the most important aspects of data science. If you can't communicate your data analysis in a simple and effective way, most of your work will go unnoticed and without impact. Using graphical resources in technical reports is widespread and helps to deliver the message. As a communicator, you need to know that a large proportion of your audience will pay more attention to your graphics than the actual text.

The easiness of which you can create and present a statistical graph, however, can be your enemy if not done correctly. Next, I'll set a few principles you should be aware when building graphical displays of data:

Visual attractiveness Always facilitate the analysis of your audience. Whenever possible, you need to make sure that the graphics state a clear and direct message. Highlight within the graphics what the audience should be looking for and how to read it. Don't expect everyone to be as technical as you. Moreover, you need to understand what your audience expects and will most care about. Case in point, don't present the same material to a group of business managers as you would for academics. Likewise, each has its own technical background, demands, and characteristics.

A figure must be self-contained Any technical information such as origin and time period of data should be clearly stated within the title, subtitle or caption of the graphic. If the reader needs to seek information about the graphical analysis in the textual report, you're doing it wrong. Sometimes this can be easier said than done but, try to communicate as much information as possible as long it does not pollute the graphic. Remember that there is a balance between elegant aesthetics and technical details.

The graphical analysis should help your analysis Just because you can make a plot, doesn't mean you must show it to the reader. The value of a graphic display is directly related to the novel information it brings in the analysis. Don't populate your report with an endless number of graphics. Stick to the ones that help you to deliver your message. When binding text and graphics, whenever you find yourselff with a figure that is not discussed by at least two paragraphs in the main text, cut it out. If you can't write two or more paragraphs about a piece of data visualization, it is probably not important.

Check your references Science and data analysis evolves as building blocks. Always check the graphical displays of your references. They will guide you on what your audience expects. Likewise, you can even use figures from previous articles to compare your results. This is especially convenient when the same or similar data-sets are used.

Previous guidelines will help you create impactful figures. Throughout this chapter, I will try to follow them as much as possible in creating all the figures.

10.1 The ggplot2 Package

R has built-in functions for creating figures, such as `graphics::plot` and `graphics::hist`. Using the native plotting functions, however, is not recommended. The customization of the graphic is not intuitive and the final result may not be visually attractive. In fact, in the past, one critic for R was its limited capacity for delivering high-quality graphics.

This deficiency was remedied by users. In 2005, Hadley Wickham, author of many other packages featured in this book, proposed a new way of structuring and creating figures in R, with a package called `ggplot2` (Wickham, 2009). It provides functions to generate graphics, structuring the process with an accessible and intuitive *layer* notation. In practice, graphics can be customized quickly and easily.

In this book, we will not go deep into `ggplot2` and all the details of its capacity. We will show the main features of the package with examples of data analysis in finance and economics. For advanced users who want to

10.2. USING GRAPHICS WINDOWS

know more about `ggplot2`, my advice is to consult the author's own book (Wickham, 2009).

For most examples given here, we will work with the data available in file `SP500-Stocks-WithRet.rds`. It contains daily closing prices and returns data for all components of the SP500 index. This file was created in chapter 8.

First, let's load the data and check its contents.

```
library(tidyverse)

# set file and load data
my_f  <- afedR::afedR_get_data_file('SP500-Stocks-WithRet.rds')
df_sp500 <- read_rds(my_f )

# print first 5 rows
glimpse(df_sp500)
```

```
R> Observations: 829,239
R> Variables: 4
R> $ price.adjusted <dbl> 68.72509, 69.69973, 69.7497...
R> $ ref.date       <date> 2010-01-05, 2010-01-06, 20...
R> $ ticker         <chr> "MMM", "MMM", "MMM", "MMM",...
R> $ ret            <dbl> -0.006263503, 0.014181794, ...
```

It is a fairly common table used in previous chapters. We have prices, dates, tickers, as well as the returns.

10.2 Using Graphics Windows

Before studying the use of `ggplot2`, we need to understand how these images are handled within the RStudio platform. When a new figure is created, as in `plot(1:20)`, it appears in the *Plots* panel (bottom right corner of RStudio). This panel, however, is small, making it difficult to visualize the figure in standard monitors. You can increase the panel's size manually, but this creates unnecessary work, as you might need to resize it again later to allow space for other panels.

A more intelligent approach to managing figures is to create an external window in RStudio, so the graphic can be displayed and resized independently of the main interface. To create a window, just use the `x11()` command before the line of code that creates the figure, as in:

```
x11()
plot(1:10)
```

The visual result in RStudio should be similar to Figure 10.1.

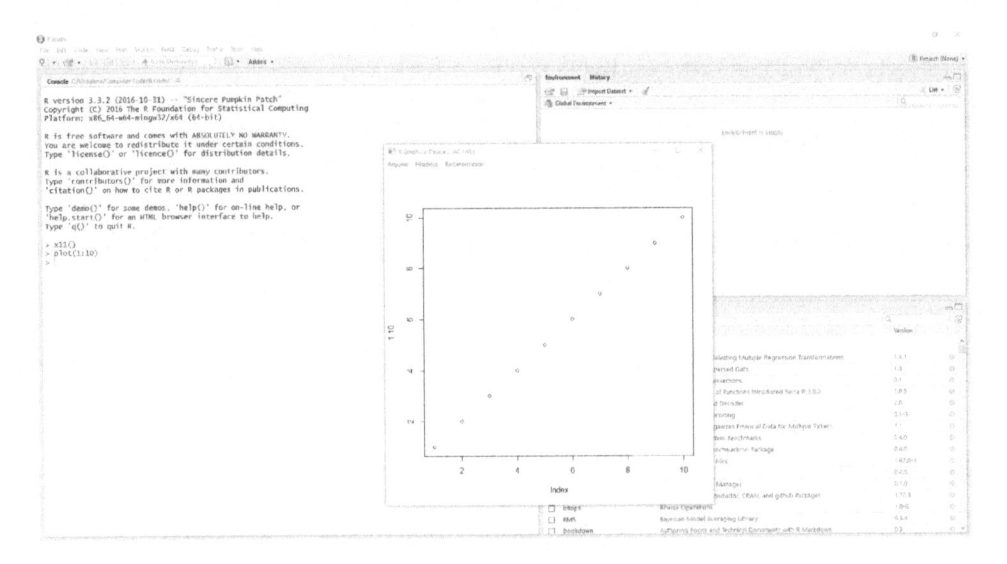

Figure 10.1: Screen of RStudio with the use of command x11()

Each call to `x11()` will create a new empty window, which we can fill with a figure later. Therefore, we can create various figures and allocate them in different windows, making it easy to analyze each individually or together, side by side.

After creating so many windows, it is best to close them. You can use `graphics.off` for that. This function, called with no argument, as in `graphics.off()`, will close all opened windows. It is common practice to use at the beginning of a research script. If you do it this way, then you are making sure that previously created plot windows do not pollute the workspace.

10.3 Creating Figures with Function qplot

Package ggplot2 has an introductory function, called qplot (*quick plot*), that mimics the behavior of the native R function plot. To use it, all you

10.3. CREATING FIGURES WITH FUNCTION QPLOT

need to know are the points that define the horizontal axis (x), the points of the vertical axis (y), and the geometric shape used in the plot.

To build a time series plot with the prices of stock MMM, we use the following code:

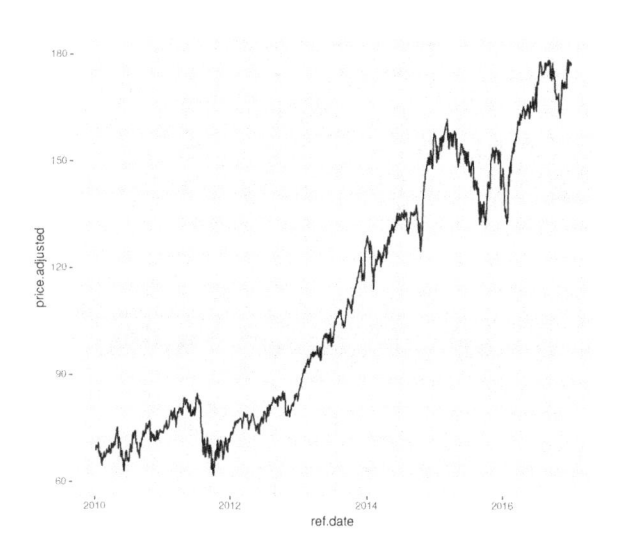

```
library(ggplot2)

# filter stock data
temp_df <- df_sp500 %>%
  filter(ticker == 'MMM')

# plot its prices
qplot(data = temp_df,
      x = ref.date,
      y = price.adjusted,
      geom = 'line')
```

In the previous example, the name of the axis corresponds to the names of the columns in `temp_df`. If we want to customize it for a specific text and set a title, we use arguments `xlab`, `ylab` and `main`:

```
qplot(data = temp_df,
      x = ref.date,
      y = price.adjusted,
      geom = 'line',
      xlab = 'Dates',
```

```
       ylab = 'Adjusted closing prices',
       main = 'Prices of MMM')
```

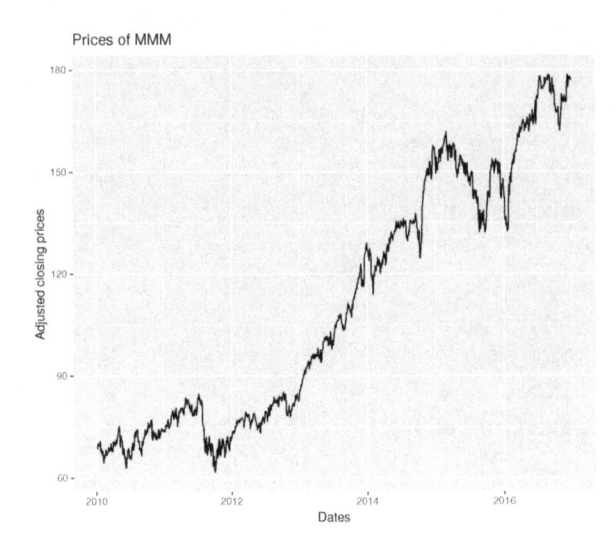

Much better! Notice how the horizontal axis of dates in the previous figures is formatted to show only the years. It adapts automatically according to the length of time in the plot. This only happened because of the `ref.date` the column is correctly defined as a `Date` object.

10.4 Creating Figures with Function `ggplot`

Using function `qplot` is recommended when you want to create a plot quickly for immediate viewing. This function, however, has restrictions in the way we customize the output. The recommended function to use in `ggplot2` is `ggplot`. It uses a clever layer framework that allows a series of complex graphical constructions.

Before presenting examples using `ggplot`, let's briefly discuss the philosophy behind how `ggplot` works. First, every figure has horizontal and vertical coordinates. These points define where the symbols or lines should be drawn. Second, we have a geometric shape placed in the coordinates. It can be a circle, a point or a line, as in the previous figures. We set the size and color of these objects and, finally, by combining all these elements, we create the full figure.

10.4. CREATING FIGURES WITH FUNCTION GGPLOT

The distinction between the steps of creating a figure is important because it is precisely this way that `ggplot2` works. We make choices for x, y, color, and size based on data, and then chose the desired format of the graphic. Everything works within each step as if we are drawing layers in the figure.

Look at the syntax of the following example that recreates the figure previously created with `qplot`.

```
p <- ggplot(data = temp_df,
            mapping = aes(x = ref.date,
                          y = price.adjusted))
p <- p + geom_line()
p <- p + labs(x = 'Dates',
              y = 'Adjusted closing prices',
              title = 'Prices of MMM')
print(p)
```

In using `ggplot`, it is always necessary to provide a `dataframe`. If you want to create figures from atomic vectors, you must allocate them to a `dataframe` first and then feed the object to function `ggplot`.

After defining the input information in argument `data`, we use function `aes` to set the aesthetics of the graph with the x and y coordinates. Here, we set the horizontal axis using column `date` and the vertical axis as prices (column `price.adjusted`). As we will soon see, it is also possible to use other information in `aes`, such as color and shapes.

Once the data and axis are defined, we save it in object p. **This object registers the current information as new layers are added with**

the plus sign (+). The second line of the code, `p <- p + geom_line()`, defines the type of figure. Here, we used the `geom_lines` function, which is a simple line graph that connects the points. In `ggplot2`, the functions that define the geometric type begins with `geom_` character. So, using the *autocomplete* function of RStudio, you can see there are many options. We can use `stringr` to find the list of functions in `ggplot2`, version 3.2.1 (2020-02-08), that starts with `geom_`:

```
library(ggplot2)
library(stringr)

# get names of functions in ggplot2
fcts <- ls('package:ggplot2')

# select those that starts with geom_
idx <- str_sub(fcts, 1, 5) == 'geom_'
fcts <- fcts[idx]

# print result
print(fcts)
```

```
R>  [1] "geom_abline"       "geom_area"
R>  [3] "geom_bar"          "geom_bin2d"
R>  [5] "geom_blank"        "geom_boxplot"
R>  [7] "geom_col"          "geom_contour"
R>  [9] "geom_count"        "geom_crossbar"
R> [11] "geom_curve"        "geom_density"
R> [13] "geom_density_2d"   "geom_density2d"
R> [15] "geom_dotplot"      "geom_errorbar"
R> [17] "geom_errorbarh"    "geom_freqpoly"
R> [19] "geom_hex"          "geom_histogram"
R> [21] "geom_hline"        "geom_jitter"
R> [23] "geom_label"        "geom_line"
R> [25] "geom_linerange"    "geom_map"
R> [27] "geom_path"         "geom_point"
R> [29] "geom_pointrange"   "geom_polygon"
R> [31] "geom_qq"           "geom_qq_line"
R> [33] "geom_quantile"     "geom_raster"
R> [35] "geom_rect"         "geom_ribbon"
R> [37] "geom_rug"          "geom_segment"
R> [39] "geom_sf"           "geom_sf_label"
R> [41] "geom_sf_text"      "geom_smooth"
```

10.4. CREATING FIGURES WITH FUNCTION GGPLOT

```
R> [43] "geom_spoke"       "geom_step"
R> [45] "geom_text"        "geom_tile"
R> [47] "geom_violin"      "geom_vline"
```

As you can see, the `ggplot2` package offers a significant quantity of geometric shapes. We'll explore many of the options within this chapter. You can find more details about each alternative in the manual[1].

Going back to our example, the third line of the code defines the name of the horizontal axis x and vertical axis y with function `labs`. Finally, we print the figure stored in `p` with function `print`. Furthermore, it is important to highlight this modular approach in using `ggplot`: each layer of the figure was created in a line of code. For example, if we did not want to set the axes as *Dates* and *Adjusted closing prices*, we can simply comment on the line in the script.

Using the **pipeline operator** is also possible. As an example, consider the same previous code but with a pipeline and sequential notation:

```
p <- temp_df %>%
  ggplot(aes(x = ref.date, y = price.adjusted)) +
  geom_line() +
  labs(x = 'Dates',
       y = 'Adjusted Closing Prices',
       title = 'Prices of MMM')
```

We advise that you make a note to show we have used symbol + and not %>% to interconnect each layer of the graph after calling `ggplot`. From now on we will use and abuse the *pipeline* notation to build the figures.

One of the great advantages of using `ggplot` is when creating figures for different groups. As an example, let's create a figure that shows, on the same axis, prices of four stocks selected randomly. The first step is to create a temporary `dataframe` that contains these stocks only.

```
# fix seed
set.seed(10)

# select 4 stocks randomly
tickers <- sample(unique(df_sp500$ticker), 4)
```

---

[1] https://ggplot2.tidyverse.org/reference/index.html

350 CHAPTER 10. CREATING AND SAVING FIGURES WITH GGPLOT2

```
# create temporary df
temp_df <- df_sp500 %>%
  filter(ticker %in% tickers)
```

In this code, we use operator `%in%` to find out the rows of `df_sp500` that contain data for the selected tickers in column `tickers`. The result is a temporary `dataframe` that contains the data of the chosen stocks. Now, we create the figure with the following code:

```
p <- temp_df %>%
  ggplot(aes(x = ref.date,
             y = price.adjusted,
             color = ticker)) +
  geom_line() +
  labs(x = 'Dates',
       y = 'Adjusted closing prices',
       title = 'Prices of four random stocks',
       subtitle = paste0('Date from ', min(temp_df$ref.date),
                         ' to ', max(temp_df$ref.date) ),
       caption = 'Data from Yahoo Finance')

print(p)
```

A difference from the previous examples is that we defined the color of the lines using argument `color` in `aes`. Each line color is defined by the elements

10.4. CREATING FIGURES WITH FUNCTION GGPLOT

in column `ticker` of `temp_df`. The actual choices of color, e.g., red, blue, and so on, is automatically defined by `ggplot`.

Notice how easy and quick it was to adjust the code for the new figure. This is one of the greatest benefits of using `ggplot2`. The layer notation and the dynamic of the aesthetics input allow for complex modifications in a single line of code.

10.4.1 The US Yield Curve

Now, let's use what we learned so far to create the current yield curve of the US market. The yield curve – or term structure – is one of the standard plots in finance, showing the market assessment of future financial returns. For a given time horizon, the yield curve sets the percentage one can expect to receive in an investment or pay in a debt. Normally, the yield curve is ascending as the interest rates rise with the increase of the time horizon. In a practical situation, this means that borrowing money becomes more expensive as the duration of the loan increases.

In the following code, we will first download the related data using package `Quandl`, structure and clean the raw data, and plot the yields for the last available date in 2019 using `ggplot2`.

```
library(Quandl)
library(tidyverse)

Quandl.api_key(my_api_key) # set yours api key here

# set symbol and dates
my.symbol <- 'USTREASURY/YIELD'
first.date <- as.Date('2010-01-01')
last_date <- Sys.Date()

# get data!
df_yc <- Quandl(code = my.symbol,
                type = 'raw',
                start_date = first.date,
                end_date = last_date)

print(head(df_yc))
```

R>   Date 1 MO 2 MO 3 MO 6 MO 1 YR 2 YR 3 YR 5 YR

```
R> 1 2020-02-07 1.57 1.58 1.56 1.57 1.49 1.41 1.39 1.41
R> 2 2020-02-06 1.59 1.59 1.57 1.58 1.51 1.44 1.43 1.45
R> 3 2020-02-05 1.55 1.56 1.57 1.57 1.49 1.44 1.43 1.46
R> 4 2020-02-04 1.55 1.57 1.57 1.57 1.48 1.41 1.40 1.42
R> 5 2020-02-03 1.56 1.57 1.57 1.56 1.46 1.36 1.34 1.35
R> 6 2020-01-31 1.56 1.57 1.55 1.54 1.45 1.33 1.30 1.32
R>   7 YR 10 YR 20 YR 30 YR
R> 1 1.51  1.59  1.89  2.05
R> 2 1.56  1.65  1.94  2.11
R> 3 1.57  1.66  1.97  2.14
R> 4 1.52  1.61  1.91  2.08
R> 5 1.45  1.54  1.84  2.01
R> 6 1.42  1.51  1.83  1.99
```

The result is a dataframe in the wide format: yields as columns, index by dates (rows). As you should expect (see chapter 9), the first step is to transform the format from wide to long and do some cleaning:

```
# change to long format and convert to factor
df_yc <- gather(data = df_yc,
                key = 'maturity',
                value = 'rate',
                -Date) %>%
  mutate(maturity = factor(maturity))

# keep only longer term yields (names with YR)
idx <- str_detect(df_yc$maturity, 'YR')
df_yc <- df_yc[idx, ]

# change name to year number with regex
# obs: regex ([0-9]+) extracts all numbers within a string
out <- str_extract_all(string = df_yc$maturity,
                       pattern = '([0-9]+)')
df_yc$maturity <- as.numeric(out)

# glimpse result
glimpse(df_yc)


R> Observations: 20,216
R> Variables: 3
R> $ Date     <date> 2020-02-07, 2020-02-06, 2020-02-...
```

10.4. CREATING FIGURES WITH FUNCTION GGPLOT

```
R> $ maturity <dbl> 1, 1, 1, 1, 1, 1, 1, 1, 1, 1, 1, ...
R> $ rate     <dbl> 1.49, 1.51, 1.49, 1.48, 1.46, 1.4...
```

We have a dataframe in the long format with three columns: Data, maturities and rates. Now we can plot the yield curve for the last available date:

```
# keep only last date of each
last_date <- max(df_yc$Date)
df_yc_lastdate <- df_yc[df_yc$Date == last_date, ]

# plot it!
p <- ggplot(df_yc_lastdate, aes(x=maturity, y=rate)) +
  geom_point(size = 2.5) + geom_line(size=1) +
  labs(x = 'Maturity (years)',
       y='Yield Rate (%)',
       title = paste0('US Yield Curve for ',last_date),
       caption = paste0('Data from Quandl table ', my.symbol, '\n',
                        'Access at ', Sys.time()))

print(p)
```

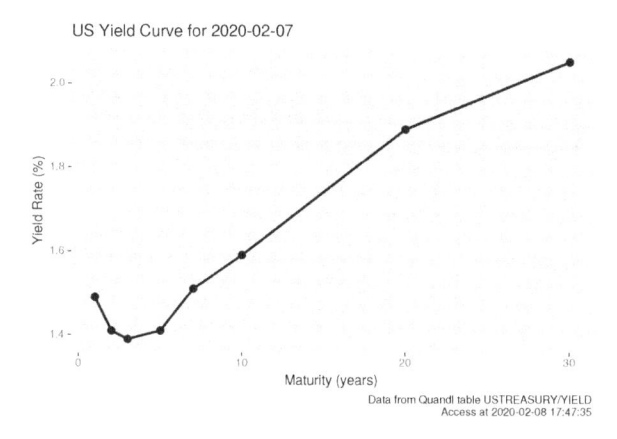

As expected, the current yield curve is upward rising in the long run, meaning the yield rate is likely to increase with the maturity of the debt. As an extension of the example, we can add some dynamic to the figure by using several dates. Have a look at the following code, where we use five yield curves covering the year of 2019.

```r
# set number of periods
n_periods <- 5
my_year <- 2019

# filter for year 2019
df_yc_my_year <- df_yc %>%
  filter(lubridate::year(Date) == my_year )

# get unique dates in data
unique_dates <- unique(df_yc_my_year$Date)

# set sequence of observations
my_seq <- floor(seq(1, length(unique_dates),
                    length.out = n_periods))

# get actual dates from sequence
my_dates <- unique_dates[my_seq]

# find rows for dates in df
idx <- df_yc_my_year$Date %in% my_dates
df_yc_periods <- df_yc_my_year[idx, ]

# plot it!
p <- ggplot(df_yc_periods, aes(x=maturity,
                               y=rate,
                               color= factor(Date))) +
  geom_point(size = 2.5) + geom_line(size = 1) +
  labs(x = 'Maturity (years)',
       y='Yield Rate (%)',
       title = paste0('US Yield Curve for ', my_year),
       color = 'Dates',
       caption = paste0('Data from Quandl table ',
                        my.symbol, '\n',
                        'Access at ', Sys.time())))

print(p)
```

US Yield Curve for 2019

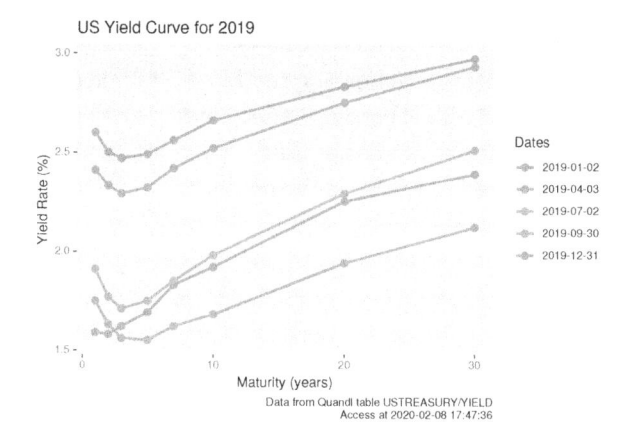

The yield curve is not static and will change over time. Whenever market expectations shift, so does the assessment of the future cost of debt. As the previous figure show, interest rates can vary significantly within a year.

10.5 Using Themes

One way of customizing graphics in `ggplot2` is using themes. A theme is a collection of options that defines the organization of the figure, its points and line colors, notation of axis, background color, and several other features. In practice, you can use preset themes or create your own. With a simple function call, you can apply it to any `ggplot` object.

Package `ggplot` has a pre-packaged collection of functions for setting themes, and their name starts with the text *theme*. Next, we show the list of theme-related functions in `ggplot`, version 3.2.1.

```
library(ggplot2)
library(stringr)

# get all functions
fcts <- ls('package:ggplot2')

# find out those that start with theme_
idx <- str_sub(fcts, 1, 6) == 'theme_'
fcts <- fcts[idx]

# print result
print(fcts)
```

```
R> [1] "theme_bw"       "theme_classic"   "theme_dark"
R> [4] "theme_get"      "theme_gray"      "theme_grey"
R> [7] "theme_light"    "theme_linedraw"  "theme_minimal"
R> [10] "theme_replace" "theme_set"       "theme_test"
R> [13] "theme_update"  "theme_void"
```

Let's try it with the theme from function `theme_bw`. From the manual: "theme_bw sets the classic dark-on-light ggplot2 theme. May work better for presentations displayed with a projector." Let's look at it visually. We need only to add a new line + `theme_bw()` in the previous code.

```
p <- temp_df %>%
  ggplot(aes(x = ref.date, y = price.adjusted, color=ticker)) +
  geom_line() +
  labs(x = 'Dates',
       y = 'Adjusted closing prices',
       title = 'Prices of four random stocks',
       caption = 'Data from Yahoo Finance') +
  theme_bw()

print(p)
```

As you can see, the new theme was a white background and a frame box.

Let's now use package `gridExtra` to create a grid of plots and check out three more themes:

10.5. USING THEMES

```
require(gridExtra)

p1 <- p +
  theme_bw() +
  labs(title = 'Theme BW')

p2 <- p +
  theme_dark() +
  labs(title = 'Theme Dark')

p3 <- p +
  theme_grey() +
  labs(title = 'Theme Grey')

p4 <- p +
  theme_light() +
  labs(title = 'Theme Light')

p5 <- p +
  theme_classic() +
  labs(title = 'Theme Classic')

p6 <- p +
  theme_minimal() +
  labs(title = 'Theme Minimal')

grid.arrange(p1, p2, p3,
             p4, p5, p6,
             ncol=2, nrow = 3)
```

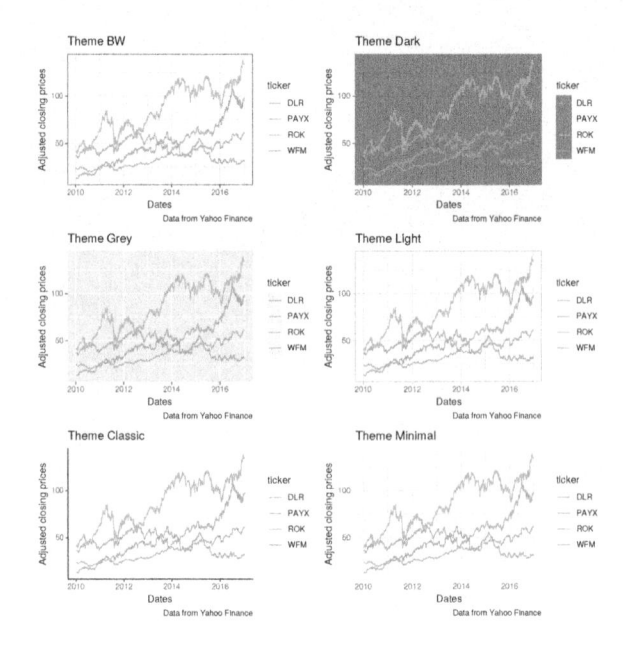

You can try other themes on your computer and see which one you like the most. You can also create your own theme. Have a look at Wickham (2009) for instructions on this specific task.

In the previous example, notice how the structure of the figure has changed, but not the colors of the lines. For example, when using `theme_bw()`, it is not unreasonable to expect that the color of lines is also set in black and white, which did not happen in the previous example. In `ggplot2`, the default `theme_*` functions have control only on the outer aspects of the plot, and not in the aesthetics.

Digging deeper, the selection of the colors follows a cycle. When the whole sequence of colors ends, it restarts. Sometimes, especially in the submission to scientific journals, it is expected that all figures have a grey theme so the article can be paper printed in black and white. For that, we can use function `scale_colour_grey` to set a colour cycle between white and black in our previous figure:

```
p <- p + 
  theme_bw() +
  scale_colour_grey(start = 0.0, end = 0.6)

print(p)
```

10.6. CREATING PANELS WITH `FACET_WRAP`

Prices of four random stocks

[Figure: Line chart showing adjusted closing prices from 2010 to 2016 for four stocks: DLR, PAYX, ROK, WFM. Data from Yahoo Finance]

The lines of the plot are now in grey. The inputs `start` and `end` at `scale_color_grey` set the minimum and maximum of "whiteness". So, never use `end = 1` with a white background. Otherwise, some lines won't be visible.

10.6 Creating Panels with `facet_wrap`

Another possibility of creating graphics for different groups within our data is to use panels, organizing each category on its own. When placed side by side and with the same axis, a visual and spatial comparison is straightforward.

Facets are possible with function `facet_wrap`, which takes as input a formula containing the name of a column with groups that will define each panel. In the following example, we use `facet_wrap` with option `facets = ~ ticker` to create a panel of prices for four selected assets.

```
library(dplyr)
# fix seed
set.seed(10)

# select 4 stocks randomly
tickers <- sample(unique(df_sp500$ticker), 4)

p <- df_sp500 %>%
  filter(ticker %in% tickers) %>%
  ggplot(aes(x = ref.date, y = price.adjusted)) +
```

```
  geom_line() +
  labs(x = 'Date',
       y = 'Adjusted closing prices',
       title = 'Prices of four random stocks',
       caption = 'Data from Yahoo Finance') +
  facet_wrap(facets = ~ticker) +
  theme_bw()

print(p)
```

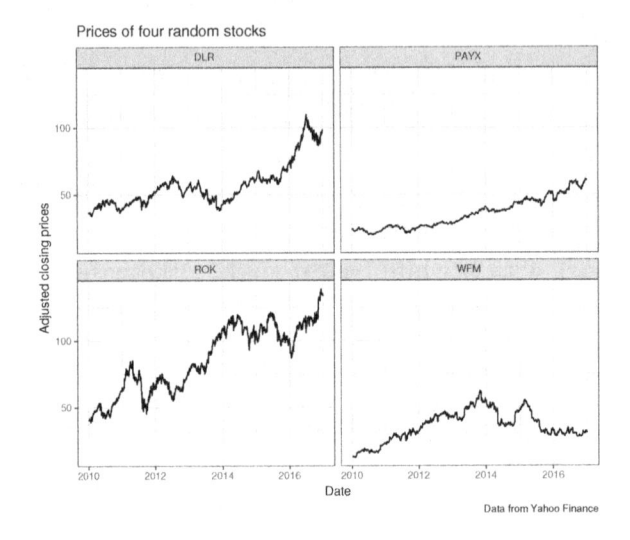

Using panels is recommended when the data of the groups are similar and often agglomerates. This makes it difficult to analyze the differences between the groups in a single graphic. One example is the case of stock returns of different assets. Next, we create a panel for the returns of four randomly selected tickers.

```
# fix seed
set.seed(25)

# select 4 stocks randomly
tickers <- sample(unique(df_sp500$ticker), 4)

p <- df_sp500 %>%
  filter(ticker %in% tickers) %>%
  ggplot(aes(x = ref.date, y = ret)) +
  geom_line(size=1) +
```

10.6. CREATING PANELS WITH `FACET_WRAP`

```
  labs(x = 'Date',
       y = 'Returns',
       title = 'Daily returns of four random stocks',
       caption = 'Data from Yahoo Finance') +
  facet_wrap(facets = ~ticker) +
  theme_bw()

print(p)
```

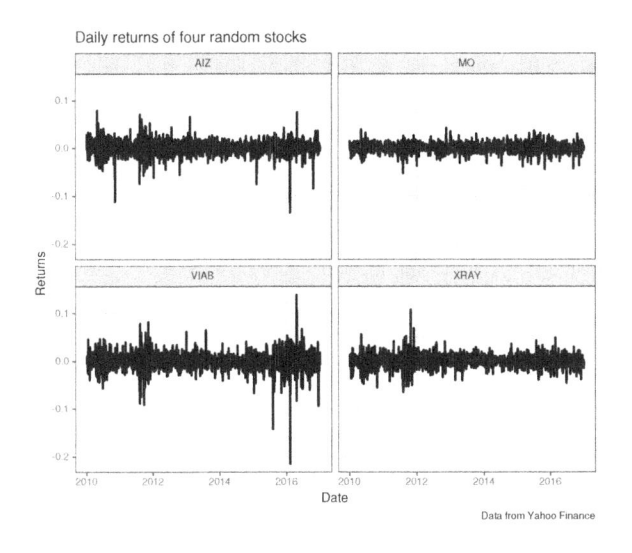

Notice how the vertical axis of the panels is fixed for all stocks, facilitating the visual analysis. We can also set the scales free by using option `scales='free'` in `facet_wrap`:

```
p <- p +
  facet_wrap(facets = ~ticker, scales = 'free_y')

print(p)
```

Daily returns of four random stocks

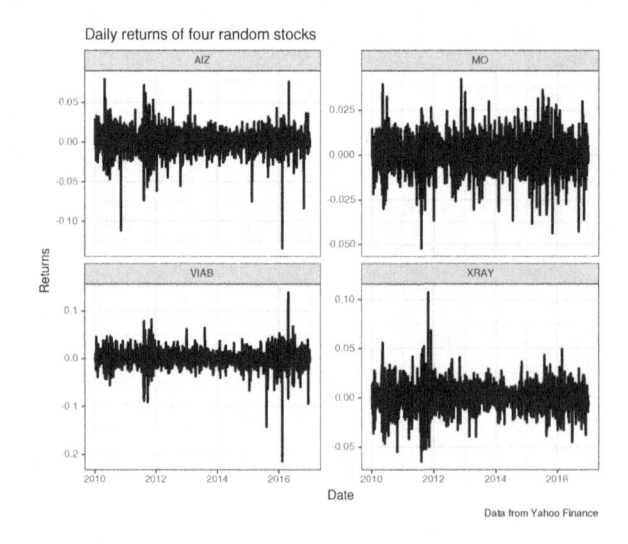

Here, both axis, x and y, have their own scale and will change according to the groups.

10.7 Using the Pipeline

We previously saw that `ggplot2` is a friend of the pipeline operator. Here we will go further and look at how we can write R code where all stages of the data analysis are fully integrated. Consider the next example, where we plot the average return and standard deviation of all stocks from the data available in `df_sp500`.

```
library(tidyverse)
library(ggplot2)

# calculated mean and sd of returns, plot result
my_f <- afedR::afedR_get_data_file(
  'SP500_Stocks_long_by_year.rds'
  )

df_sp500 <- read_rds(my_f)

p <- df_sp500 %>%
  na.omit() %>%
  group_by(ticker) %>%
  summarise(mean_ret = mean(ret.adjusted.prices),
            std_ret = sd(ret.adjusted.prices)) %>%
```

10.7. USING THE PIPELINE

```
    ggplot(aes(x = std_ret, y = mean_ret)) +
    geom_point() +
    labs(x = 'Standard Deviation of Yearly returns',
         y = 'Average Yearly Returns',
         title = 'Expected Return and Risk for SP500 Stocks',
         subtitle = paste0('Annual price data from 2010 to 2019, ',
                           length(unique(df_sp500$ticker)),
                           ' stocks included'),
         caption = 'Data imported from Yahoo Finance') +
    scale_y_continuous(labels = scales::percent) +
    scale_x_continuous(labels = scales::percent) +
    theme_bw()

print(p)
```

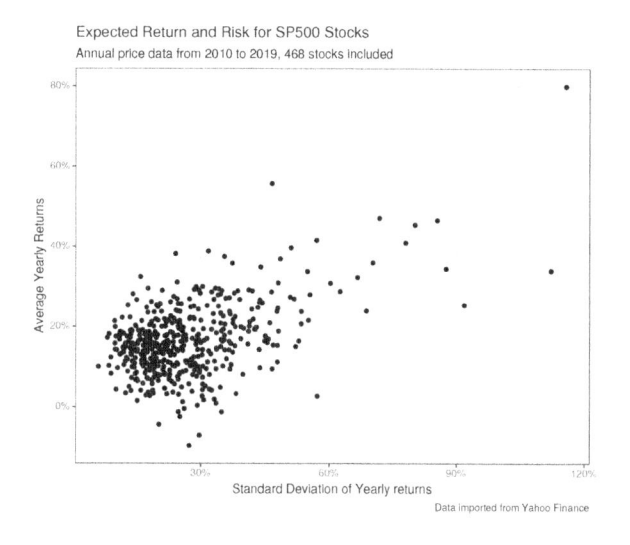

![Expected Return and Risk for SP500 Stocks scatter plot. Annual price data from 2010 to 2019, 468 stocks included. Data imported from Yahoo Finance.]

The previous code is self-contained, easy to read, and elegant. It goes from raw data to the plot, with no object created in the intermediate steps. With a few lines of code, anyone can see what is going on and how the plot was built. Modifications in the data processing stage are also straightforward.

This is another example of an elegant code producing quality results. The plot should be familiar for anyone that ever studied investments in the stock market. The graph, also known as mean-variance map, shows the relationship of expected returns (average) and risk (standard deviation) and plays a large role in a theoretical asset pricing model called CAPM (Capital Asset Pricing Model). As we can see from the data, the higher the measured risk, the higher the expected return.

10.8 Creating Statistical Graphics

Package `ggplot` has several options for creating graphs with statistical content. This includes histograms, boxplot (dispersion) graphics, QQ plots, and more.

10.8.1 Creating Histograms

A histogram shows the empirical distribution of the data. We can easily create them with `ggplot` and function `geom_histogram`. An example is given in the following code, where we generate a histogram for all returns found in `df_sp500`. But, before we build the plot, we need to remove outliers from the data. For that, we use function `afedR::afedR_replace_outliers`.

```
# set file and load data
my_f <- afedR::afedR_get_data_file('SP500-Stocks-WithRet.rds')
df_sp500 <- read_rds(my_f )

# remove outliers
my_prob_outliers <- 0.01
df_sp500$ret <- afedR::afedR_replace_outliers(
  df_sp500$ret,
  my_prob = my_prob_outliers
  )

# plot the data
p <- ggplot(data = df_sp500, aes(x = ret)) +
  geom_histogram(bins = 100) +
  labs(y = 'Frequency',
       x = 'Returns',
       title = paste0('Distribution of returns for ',
                      'all stocks in the SP500 index'),
       subtitle = paste0('Data from 2010 to 2019\n',
                         'Distribution based quantiles at the ',
                         scales::percent(my_prob_outliers),
                         ' were removed'),
       caption = 'Data from Yahoo Finance'
  ) +
  scale_x_continuous(labels = scales::percent) +
  theme_bw()
```

10.8. CREATING STATISTICAL GRAPHICS

```
print(p)
```

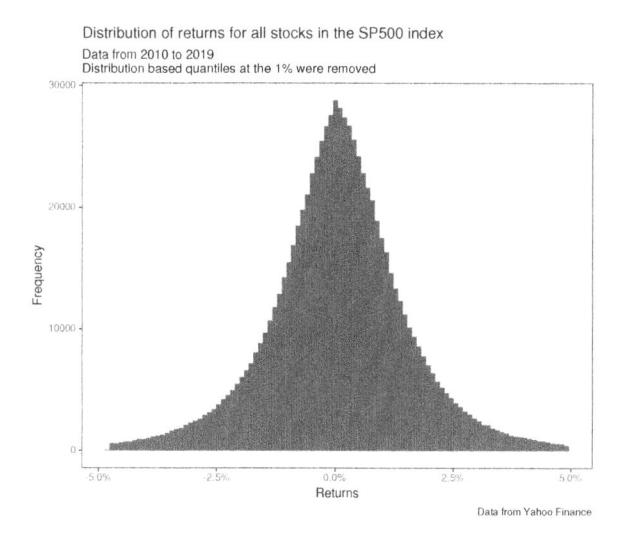

Distribution of returns for all stocks in the SP500 index
Data from 2010 to 2019
Distribution based quantiles at the 1% were removed

Data from Yahoo Finance

Here, we only need to define the x value, without the y. The size of the intervals in the histogram is defined by input `bins`.

We can also use groups and facets as we did for point and line plots. Have a look.

```
# fix seed
set.seed(30)

# select 4 stocks randomly
tickers <- sample(unique(df_sp500$ticker), 4)

p <- df_sp500 %>%
  filter(ticker %in% tickers) %>%
  ggplot(aes(x = ret)) +
  geom_histogram(bins = 50) +
  labs(y = 'Frequency',
       x = 'Returns',
       title = 'Distribution of returns for four random stocks',
       subtitle = paste0('Data from 2010 to 2019\n',
                         'Quantiles at the ',
                         scales::percent(my_prob_outliers),
                         ' of the distribution were removed'),
       caption = 'Data from Yahoo Finance'
```

```
  ) +
  scale_x_continuous(labels = scales::percent) +
  theme_bw() +
  facet_wrap(facets = ~ticker)

print(p)
```

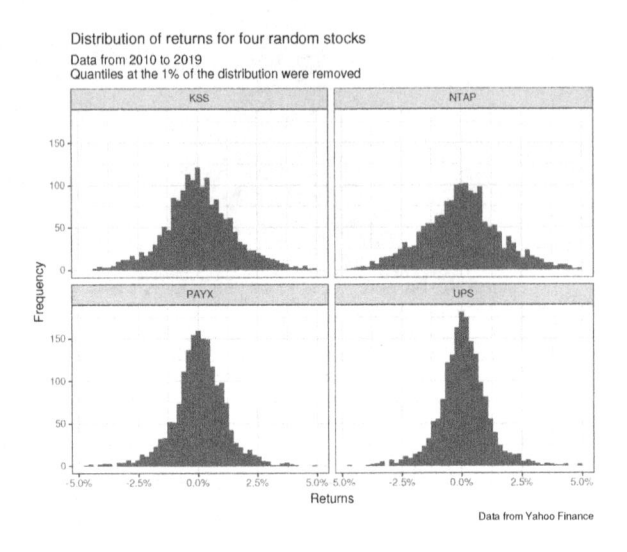

[Figure: Distribution of returns for four random stocks, Data from 2010 to 2019, Quantiles at the 1% of the distribution were removed — histograms for KSS, NTAP, PAYX, UPS. Data from Yahoo Finance]

A histogram with the empirical densities of the data can be created using function `geom_density`. While histograms built with `geom_histogram` count the number of times the data is located within an interval, a density histogram uses the relative frequency and interpolates the values, resulting in a more visually appealing representation of a distribution. See an example next.

```
p <- df_sp500 %>%
  filter(ticker %in% tickers) %>%
  ggplot(aes(x = ret)) +
  geom_density() +
  facet_wrap(facets = ~ticker) +
  labs(y = 'Interpolated Frequency',
       x = 'Returns',
       title = paste0('Interpolated distribution of returns',
                      'for all stocks in the SP500 index'),
       subtitle = paste0('Data from 2010 to 2019\n',
                         'Quantiles at the ',
                         scales::percent(my_prob_outliers),
```

10.8. CREATING STATISTICAL GRAPHICS

```
                          ' of both sides of the distribution',
                          'were removed'),
      caption = 'Data from Yahoo Finance'
  ) +
  scale_x_continuous(labels = scales::percent) +
  theme_bw()

print(p)
```

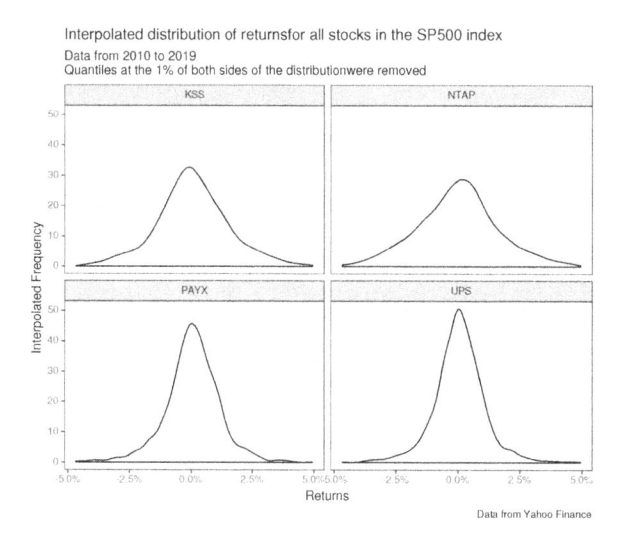

The previous figure allows a clear visual comparison of the differences between the distributions of returns of the different stocks.

10.8.2 Creating *boxplot* Figures

Figures of type *boxplot*, or box and whisker diagram, show the distribution of a variable conditional on some category or group. Using the median, maximum, minimum, and quartiles of the data, this statistical display highlights the distribution of a variable in a specific visual pattern. See an example next, where we show the price distribution of four randomly selected stocks.

```
# fix seed
set.seed(30)

# select 4 stocks randomly
tickers <- sample(unique(df_sp500$ticker), 4)
```

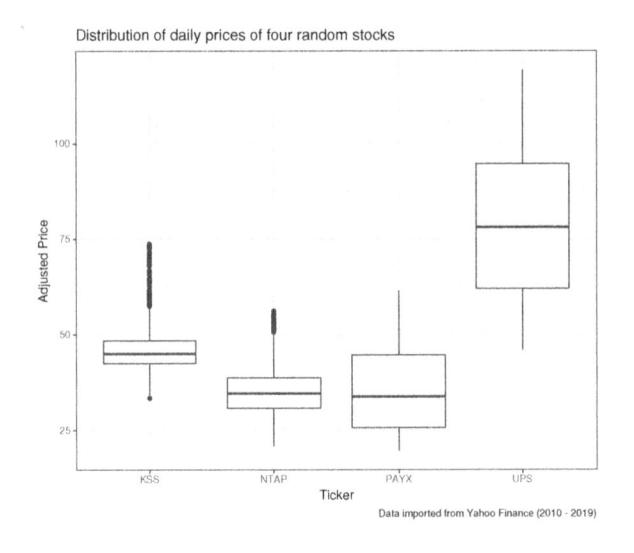

```r
p <- df_sp500 %>%
  filter(ticker %in% tickers) %>%
  ggplot(aes(x = ticker, y = price.adjusted)) +
  geom_boxplot() +
  labs(y = 'Adjusted Price',
       x = 'Ticker',
       title = paste0('Distribution of daily prices',
                      ' of four random stocks'),
       caption = paste0('Data imported from Yahoo Finance',
                        ' (2010 - 2019)')
       ) +
  theme_bw()

print(p)
```

We define a box plot by setting the x and y columns in aes. Here we are telling ggplot to build a boxplot of prices for each ticker. As we can see from the previous figure, the stocks have different distributions for their prices. The middle line defines the median value, while the upper and lower lines of the box define the first and third quartile.

Another interesting application of boxplot figures is to look at the distribution of daily yield rates across different maturities. Do you remember that we downloaded current US yield rates, for the previous example, starting with 2010. For each day, we have several rates of return for different maturities. If we are interested in better understanding the impact of the maturity over interest rates, a boxplot figure can help:

10.8. CREATING STATISTICAL GRAPHICS

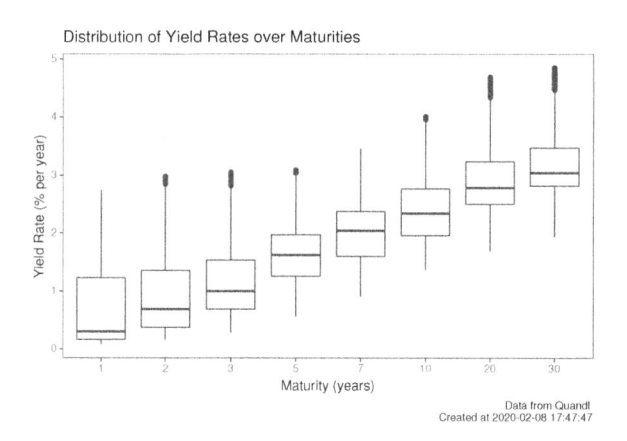

```
p <- ggplot(df_yc, aes(x = factor(maturity), y = rate)) +
  geom_boxplot() +
  labs(title = 'Distribution of Yield Rates over Maturities',
       x = 'Maturity (years)',
       y = 'Yield Rate (% per year)',
       caption = paste0('Data from Quandl \n',
                        'Created at ', Sys.time()) ) +
  theme_bw()

print(p)
```

The statistical plot shows the upward pattern for yield rates: as maturity increases, so does the returns of an investor and the cost of capital for a debtor. However, the distribution of yields also seems homogeneous. Overall, a long term rate has a similar daily variation than a short term rate. We can also use the plot for some simple extrapolations. For example, a simple prediction for a seven-year term rate for the US market is its median, around 2%.

10.8.3 Creating *QQ* Plots

QQ plots show a comparison between the empirical (observed) distribution of a variable and a theoretical distribution, such as the Normal. In other words, it is a scatter plot between cumulative distributions. The closest to a straight line, the more similar is the empirical distribution to the theoretical.

Let's try an example with some simulated data.

```r
# fix seed
set.seed(40)

# set options
N <- 10000
my_mean <- 10
my_sd <- 2

# create tibble
temp_df <- tibble(y=rnorm(n = N,
                          mean = my_mean,
                          sd = my_sd))

# plot QQ
p <- ggplot(data = temp_df, aes(sample = y)) +
  geom_qq(distribution = qnorm,
          dparams = c(mean=my_mean, sd=my_sd)) +
  labs(title = 'QQ plot of simulated Normal Distribution')

print(p)
```

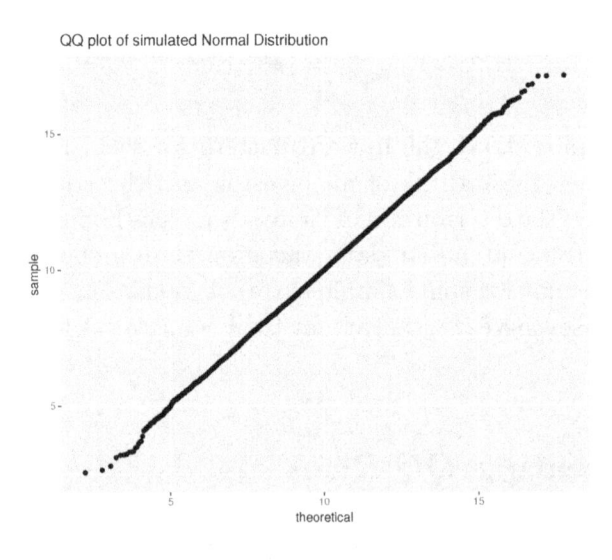

In the previous code, we simulate random normal variables with mean 10 and standard deviation equal to 2. As you can see, the QQ plot is close to a straight line, meaning the empirical distribution of the simulated data is close to a Normal distribution. Since we used artificial data from the distribution, this result is not surprising!

10.8. CREATING STATISTICAL GRAPHICS

Now, let's try it for our table of stock's returns. We will randomly select 4 stocks, create a new column, called `norm_ret`, with the normalized values of the returns. The normalization procedure works as follows; we subtract the mean for each return and divide the result by the standard deviation. This procedure must be executed individually for each stock. After that, we compare the resulting distribution against a standard Normal with mean zero and deviation equal to 1. The following code does this operation.

```
# fix seed
set.seed(10)

# select 4 stock randomly and filter
tickers <- sample(unique(df_sp500$ticker), 4)

temp_df <- df_sp500 %>%
  filter(ticker %in% tickers)

# set function for normalization
norm_vec <- function(y){
  # Normalizes a vector by subtracting mean and dividing
  # by the standard deviation
  #
  # Args:
  #   y - numerical vector
  #
  # Returns:
  #   A normalized vector
  
  y.norm <- (y-mean(y, na.rm = TRUE))/sd(y, na.rm = TRUE)
  return(y.norm)
}

# apply function
my_l <- tapply(X = temp_df$ret,
               INDEX = factor(temp_df$ticker),
               FUN = norm_vec)

# reorder list (tapply sorts alphabetically)
my_l <- my_l[as.character(unique(temp_df$ticker))]

# save new column norm.ret
temp_df$norm_ret <- unlist(my_l)
```

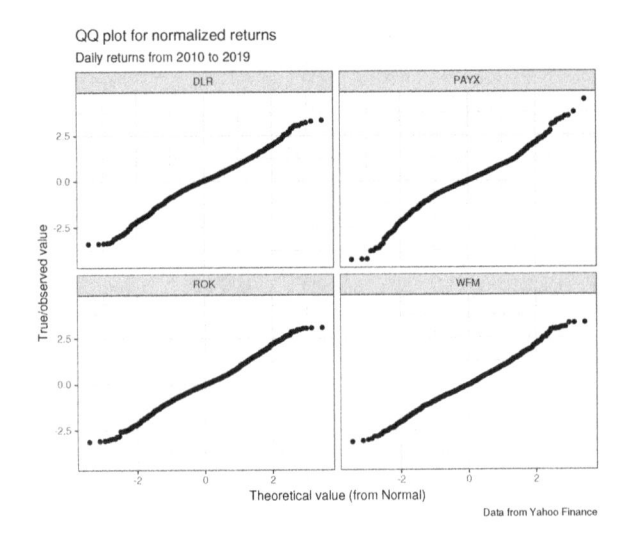

```r
# plot it!
p <- ggplot(data = temp_df, aes(sample = norm_ret)) +
  geom_qq() +
  facet_wrap(~ticker) +
  labs(title = 'QQ plot for normalized returns',
       subtitle = 'Daily returns from 2010 to 2019',
       x = 'Theoretical value (from Normal)',
       y = 'True/observed value',
       caption = 'Data from Yahoo Finance') +
  theme_bw()

print(p)
```

As you can see, the result is not visually similar to the result found for the simulated distribution, especially at the tails. We see a higher proportion of cases at the extremes. Such a result is a well-known financial fact, conveniently called *fat tails*. It means the Normal distribution does a bad job describing empirical returns from the stock market. In other words, the extreme returns, positive or negative, are more likely to occur than expected. In particular, this issue is an important aspect when it comes to calculating the risk estimates, where a *fat tail* will underestimate the likelihood of an extreme loss.

10.9 Saving Graphics to a File

To save pictures created with **ggplot**, use function **ggsave**. It takes as input the name of the file, including path and extension (*.jpg*, *.png*, etc). If the figure object p is not explicitly set, the last generated graph will be saved. Additionally, one suggestion is to give preference to the *png* format, which is more commonly accepted for publication due to its higher printing quality. If necessary, you can set the resolution using the argument **dpi**.

Consider the following example, where we create a graph and save it to a file, called MyPrices.png, available at folder fig_ggplot:

```
library(tidyverse)

# fix seed
set.seed(40)

# select 4 stocks randomly
tickers <- sample(unique(df_sp500$ticker), 4)

p <- df_sp500 %>%
  filter(ticker %in% tickers) %>%
  ggplot(aes(x = ref.date,
             y = price.adjusted,
             color = ticker)) +
  geom_line() +
  labs(x = 'Date',
       y = 'Adjusted closing prices',
       title = 'Prices of four random stocks',
       caption = 'Data from Yahoo Finance')

# save file
my_fig_file <- 'fig_ggplot/MyPrices.png'
ggsave(filename = my_fig_file,
       plot=p,
       dpi = 600)
```

You can verify the creation of the file with function list.files:

```
print(list.files('fig_ggplot'))
```

```
R> [1] "MyPrices.png"
```

As expected, the file is available in folder `fig_ggplot`, and it is ready to be inserted into a technical report or scientific article.

10.10 Exercises

1. Download Facebook (FB) stock data with the `BatchGetSymbols` package for the past 500 days. Display a line graph of the adjusted prices over time using the `ggplot2::ggplot` function. Make sure that:

   - The x and y-axis is correctly named;
   - The plot has a title ("Prices for 1 stock"), subtitle ("Data from YYYY-MM-DD to YYYY-MM-DD") and a caption ("Beautiful solution of exercise 01, chapter 10.")

2. Download Google (GOOG), Facebook (FB) and Dropbox (DBX) stock data with `BatchGetSymbols` for the last 1500 days. Use function `ggplot` to create a single chart for all stock prices, where each ticker has a different line color. Maintain all other aspects of the plot from the previous exercise.

3. For the previous chart, add points to the lines.

4. For the same chart, separate stock prices into different panels with the `ggplot::facet_wrap` function. Also "release" the y axis for the different stocks so that each stock has its own vertical axis.

5. Modify the previous chart theme to greyscale for both the chart area and the line colors.

6. For the previous data, create the histogram of the returns of the different stocks in different panels and save the result in a file named `'histograms.png'`.

7. Use function `tidyquant::tq_exchange` to find out all tickers from the NYSE exchange. Using `BatchGetSymbols::BatchGetSymbols`, download **annual** return data for all stocks in the exchange from 2010 until the current day. After that, create the mean/variance map by plotting the average annual return against its standard deviation. Tip: Use the parallel option at `BatchGetSymbols` to speed things up. You will find many outlier returns in the raw data. Make sure the plot is visible by limiting the x and y-axis (see functions `ggplot2::xlim` and `ggplot2::ylim`)

8. Head over to the Kaggle data website[2] and choose a particular dataset for your analysis. It need not be related to economics or finance. Feel free to make a decision based on your own interests. After downloading the data, create a visual analysis of the data. Fell free to try out one or more plots of interest.

---

[2]https://www.kaggle.com/datasets

Chapter 11

Financial Econometrics with R

The modeling tools from econometrics and statistics allow the researcher to simulate stochastic processes, make predictions, and test a particular hypothesis about the data. Furthermore, empirical applications are exhaustive. Briefly, we estimate a model to learn something from the data. This model can later provide quantitative insights, which will help when it comes to the decision-making process on a large scale. The main benefit of modeling data is the gain in efficiency of analysis. With modern computers, a large batch of models can be quickly estimated and drive corporate decisions such as pricing products and targeting consumer advertising.

The variety of models used in financial econometrics is huge. It would be impossible to cover all possible models and their particularities. However, some types are used more often than others. In this chapter, we will deal with these types of models and their applications:

- Linear models (OLS)
- Generalized linear models (GLS)
- Panel data models
- Arima models (Integrated Autoregressive Moving Averages)
- Garch models (Generalized Autoregressive Conditional Heteroskedasticity).
- Markov Regime switching models

We will not present a full description of the underlying theory behind the representation, estimation, and possible tests related to each type of model. The focus of this chapter is to present the main motivation and the computational details of working with these models in R, including the packages.

While we will give quantitative context, providing examples with simulated and real data, these will not be deep. This chapter should be studied alongside the main literature of financial econometrics (Campbell et al., 1997, Brooks (2014), Hamilton (1994), Greene (2003)). As a suggestion, more dense material on using R for Econometrics is found in Kleiber and Zeileis (2008) and Hanck et al. (2019).

11.1 Linear Models (OLS)

A linear model is, without a doubt, one of the most used econometric models in R and finance. Whenever you need to estimate a linear relationship from the data, you will likely use a linear model of the OLS (*ordinary least squares*) type. Its main advantage is simplicity and speed. Since the model is estimated using a closed formula, its estimation, even for large amounts of data, is blazing fast.

In finance, the most direct and popular use of linear models is in the estimation of beta coefficients and factor models, measures of systematic risk in investments. The beta, for example, indicates the strength of the relationship of a stock with the overall market. If the stock has a high value of beta, it strongly follows the market and has a high systematic risk. Likewise, if the absolute value of beta is low, it means the stock has low sensitivity to market conditions, and its returns tend to diverge from the market.

A linear model with N explanatory variables can be represented:

$$y_t = \alpha + \beta_1 x_{1,t} + \beta_2 x_{2,t} + ... + \beta_N x_{N,t} + \epsilon_t$$

The left side of the equation, (y_t), is the dependent (or explanatory) variable. This is the vector of information we are trying to explain and create predictions. Variables y_t and $x_{i,t}$ with $i = 1..N$ are the vectors with data. In R, they are the information we use as input in the estimation function. When we estimate the model, we find the values of α and β_i that minimize the sum of squared errors. In simpler words, we find the parameters that give the highest possible accuracy when predicting real data.

11.1.1 Simulating a Linear Model

Consider the following equation:

$$y_t = 0.5 + 2x_t + \epsilon_t$$

11.1. LINEAR MODELS (OLS)

We can use R to simulate *1.000* observations for y_t. We first define x_t and the model's error, ϵ_t, as random variables from the Normal distribution with zero mean and variance equal to one. The full simulation of y_t is performed with the following code:

```r
set.seed(50)

# number of obs
n_T <- 1000

# set x as Normal (0, 1)
x <- rnorm(n_T)

# set coefficients
my_alpha <- 0.5
my_beta <- 2

# build y
y <- my_alpha + my_beta*x + rnorm(n_T)
```

Using `ggplot`, we can create a scatter plot to visualize the correlation between objects x and y.

```r
library(tidyverse)

# set temp df
temp_df <- tibble(x = x,
                  y = y)

# plot it
p <- ggplot(temp_df, aes(x = x, y = y)) +
  geom_point(size=0.5) +
  labs(title = 'Example of Correlated Data') +
  theme_bw()

print(p)
```

Example of Correlated Data

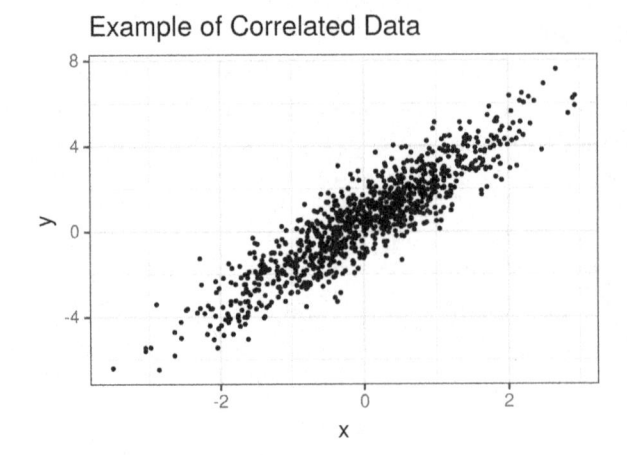

Clearly, there is a positive linear correlation; an upward straight line would be a good approximation for the relationship between x and y. We can check this result with the calculation of the linear correlation coefficient with the command `cor(temp_df$x, temp_df$y)`. Here, the correlation between y and x is 0.901, a very high value as linear correlations have a maximum value of 1.

11.1.2 Estimating a Linear Model

In R, the main function for estimating a linear model is `lm`. Let's use it to estimate a model from the previous simulated data.

```
# set df
lm_df <- tibble(x, y)

# estimate linear model
my_lm <- lm(data = lm_df, formula = y ~ x)
print(my_lm)
```

```
R> 
R> Call:
R> lm(formula = y ~ x, data = lm_df)
R> 
R> Coefficients:
R> (Intercept)            x
R>      0.5083       1.9891
```

11.1. LINEAR MODELS (OLS)

The `formula` argument defines the shape of the linear model. If we had another column, called x2, and wanted to include it in the model, we could write `formula = y ~ x1 + x2`. Notice the intercept (α) is, by default, included in the estimation. If we needed to omit the intercept, we could write `formula = y ~ 0 + x1` or `formula = y ~ -1 + x1`.

Argument `formula` allows other custom options, including interactions between the explanatory variables. Let's create another artificial dataset and look at some of these options:

```
set.seed(15)

# set simulated dataset
N <- 100
df <- tibble(x = runif(N),
             y = runif(N),
             z = runif(N),
             group = sample(LETTERS[1:3],
                            N,
                            replace = TRUE ))

# Vanilla formula
#
# example: y ~ x + z
# model: y(t) = alpha + beta(1)*x(t) + beta(2)*z(t) + error(t)
my_formula <- y ~ x + z
print(lm(data = df,
         formula = my_formula))


R>
R> Call:
R> lm(formula = my_formula, data = df)
R>
R> Coefficients:
R> (Intercept)            x            z
R>     0.44971      0.14223     -0.03781

# vannila formula with dummies
#
# example: y ~ group + x + z
# model: y(t) = alpha + beta(1)*D_1(t)+beta(2)*D_2(t) +
```

```
#                 beta(3)*x(t) + beta(4)*z(t) + error(t)
# D_i(t) - dummy for group i
my_formula <- y ~ group + x + z
print(lm(data = df,
         formula = my_formula))
```

```
R>
R> Call:
R> lm(formula = my_formula, data = df)
R>
R> Coefficients:
R> (Intercept)        groupB        groupC             x
R>    0.436513      0.003993      0.041217      0.141471
R>           z
R>   -0.042747
```

```
# Without intercept
#
# example: y ~ -1 + x + z
# model: y(t) = beta(1)*x(t) + beta(2)*z(t) + error(t)
my_formula <- y ~ -1 + x + z
print(lm(data = df,
         formula = my_formula))
```

```
R>
R> Call:
R> lm(formula = my_formula, data = df)
R>
R> Coefficients:
R>      x       z
R> 0.5183  0.3133
```

```
# Using combinations of variables
# example: y ~ x*z
# model: y(t) = alpha + beta(1)*x(t) + beta(2)*z(t) +
#               beta(3)*x(t)*z(t) + error(t)
my_formula <- y ~ x*z
print(lm(data = df,
         formula = my_formula))
```

11.1. LINEAR MODELS (OLS)

```
R>
R> Call:
R> lm(formula = my_formula, data = df)
R>
R> Coefficients:
R> (Intercept)            x            z          x:z
R>     0.39827      0.22970      0.05129     -0.15464

# Interacting variables
# example: y ~ x:group + z
# model: y(t) = alpha + beta(1)*z(t) + beta(2)*x(t)*D_1(t) +
#              beta(3)*x(t)*D_2(t) + beta(4)*x(t)*D_3(t) +
#              error(t)
# D_i(t) - dummy for group i
my_formula <- y ~ x:group + z
print(lm(data = df,
         formula = my_formula))


R>
R> Call:
R> lm(formula = my_formula, data = df)
R>
R> Coefficients:
R> (Intercept)            z     x:groupA     x:groupB
R>     0.44967     -0.03636      0.11278      0.16477
R>     x:groupC
R>     0.14108
```

The different options in the `formula` input allow a diversified range of linear models. Using common mathematical operations, such as `log(x)`, is also possible. More details about advanced uses of `formula` input is available in the manual[1].

Moreover, when it comes to the output of `lm`, then it is important that you understand that it is an object similar to a `list`. Therefore, its elements can be accessed using the $ operator. Let's print all available names:

```
# print names in model
print(names(my_lm))
```

---

[1] https://stat.ethz.ch/R-manual/R-devel/library/stats/html/formula.html

```
R>  [1] "coefficients"   "residuals"      "effects"
R>  [4] "rank"           "fitted.values"  "assign"
R>  [7] "qr"             "df.residual"    "xlevels"
R> [10] "call"           "terms"          "model"
```

As you can see, there is a slot called coefficients. Let's check its contents.

```
print(my_lm$coefficients)
```

```
R> (Intercept)           x
R>   0.5083045    1.9890616
```

The result is a simple atomic vector that increases in length, according to the number of explanatory variables in the model.

In our example of using lm with simulated data, the estimated coefficients are close to the actual values of 0.5 and 2. Remember, in the previous code, we set these values as my_alpha <- 0.5 and my_beta <- 2.

Experienced researchers have probably noted that, from the econometric viewpoint, using function print in the output of lm results in little information. Besides the values of the coefficients, many other aspects of a linear model must be analyzed, such as goodness of fit. In R, to obtain more information about the model that we estimated previously. Likewise, we use the function summary. See next.

```
print(summary(my_lm))
```

```
R>
R> Call:
R> lm(formula = y ~ x, data = lm_df)
R>
R> Residuals:
R>     Min      1Q  Median      3Q     Max
R> -3.0444 -0.6906 -0.0244  0.6807  3.2892
R>
R> Coefficients:
R>             Estimate Std. Error t value Pr(>|t|)
R> (Intercept)  0.50830    0.03107   16.36   <2e-16 ***
R> x            1.98906    0.03031   65.61   <2e-16 ***
R> ---
```

11.1. LINEAR MODELS (OLS)

```
R> Signif. codes:
R> 0 '***' 0.001 '**' 0.01 '*' 0.05 '.' 0.1 ' ' 1
R>
R> Residual standard error: 0.9824 on 998 degrees of freedom
R> Multiple R-squared:  0.8118, Adjusted R-squared:  0.8116
R> F-statistic:  4305 on 1 and 998 DF,  p-value: < 2.2e-16
```

The estimated coefficients have high T values, and the model has an outstanding fit of the data, with an adjusted R^2 value of 0.8116. This positive result is not surprising. The data were simulated in a linear process, and the correlation was introduced artificially.

Additional information is available in the resulting object from `summary`. Let's look at the names of the output:

```
my_summary <- summary(my_lm)
print(names(my_summary))
```

```
R>  [1] "call"          "terms"         "residuals"
R>  [4] "coefficients"  "aliased"       "sigma"
R>  [7] "df"            "r.squared"     "adj.r.squared"
R> [10] "fstatistic"    "cov.unscaled"
```

Each element contains information that can be reported using an estimation table. More, we could export the values of coefficients, T statistics, and others to a spreadsheet tool and create a custom table to report the results. This, however, is not recommended. In section 12.2, we will discuss the best ways of reporting a model using specialized packages. You'll be able to export your model result to Word, LaTeX or HTML.

Now, let's move to an example with real data. For that, we will estimate the beta coefficient of a randomly selected stock. The beta specification, also called market model, is given by:

$$R_t = \alpha + \beta R_{M,t} + \epsilon_t$$

First, let's load the SP500 dataset.

```
library(tidyverse)

# load stock data
```

```r
my_f <- afedR::afedR_get_data_file('SP500-Stocks-WithRet.rds')
my_df <- read_rds(my_f)

# select rnd asset and filter data
set.seed(10)

my_asset <- sample(my_df$ticker,1)
my_df_asset <- my_df[my_df$ticker == my_asset, ]

# load SP500 data
df_sp500 <- read.csv(file = 'data/SP500.csv',
                     colClasses = c('Date','numeric'))

# calculate return
calc_ret <- function(P) {
  N <- length(P)
  ret <- c(NA, P[2:N]/P[1:(N-1)] -1)
}

df_sp500$ret <- calc_ret(df_sp500$price)

# print number of rows in datasets
print(nrow(my_df_asset))
```

R> [1] 1761

```r
print(nrow(df_sp500))
```

R> [1] 2264

You can see the number of rows of the dataset for stock SWKS doesn't match the rows of the SP500 index. While the stock dataset has 1761 rows, the SP500 date has 2264. In other words, the dates of the different `dataframes` are not synchronized. So, the first step is to add a column in `my_df_asset` with the returns of the market index. For that, we use the function `match` to find the indices that synchronize the dates.

```r
# find location of dates in df_sp500
idx <- match(my_df_asset$ref.date, df_sp500$ref.date)
```

11.1. LINEAR MODELS (OLS)

```r
# create column in my_df with sp500 returns
my_df_asset$ret_sp500 <- df_sp500$ret[idx]
```

As a start, let's create a scatter plot with the returns of the stock and the market index, adding a linear trend.

```r
library(ggplot2)

p <- ggplot(data = my_df_asset,
            aes(x=ret_sp500, y=ret)) +
  geom_point(size = 0.5) +
  geom_smooth(method = 'lm') +
  labs(x = 'SP500 Returns',
       y = paste0(my_asset, ' Returns'),
       title = paste0(my_asset, ' and ', ' the SP500' ),
       caption = 'Data from Yahoo Finance') +
  theme_bw()

print(p)
```

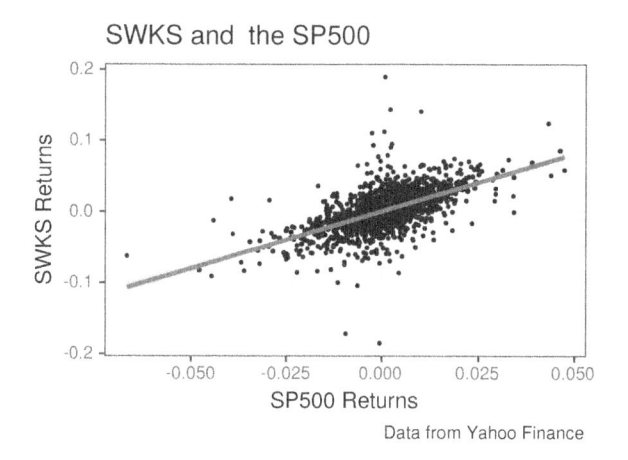

SWKS and the SP500

The figure shows a clear linear tendency; the returns from the market index are a good predictor of the returns of the stock. Now, let's estimate the linear model.

```r
# estimate beta model
my_beta_model <- lm(data = my_df_asset,
                    formula = ret ~ ret_sp500)
```

```
# print it
print(summary(my_beta_model))
```

```
R>
R> Call:
R> lm(formula = ret ~ ret_sp500, data = my_df_asset)
R>
R> Residuals:
R>      Min       1Q    Median       3Q      Max
R> -0.184605 -0.010994 -0.000278  0.010956  0.187526
R>
R> Coefficients:
R>              Estimate Std. Error t value Pr(>|t|)
R> (Intercept) 0.0006054  0.0005275   1.148    0.251
R> ret_sp500   1.6117910  0.0538714  29.919   <2e-16 ***
R> ---
R> Signif. codes:
R> 0 '***' 0.001 '**' 0.01 '*' 0.05 '.' 0.1 ' ' 1
R>
R> Residual standard error: 0.02211 on 1759 degrees of freedom
R> Multiple R-squared:  0.3373, Adjusted R-squared:  0.3369
R> F-statistic: 895.2 on 1 and 1759 DF,  p-value: < 2.2e-16
```

The output shows that stock SWKS has a beta equal to 1.61. This means this is an aggressive stock with high sensitivity to market movements.

11.1.3 Statistical Inference in Linear Models

After estimating a model with function lm, the next step is to test some hypotheses about the coefficients. The F-test verifies the most basic condition for a model to justify its existence – all coefficients, excluding the intercept, are equal to zero. When function summary is applied to an lm output, the F-test is provided by default in the last line of the text output. The null hypothesis of the test is that all slopes are equal to zero. Let's try it:

```
n_T <- 100
df <- data.frame(y = runif(n_T),
                 x_1 = runif(n_T),
                 x_2 = runif(n_T))
```

11.1. LINEAR MODELS (OLS)

```
my_lm <- lm(data = df,
            formula = y ~ x_1 + x_2)

print(summary(my_lm))


R>
R> Call:
R> lm(formula = y ~ x_1 + x_2, data = df)
R>
R> Residuals:
R>      Min       1Q   Median       3Q      Max
R> -0.43249 -0.21260 -0.01412  0.18636  0.51835
R>
R> Coefficients:
R>             Estimate Std. Error t value Pr(>|t|)
R> (Intercept)  0.43888    0.07562   5.804 8.16e-08 ***
R> x_1         -0.01240    0.09427  -0.132    0.896
R> x_2          0.01549    0.08765   0.177    0.860
R> ---
R> Signif. codes:
R> 0 '***' 0.001 '**' 0.01 '*' 0.05 '.' 0.1 ' ' 1
R>
R> Residual standard error: 0.2645 on 97 degrees of freedom
R> Multiple R-squared:  0.0005405, Adjusted R-squared:  -0.02007
R> F-statistic: 0.02623 on 2 and 97 DF,  p-value: 0.9741
```

In this example, the F statistic is 0.0262284. The associated p-value is higher than 10%, indicating strong statistical evidence, which is in line with the null hypothesis. We failed to reject the hypothesis that the parameters attached to x_1 and x_2 are equal to zero. The association between the explained variable and these vectors is almost null. For example, for the rejection of the null hypothesis of the F test, see the estimation of a model with artificial data in section 11.1.2.

Another type of test automatically executed by the lm and summary function is the T test. While the F statistics test the joint hypothesis that **all** coefficients are zero, the T statistic tests it for **individual** parameters. It verifies the hypothesis that a specific parameter is equal to zero. It is not accidental that T tests are very common in financial and economic research. It allows testing the significance of a particular effect in the data. For example, if you wanted to study the relationship between the stock prices of two companies, you could regress their returns on each other and use the T test of the beta coefficient to checker whether the hypothesis of the numerical association is corroborated by the data or not.

In the practice of research, it is likely that both tests, T and F, will suffice in most cases. They will give you information about the statistical relationships in the data. However, you can also test a custom hypothesis, such as the sum or product of parameters equal to a particular value, using the `car` (Fox and Weisberg, 2011) package. Additionally, the tested hypotheses are usually provided from a theoretical model or analysis. For example, let's assume you want to study the performance of a forecasting algorithm. We can test the performance of the forecasts by estimating a linear model with the actual values of the variable as dependent and the forecasts as independent (explanatory). If the forecasting model works well, the intercept from the resulting model should be zero, and the slope should be equal to one. We can jointly test this hypothesis and calculate a p-value associated with it.

As a simple example, let's test a linear hypothesis for a simulated model. Here, we will create artificial data and test the formal hypothesis that the estimated coefficients are equal to the actual values provided in the simulation.

```
set.seed(10)

# number of time periods
n_T <- 1000

# set parameters
my_intercept <- 0.5
my_beta <- 1.5

# simulate
x <- rnorm(n_T)
y <- my_intercept + my_beta*x + rnorm(n_T)

# set df
df <- tibble(y, x)

# estimate model
my_lm <- lm(data = df,
            formula = y ~ x )
```

After the estimation of the model, we use the function `LinearHypothesis` from package `car` (Fox and Weisberg, 2011) to implement our formal test.

11.1. LINEAR MODELS (OLS)

Before using it, we need to understand its arguments. The first input, model, is the estimated model from the previous chunk. Inputs hypothesis.matrix and RHS determine the linear hypothesis of the test in a matrix format. The object in hypothesis.matrix will be multiplied in matrix notation by a vertical vector of the coefficients from the model. The RHS (right-hand side) determines the hypothesized result from this calculation. In our case, the resulting matrix operation is:

$$\underbrace{\begin{bmatrix} 1 & 0 \\ 0 & 1 \end{bmatrix}}_{hypothesis.matrix} \begin{bmatrix} \alpha \\ \beta \end{bmatrix} = \underbrace{\begin{bmatrix} 0.5 \\ 1.5 \end{bmatrix}}_{rhs}$$

With this matrix operation, we test the joint hypothesis that the intercept is equal to 0.5 and the slope equals 1.5. Notice that using matrices gives flexibility to the user. We could test many other linear hypotheses by changing the shape of hypothesis.matrix and RHS. The actual R code that implements the test is given next.

```
library(car)

# set test matrix
test_matrix <- matrix(c(my_intercept,   # alpha test value
                        my_beta))       # beta test value

# hypothesis matrix
hyp_mat <- matrix(c(1,0,
                    0,1),nrow = 2)

# do test
my_waldtest <- linearHypothesis(my_lm,
                                hypothesis.matrix = hyp_mat,
                                rhs = test_matrix)

# print result
print(my_waldtest)
```

```
R> Linear hypothesis test
R>
R> Hypothesis:
R> (Intercept) = 0.5
R> x = 1.5
R>
```

```
R> Model 1: restricted model
R> Model 2: y ~ x
R>
R>   Res.Df     RSS Df Sum of Sq      F Pr(>F)
R> 1   1000  1089.1
R> 2    998  1086.8  2     2.3766 1.0912 0.3362
```

As we can see, the test fails to reject the null hypothesis. This means our simulation worked. The parameters are correctly estimated, as expected.

Another family of tests commonly applied to linear models is related to its assumptions. Every linear model of type OLS assumes several conditions to its errors, including: 1) independence, 2) homoscedasticity (constant variance), and 3) adherence to the Normal distribution. If these assumptions are not true, the model may be inefficient or biased, meaning some modification or use of robust estimates is required. More details about why these assumptions must hold and possible workarounds are found in any comprehensive Econometric textbook, such as Maddala (2001), Greene (2003) and Brooks (2014).

In R, we can use the package `lmtest` (Zeileis and Hothorn, 2002) to test for independence with the Breush-Godfrey and Durbin Watson test. The Shapiro-Wilk test for normality is available in package `stats`. Next, we provide an example of usage for the previously estimated model with random data.

```
library(lmtest)

# Breush Pagan test 1 - Serial correlation
# Null Hypothesis: No serial correlation in residual
print(bgtest(my_lm, order = 5))

# Breush Pagan test 2 - Homocesdasticity of residuals
# Null Hypothesis: homocesdasticity
#                  (constant variance of residuals)
print(ncvTest(my_lm))

# Durbin Watson test - Serial correlation
# Null Hypothesis: No serial correlation in residual
print(dwtest(my_lm))

# Shapiro test  - Normality
# Null Hypothesis: Data is normally distributed
print(shapiro.test(my_lm$residuals))
```

11.1. LINEAR MODELS (OLS)

```
R> 
R> 	Breusch-Godfrey test for serial correlation of
R> 	order up to 5
R> 
R> data:  my_lm
R> LM test = 4.2628, df = 5, p-value = 0.5122
R> 
R> Non-constant Variance Score Test
R> Variance formula: ~ fitted.values
R> Chisquare = 1.54328, Df = 1, p = 0.21413
R> 
R>  Durbin-Watson test
R> 
R> data:  my_lm
R> DW = 2.092, p-value = 0.9271
R> alternative hypothesis: true autocorrelation is greater than 0
R> 
R> 
R>  Shapiro-Wilk normality test
R> 
R> data:  my_lm$residuals
R> W = 0.99803, p-value = 0.2964
```

As expected, the model with artificial data passed all tests.

Another interesting approach for validating linear models is to use the `gvlma` (Pena and Slate, 2014) package. It provides a top-level function that can execute all sorts of tests in linear models, including the ones described before. The main advantage is that it outputs all tests in a single function call. Let's try it:

```
library(gvlma)

# global validation of model
gvmodel <- gvlma(my_lm)

# print result
summary(gvmodel)
```

```
R>
```

```
R> Call:
R> lm(formula = y ~ x, data = df)
R>
R> Residuals:
R>     Min      1Q  Median      3Q     Max
R> -3.2703 -0.6898  0.0063  0.7346  3.8266
R>
R> Coefficients:
R>             Estimate Std. Error t value Pr(>|t|)
R> (Intercept)  0.51510    0.03300   15.61   <2e-16 ***
R> x            1.54658    0.03329   46.46   <2e-16 ***
R> ---
R> Signif. codes:
R> 0 '***' 0.001 '**' 0.01 '*' 0.05 '.' 0.1 ' ' 1
R>
R> Residual standard error: 1.044 on 998 degrees of freedom
R> Multiple R-squared:  0.6838, Adjusted R-squared:  0.6835
R> F-statistic:  2159 on 1 and 998 DF,  p-value: < 2.2e-16
R>
R>
R> ASSESSMENT OF THE LINEAR MODEL ASSUMPTIONS
R> USING THE GLOBAL TEST ON 4 DEGREES-OF-FREEDOM:
R> Level of Significance =  0.05
R>
R> Call:
R>   gvlma(x = my_lm)
R>
R>                     Value p-value
R> Global Stat        3.6404  0.4569
R> Skewness           1.7814  0.1820
R> Kurtosis           0.1738  0.6767
R> Link Function      0.6628  0.4156
R> Heteroscedasticity 1.0224  0.3119
R>                                      Decision
R> Global Stat        Assumptions acceptable.
R> Skewness           Assumptions acceptable.
R> Kurtosis           Assumptions acceptable.
R> Link Function      Assumptions acceptable.
R> Heteroscedasticity Assumptions acceptable.
```

The output of `gvlma` shows several tests performed in the model. The result is also positive, as the decision from the model is that the OLS assumptions

11.2 Generalized Linear Models (GLM)

The generalized linear model (GLM) is a flexible alternative to a linear model. It allows the user to change the distribution of the error and the link function, a systematic way that quantifies how the explained variable will be affected by the response variable. GLM models are best suited when the OLS assumptions, such as normality of residuals, don't hold. For example, suppose you want to understand the factors – age, income and so on – that explain the default, a missing payment, in personal debt. The explained variable is binary, one for default and zero for no default. We cannot use the OLS model in this problem as the distribution assumption of Normality does not hold. For that, we have a GLM model.

We can write a general univariate GLM specification as:

$$E(y_t) = g\left(\alpha + \sum_{i=1}^{N} \beta_i x_{i,t}\right)$$

The main difference of a GLM model and a OLS model is the use of a link function $g()$ and a custom distribution assumption for the error term. Function $g()$ can take many shapes. For example, if we are modelling a binary variable, we can use $g()$ as the *logit* function:

$$g(x) = \frac{\exp(x)}{1 + \exp(x)}$$

Did you notice that function $g()$ ensures any value of x will result in a number between 0 and 1 in this case? Consequently, the response of the explained variable to the explanatory will be nonlinear.

11.2.1 Simulating a GLM Model

As an example, let's simulate the following GLM model, where the response vector y_t is a Bernoulli variable that takes value 1 with probability p_t. The probabilities are calculated from the non linear transformation of x_t:

$$p_t = \frac{\exp(2 + 5x_t)}{1 + \exp(2 + 5x_t)}$$

In R, we use the following code to build the response vector.

```
set.seed(15)

# set number of obs
n_T <- 500

# set x
x = rnorm(n_T)

my_alpha <- 2
my_beta <- 5

# set probabilities
z = my_alpha + my_beta*x
p = exp(z)/(1+exp(z))

# set response variable
y = rbinom(n = n_T,
           size = 1,
           prob = p)
```

Function **rbinom** creates a vector of 1s and 0s, based on the probabilities of input **prob**. Let's look at its content.

```
summary(y)
```

```
R>    Min. 1st Qu. Median  Mean 3rd Qu.  Max.
R>    0.00    0.00   1.00  0.67    1.00  1.00
```

Object y contains zeros and ones, as expected.

11.2.2 Estimating a GLM Model

In R, the estimation of GLM models is accomplished with function **stats::glm**. It works similarly to **lm** but contains several extra arguments

11.2. GENERALIZED LINEAR MODELS (GLM)

that control the details of the models, such as the type of link function and distributing the residuals.

Let's use the previously simulated data to estimate a *logit* model:

```
# estimate GLM
df <- tibble(x, y)
my_family <- binomial(link = "logit")
my_glm <- glm(data = df,
              formula = y ~ x ,
              family = my_family)

# print it with summary
print(summary(my_glm))
```

```
R>
R> Call:
R> glm(formula = y ~ x, family = my_family, data = df)
R>
R> Deviance Residuals:
R>     Min       1Q    Median       3Q      Max
R> -2.99392  -0.13689   0.04087   0.23250  2.91383
R>
R> Coefficients:
R>              Estimate Std. Error z value Pr(>|z|)
R> (Intercept)   2.1488     0.2622   8.197 2.47e-16 ***
R> x             4.9050     0.5110   9.598  < 2e-16 ***
R> ---
R> Signif. codes:
R> 0 '***' 0.001 '**' 0.01 '*' 0.05 '.' 0.1 ' ' 1
R>
R> (Dispersion parameter for binomial family taken to be 1)
R>
R>     Null deviance: 634.18  on 499  degrees of freedom
R> Residual deviance: 214.14  on 498  degrees of freedom
R> AIC: 218.14
R>
R> Number of Fisher Scoring iterations: 7
```

The estimated coefficients are close to what we've set in `my_alpha` and `my_beta`. As expected, the model has a good fitness of the data, with both parameters being statistically significant at 1%.

Function `glm` offers many options for setting a customized model. From the help files, we have these alternatives for the distribution and link function and their corresponding inputs:

Family	Default Link Function
binomial	link = "logit"
gaussian	link = "identity"
Gamma	link = "inverse"
inverse.gaussian	link = "1/mu^2"
poisson	link = "log"
quasi	link = "identity", variance = "constant"
quasibinomial	link = "logit"
quasipoisson	link = "log"

The first step in using a GLM model is to identify the distribution and link function that best suits your data. After that, you can use the previous table to set the input of function `glm`.

As an example, with real data, we'll use a credit card dataset from Kaggle[2] to model credit risk. First, let's import the original series and have a look at its content.

```
library(tidyverse)

# read default data
my_f <- afedR::afedR_get_data_file('UCI_Credit_Card.csv')
df_default <- read_csv(my_f,
                       col_types = cols())

glimpse(df_default)
```

```
R> Observations: 30,000
R> Variables: 25
R> $ ID              <dbl> 1, 2, 3, 4, 5, ...
R> $ LIMIT_BAL       <dbl> 20000, 120000, ...
R> $ SEX             <dbl> 2, 2, 2, 2, 1, ...
R> $ EDUCATION       <dbl> 2, 2, 2, 2, 2, ...
R> $ MARRIAGE        <dbl> 1, 2, 2, 1, 1, ...
R> $ AGE             <dbl> 24, 26, 34, 37,...
R> $ PAY_0           <dbl> 2, -1, 0, 0, -1...
R> $ PAY_2           <dbl> 2, 2, 0, 0, 0, ...
R> $ PAY_3           <dbl> -1, 0, 0, 0, -1...
```

---

[2]https://www.kaggle.com/uciml/default-of-credit-card-clients-dataset

11.2. GENERALIZED LINEAR MODELS (GLM)

```
R> $ PAY_4                   <dbl> -1, 0, 0, 0, 0,...
R> $ PAY_5                   <dbl> -2, 0, 0, 0, 0,...
R> $ PAY_6                   <dbl> -2, 2, 0, 0, 0,...
R> $ BILL_AMT1               <dbl> 3913, 2682, 292...
R> $ BILL_AMT2               <dbl> 3102, 1725, 140...
R> $ BILL_AMT3               <dbl> 689, 2682, 1355...
R> $ BILL_AMT4               <dbl> 0, 3272, 14331,...
R> $ BILL_AMT5               <dbl> 0, 3455, 14948,...
R> $ BILL_AMT6               <dbl> 0, 3261, 15549,...
R> $ PAY_AMT1                <dbl> 0, 0, 1518, 200...
R> $ PAY_AMT2                <dbl> 689, 1000, 1500...
R> $ PAY_AMT3                <dbl> 0, 1000, 1000, ...
R> $ PAY_AMT4                <dbl> 0, 1000, 1000, ...
R> $ PAY_AMT5                <dbl> 0, 0, 1000, 106...
R> $ PAY_AMT6                <dbl> 0, 2000, 5000, ...
R> $ default.payment.next.month <dbl> 1, 1, 0, 0, 0, ...
```

This is a comprehensive dataset with several pieces of information about the clients, including; sex, marital status, education, transactions and their credit history — more detailed information about each column found in Kaggle. For now, let's simplify the analysis and focus on four columns: sex, education, marriage and age. For that, we'll also need to decode the values in some columns. We can find such information from the website.

```
library(tidyverse)

# read credit card data
# source:
# www.kaggle.com/uciml/default-of-credit-card-clients-dataset
# COLUMNS: GENDER: (1 = male; 2 = female).
#          EDUCATION: 1 = graduate school;
#                     2 = university;
#                     3 = high school;
#                     4 = others.
#          MARRIAGE: 1 = married;
#                    2 = single;
#                    3 = others
df_default <- df_default %>%
  mutate(default = (default.payment.next.month == 1),
         D_male_gender = (SEX == 1),
         age = AGE,
         educ = dplyr::recode(as.character(EDUCATION),
```

```
                              '1' = 'Grad',
                              '2' = 'University',
                              '3' = 'High School',
                              '4' = 'Others',
                              '5' = 'Unknown',
                              '6' = 'Unknown'),
         D_marriage = (MARRIAGE == 1)) %>%
  select(default, D_male_gender, age, educ, D_marriage)

glimpse(df_default)


R> Observations: 30,000
R> Variables: 5
R> $ default       <lgl> TRUE, TRUE, FALSE, FALSE, FA...
R> $ D_male_gender <lgl> FALSE, FALSE, FALSE, FALSE, ...
R> $ age           <dbl> 24, 26, 34, 37, 57, 37, 29, ...
R> $ educ          <chr> "University", "University", ...
R> $ D_marriage    <lgl> TRUE, FALSE, FALSE, TRUE, TR...
```

Much better! Now we only have the columns of interest, with more appealing names and content. Let's proceed to the estimation of the glm model.

```
# estimate glm model
glm_credit <- glm(data=df_default,
                  formula = default ~ D_male_gender + age +
                                      educ + D_marriage,
                  family = binomial(link = "logit"))

# show output
summary(glm_credit)


R>
R> Call:
R> glm(formula = default ~ D_male_gender + age + educ + D_marriage,
R>     family = binomial(link = "logit"), data = df_default)
R>
R> Deviance Residuals:
R>     Min       1Q   Median       3Q      Max
R> -0.8362  -0.7338  -0.6891  -0.6135   2.4413
R>
```

11.2. GENERALIZED LINEAR MODELS (GLM)

```
R> Coefficients:
R>                    Estimate Std. Error z value
R> (Intercept)      -12.632131  86.643961  -0.146
R> D_male_genderTRUE  0.208046   0.028503   7.299
R> age               -0.002406   0.001736  -1.386
R> educGrad          11.144137  86.643942   0.129
R> educHigh School   11.475660  86.643944   0.132
R> educOthers         9.774018  86.644813   0.113
R> educUniversity   11.401911  86.643941   0.132
R> educUnknown      10.107622  86.644179   0.117
R> D_marriageTRUE     0.130295   0.031604   4.123
R>                   Pr(>|z|)
R> (Intercept)         0.884
R> D_male_genderTRUE 2.90e-13 ***
R> age                 0.166
R> educGrad            0.898
R> educHigh School     0.895
R> educOthers          0.910
R> educUniversity      0.895
R> educUnknown         0.907
R> D_marriageTRUE    3.74e-05 ***
R> ---
R> Signif. codes:
R> 0 '***' 0.001 '**' 0.01 '*' 0.05 '.' 0.1 ' ' 1
R>
R> (Dispersion parameter for binomial family taken to be 1)
R>
R>     Null deviance: 31705  on 29999  degrees of freedom
R> Residual deviance: 31458  on 29991  degrees of freedom
R> AIC: 31476
R>
R> Number of Fisher Scoring iterations: 11
```

We find that the only coefficients with statistical significance at 5% is `D_male_gender` and `D_marriage`. Its positive values imply that married male applicants are more likely to default on a credit card payment. It is also interesting to see that formal education, columns `educ*`, seems to have no effect on default rates.

11.3 Panel Data Models

Panel data models are advised when the modeled data is multidimensional, covering information about individuals or companies that spawn over time. A dataset with financial information about several companies for many years is a classic case of panel data. We have a column identifying the company, another column for the time, and one or more columns identifying the financial indicators. In a cross-section of time, we have several companies and several financial ratios. The dataset can be further categorized as balanced, where all companies have information on all dates, and unbalanced, where not all companies have data for all dates.

The main motivation to use panel data models is to allow common effects within the groups. If a standard OLS estimation is used for each group, such as companies, we implicitly assume the models are independent. If the assumption of independence is not true, our econometric analysis is jeopardized by a possible bias. Using panel data models allows for more flexible representations. Some parameters can be individual to each group, while others are shared. Using panel data models requires careful thought about how the model is identified. Many statistical tests are available for this purpose.

We can represent the simplest case of a panel data model as:

$$y_{i,t} = \alpha_i + \beta x_{i,t} + \epsilon_{i,t}$$

Notice we now use index i in the dependent and independent variables. This index controls for the groups, such as different companies. In our specific model, all i cases have different intercepts but share the same beta. Depending on the assumptions about the intercept, the previous equation can represent a panel data model of type *fixed* or *random effects* . There are many other ways to customize a panel data model and set dynamic effects, such as lagged terms. You can find more details in Hsiao (2014).

11.3.1 Simulating Panel Data Models

Let's simulate a balanced panel data with fixed effects for twelve different firms and five time periods. This is a classic case of panel data, with large N (number of companies) and small T (number of time periods). Each company will have an explanatory variable, called x, that varies over different dates. The following code uses matrix operations to simulate all cases. Notice the many uses of the `sapply` function. After creating the multivariate data, we stack it in single vectors and save it in a `dataframe`.

11.3. PANEL DATA MODELS

```
set.seed(25)

# number of obs for each case
n_T <- 5

# set number of groups
N <- 12

# set possible cases
possible_cases <- LETTERS[1:N]

# set parameters
my_alphas <- seq(-10, 10,
                 length.out = N)
my_beta <- 1.5

# set indep var (x) and dates
indep_var <- sapply(rep(n_T,N), rnorm)
my_dates <- Sys.Date() + 1:n_T

# create response matrix (y)
response_matrix <- matrix(rep(my_alphas,
                              n_T),
                          nrow = n_T,
                          byrow = TRUE) +
  indep_var*my_beta + sapply(rep(n_T,N),rnorm, sd = 0.25)

# set df
sim_df <- tibble(firm = as.character(sapply(possible_cases,
                                            rep,
                                            times=n_T )),
                 dates = rep(my_dates, times=N),
                 y = as.numeric(response_matrix),
                 x = as.numeric(indep_var),
                 stringsAsFactors = FALSE)

# print result
glimpse(sim_df)

R> Observations: 60
R> Variables: 5
R> $ firm              <chr> "A", "A", "A", "A", "A", ...
```

```
R> $ dates            <date> 2020-02-09, 2020-02-10, ...
R> $ y                <dbl> -10.676541, -11.550739, -...
R> $ x                <dbl> -0.21183360, -1.04159113,...
R> $ stringsAsFactors <lgl> FALSE, FALSE, FALSE, FALS...
```

The result is a `dataframe` object with 60 rows and 5 columns. We can look at the scatter plot of x and y for each firm using `ggplot2`:

```
library(ggplot2)

p <- ggplot(sim_df, aes(x = x,
                        y = y)) +
  geom_point() + geom_line() +
  facet_wrap(~ firm) +
  labs(title = 'Simulated Panel Data') +
  theme_bw()

print(p)
```

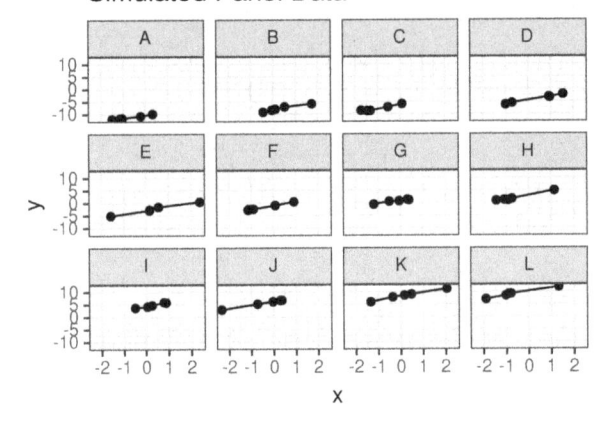

The figure shows the strong linear relationship shared between x and y in the different groups. The slope (*beta*) in all groups is the same. However, do notice that the intercept (*alpha*) changes for each firm. If we estimated a linear model from this data, we would have to allow a different intercept for each group, which is exactly what a standard panel model does.

11.3.2 Estimating Panel Data Models

With the artificial data simulated in the previous step, let's estimate the model using package `plm` (Croissant and Millo, 2008). This is a great package

11.3. PANEL DATA MODELS

that offers a comprehensive set of tools in testing and estimating panel data models. The interface of function `plm` is similar to `lm`. However, we need to define the panel data model in the argument `model` and the names of columns that define the groups and time reference in the input `index`.

```
library(plm)

# estimate panel data model with fixed effects
my_pdm <- plm(data = sim_df,
              formula = y ~ x,
              model = 'within',
              index = c('firm','dates'))

# print coeficient
print(coef(my_pdm))
```

```
R>        x
R> 1.479366
```

As expected, the slope parameter was correctly retrieved from the data, with a small difference from the actual value defined in `my_beta`. Be aware that the different intercepts were not printed in the `summary` output. We can retrieve them using function `fixef`:

```
print(fixef(my_pdm))
```

```
R>           A           B           C           D
R> -10.0934047  -8.2435523  -6.3253831  -4.6552624
R>           E           F           G           H
R>  -2.8087407  -0.9794636   0.9609360   2.7568233
R>           I           J           K           L
R>   4.4134081   6.2113577   8.1880249  10.0337231
```

Again, the simulated intercept values are close to the ones obtained from the estimation.

As an example with real data, let's use the dataset from Grunfeld (1958). This research paper studied the components of corporate investments using data for ten companies for twenty years. The data is available with package `plm`, and we can load it with function `data`. Let's import it and take a look at its content.

```
library(plm)

# data from Grunfeld
data("Grunfeld")

# print it
glimpse(Grunfeld)


R> Observations: 200
R> Variables: 5
R> $ firm    <int> 1, 1, 1, 1, 1, 1, 1, 1, 1, 1, 1, 1...
R> $ year    <int> 1935, 1936, 1937, 1938, 1939, 1940...
R> $ inv     <dbl> 317.6, 391.8, 410.6, 257.7, 330.8,...
R> $ value   <dbl> 3078.5, 4661.7, 5387.1, 2792.2, 43...
R> $ capital <dbl> 2.8, 52.6, 156.9, 209.2, 203.4, 20...
```

The `Grunfeld` dataset contains company information about gross investment, market value, and capital (plant and equipment). The `dataframe` is in the long format and ready to be used. In the model, column `inv` is set as the dependent variable. Columns `firm` and `year` are the index of panel data estimation. The remaining columns, `value` and `capital`, are explanatory variables. You can find more details about the Grunfeld data, including information about different versions of the dataset and its historical usage, in Kleiber and Zeileis (2010).

A note here is important; given its high number of time periods in proportion to the number of firms, the Grunfeld data is best suited for a more advanced econometric model of type SUR (seemly unrelated regression). Next, for educational purposes of learning R, we will explore other types of panel models with this dataset. See Greene (2003) for more details.

First, let's explore the raw data by estimating a different OLS model for each firm. This is also called the pooled model. We can use the function `by` with a custom function for this purpose (see chapter 8 for details).

```
est_lm <- function(df) {
  # Estimates a linear model from Grunfeld data
  #
  # Args:
  #   df - dataframe from Grunfeld
  #
  # Returns:
```

11.3. PANEL DATA MODELS

```
#    lm object

my_model <- lm(data = df,
               formula = inv ~ value + capital)

return(my_model)
}

# estimate model for each firm
my_l <- by(Grunfeld,
           INDICES = Grunfeld$firm,
           FUN = est_lm)

# print result
my_coefs <- sapply(my_l, coef)
print(my_coefs)
```

```
R>                         1            2           3
R> (Intercept) -149.7824533 -49.1983219 -9.95630645
R> value          0.1192808   0.1748560  0.02655119
R> capital        0.3714448   0.3896419  0.15169387
R>                         4            5           6
R> (Intercept)  -6.18996051 22.707116014 -8.68554338
R> value         0.07794782  0.162377704  0.13145484
R> capital       0.31571819  0.003101737  0.08537427
R>                         7            8           9
R> (Intercept)  -4.4995344  -0.50939018 -7.72283708
R> value         0.0875272   0.05289413  0.07538794
R> capital       0.1237814   0.09240649  0.08210356
R>                        10
R> (Intercept) 0.161518567
R> value       0.004573432
R> capital     0.437369190
```

The results show a great discrepancy between the coefficients obtained for each firm. This is especially true for the intercept value. It ranges from -149.8 to 22.71. This result shows evidence it might be more realistic to assume different coefficients for the different firms. We can formally test this hypothesis with a function `polltest` from `plm`. It tests the null hypothesis that all coefficients are the same across the cases, against the alternative hypothesis they are not. Let's use it.

```
# test if all coef are the same across firms
my_pooltest <- pooltest(inv ~ value + capital,
                        data = Grunfeld,
                        model = "pooling")

# print result
print(my_pooltest)
```

```
R>
R>  F statistic
R>
R> data:  inv ~ value + capital
R> F = 27.749, df1 = 27, df2 = 170, p-value <
R> 2.2e-16
R> alternative hypothesis: unstability
```

The high F test and small p-value suggest the rejection of the null hypothesis. The evidence that the same coefficients can be applied to all firms is minimal. The motivation for using panel data models for the Grunfeld dataset is justified.

Before estimating the model, we need to understand which kind of panel data model is best suited for the data. For simplicity, let's assume only two possible choices, fixed or random effects. In both models, each group has unobserved individual effects but share the same impact (beta) of the observed explanatory variables. The difference between the models is how the unobserved individual effect is perceived. Individual effects are correlated to the explanatory variables in the fixed-effect model, while in the random effects, they are random variables. The correct estimation of the model and econometric analysis will change according to the underlying correlation structure. See Greene (2003) for more technical details about the difference between fixed and random effects models.

We can test the model specification using the `plm` package. Likewise, the `phtest` function executes the Hausman test (Hausman, 1978), a statistical procedure that tests the null hypothesis that the best model is the random effects and not the fixed effect. Let's try it for our data.

```
# set options for Hausman test
my_formula <- inv ~ value + capital
my_index <- c('firm','year')
```

11.3. PANEL DATA MODELS

```
# do Hausman test
my_hausman_test <- phtest(x = my_formula,
                          data = Grunfeld,
                          model = c('within', 'random'),
                          index = my_index)

# print result
print(my_hausman_test)
```

```
R>
R>   Hausman Test
R>
R> data:  my_formula
R> chisq = 2.3304, df = 2, p-value = 0.3119
R> alternative hypothesis: one model is inconsistent
```

The p-value of 31.19% is higher than an acceptable threshold of 10%. Therefore, we fail to reject the null hypothesis that the most efficient panel data model is the random effects. We have strong statistical evidence that a random effect model is better suited than a fixed effect type for the Grunfeld dataset.

After identifying the model, let's estimate it using function plm.

```
# set panel data model with random effects
my_model <- 'random'
my_formula <- inv ~ value + capital
my_index <- c('firm','year')

# estimate it
my_pdm_random <- plm(data = Grunfeld,
                     formula = my_formula,
                     model = my_model,
                     index = my_index)

# print result
print(summary(my_pdm_random))
```

```
R> Oneway (individual) effect Random Effect Model
R>    (Swamy-Arora's transformation)
R>
```

```
R> Call:
R> plm(formula = my_formula, data = Grunfeld, model = my_model,
R>     index = my_index)
R>
R> Balanced Panel: n = 10, T = 20, N = 200
R>
R> Effects:
R>                   var std.dev share
R> idiosyncratic 2784.46   52.77 0.282
R> individual    7089.80   84.20 0.718
R> theta: 0.8612
R>
R> Residuals:
R>      Min.    1st Qu.    Median    3rd Qu.      Max.
R> -177.6063  -19.7350    4.6851    19.5105   252.8743
R>
R> Coefficients:
R>               Estimate Std. Error z-value Pr(>|z|)
R> (Intercept) -57.834415  28.898935 -2.0013  0.04536 *
R> value         0.109781   0.010493 10.4627  < 2e-16 ***
R> capital       0.308113   0.017180 17.9339  < 2e-16 ***
R> ---
R> Signif. codes:
R> 0 '***' 0.001 '**' 0.01 '*' 0.05 '.' 0.1 ' ' 1
R>
R> Total Sum of Squares:    2381400
R> Residual Sum of Squares: 548900
R> R-Squared:       0.7695
R> Adj. R-Squared: 0.76716
R> Chisq: 657.674 on 2 DF, p-value: < 2.22e-16
```

As expected, the coefficients are significant at 1%. The adjustment of the model is also high, with an adjusted R-squared equal to 0.77. This means a great proportion of the variation in the data was explained by the model. The results from the panel data model indicate the value of the firms and their current assets are positively related to the number of investments. The firms with higher market value and more assets will often invest more.

For one last example of using R in panel models, let's estimate a SUR (seemingly unrelated regression) model for the Grunfeld data. The SUR specification assumes the different models for each group can be estimated individually, with a correlation between the disturbances across models. It

11.3. PANEL DATA MODELS

is best suited when we have many time periods and a few groups, such as in the `Grunfeld` data.

The `systemfit` package offers a function with the same name for the estimation of the SUR model. The first step in using `systemfit` is to allocate the `Grunfeld` data to a specific `data.frame.` format with function `plm::pdata.frame`. Let's try it.

```
library(systemfit)

# set pdataframe
p_Grunfeld <- pdata.frame(Grunfeld, c( "firm", "year" ))

# estimate sur
my_SUR <- systemfit(formula = inv ~ value + capital,
                    method = "SUR",
                    data = p_Grunfeld)
print(my_SUR)
```

```
R>
R> systemfit results
R> method: SUR
R>
R> Coefficients:
R>    1_(Intercept)        X1_value        X1_capital
R>      -135.6061364       0.1138135         0.3861235
R>   10_(Intercept)       X10_value       X10_capital
R>         1.9893500      -0.0161291         0.3768475
R>    2_(Intercept)        X2_value        X2_capital
R>       -10.9059829       0.1627658         0.3406261
R>    3_(Intercept)        X3_value        X3_capital
R>       -15.8959008       0.0349626         0.1257302
R>    4_(Intercept)        X4_value        X4_capital
R>         1.8043270       0.0678437         0.3075528
R>    5_(Intercept)        X5_value        X5_capital
R>        26.4673602       0.1274473         0.0119871
R>    6_(Intercept)        X6_value        X6_capital
R>        -6.1934512       0.1333107         0.0540052
R>    7_(Intercept)        X7_value        X7_capital
R>        -9.7701305       0.1134649         0.1281802
R>    8_(Intercept)        X8_value        X8_capital
R>         3.1490972       0.0537015         0.0433622
```

```
R>  9_(Intercept)        X9_value         X9_capital
R>     -3.1568643       0.0765949         0.0654245
```

The output object `my_SUR` contains the estimation of all equations, firm by firm. Using `print` is limited in this case; it only shows the estimated coefficients. Function `summary` provides more information, including the correlation structure between the disturbances. But, its output is extensive and would fill several pages of this book. We leave it as an exercise.

11.4 Arima Models

Arima is a special type of model that uses the past of a time series to explain its future. Estimating an Arima model for stock returns can tell how the returns today are related to past returns. If we find a negative correlation, it means a positive return yesterday is likely to be followed by a positive return today. In a forecasting "horse race," an arima model can be a benchmark and we compare the predictive performance of forecasting candidates against it.

A simple example of an Arima model is defined by the following equation:

$$y_t = 0.5 y_{t-1} - 0.2 \epsilon_{t-1} + \epsilon_t$$

In this example, we have an ARIMA(AR = 1, D = 0, MA = 1) model without the intercept. This specific notation informs the configuration of the model and the number of used parameters. The first value in (1, 0, 1) indicates the maximum lag used in y_t in the right hand side of the equation. The second value indicates the degree of differentiation of the time series (Hamilton, 1994). If $D = 1$, we use the first difference of y_t as the dependent variable. The third component, MA, shows the maximum lag used for the error of the model. This identification process can be arbitrary or not. A common procedure is to search for the combination of AR, D, and MA terms, which can maximize an adjustment function, (as shown in section 11.4.2.

11.4.1 Simulating Arima Models

First, let's simulate an Arima model using function `arima.sim` from `stat`. This package is loaded by default, and we need not source it with the `library`.

11.4. ARIMA MODELS

```
set.seed(1)

# set number of observations
my_T <- 5000

# set model's parameters
my_model <- list(ar = 0.5,
                 ma = -0.1)
my_sd <- 1

# simulate model
my_ts <- arima.sim(n = my_T,
                   model = my_model ,
                   sd = my_sd)
```

We can look at the result of the simulation by creating a plot with the artificial time series:

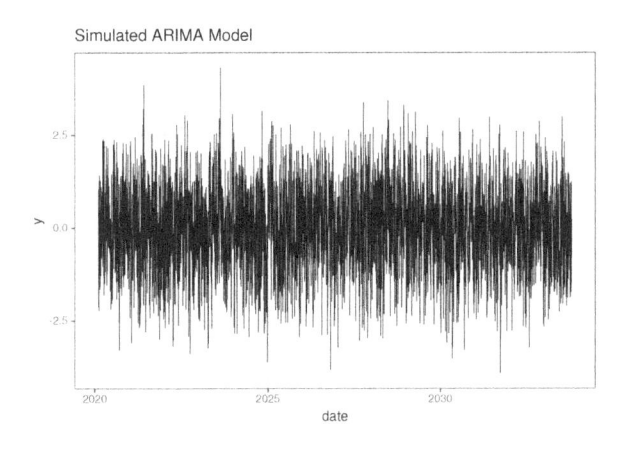

```
library(ggplot2)

# set df
temp_df <- data.frame(y = unclass(my_ts),
                      date = Sys.Date() + 1:my_T)

p <- ggplot(temp_df, aes(x = date, y = y)) +
  geom_line(size=0.25) +
  labs(title = 'Simulated ARIMA Model') +
  theme_bw()

print(p)
```

The graph shows a time series with an average close to zero and strong instability. These are typical properties of an Arima model.

11.4.2 Estimating Arima Models

To estimate an Arima model, we use function `arima` from the same package. Let's estimate a model for our simulated data.

```
# estimate arima model
my_arima <- arima(my_ts, order = c(1,0,1))

# print result
print(coef(my_arima))
```

```
R>            ar1           ma1      intercept
R>   0.482547196  -0.077376754  -0.007458499
```

As expected, the estimated parameters are close to the simulated values, with *ar1* equal to 0.4825 and *ma1* equal to -0.07738. As we did for a `lm` and `plm` model, we can also use function `summary` to get more information from the estimation of the Arima model. Let's look at all elements available in `summary(my_arima)`:

```
attributes(summary(my_arima))
```

```
R> $dim
R> [1] 14  3
R>
R> $dimnames
R> $dimnames[[1]]
R>  [1] "coef"      "sigma2"    "var.coef"  "mask"
R>  [5] "loglik"    "aic"       "arma"      "residuals"
R>  [9] "call"      "series"    "code"      "n.cond"
R> [13] "nobs"      "model"
R>
R> $dimnames[[2]]
R> [1] "Length" "Class"  "Mode"
R>
R>
R> $class
R> [1] "summaryDefault" "table"
```

11.4. ARIMA MODELS

We have the adjustment criteria in `aic`, residuals in `residuals`, coefficients in `coef`, the covariance matrix of estimated coefficients in `var.coef`, and many more.

The identification of the Arima model, defining values AR, D, MA in Arima (AR, D, MA), can also be performed automatically. Package `forecast` (Hyndman and Khandakar, 2007) offers function `auto.arima` that automates this process by choosing the best model according to an adjustment criterion, such as AIC (*Akaike information criteria*) and BIC (*Bayesian information criteria*). This is a very useful function. We allow the data to speak for itself, avoiding a possible bias in the identification of the model.

In the next example, we use the function `auto.arima` to find the best model for the daily returns of the SP500 index.

```
library(BatchGetSymbols)

df_SP500 <- BatchGetSymbols(tickers = '^GSPC',
                            first.date = '2015-01-01',
                            last.date = '2019-01-01')$df.tickers
```

Before estimating the model, we need to check the stationarity of the return data. If the data is not stationary, it might be necessary to use the first differences of the original series (Maddala, 2001). Since we are modeling returns, the raw data of prices was already differentiated. It is worth testing this property of the data before estimating the Arima model. Package `tseries` (Trapletti and Hornik, 2017) provides a function called `adf.test` that will check if the data has unit root (not stationary). The null hypothesis of the test is the non-stationarity of the data, i.e., the existence of unit-roots.

```
library(tseries)
print(adf.test(na.omit(df_SP500$ret.adjusted.prices)))
```

```
R>
R>   Augmented Dickey-Fuller Test
R>
R> data:  na.omit(df_SP500$ret.adjusted.prices)
R> Dickey-Fuller = -10.34, Lag order = 10, p-value
R> = 0.01
R> alternative hypothesis: stationary
```

The result of the test shows a small p-value that strongly suggests the rejection of the null hypothesis. The evidence indicates that the return vector can be considered stationary. For curiosity, let's also try the test on the price series:

```
print(adf.test(df_SP500$price.close))
```

```
R>
R>    Augmented Dickey-Fuller Test
R>
R> data:  df_SP500$price.close
R> Dickey-Fuller = -1.6599, Lag order = 10, p-value
R> = 0.7223
R> alternative hypothesis: stationary
```

This time, we easily fail to reject the null hypothesis with a large p-value. The test strongly suggests the price series is not stationary. Further, we are correct in estimating an Arima model for returns, not prices, from the econometric viewpoint.

One issue in working with Arima models is with the arbitrary identification of the parameters. Do you remember that we always defined the structure of the model by picking the maximum lags for the AR and MA components in the argument `order` of function `arima` in the previous examples? Such practice is not recommended as we can forcibly induce a bias in our model. A more clever and unbiased approach would be to let the data speak for itself. Therefore, that is to say, selecting a combination of AR, MA and D that results in the best fit of the time series. However, for that, function `forecast::auto.arima` estimates na Arima model with automatic identification of the best model using fitting criteria. So, let's try its default options:

```
library(forecast)

# estimate arima model with automatic identification
my_autoarima <- auto.arima(x = df_SP500$ret.closing.prices)

# print result
print(my_autoarima)
```

```
R> Series:
```

11.4. ARIMA MODELS

```
R> ARIMA(2,0,0) with zero mean
R>
R> Coefficients:
R>          ar1      ar2
R>       -0.0106  -0.0527
R> s.e.   0.0316   0.0316
R>
R> sigma^2 estimated as 7.401e-05:  log likelihood=3354.39
R> AIC=-6702.78   AICc=-6702.76   BIC=-6688.04
```

The result tells us the best model for the returns of the SP500 index is an Arima (2, 0, 0). This result implies the return series of the financial index has low memory and only the previous two returns have predictive power over the current returns. Here, since we find negative coefficients, a positive return is more likely to be followed by a negative return.

11.4.3 Forecasting Arima Models

We can obtain the forecasts of an Arima model with the `forecast` function is also from package `forecast`. The forecast is of the static type; only information up to time t is used to make forecasts in $t+k$. In the following example, we calculate the forecasts for five periods ahead, with their corresponding confidence interval.

```
# forecast model
print(forecast(my_autoarima, h = 5))
```

```
R>      Point Forecast        Lo 80       Hi 80        Lo 95
R> 1007  -2.467578e-05  -0.01104984  0.01100049  -0.01688621
R> 1008  -4.476926e-04  -0.01147348  0.01057809  -0.01731017
R> 1009   6.054784e-06  -0.01103499  0.01104710  -0.01687977
R> 1010   2.355023e-05  -0.01101750  0.01106460  -0.01686228
R> 1011  -5.694085e-07  -0.01104166  0.01104052  -0.01688646
R>              Hi 95
R> 1007    0.01683686
R> 1008    0.01641479
R> 1009    0.01689188
R> 1010    0.01690938
R> 1011    0.01688533
```

11.5 GARCH Models

GARCH (Generalized Autoregressive Conditional Heterocesdasticity) models relate to the seminal work of Engle (1982) and Bollerslev (1986). The main innovation in this class of models is that the variance of the residual can change. Garch models became very popular mainly because they replicate characteristics of financial asset returns, such as the existence of fat tails in their distribution and the clustering of volatile periods. In practice, Garch models are mostly used when market risk is being assessed and managed.

A GARCH model is modular. In its simplest format, you have two main equations: a process that sets the conditional mean, and another that defines the variance of the error. See the following example for an ARIMA(1,0,0)-GARCH(1,1) model:

$$y_t = \mu + \theta y_{t-1} + \epsilon_t$$
$$\epsilon_t \sim N(0, h_t)$$
$$h_t = \omega + \alpha \epsilon_{t-1}^2 + \beta h_{t-1}$$

The y_t equation sets the process for the conditional mean, an AR model with one lag. This is the actual observed value of the time series. Variable h_t defines the variance of the error, the instability of the model. Different Garch models will use different equations for h_t and different distributions of the error term. In its simplest case, the one presented here, we use the Normal distribution. In addition, it is important to have an understanding of the modular notation for Garch models, because R functions will follow the same logic.

11.5.1 Simulating Garch Models

In CRAN, we can find two main packages related to Garch models. The first is the package fGarch (Wuertz et al., 2016) and the second is rugarch (Ghalanos, 2015). Both have great features and are optimized for agile estimations. You will be well served in choosing either of them. For simplicity, we will give preference to package fGarch, as it works with an interface similar to the Arima models from the previous section.

In fGarch, we simulate a model using function garchSim. The first step is to load the package fGarch and create the model specification:

11.5. GARCH MODELS

```
library(fGarch)

# set list with model spec
my_model = list(omega=0.001,
                alpha=0.15,
                beta=0.8,
                mu=0.02,
                ar = 0.1)

# set garch spec
spec = garchSpec(model = my_model)

# print it
print(spec)


R>
R> Formula:
R>  ~ ar(1) + garch(1, 1)
R> Model:
R>  ar:     0.1
R>  mu:     0.02
R>  omega:  0.001
R>  alpha:  0.15
R>  beta:   0.8
R> Distribution:
R>  norm
R> Presample:
R>    time         z     h          y
R> 1     0   0.73715  0.02  0.02222222
```

The previous code defines a Garch model equivalent to these equations.

$$y_t = 0.02 + 0.1 y_{t-1} + \epsilon_t$$
$$\epsilon_t \sim N(0, h_t)$$
$$h_t = 0.001 + 0.15 \epsilon_{t-1}^2 + 0.8 h_{t-1}$$

To simulate *1000* observations of this model, we use function `garchSim`:

```
set.seed(20)
# simulate garch model
sim_garch = garchSim(spec, n = 1000)
```

We can visualize the artificial time series generated by creating a plot with ggplot:

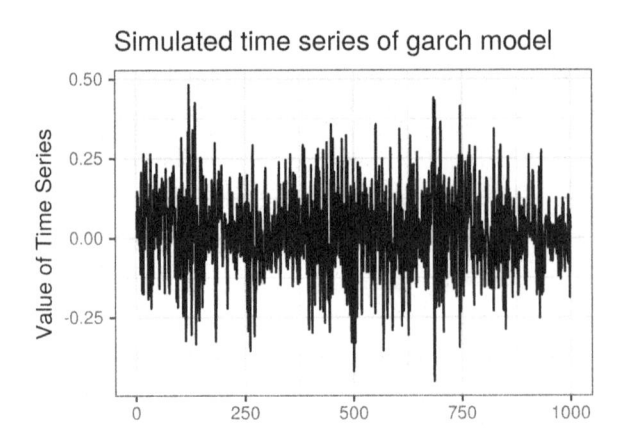

```
# set df for ggplot
temp_df <- tibble(sim.ret = sim_garch$garch,
                  idx=seq_along(sim_garch$garch))

p <- ggplot(temp_df, aes(x = idx,
                         y = sim.ret)) +
  geom_line() +
  labs(title = 'Simulated time series of garch model',
       y = 'Value of Time Series',
       x = '') +
  theme_bw()

print(p)
```

The behavior of the simulated series is similar to the return series of the stocks in chapter 10. It is often difficult to set apart an artificial return series of a Garch model from a real one. Unlike other models, where the instability is constant, a Garch model can portray a return series more realistically by assuming a time changing volatility.

11.5.2 Estimating Garch Models

The estimation of the parameters from a GARCH model is usually achieved using a technique called *maximum-likelihood*. This procedure finds the parameters that make the shape of the model as close as possible to the shape of the time series of interest. It involves a numerical optimization process

11.5. GARCH MODELS

that requires a reasonable amount of processing time. Fortunately, package `fGarch` provides a function, called `garchFit`, that performs the whole operation.

In the following example, we estimate a Garch model for the artificial data created in the previous section. We set the option `trace = FALSE` to prevent the presentation of the details of the optimization process, as they are extensive and would occupy several pages of this book.

```
# estimate garch model
my_form <- formula('sim.ret ~ arma(1,0) + garch(1,1)')

my_garchfit <- garchFit(
  data = sim_garch,
  formula = my_form,
  trace = FALSE)
```

To learn more about the estimated model, we can present it on the screen with the command `print`:

```
print(my_garchfit)
```

```
R> 
R> Title:
R>  GARCH Modelling
R> 
R> Call:
R>  garchFit(formula = my_form, data = sim_garch, trace = FALSE)
R> 
R> Mean and Variance Equation:
R>  data ~ arma(1, 0) + garch(1, 1)
R> <environment: 0x5629dfe57f20>
R>  [data = sim_garch]
R> 
R> Conditional Distribution:
R>  norm
R> 
R> Coefficient(s):
R>         mu         ar1       omega      alpha1       beta1
R>  0.0164569   0.0695426   0.0010592   0.1292773   0.8175428
R> 
R> Std. Errors:
```

```
R>   based on Hessian
R>
R> Error Analysis:
R>          Estimate   Std. Error  t value Pr(>|t|)
R> mu       0.0164569  0.0039213    4.197  2.71e-05 ***
R> ar1      0.0695426  0.0327651    2.122  0.0338   *
R> omega    0.0010592  0.0004267    2.482  0.0131   *
R> alpha1   0.1292773  0.0282136    4.582  4.60e-06 ***
R> beta1    0.8175428  0.0405740   20.149  < 2e-16  ***
R> ---
R> Signif. codes:
R> 0 '***' 0.001 '**' 0.01 '*' 0.05 '.' 0.1 ' ' 1
R>
R> Log Likelihood:
R>   604.189   normalized:  0.604189
R>
R> Description:
R>   Sat Feb  8 17:48:00 2020 by user:
```

The resulting parameters from the estimation are close to the values defined arbitrarily in the call to `garchSpec`. We can achieve higher accuracy by increasing the number of observations in the simulated model. Function `summary` also works for Garch models. However, due to the large volume of information on the prompt, we will leave it as an exercise for you.

Now, we will conduct another example using real data. So, let's estimate a Garch model for the SP500 index. The data is loaded from section 11.4.2, so we can use it directly. First, let's execute the LM Arch test (Engle, 1982; Tsay, 2005) to verify if the returns of the market index have the Arch effect. Function `archTest` from MTS (Tsay and Wood, 2018) can perform this task.

```
library(MTS)

# test for Arch effects
archTest(rt = na.omit(df_SP500$ret.adjusted.prices))
```

```
R> Q(m) of squared series(LM test):
R> Test statistic:  313.3114  p-value:  0
R> Rank-based Test:
R> Test statistic:  227.5087  p-value:  0
```

11.5. GARCH MODELS

The evidence is strong for Arch effects in the SP500 returns. The null hypothesis of the test is the non-existence of the Arch effects, and we can easily reject it at 1%. Let's estimate a Arma(1,0)-Garch(1,1) for the returns.

```
# set object for estimation
df_est <- as.timeSeries(na.omit(df_SP500))

# estimate garch model for SP500
my_garchfit_SP500 <- garchFit(
  data = df_est,
  formula = ret.adjusted.prices ~ arma(1,0) +
                                  garch(1,1),
  trace = FALSE)

# print model
print(my_garchfit_SP500)
```

```
R>
R> Title:
R>  GARCH Modelling
R>
R> Call:
R>  garchFit(formula = ret.adjusted.prices ~ arma(1, 0) + garch(1,
R>     1), data = df_est, trace = FALSE)
R>
R> Mean and Variance Equation:
R>  ret.adjusted.prices ~ arma(1, 0) + garch(1, 1)
R>  [data = df_est]
R>
R> Conditional Distribution:
R>  norm
R>
R> Coefficient(s):
R>          mu         ar1        omega       alpha1
R>  7.5092e-04  -7.7746e-02   3.9465e-06   1.9936e-01
R>       beta1
R>  7.5464e-01
R>
R> Std. Errors:
R>  based on Hessian
R>
R> Error Analysis:
```

```
R>              Estimate    Std. Error   t value  Pr(>|t|)
R> mu           7.509e-04   1.992e-04     3.769  0.000164 ***
R> ar1         -7.775e-02   3.541e-02    -2.195  0.028143 *
R> omega        3.947e-06   8.493e-07     4.647  3.37e-06 ***
R> alpha1       1.994e-01   3.348e-02     5.955  2.60e-09 ***
R> beta1        7.546e-01   3.447e-02    21.892   < 2e-16 ***
R> ---
R> Signif. codes:
R> 0 '***' 0.001 '**' 0.01 '*' 0.05 '.' 0.1 ' ' 1
R>
R> Log Likelihood:
R>  3517.352    normalized:   3.499853
R>
R> Description:
R>  Sat Feb  8 17:48:00 2020 by user:
```

As expected, all Garch coefficients are significant at 1%. As for the mean equation, we again find a negative value for `ar1`, with a p-value close to 3%. We could use the previously estimated Garch model to simulate future returns and prices of the SP500 index.

11.5.3 Forecasting Garch Models

Forecasting Garch models involves two elements: a forecast for the conditional mean (see the first equation in the Garch formula) and a forecast for future values of conditional volatility (see the second equation). Although the initial forecast sets for the next values of the analyzed series, the second quantifies the uncertainty of this forecast. The more uncertain the forecast, less we can trust it to be correct.

In package `fGarch`, both forecasts are calculated using the function `predict` that, just like `summary`, is a generic function that can be used for different models. Consider the following example, where we forecast the next values and the future volatilities of the Garch model fitted with the SP500 returns.

```
# static forecast for garch
my_garch_forecast <- predict(my_garchfit_SP500, n.ahead = 3)

# print df
print(my_garch_forecast)
```

11.6. REGIME SWITCHING MODELS

```
R>    meanForecast   meanError standardDeviation
R> 1 9.066349e-05 0.01865103          0.01865103
R> 2 7.438703e-04 0.01838229          0.01832501
R> 3 6.930862e-04 0.01806510          0.01800848
```

The first column of the previous result is the forecast of the conditional mean; the second presents the expected error of the previous forecast, and the third indicates the expected volatility in standard deviation (the root of the variance). All forecasts are the static type, that is, information up to time t is used to make forecasts for $t+k$.

11.6 Regime Switching Models

Markov regime-switching models are a specification in which the selling point is the flexibility in handling processes driven by heterogeneous states of the world (Hamilton, 1994). In financial markets, we can have two regimes for volatility, one regime where volatility is high and others where it is low. We can justify these regimes as time periods with a greater or lesser amount of new information and uncertainty. Each regime can have its own characteristics. As a researcher, we need to understand how to identify these regimes and estimate the parameters from our models separately.

If we want to motivate the model, we need to consider the following econometric process:

$$y_t = \mu_{S_t} + \epsilon_t$$

where $S_t = 1..k$ and ϵ_t follows a Normal distribution with zero mean and variance given by $\sigma^2_{S_t}$. This is the simplest case of a model with a switching dynamic. If there are k states of the world, there will be k values for the conditional mean and conditional variance. If there is only one state of the world ($k=1$), the previous formula becomes a simple linear regression model under general conditions.

Now, let's assume the previous model has two states ($k=2$). An alternative representation is:

$$y_t = \mu_1 + \epsilon_t \quad \text{for State 1}$$
$$y_t = \mu_2 + \epsilon_t \quad \text{for State 2}$$

where:

$$\epsilon_t \sim (0, \sigma_1^2) \quad \text{for State 1}$$
$$\epsilon_t \sim (0, \sigma_2^2) \quad \text{for State 2}$$

This representation implies two processes for the dependent variable. When the state of the world for time t is 1, the expectation of the dependent variable is μ_1 and the volatility of the innovations is σ_1^2. Likewise, when the state is 2, the mean and volatility take other values.

We will now look at a financial example where the dependent variable y_t can represent a vector of log returns. The value of μ_1 is the expected return on a bull market state, which implies a positive trend for financial prices and consequently a positive log return. The lower, and possibly negative, value of μ_2 measures the expected log return for the bear market state, where asset prices have a tendency to go down.

The different volatilities represent higher uncertainty regarding the predictive power of the model in each state of the world. We can expect the bear market state to be more volatile than the bull market, i.e., prices go down faster than they go up. The usual explanation for this effect is that traders react faster to bad news when comparing to the good news. This can also be explained by limit loss orders, which will sell at market prices once a particular threshold in the prices has been breached. When used by a significant number of traders and at different threshold levels, these limit loss orders will create a cascade effect, accelerating the downfall of prices. This means we can expect the volatility in state 2 (bear market) to be higher than the volatility in state 1 (bull market).

The changes in the states in the model can be set in a deterministic way. We could've set state 1 to be true for time t when another time series is higher or lower than a known threshold. This greatly simplifies the model as each state is observable; therefore, we can treat the model as a regression with dummy variables. Function `lm` could be used for the estimation of this model.

Markov switching is a special type of model for regime changes. Its main difference from the regression with dummy variables is the identification of states is part of the estimation process. **The model learns the regime shifts from the data!** The transition of states in a Markov switching model is not deterministic; it is stochastic. This means one is never sure whether there will be a switch of state. But, the dynamics behind the switching process are known and driven by a transition matrix. This matrix, also

11.6. REGIME SWITCHING MODELS

estimated from the data, will control the probabilities of making a switch from one state to the other. It can be represented as:

$$P = \begin{bmatrix} p_{11} & \cdots & p_{1k} \\ \vdots & \ddots & \vdots \\ p_{k1} & \cdots & p_{kk} \end{bmatrix}$$

In the previous matrix, row i, column j controls the probability of a switch from state j to state i. Consider that, for some time t, the state of the world is 2. This means the probability of a switch from state 2 to state 1 between time t and $t+1$ will be given by p_{12}. Likewise, the probability of staying in state 2 is determined by p_{22}. This is one of the central points of the structure of a Markov regime-switching model: the switching of states is a stochastic process.

11.6.1 Simulating Regime Switching Models

In R, two packages are available for handling univariate Markov regime-switching models, MSwM (Sanchez-Espigares and Lopez-Moreno, 2014) and fMarkovSwitching (Perlin, 2014). The last one also includes functions for simulating a time series. Before using it, let's install fMarkovSwitching from the R-Forge repository. Be aware this package is not available in CRAN.

```
install.packages("fMarkovSwitching",
                 repos="http://R-Forge.R-project.org")
```

Once it is installed, let's look at its functions:

```
library(fMarkovSwitching)

print(ls('package:fMarkovSwitching'))
```

```
R> [1] "dim.MS_Model"      "MS_Regress_Fit"
R> [3] "MS_Regress_For"    "MS_Regress_Lik"
R> [5] "MS_Regress_Simul"  "plot.MS_Model"
R> [7] "plot.MS_Simul"     "print.MS_Model"
R> [9] "print.MS_Simul"
```

The package includes functions for simulating, estimating, and forecasting an univariate markov switching model. Now, to conduct another example, we will simulate the regime switching model by using these equations:

$$y_t = +0.5x_t + \epsilon_t \quad \text{State 1}$$
$$y_t = -0.5x_t + \epsilon_t \quad \text{State 2}$$
$$\epsilon_t \sim N(0, 0.25) \quad \text{State 1}$$
$$\epsilon_t \sim N(0, 1) \quad \text{State 2}$$

The transition matrix will be given by:

$$P = \begin{bmatrix} 0.90 & 0.2 \\ 0.10 & 0.8 \end{bmatrix}$$

This model has two states with different volatilities. In each state, the impact of the explanatory variable will be different. From package fMarkovSwitching, we can use function MS_Regress_Simul to simulate this model. Look at the following code, where we simulate the model from the previous equations.

```
set.seed(10)
library(fMarkovSwitching)

# number of obs
n_T <- 500

# distribution of residuals
distrib <- "Normal"

# number of states
k <- 2

# set transition matrix
P <- matrix(c(.9 ,.2,
              .1 ,.8),
            nrow = 2,
            byrow = T)

# set switching flag
S <- c(0,1)

# set parameters of model (see manual for details)
nS_param <- matrix(0)
S_param <- matrix(0,sum(S),k)
```

11.6. REGIME SWITCHING MODELS

```
S_param[,1] <-  .5
S_param[,2] <- -.5

# set variance of model
sigma <- matrix(0, 1, k)
sigma[1,1] <- sqrt(0.25)    # state 1
sigma[1,2] <- 1             # state 2

# build list
Coeff <- list(P = P              ,
              S = S              ,
              nS_param = nS_param ,
              S_param = S_param   ,
              sigma = sigma      )

# simulate model
my_ms_simul <- MS_Regress_Simul(nr = n_T,
                                Coeff = Coeff,
                                k = k,
                                distrib = distrib)
```

In the simulation function, argument `nS_param` sets the non-switching parameters. These are the coefficients on the right-hand side of the econometric equation that will not switch states. We use a value of zero, as our simulated model has no non-switching coefficients. Even if not used, we need to set this argument in `MS_Regress_Simul`; otherwise, the function will return an error. The elements in `S_param` define the coefficients in each state for the switching parameters. In our example, we have a positive effect of x_t in y_t in state one and a negative effect in state two. Finally, the `sigma` input defines the volatility (standard deviation) of the residual in each regime.

Once the model is simulated and available, let's plot the time series of artificial values. A note here is important; the output from `my_ms_simul` is an S3 object was custom designed to interact with the common functions `print` and `plot`. To access its elements, we use @ instead of $.

```
library(ggplot2)
df_to_plot <- tibble(y = my_ms_simul@dep,
                     x = Sys.Date()+1:my_ms_simul@nr,
                     states = my_ms_simul@trueStates[, 1])

p <- ggplot(data = df_to_plot,
```

```
                aes(y = y, x = seq_along(y))) +
    geom_line() +
    labs(title = 'Simulated markov switching process',
         x = '',
         y = 'Value') +
    theme_bw()

print(p)
```

Simulated markov switching process

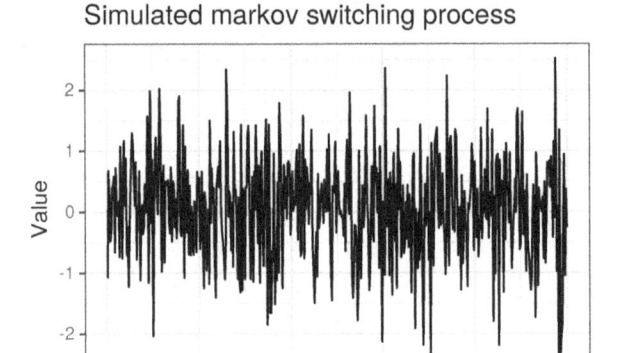

We can also look at the simulated states:

```
library(ggplot2)
df_to_plot <- tibble(y = my_ms_simul@dep,
                     x = Sys.Date()+1:my_ms_simul@nr,
                     states = my_ms_simul@trueStates[,1])

p <- ggplot(data = df_to_plot,
            aes(y = states, x = x)) +
    geom_line() +
    labs(y = 'Probability of state 1') +
    theme_bw()

print(p)
```

11.6. REGIME SWITCHING MODELS

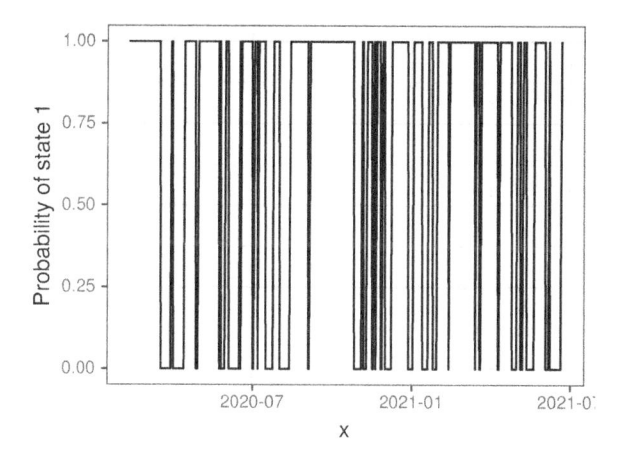

[Figure: Probability of state 1 plotted against x from 2020-07 to 2021-07]

As expected, the model is switching from one state to the other. Either state is strongly predominant over time, but state one seems to have a longer duration than state two. This property is controlled by the transition probabilities set in the object `P`.

11.6.2 Estimating Regime Switching Models

We can estimate a univariate Markov switching model with function `MS_Regress_Fit`. Let's try it for the previously simulated time series.

```
# set dep and indep
dep <- my_ms_simul@dep
indep <- my_ms_simul@indep

# set switching parameters and distribution
S <- c(0,1)
k <- 2
distIn <- "Normal"

# estimate the model
my_ms_model <- MS_Regress_Fit(dep, indep, S, k)
```

Argument `dep` and `indep` sets the variables in the estimation, left, and right side of the econometric equation. Input `S` only takes values zero and one. It defines where the switching effect will occur. Since we only have two independent variables where the first does not switch states, we use `S <- c(0,1)`. Object `k` sets the number of states in the model, in this case, two. After finishing the estimation, let's look at the output.

```
# print estimation output
print(my_ms_model)


R>
R>
R> ***** Numerical Optimization for MS Model Converged *****
R>
R> Final log Likelihood: -544.5191
R> Number of parameters: 7
R> Distribution Assumption -> Normal
R>
R> ***** Final Parameters *****
R>
R> ---> Non Switching Parameters <---
R>
R>   Non Switching Parameter at Indep  Column  1
R>       Value:       -0.0333
R>       Std error: 0.0266 (0.21)
R>
R> --->    Switching Parameters    <---
R>
R>   State 1
R>       Model Standard Deviation: 0.5082
R>       Std Error:                0.0235 (0.00)
R>   State 2
R>       Model Standard Deviation: 0.9584
R>       Std Error:                0.0613 (0.00)
R>
R>   Switching Parameters for Indep  Column  2
R>
R>   State  1
R>       Value:       0.5471
R>       Std error:   0.0313 (0.00)
R>   State  2
R>       Value:       -0.4563
R>       Std error:   0.0979 (0.00)
R>
R> ---> Transition Probabilities Matrix <---
R>
R>        0.90   0.21
R>        0.10   0.79
R>
```

11.6. REGIME SWITCHING MODELS

```
R> ---> Expected Duration of Regimes <---
R> 
R>      Expected duration of Regime #1: 10.52 time periods
R>      Expected duration of Regime #2: 4.81 time periods
```

The estimated coefficients are close to the ones from the simulation. The estimation recognized the parameters from the simulated data. The output object from `MS_Regress_Fit` can also be used with a `plot` for a custom figure. Have a look.

```
plot(my_ms_model)    # plotting output
```

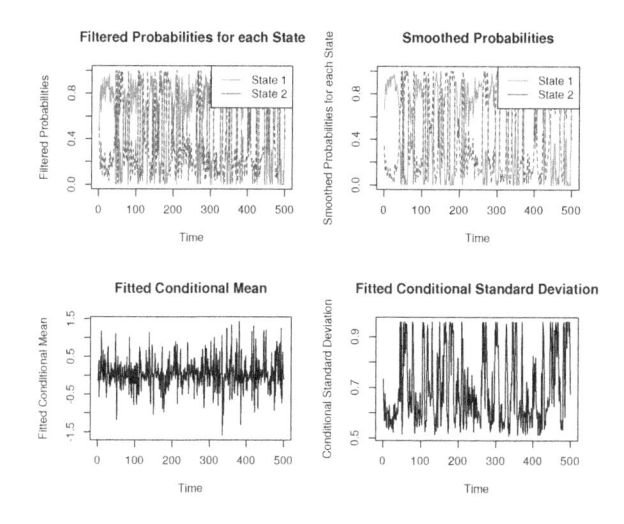

As an example with real data, let's estimate the same Markov regime-switching model for the SP500 returns over a long time period.

```
library(BatchGetSymbols)

df_SP500 <- BatchGetSymbols(tickers = '^GSPC',
                            first.date = '2010-01-01',
                            last.date = '2019-01-01')$df.tickers


# set input objects to MS_Regress_Fit
ret <- na.omit(df_SP500$ret.closing.prices)
dep <- matrix(ret, nrow = length(ret))
indep <- matrix(rep(1, length(dep)),nrow = length(dep))
```

```
S <- c(1)     # where to switch (in this case in the only indep)
k <- 2        # number of states
distIn <- "Normal" #distribution assumption

# estimating the model
my_SP500_MS_model <- MS_Regress_Fit(dep, indep, S, k)
```

And now, we check the result.

```
# printing output
print(my_SP500_MS_model)
```

```
R>
R>
R> ***** Numerical Optimization for MS Model Converged *****
R>
R> Final log Likelihood: 7703.969
R> Number of parameters: 6
R> Distribution Assumption -> Normal
R>
R> ***** Final Parameters *****
R>
R> ---> Non Switching Parameters <---
R>
R> There was no Non Switching Parameters. Skipping this result
R>
R> --->    Switching Parameters    <---
R>
R>    State 1
R>       Model Standard Deviation: 0.0052
R>       Std Error:                0.0002 (0.00)
R>    State 2
R>       Model Standard Deviation: 0.0139
R>       Std Error:                0.0004 (0.00)
R>
R>    Switching Parameters for Indep  Column  1
R>
R>    State  1
R>      Value:       0.0010
R>      Std error:   0.0001 (0.00)
R>    State  2
```

11.6. REGIME SWITCHING MODELS

```
R>        Value:       -0.0007
R>        Std error:   0.0005 (0.18)
R>
R> ---> Transition Probabilities Matrix <---
R>
R>        0.97    0.05
R>        0.03    0.95
R>
R> ---> Expected Duration of Regimes <---
R>
R>        Expected duration of Regime #1: 33.46 time periods
R>        Expected duration of Regime #2: 19.48 time periods
```

The model identified two volatility regimes from the SP500 returns. In the first, low volatility regime, the standard deviation of the returns is 0.518%. In the second state with high uncertainty, the value of the standard deviation is 1.39%. As we expected, the high volatility state has a negative mean of -0.0658%, and the low volatility state has a positive mean of 0.102%. The information from the model is that the SP500 index goes down faster than it goes up. More interesting information is related to the expected duration of the states. A bull market, with positive average returns, tends to last approximately 33 days, while a bear market cycle lasts 19 days. To the point, US equity prices go up slowly and fall fast.

A common figure in the analysis of Markov switching models is the price dynamic in different states. It is a time series plot with overlapped information. First, we separate the variables of interest and then use ggplot2::facet_wrap to create the panels.

```
# get variables for plot
smooth.prob <- as.numeric(my_SP500_MS_model @smoothProb[ , 1])
price <- df_SP500$price.close[2:nrow(df_SP500)]
ref_dates <- df_SP500$ref.date[2:nrow(df_SP500)]

# build long df to plot
df.to.plot <- tibble(type = c(rep('Probabilities Bull Market',
                                  length(smooth.prob)),
                              rep('SP500',
                                  length(smooth.prob))),
                     ref.date = rep(ref_dates ,2),
                     value = c(smooth.prob,
                               price) )
```

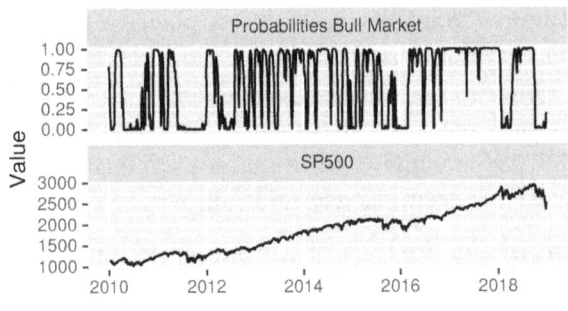

```
# plot with ggplot
p <- ggplot(df.to.plot, 
            aes(y=value, x =ref.date)) + 
  geom_line(size = 0.5) + 
  facet_wrap(~type, nrow = 2, scales = 'free_y') + 
  labs(x = '',
       y = 'Value',
       title = 'SP500 and its bull market states',
       subtitle = 'Prob. from a markov regime switching model',
       caption = 'Data from Yahoo Finance')

# plot it!
print(p)
```

SP500 and its bull market states
Prob. from a markov regime switching model

Data from Yahoo Finance

The figure shows how the price increases in state 1 and decreases in state 2. From 2017 to 2018, we can clearly see a bull market trend for SP500 prices.

11.6.3 Forecasting Regime Switching Models

Package `MS_Regress` provides function `MS_Regress_For` for statically forecasting a univariate Markov switching model. Its inputs are: a model estimated with `MS_Regress_Fit`, argument `myModel`, and the set of new explanatory variables in input `newIndep`. Let's use it to forecast the next day's return of the SP500. In our case, since the regime-switching model only had an intercept, we set `newIndep = 1`.

11.7. DEALING WITH SEVERAL MODELS

```
# make static forecast of regime switching model
newIndep <- 1

my_for <- MS_Regress_For(my_SP500_MS_model , newIndep)

# print output
print(my_for)


R> $condMean
R>                   [,1]
R> [1,] -0.0002773977
R>
R> $condStd
R>               [,1]
R> [1,] 0.01192185
```

The model predicts, the day after the last date available in the SP500 data (2018-12-31), the stock market index will change its value in -0.028%, with a volatility of 1.2%.

11.7 Dealing with Several Models

In the practice of research, we will likely estimate more than one model. We might want to test different models, have different study cases, or run a robustness test by estimating the same model in different time periods. This issue becomes crucial as the scale of the research increases. More data and more models require an efficient computational structure.

In chapter 8, we learned we could use functions from the `apply` family or package `dplyr` to do iterative data tasks. As you probably suspect, we can also use it to estimate several models from the data. Let's start with an example. Here, we will estimate an Arima model for the returns of four random stocks. The extra information to be included in the code from section 11.4.2 is the vector with the stock's tickers. First, let's load the data.

```
set.seed(10)

# set number of stocks
n_stocks <- 4
```

```r
# load data from .rds
my_f <- afedR::afedR_get_data_file('SP500-Stocks-WithRet.rds')
df_stocks <- read_rds(my_f)

# select tickers
my_tickers <- sample(unique(df_stocks$ticker), n_stocks)

# set my_df
df_temp <- df_stocks %>%
  dplyr::filter(ticker %in% my_tickers)

# renew factors in ticker
df_temp$ticker <- as.factor(as.character(df_temp$ticker))
```

Now, what we want to do with this data is separate the returns by ticker and use function `arima` to estimate a model for each stock. One solution is to use function `tapply`:

```r
my_l <- tapply(X = df_temp$ret,
               INDEX = df_temp$ticker,
               FUN = arima,
               order = c(1, 0, 0))
```

Each model is available in `my_l`. To retrieve all coefficients, we can use `sapply` and function `coef`:

```r
# print all coefficients
print(sapply(X = my_l,
             FUN = coef))
```

```
R>                    DLR           PAYX           ROK
R> ar1         0.0018378305  -0.037686589  -0.0123418378
R> intercept   0.0006851939   0.000597599   0.0008427853
R>                    WFM
R> ar1         0.0028082571
R> intercept   0.0006894975
```

A limitation is, by using `tapply`, we are restricted to using a single column of `df_stocks`. Notice how to input `X` of `tapply` only accepts one vector. If we want to use more columns of the `dataframe` in a group type operation,

11.7. DEALING WITH SEVERAL MODELS

we can use the `by` function. So, based on a factor or character object, this function will break a `dataframe` into several smaller ones and save them into a list. We can then write a function to be applied to each `dataframe`.

For an example, we are going to estimate several models with the `by` function, so let's calculate the beta coefficient for all stocks in our database. First, let's load the index data and add a new column in `df_stocks` with the returns of the SP500 index.

```
# load SP500 data
df_sp500 <- read.csv(file = 'data/SP500.csv',
                     colClasses = c('Date','numeric'))

# calculate return
df_sp500$ret <- calc.ret(df_sp500$price.close)


# find location of dates in df_sp500
idx <- match(df_stocks$ref.date,
             df_sp500$ref.date)

# create column in my_df with sp500 returns
df_stocks$ret.sp500 <- df_sp500$ret[idx]
```

The next step is to create a function that will take a `dataframe` as input, use the returns of the asset and the returns of the SP500 index to output the beta. Have a look:

```
estimate_beta <- function(df) {
  # Function to estimate beta from dataframe of stocks returns
  #
  # Args:
  #   df - Dataframe with columns ret and ret.sp500
  #
  # Returns:
  #   The value of beta
  
  my_model <- lm(data = df,
                 formula = ret ~ ret.sp500)
  
  return(coef(my_model)[2])
}
```

Now, we can use the previous function with `by`.

```
# calculate beta for each stock
my_betas <- by(data = df_stocks,
               INDICES = df_stocks$ticker,
               FUN = estimate_beta)

glimpse(as.numeric(my_betas))
```

```
R>   num [1:471] 1.458 1.433 0.76 0.942 0.715 ...
```

The values of the different `betas` are available in object `my_betas`. Let's look at the distribution of our betas using a histogram:

```
library(ggplot2)

df_to_plot <- tibble(betas = as.numeric(my_betas))

p <- ggplot(df_to_plot, aes(x = my_betas)) +
  geom_histogram(bins = 40) +
  labs(x = 'Betas',
       y = 'Frequency',
       title = 'Histogram of Betas for SP500 stocks',
       subtitle = paste0('Market models estimated with data from ',
                         min(df_stocks$ref.date), ' to ',
                         max(df_stocks$ref.date), '\n',
                         length(unique(df_stocks$ticker)),
                         ' stocks included'),
       caption = 'Data from Yahoo Finance') +
  theme_bw()

print(p)
```

11.7. DEALING WITH SEVERAL MODELS

Histogram of Betas for SP500 stocks
Market models estimated with data from 2010-01-05
471 stocks included

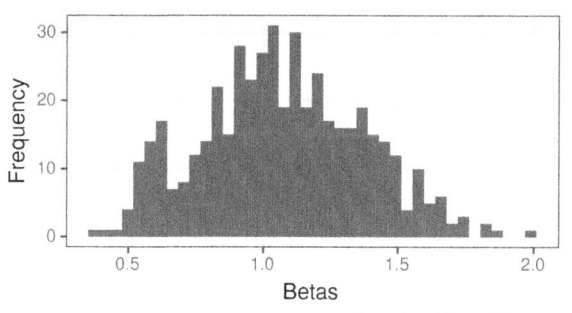

Data from Yahoo Finance

For the SP500 data, we find no negative value of beta. Not surprisingly, the average beta is very close to one.

Another way of storing and managing several models is to use the capabilities of list-columns with `dplyr`. Look at the next example of code, where we replicate the previous procedure of estimating an Arima model for several stocks using functions from `dplyr`.

```
library(dplyr)

my_tab <- df_stocks %>%
  group_by(ticker) %>%
  do(my_model = arima(x = .$ret, order = c(1,0,0)))

glimpse(my_tab)


R> Observations: 471
R> Variables: 2
R> $ ticker   <chr> "A", "AAL", "AAP", "AAPL", "ABC",...
R> $ my_model <list> [<-0.0101153599, 0.0006101093, 0...
```

We have a list-column, called `my_model`, storing the objects with each result from the estimation. We can also use `mutate` to get information about the model. Look at the next code, where we present the coefficients of the model in the same object.

```
my_model_tab <- df_stocks %>%
  group_by(ticker) %>%
```

```
  do(my_model = arima(x = .$ret, order = c(1,0,0))) %>%
  mutate(alpha = coef(my_model)[2],
         ar1 = coef(my_model)[1])
```

```
glimpse(my_model_tab)
```

```
R> Observations: 471
R> Variables: 4
R> $ ticker    <chr> "A", "AAL", "AAP", "AAPL", "ABC",...
R> $ my_model  <list> [<-0.0101153599, 0.0006101093, 0...
R> $ alpha     <dbl> 0.0006101093, 0.0017778322, 0.000...
R> $ ar1       <dbl> -0.010115360, 0.006841853, -0.026...
```

Another trick in handling models with `dplyr` is to use package `broom` (Robinson, 2017) to access the estimated coefficients. In the previous use of `mutate`, we added two columns in `my_tab` with the *alpha* and *ar1* coefficients. A simpler, more direct way of accessing information for all coefficients is to use function `tidy` from `broom`. Have a look:

```
library(broom)
```

```
# get coefs with tidy
my_coef_tab <- my_model_tab %>%
  tidy(my_model)
```

```
# print result
print(head(my_coef_tab))
```

```
R> # A tibble: 6 x 6
R> # Groups:   ticker, alpha, ar1 [3]
R>   ticker    alpha      ar1 term       estimate std.error
R>   <chr>     <dbl>    <dbl> <fct>         <dbl>     <dbl>
R> 1 A       0.000610 -0.0101 ar1        -1.01e-2    0.0238
R> 2 A       0.000610 -0.0101 intercept   6.10e-4    0.000443
R> 3 AAL     0.00178   0.00684 ar1         6.84e-3    0.0239
R> 4 AAL     0.00178   0.00684 intercept   1.78e-3    0.000737
R> 5 AAP     0.000973 -0.0261 ar1        -2.61e-2    0.0238
R> 6 AAP     0.000973 -0.0261 intercept   9.73e-4    0.000400
```

Notice how function `tidy` included the estimated errors from the model. If we had more coefficients, they would also be reported in `my_coef_tab`. As for general information about the model, we can use the function `glance`:

11.8. EXERCISES

```
# get info on models
my_info_models <- my_model_tab %>%
  glance(my_model)

print(head(my_info_models))
```

```
R> # A tibble: 6 x 7
R> # Groups:   ticker, alpha, ar1 [6]
R>   ticker   alpha      ar1  sigma logLik     AIC     BIC
R>   <chr>    <dbl>    <dbl>  <dbl>  <dbl>   <dbl>   <dbl>
R> 1 A      6.10e-4 -0.0101  0.0188  4503.  -9000.  -8984.
R> 2 AAL    1.78e-3  0.00684 0.0307  3636.  -7266.  -7249.
R> 3 AAP    9.73e-4 -0.0261  0.0172  4656.  -9305.  -9289.
R> 4 AAPL   9.46e-4  0.0221  0.0165  4729.  -9453.  -9436.
R> 5 ABC    7.55e-4 -0.0497  0.0132  5121. -10237. -10220.
R> 6 ABT    3.93e-4  0.00173 0.0116  5346. -10686. -10670.
```

It includes information about coefficients and statistics about each model, such as log-likelihood, AIC (Akaike Information Criteria), and BIC (Bayesian Information Criteria).

11.8 Exercises

1. Simulate the following linear process in R:

```
set.seed (5)

# number of obs
nT <- 100

# set x as Normal (0, 1)
x <- rnorm (nT)

# set coefficients
my_alpha <- 1.5
my_beta <- 0.5

# build y
y <- my_alpha + my_beta * x + rnorm (nT, sd = 5)
```

Using the simulated data, x and y estimate a linear model where x is the explanatory variable, and y is the explained variable. Use the `summary` function on the returned object from `lm` to find more details about the model. Is the beta coefficient significant at 5%?

2. Using package `car` and the data we previously simulated, test the joint hypothesis that the value of alpha equals to 1.5 and beta equals to 0.5. Is the null hypothesis of the test rejected at 5%?

3. Use package `gvlma` to test the OLS assumptions for the previously estimated model. Does the model pass all tests? If not, increase the value of `nT` to 5000 and try again.

4. **CHALLENGE** - Using your programming skills, conduct a study to see how the value of `nT` impacts the test of the joint hypothesis from the previous exercise. Thus, that is to say, and we need to keep everything else constant and, for each test of `nT`, simulate 1,000 series and estimate the same model for each one. Check for each `nT` the null hypothesis of the test. A scatter-plot was showing the relationship between `nT`, and the p-values of the test would be interesting for the analysis.

5. From package `BatchGetSymbols`, use functions `GetSP500Stocks` and `BatchGetSymbols` to download the past three years price data for all stocks belonging to the current SP500 index. Calculate the systemic risk (beta) for each stock and display the histogram of the estimated *betas*.

6. For the same stock data from the previous exercise, estimate a panel data version of the market model, that is, each stock has a different *alpha*, but the same *beta*. Is the estimated beta significant at 5%?

7. Using the tidyverse functions `dplyr::group_by` and `dplyr::do`, estimate an ARIMA(1, 0, 0) model for the returns of each stock using the same data as the previous exercise. On the same `tibble`, create a new column with the return forecast at *t+1* for each ticker. Which stock has the highest expected return for the next day?

8. Using the same "pipeline" code as the previous question, use package `fGarch` to add a new list-column with the estimation of an ARMA(1,0)-GARCH(1,1) model for the returns of each stock. Add another column with the volatility forecast (standard deviation) and the return, both at $t + 1$. Increment the table by creating a trade index, the result of dividing the expected return (mean forecast)

11.8. EXERCISES

calculated in the previous item by the predicted risk (standard deviation forecast). Which stock is more attractive and has a higher value of this index? Tip: Ensure that you remove all of the NA values before estimating the ARMA-GARCH model.

9. For the same SP500 database, set set.seed(10) and filter data for four randomly selected stocks. Again, make sure all NA values are removed from the dataframe. For each stock, estimate a simple Markov regime-switching model for its returns. Such a model will have two states for intercept and volatility. The structure of the model is equivalent to the first model in the section "Estimating Regime Switching Models" of chapter 11. Use the plot function to display the smoothed probability plot and use png::jpeg and grDevices::dev.off to save each figure in a folder named 'fig'.

Chapter 12

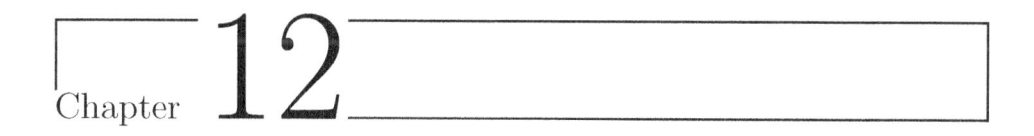

Reporting Results

In previous chapters, we learned how to use R to manipulate data, create figures and estimate models. Now, it is to time to study the best way to report our results, exporting tables and figures to a written document. This is the final stage of the research and we must consider two points: quality and ease of making changes.

Quality relates to the visual attractiveness of the exported materials. For example, a figure can be exported with high resolution. Likewise, a table with statistical tests can be organized with a particular structure, highlighting the most significant results. For example, it is very common in a model estimation table that statistically significant coefficients are highlighted with asterisks or in bold. This facilitates the reader's analysis, whose attention will be drawn to the most important numerical results.

The ease of change relates to how we edit and finalize exported items. A table can be manually edited to achieve high quality. We can copy the information to spreadsheet software, such as Excel, and modify the table until it reaches the desired format. However, every time we modify the original data or the models, we must re-copy and reformat the table in the spreadsheet software.

If you have many tables and figures in your report, a large amount of time will be wasted on manually formatting the information. Ideally, we should aim for a work cycle where the manipulation of data is integrated with the creation of the tables and figures. So, a change in the raw data does not entail extra work in exporting the results to a report. Time is scarce and should be allocated to more productive activities. Fortunately, as you probably suspect, R has packages that facilitate and automate this process. Usually and especially for Latex users, exporting figures and tables is fluid and requires no additional work. Any change in the data will require no manual re-formatting of any sort.

There are two strategies for reporting research results in R. The first, and most common, is to separate the table and figure creation stage from the writing stage. Here, figures and tables are exported from R as local files and can be copied directly to text editors such as *Word/Writer/LaTeX*. It is noteworthy that using LaTeX greatly facilitates this process because each table becomes a local file that can be imported in the main LaTeX code. The second way to write articles in R is to use the dynamic reporting capability of **Rmarkdown**, which is where text and code are merged within the same file. Let's start by exploring the first strategy.

12.1 Reporting Tables

Simple tables, such as descriptive statistics of the data, must be created from a `dataframe`. Let's start with an example using LaTeX. In the next code, we will import data for four stocks using `BatchGetSymbols` and from these, a descriptive table will be exported to a LaTeX file using the `xtable` package.

```
library(tidyverse)
library(BatchGetSymbols)
library(DistributionUtils)

# set number of rows in table
my_tickers <- c('FB', 'GOOGL',
                'JPM', 'BRK-B')

first_date = '2015-01-01'
last_date = '2018-01-01'

df_stocks <- BatchGetSymbols(tickers = my_tickers,
                             first.date = first_date,
                             last.date = last_date,
                             bench.ticker = '^BVSP')[[2]]

# create descriptive table
my_desc_table <- df_stocks %>%
  group_by(Ticker = ticker ) %>%
  summarise('Mean Ret' = mean(ret.adjusted.prices, na.rm = TRUE),
```

12.1. REPORTING TABLES

```
                       'StDev Ret' = sd(ret.adjusted.prices, na.rm = TRUE),
                       'Max Ret' = max(ret.adjusted.prices, na.rm = TRUE),
                       'Min Ret' = min(ret.adjusted.prices, na.rm = TRUE),
                       Assimetry = skewness(ret.adjusted.prices, na.rm = TRUE),
                       Kurtosis = kurtosis(ret.adjusted.prices, na.rm = TRUE))

print(my_desc_table)


R> # A tibble: 4 x 7
R>   Ticker `Mean Ret` `StDev Ret` `Max Ret` `Min Ret`
R>   <chr>       <dbl>       <dbl>     <dbl>     <dbl>
R> 1 BRK-B    0.000419     0.00922    0.0381   -0.0430
R> 2 FB        0.00119      0.0152     0.155   -0.0581
R> 3 GOOGL     0.00101      0.0140     0.163   -0.0541
R> 4 JPM      0.000906      0.0134    0.0833   -0.0695
R> # ... with 2 more variables: Assimetry <dbl>,
R> #   Kurtosis <dbl>
```

In creating the **dataframe**, notice how we define column names as text (quotation marks). This is necessary as we are using spaces in the names. Now that we have our table, let's export it to LaTeX.

```
library(xtable)

# set xtable object
my_xtable <- xtable(x = my_desc_table,
                    label = 'tab:DescRetStats',
                    caption = 'Descriptive Statistics for Returns',
                    digits = 4)

# check if folder exists
if (!dir.exists('tabs')) {
    dir.create('tabs')
}

# print output to latex file
my_tex_file <- 'tabs/MyTable.tex'

# save it
print(my_xtable,
      include.rownames = FALSE,
```

```
              file = my_tex_file,
              type='latex')
```

In the `xtable` function, we only use `label` and `caption` entries to edit the table details. There are several other options available in the `xtable` function. The resulting LaTeX file is saved in the `tabs` folder of the current directory. The code checks for the existence of this directory and, if it does not exist, it creates it. After compiling the LaTeX file, the result will be identical to 12.1, a printable table in an article or scientific report.

Ticker	Mean Ret	StDev Ret	Max Ret	Min Ret	Assimetry	Kurtosis
BRK-B	0.0004	0.0092	0.0381	-0.0430	0.1225	1.8834
FB	0.0012	0.0152	0.1552	-0.0581	1.1721	14.9905
GOOGL	0.0010	0.0140	0.1626	-0.0541	2.1183	25.1883
JPM	0.0009	0.0134	0.0833	-0.0695	0.1353	4.0590

Table 1: Descriptive Statistics for Returns

Figure 12.1: Example of LaTeX table with xtable

As for exporting tables to *Word* (*Microsoft*) or *Writer* (*Libreoffice*) files, there is no direct way to do this using `xtable`. But a simple solution is to use the package to export the table to a temporary file with an *html* or *doc* extension and then copy and paste the result into the final report. This operation works because files with the extension *html* and *doc* share a similar format for tables. As an example, let's perform this operation with the same table:

```
# set html file for output
my_html_file <- 'tabs/MyTable.html'

# write it!
print(x = my_xtable,
      file = my_html_file,
      type = 'html',
      include.rownames = FALSE )
```

Once the file is available, we can open tabs/MyTable.html with any web browser, select and copy the table, and finally paste it into our document. The result should look similar to the table in Figure 12.2.

Going further, if you are dealing with several figures and tables in *.docx* (Word/Writer) or *.ppt* (Powerpoint/Impress) files, the `ReporteRs` (Gohel,

12.2. REPORTING MODELS

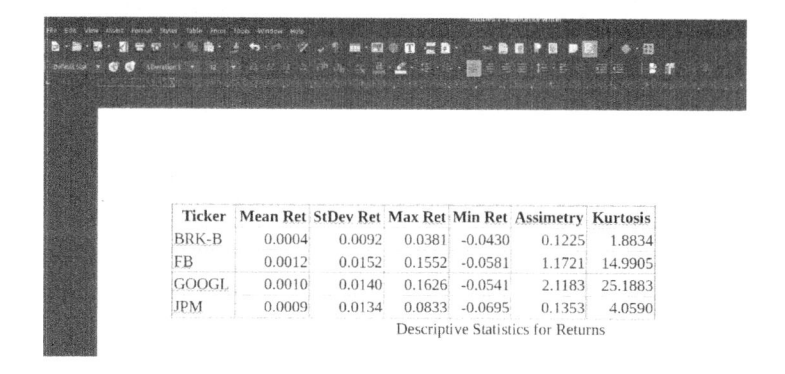

Figure 12.2: Example of table in Writer (LibreOffice)

2017) package can save you a lot of time and effort. It offers a very interesting way to automate the reporting process in the Microsoft Office format. Instead of explicitly exporting tables and figures with local files, you can define *placeholders* in the text of the *.docx* file to insert tables and figures straight from the code. For example, you could type the text `FIGURE_1_HERE` in the *Word* file and, from R, replace the text with any `ggplot` figure. Readers interested in this format of work can find more information in the Github page[1].

12.2 Reporting Models

Reporting the estimation of models requires a special type of table, with an unique structure in the presentation of different performance measures, comparison of coefficients for different models, besides the individual parameters and their statistics. Fortunately for R users, different packages make it easy to build and customize estimation tables for one or more models. The most popular are `xtable`, `texreg` and `stargazer`.

As an example, let's use the `texreg` package to report the results of the *beta* calculation of four different stocks. We load the data, estimate the models and then use the `screenreg` function to display a representation of the models in text format.

```
library(texreg)
library(dplyr)
library(BatchGetSymbols)
```

---

[1]https://davidgohel.github.io/ReporteRs/

```r
# get Ibov data
my_tickers <- c('^GSPC')

first_date = '2015-01-01'
last_date = '2019-01-01'

df_sp500 <- BatchGetSymbols(tickers = my_tickers,
                            first.date = first_date,
                            last.date = last_date)[[2]]

# set sp500 ret column
idx <- match(df_stocks$ref.date, df_sp500$ref.date)
df_stocks$ret_mkt <- df_sp500$ret.adjusted.prices[idx]

# estimate betas
beta_tab <- df_stocks %>%
  group_by(ticker) %>%
  do(beta_model = lm(data=., ret.adjusted.prices ~ ret_mkt))

# report result
est_table <- screenreg(l = beta_tab$beta_model,
                       custom.model.names = beta_tab$ticker,
                       custom.coef.names = c('Alpha', 'Beta'),
                       digits = 2)

# print it
print(est_table)
```

```
R>
R> ============================================================
R>             BRK-B        FB          GOOGL        JPM
R> ------------------------------------------------------------
R> Alpha       0.00         0.00        0.00         0.00
R>            (0.00)       (0.00)      (0.00)       (0.00)
R> Beta        0.96 ***     1.10 ***    1.04 ***     1.33 ***
R>            (0.03)       (0.06)      (0.05)       (0.04)
R> ------------------------------------------------------------
R> R^2         0.65         0.31        0.34         0.59
R> Adj. R^2    0.65         0.31        0.34         0.59
R> Num. obs.   754          754         754          754
R> RMSE        0.01         0.01        0.01         0.01
R> ============================================================
```

12.2. REPORTING MODELS

```
R> *** p < 0.001, ** p < 0.01, * p < 0.05
```

In the previous code, `beta_model` column of `beta_tab` contains all estimated models in a list type object. The `custom.model.names` argument in `screenreg` defines the name of the models (top row of the table), while `custom.coef.names` allows the use of custom coefficient names. For our case, we can clearly see that the *betas* of the stocks are positive and statistically significant, as expected.

The `texreg` package also offers several other options for the user. You can customize your own table. Exporting to other formats such as LaTeX and *html* is possible and recommended. For Microsoft Office users, the `htmlreg` function also lets you export a table to a Word file. You can do this by setting `file` input as a *.doc* file. If you work with estimation tables on a daily basis, the `texreg` package will save you a lot of time.

The following chunk is an example of using `texreg` to export a LaTeX table:

```
# report result
est_table <- texreg(l = beta_tab$beta_model,
                    file = 'tabs/Example_texreg.tex',
                    custom.model.names = beta_tab$ticker,
                    custom.coef.names = c('Alpha', 'Beta'),
                    digits = 2)
```

The result in a LaTex file compiled for pdf will equal figure 12.3.

	BRK-B	FB	GOOGL	JPM
Alpha	0.00	0.00	0.00	0.00
	(0.00)	(0.00)	(0.00)	(0.00)
Beta	0.96***	1.10***	1.04***	1.33***
	(0.03)	(0.06)	(0.05)	(0.04)
R^2	0.65	0.31	0.34	0.59
Adj. R^2	0.65	0.31	0.34	0.59
Num. obs.	754	754	754	754
RMSE	0.01	0.01	0.01	0.01

***$p < 0.001$, **$p < 0.01$, *$p < 0.05$

Table 3: Statistical models

Figure 12.3: Example of LaTeX table with texreg

12.3 Creating Reports with *RMarkdown*

RMarkdown innovates the process of writing reports by merging text with code. The great benefit is the entire production of technical reports is contained in a single file with extension *.Rmd*. Any change in the code will automatically have an impact in the tables, figures and also inline text.

Rmarkdown's text structure is based on **markdown**[2], a language for writing and formatting text on the internet. The difference from text editing software such as *Word* and *Writer* is that all text formatting is performed with code. For example, bold text in *markdown* is written as `**bold text**` and italic as `_italic text_`. A compiler reads the original code and transforms it into formatted text of any kind; this could be a web page, a Word document or a pdf. LaTeX users are likely to feel comfortable when writing in *RMarkdown* as both formats use commands to format the text output.

Let's explore how `Rmarkdown` works with a practical example. Open RStudio and click *New Files* and then *New R Markdown*. A dialog box should appear with options for *Document, Presentation, Shiny,* and *From Template*. The first case, *Document* refers to the writing of traditional text documents; namely, articles and technical reports. The second option, *Presentation*, is about creating *slides*, comparable to *Powerpoint/Impress* and LaTeX (*beamer*) files. The third option, `Shiny`, creates internet applications using the technology of the same name. It is not appropriate here to explain the functionalities of all cases. We will, therefore, give preference to the *Document* option, which we are most interested in.

Going forward, we will edit the report title as `"My First RMarkdown Report"` and the author's name as, well, `"Marcelo S. Perlin"`. The result of our choices should be similar to the screen highlighted in Figure 12.4.

The next choices relate to the output when compiling the report: html, pdf, or Word. The contents of the document will originally be written in *RMarkdown* and then compiled into one format. The result will be a file with one of the three extensions. What is the best format? The answer depends on your audience and how they will read the document. Personally, I particularly like the *html* format because of its ease of distribution. Today, any computer or mobile/tablet has a pre-installed internet browser. The PDF and Word formats, however, are more popular. Either way, don't worry about it too much; you can use the same RMarkdown file and modify the output format in the future. Note that PDF production requires the installation of a LaTex

---

[2]https://daringfireball.net/projects/markdown/

12.3. CREATING REPORTS WITH RMARKDOWN

Figure 12.4: Creating a Rmarkdown Report

compiler – miktex[3] in Windows, TeXLive[4] in Linux/Mac. A simple trick for installing LaTeX is calling function `tinytex::install_tinytex()`, which will automatically select and install a LaTeX flavour for your operating system.

After pressing *OK*, a file will appear in the *scripts* editing screen. Let's dissect its elements with screenshots. The first part is the file header, Figure 12.5.

Figure 12.5: Header Code in Rmarkdown

The document header is identified using the `---` separator. Each item is predefined and recognized by `RMarkdown`, including title (`title:`), author (`author:`), document date (`date:`) and output type (`output:`). There are several other customization options. You can configure page size, output text style, picture size, and more[5].

The next piece of text is identified in Figure 12.6. This is the report setup code. The term *setup* is the optional identifier of the chunk of R code,

---

[3]https://miktex.org/
[4]https://www.tug.org/texlive/
[5]https://rmarkdown.rstudio.com/index.html

which might be used in the future. In *RMarkdown*, all code starts and ends with triple inverse accents. The `r` item indicates the language used to run the code, in this case, R. We could, however, execute code from another language, such as *Python*, *SQL* or *Bash*.

The `include = FALSE` item is a specific option for that chunk of code. The `include = FALSE` command tells RMarkdown not to include that specific piece of setup code output, but to run the code in it. There are several other options for each piece of code. The *knitr* manual[6], available on the internet, dissects all possibilities. For now, I suggest knowing only the simplest options. Here, besides the `include` entry, you should know the `eval = TRUE | FALSE` option, which defines whether this code will be executed and `echo = TRUE | FALSE`, allowing you to hide or show the code in the text of the compiled document.

```
8   ```{r setup, include=FALSE}
9   knitr::opts_chunk$set(echo = TRUE)
10  ```
```

Figure 12.6: Rmarkdown code

For the first chunk of code, the `knitr::opts_chunk$set(echo = TRUE)` line sets a global option for all future chunks of code. Here, `echo = TRUE`, defines that all code will be displayed in the final document. This option will be *default* and respected throughout the rest of the document unless a particular chunk of code defines the `echo = FALSE` option explicitly.

An important point here is that, at the time of compiling the *Rmarkdown* file, the working directory will always be the source file location. Therefore, unlike other R scripts, it is **unnecessary to change directories in code with the `setwd` function**.

Moving on, the `## R Markdown` text in Figure 12.7 defines a title, in this case at the second level of depth. In *Word/Writer*, this format would be named *Title 2*. The depth of the title defines the size and font of the title letters, and the structure of the summary. If necessary, a first level title could be set as `# Title 1` and a third level title as `### Title 3` and so on. Do notice that the amount of *hashtags* (#) defines the level of the title's depth.

The second part of 12.7 is the text itself. Here you can write freely, paying attention only to the formatting structure. For example, bold text is written as `**bold text**`, italics as `*italic text*` or `_italic text_`, internet links with the format `(link text)[url]`. As for the previous cases, there are several other options. See the Rmarkdown manual[7] for more details.

---

[6]https://yihui.name/knitr/options/#code-evaluation
[7]https://rmarkdown.rstudio.com/index.html

12.3. CREATING REPORTS WITH RMARKDOWN

```
12   ## R Markdown
13
14   This is an R Markdown document. Markdown is a simple formatting syntax for
     authoring HTML, PDF, and MS Word documents. For more details on using R
     Markdown see <http://rmarkdown.rstudio.com>.
15
16   When you click the **Knit** button a document will be generated that includes
     both content as well as the output of any embedded R code chunks within the
     document. You can embed an R code chunk like this:
17
18   ```{r cars}
19   summary(cars)
20   ```
```

Figure 12.7: Text in RMarkdown

An important point here is the use of code (or variables) in plain text, which is not part of the *RMarkdown template* document. To explain, imagine a situation where you need to report the value of a statistical test in the main text, such as in the phrase:

> "The estimated value of beta is X_1, with a T test equal to X_2. Therefore, at a threshold value of X_3, we find Y_1 statistical significance for the coefficient beta."

where _X*_ are numerical results from the code and _Y_1_ is the word "not" or empty. Here, we need to use inline code to substitute the text with values. See an example in Figure 12.8

```
33   ```{r}
34   x <- runif(100)
35   y <- runif(100)
36
37   my_lm <- lm(formula = x ~ y)
38
39   threshold_pvalue <- 0.05
40   pvalue_beta <- summary(my_lm)$coefficients[2, 4]
41
42   if (pvalue_beta >= threshold_pvalue) {
43     pvalue_decision_txt <- 'no'
44   } else {
45     pvalue_decision_txt <- ''
46   }
47
48   value_beta <-
49   my_ttest <- format(summary(my_lm)$coefficients[2, 3], digits = 3)
50   ```
51
52   The estimated value of beta is `r value_beta`, with a T test equal to `r my_ttest`.
     Therefore, at a threshold value of `r scales::percent(threshold_pvalue)`, we find `r
     pvalue_decision_txt` statistical significance for coefficient $\beta$.
```

Figure 12.8: Example of R code in inline text

R will evaluate the value of objects `value_beta`, `my_ttest`, `threshold_pvalue` and `pvalue_decision_txt` at compile time and build the paragraph with actual text. The result is given in Figure 12.9

Note here the great advantage of *RMarkdown*, text and results are dynamically integrated. If we changed the input data, it would not be necessary to

The estimated value of beta is 0.751, with a T test equal to 0.751. Therefore, at a threshold value of 5.00%, we find no statistical significance for coefficient β.

Figure 12.9: Result of inline R code

rewrite the sentence since it would not lose its meaning. All variables would be updated and the text would still be correct.

The last part in 12.7 displays the `summary(cars)` code, that is, it summarizes an object. This code will be shown in the text (see the use of `echo = TRUE` in `knitr::opts_chunk`) and will display the result of its execution in compiled text. Displaying results is not only relative to the `print` command. You can also use the `cat` command to display output texts in the final document.

Figure 12.10 shows the last section of the example. This creates and displays a figure in the final report. To do so, simply call the `plot` function or `ggplot2` functions normally, as learned in chapter 10. If you create more than one chart, they will be displayed one below the other in the document. An important note, **never use `x11()` to create windows in a *Rmarkdown* file. This will cause an error in the compilation**.

```
22  ## Including Plots
23
24  You can also embed plots, for example:
25
26  ```{r pressure, echo=FALSE}
27  plot(pressure)
28  ```
29
30  Note that the `echo = FALSE` parameter was added to the code chunk to prevent
    printing of the R code that generated the plot.
```

Figure 12.10: Figures in Rmarkdown

Now that we understand the components that make up our *Rmarkdown* report, it's time to compile and analyze the final result. First save the *Rmd* file to a local folder. After that, click the *Knit* button at the top of the RStudio editor and select *Knit to html*. In the lower-left corner of RStudio the process output will appear. Finally, a new window with the already compiled document will show up. You can click *Open in Browser* to open the file in your default web browser. The compiled file will have the same name and folder location as the original *Rmd* file, but with extension *html*. The result should be identical to the one in Figure 12.11. As an exercise, I suggest compiling the file into other formats, *pdf* and *docx*, and checking the result.

It's important to know that the table export procedures using `xtable` and `texreg` packages are also valid. Therefore, at your disposal, you have all the

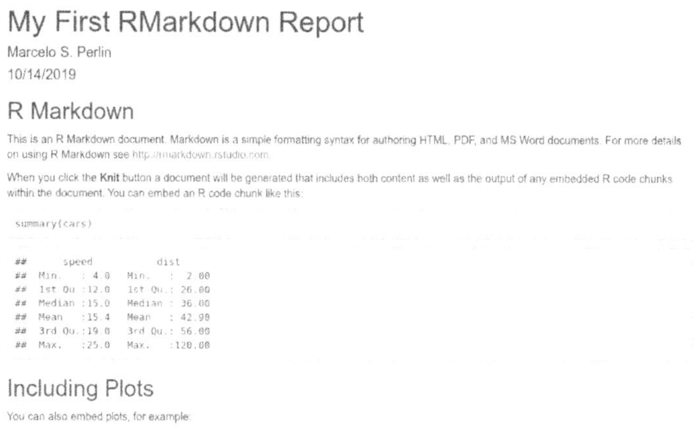

My First RMarkdown Report

Marcelo S. Perlin

10/14/2019

R Markdown

This is an R Markdown document. Markdown is a simple formatting syntax for authoring HTML, PDF, and MS Word documents. For more details on using R Markdown see http://rmarkdown.rstudio.com.

When you click the **Knit** button a document will be generated that includes both content as well as the output of any embedded R code chunks within the document. You can embed an R code chunk like this:

```
summary(cars)
```

```
##      speed           dist       
##  Min.   : 4.0   Min.   :  2.00  
##  1st Qu.:12.0   1st Qu.: 26.00  
##  Median :15.0   Median : 36.00  
##  Mean   :15.4   Mean   : 42.98  
##  3rd Qu.:19.0   3rd Qu.: 56.00  
##  Max.   :25.0   Max.   :120.00  
```

Including Plots

You can also embed plots, for example:

Figure 12.11: Example of compiled report in html

tools needed to create scientific articles in *RMarkdown*, with both code and text integrated.

This section showed a small portion of the universe of possibilities in using *RMarkdown*. Readers interested in learning more, I suggest consulting the featured manual[8]. It also offers a gallery of Rmarkdown user cases. Alternatively, a collection of *RMarkdown templates* is offered at GitHub[9].

12.4 Exercises

1. Consider the Grunfeld data available at link https://eeecon.uibk.ac.at/~zeileis/grunfeld/Grunfeld.csv. Import the data in R and create a descriptive table of the variables. This table should provide enough information for the reader to understand the data. Use `xtable` package to report it in LaTeX or Word/Writer format.

2. Using `BatchGetSymbols::GetSP500Stocks` function, select four random stocks and download stock prices for the previous 3 years. Estimate an ARIMA (1,0,1) model for each stock and report the result on the R screen with `texreg::screenreg` function.

3. Create a new report in *Rmarkdown* covering the two previous exercises. Compile the report in html and open it in your *browser*.

[8]https://rmarkdown.rstudio.com/index.html

[9]https://github.com/svmiller/svm-r-markdown-templates

4. [**CHALLENGE**] - Download SP500 components data for the past three years. Estimate an ARMA(1, 1) - Garch(1, 1) model for the returns of each stock. Now, let's automate a reporting procedure. Write a function that takes as input a Garch model and output a text with the report of the results. Use this function in a rmarkdown document, providing a paragraph for each stock in the database.

Chapter 13

Optimizing Code

In this chapter, we will study how to be more efficient in writing R scripts. Here, efficiency means to achieve the same results with our R code, but spending far less time working on it. We can divide the total working time into programming and code execution. Let's go deeper into each of these subjects.

However, before we start you need to understand that code optimization is an advanced and complex topic. So, you should only read this chapter if you feel comfortable with the information in the previous ones. Improving code execution, for example, is a deep subject that can be tackled in different ways, from hardware configuration to package selection. Here, we will focus mostly on the most obvious cases of the code improvement. Plus, you can find a very comprehensive material on the topic in Gillespie and Lovelace (2016).

13.1 Optimizing your Programming Time

The first topic you must consider when thinking about optimizing your work is the code format. Just like we can improve the content in an essay, we can also optimize the way we write code: keep it clear, organized, simple and easy to follow. Thus, with this in mind, we must consider these guidelines:

DRY (don't repeat yourself) Whenever you find yourself writing similar code lines, or copying and pasting in different parts of the code, consider writing a function (see chapter 8). Some time will be spend organizing inputs and outputs and writing comments, but the benefits are clear. You'll be able to use it in all your future code, forever. If you can, invest time in making powerful functions, which you can reuse in many different projects.

KISS (keep it simple and *stunning*) The simplest and most-straightforward your code, the better. You should aim to have a code structure so obvious that even a novice programmer can understand what is happening within the script, even if he/she cannot replicate it. You can easily do that by using, established packages or custom functions in order of preference. However, whenever your code is becoming too complex, take a break and rethink if the current state is the most optimal structure for solving the problem.

Folder structure Organize all elements of the scripts in relative folders (see chapter 3). As an example, all raw data files should go to folder `data`, all output figures to `figs` and so on. Scripts that produce contents should be named and organized in a sequence (e.g. `'01_load_data.R'`, `'02_clean_data.R'`). This simple organization will make it easier to change and execute the code in the future.

Comments are your timeless friend Even when writing just to yourself, keep comments alive and instructive. Write about the problems you had to solve while writing the code and external dependencies of your script. Anything that is not obvious from the code should be noted by making an explicit comment. In addition, you need to remember that you will probably continue using the same code for years to come, even if you get a fresh new computer. Actually, taking a few minutes to write good comments or taking notes today can save you hours in the future.

Keep a clear notation Code notation is the personal touch you bring to your work. It sets how you name variables and functions and how you write code in general. Try not to be the person in the room with the strangest code notation. There is wisdom in following community guidelines, especially if collaboration is part of your work. Here, let's explore the official conventions for `tidyverse`, found at its website[1].

Filenames and paths: Names and paths of files should help identify their content.

```
# GOOD
my_f <- '01_Run_Research.R'
my_f <- '02_Import_and_Clean_Data.R'
```

---

[1] https://style.tidyverse.org/

13.1. OPTIMIZING YOUR PROGRAMMING TIME

```r
my_f <- 'data/gdp.rds'
my_f <- 'fcts/report_functions.R'

# BAD
my_f <- 'functions.R'
my_f <- 'R/script.R'
my_f <- 'New folder/script_ver_03.R'
my_f <- 'New folder/script_ver_05_with_clean_data.R'
```

Sections of code: Use dashes within the script to break sections of the code. Remember that RStudio will create shortcuts for each stage in a small window just above the prompt and below the editor.

```r
# Import data ----



# Clean data ----



# Estimate models ----
```

Variable and function names: Use these guidelines for naming objects, including functions:

- Give preference to lowercase characters when naming objects;
- Keep names short, concise and intuitive (easier said than done, but try your best..);
- Use the first few words to identify the class of an object (e.g. dataframe `df_gdp`, list `l_args`);
- Avoid the use of dots (.) when connecting words in the object's names. The dot has a special use when calling S3 objects[2], an object-oriented approach in R, not discussed in this book. In substitution, use underscore (_) to link words in a name.

```r
# GOOD
my_seq <- 1:100 # simple and clean
df_prices <- tibble() # for sure it is a dataframe with prices!
fct_plot_prices <- function() # I know what it does before executing it!
    l_args <- list() # also nice and clean
```

---

[2]http://adv-r.had.co.nz/S3.html

```
# BAD
DF <- tibble() # all uppercase and generic
DataFrame <- tibble() # camel case and same name as object
list <- list() # Same name as constructor. Does it even work?
# It does..
Prices_of_Facebook <- tibble() # very informative,
# but too long!
DATAFRAME_WITH_SPECIAL_DATA <- tibble() # too long!
# Why SHOUT in code?
# be nice
df.prices <- tibble() # use of dots
```

Other code conventions:

- Always put a space around operators (=, >, <, ...) and use parenthesis to indicate logical tests:

```
# GOOD
x <- 10
flag <- (x > 0)

# BAD
x<-0
flag<-x>0
```

- Always set a space after using comma, just like you would when writing:

```
# GOOD
my_fct(1, 2, 3)
my_x <- c(1, 2, 3)

# BAD
my_fct(1,2,3)
my_x <- c(1,2,3)
```

These are simple and important rules you can follow for keeping your code more readable. Additionally, you can find a more complete description in the tidyverse style guide[3]. If writing R code is a large part of your work, make

---

[3] https://style.tidyverse.org/

13.2 Optimizing Code Speed

sure you understand and follow such rules. You'll be surprised by how much you can know about a programmer experience just by looking at his/her code structure.

For most R users, code execution time is not much of a concern. If you are using the platform to analyze tables and produce technical reports, it is unlikely that you will stumble upon a programming problem where the execution time becomes a **real** issue. Today we can buy domestic computers with high hardware specifications, which facilitate the analysis of large tables.

Moreover, time can also be abundant. For example, my experience tells me that an academic research cycle – from idea to written article – takes around 6 months. Even if the code execution time takes three hours to complete, which is rare, I can pay the price of waiting for it. Likewise, in a corporate scenario, if an RMarkdown report takes five minutes to compile instead of 30 seconds, then it isn't really harmful. In fact, it might just be a nice excuse for another cup of coffee. So, you should be aware that it could be the case where **you spend more time trying to optimize a code than the actual benefit you can potentially get!** In other words, it makes **no sense** to spend three hours trying to optimize a code that runs in 5 minutes, every month. Whenever you think about optimizing R code, make sure that your net gain is positive and the investment of time pays off.

The execution time becomes an issue when the R code is serving something else in a live setup. For example, if the Google search algorithm was written in R, there is a real and economic benefit in improving its execution and dropping a millisecond. Likewise, if one is serving an R shiny app on the internet and its interface feels sluggish, code optimization should be a priority.

Back to the code, optimizing speed in R scripts is a two-stage process: we first need to identify the parts of the code that are taking more time – the so-called profiling stage – and then try to fix it.

13.2.1 Profiling Code

There are different routes to profile an R code. A simple and easy way of doing this is providing messages of the stages of the script in the prompt.

When you watch the code run live, it will be easy to notice which parts are taking more time to run and where we should try to optimize.

As an example, I'll first write a function that will simulate some data, pause for one second and then estimate a linear model. The pause is the bottleneck, the part that will take most of the execution time.

```
my_bench_fct <- function() {

  require(tictoc)
  require(tidyverse)

  cat('01-Set parameters\n')
  my_n <- 1000000

  cat('02-Build variables\n')
  x <- runif(my_n)
  y <- x + rnorm(my_n)

  cat('03-Pause for a while -- the bottleneck\n')
  profvis::pause(1)

  cat('04-Estimate a linear model\n')
  lm_model <- lm(data = tibble(x = x, y = y),
                 formula = y ~ x)

  return(lm_model)
}

out <- my_bench_fct()
```

```
R> 01-Set parameters
R> 02-Build variables
R> 03-Pause for a while -- the bottleneck
R> 04-Estimate a linear model
```

Whenever you make a call to function `my_bench_fct` you'll see the messages scrolling down in R's prompt. You'll be looking for the time it takes for each message to appear. It is simple but effective. You'll be able to easily spot which section of the code is taking more time. Here, it becomes clear when watching the execution that stage 03 is the bottleneck.

13.2. OPTIMIZING CODE SPEED

For complex and extensive code, however, using `cat` to print messages may not help much, especially when each stage of the script has many lines of code. For that, we use the function `base::Rprof` to profile the code. What it will do is to measure the time taken for each line of the code to run. It will save the result in a file that can be later analyzed.

Function `base::Rprof` works by first calling it with the location of a file to save the results. Any code executed after the call to `Rprof`, will be evaluated for its execution time. When finished, we pause profiling by calling `Rprof(NULL)`. See an example next:

```r
# set temporary file for results
profiling_file <- tempfile(pattern = 'profiling_example',
                           fileext = '.out')

# initialize profiling
Rprof(filename = profiling_file)

cat('01-Set parameters\n')
my_n <- 1000000

cat('02-Build variables\n')
x <- runif(my_n)
y <- x + rnorm(my_n)

cat('03-Pause for a while -- the bottleneck\n')
profvis::pause(1)

cat('04-Estimate a linear model\n')
lm_model <- lm(data = tibble(x = x, y = y),
               formula = y ~ x)

# stop profiling
Rprof(NULL)
```

```
R> 01-Set parameters
R> 02-Build variables
R> 03-Pause for a while -- the bottleneck
R> NULL
R> 04-Estimate a linear model
```

The actual results can be imported with `base::summaryRprof`:

```r
# check results
df_res <- summaryRprof(profiling_file)$by.total

# print it
print(head(df_res))
```

```
R>                        total.time total.pct self.time
R> "block_exec"                  1.5       100         0
R> "call_block"                  1.5       100         0
R> "evaluate_call"               1.5       100         0
R> "evaluate::evaluate"          1.5       100         0
R> "evaluate"                    1.5       100         0
R> "generator$render"            1.5       100         0
R>                         self.pct
R> "block_exec"                   0
R> "call_block"                   0
R> "evaluate_call"                0
R> "evaluate::evaluate"           0
R> "evaluate"                     0
R> "generator$render"             0
```

In this `dataframe` we see the top 5 lines of code that took more execution time: `profivs::pause` and `lm`. The next step of the code optimization is to further analyze it and check whether any line of code can be improved. The solution, in this case, is to remove the `profivs::pause` line, making our code run one second faster.

Another solution for profiling is package `profvis`. Based on the output file from `base::Rprof`, it can create a dynamic shiny site with the actual code lines and its evaluation. The next lines of code will run our previous example.

```r
library(profvis)

# use profvis
profiling <- profvis(expr = {
  require(tictoc)
  require(tidyverse)
  
  cat('01-Set parameters\n')
  my_n <- 1000000
```

13.2. OPTIMIZING CODE SPEED

```
  cat('02-Build variables\n')
  x <- runif(my_n)
  y <- x + rnorm(my_n)

  cat('03-Pause for a while -- the bottleneck\n')
  profvis::pause(1)

  cat('04-Estimate a linear model\n')
  lm_model <- lm(data = tibble(x = x, y = y),
                 formula = y ~ x)

})

# create visualization
htmlwidgets::saveWidget(profiling , "profile.html")

# Can open in browser from R
browseURL("profile.html")
```

The result will be similar to Figure 13.1.

Figure 13.1: The html output of profvis

Again we find the same result – line 13 (`profvis::pause(1)`) is the bottleneck –, but in a nice web interface.

13.2.2 Simple Strategies to Improve Code Speed

Once you identify the bottleneck in your code, its time to fix it. Here we'll discuss the most obvious ways you can improve the execution time of R code.

13.2.2.1 Use Vector Operations

Whenever you are working with atomic vectors in R, you should understand that "manual" insertions and modifications of elements are not efficient. As a rule of thumb, always use a native vectorized function for any operation. These are written in C code and can be very, very fast.

As an example, let's look at the case of building a numeric vector y based on another vector x. The vectorized version of the solution is simple: `y <- x + 1`. But, we'll explore alternatives using loops and preallocation. In the next chunk of code, we use package `tictoc`, a simple watch-clock, to assess the execution time of each part of the code.

```
library(tictoc)

N <- 10000000
x <- 1:N

tic('Using loops without preallocation') # start timer
y <- numeric()
for (i in seq_along(x)) {
  y[i] <- x[i] + 1
}
toc() # end timer


tic('Using loops with preallocation') # start timer
y <- numeric(length = N)
for (i in seq_along(x)) {
  y[i] <- x[i] + 1
}
toc() # end timer

tic('Using vectors') # start timer
y <- x + 10
toc() # end timer


R> Using loops without preallocation: 3.511 sec elapsed
R> Using loops with preallocation: 0.926 sec elapsed
R> Using vectors: 0.325 sec elapsed
```

In the first version with loop, we set `y <- numeric()`, that is, an empty vector. Here, there is no preallocation of vectors. The result is the worst

13.2. OPTIMIZING CODE SPEED

execution time. In the second case, we preallocate memory for the vector in `y <- numeric(length = N)` and run the same loop. This simple preallocation technique decreased execution time significantly. However, notice how the vectorized version of the code was able to perform the same operation in a fraction of the time.

The lesson here is: **always seek vectorized versions of functions**. These are mostly written in low-level languages and can execute a lot faster. When possible, avoid creating or expanding vectors within loops.

13.2.2.2 Repetitive binding of `dataframes`

Another common mistake when it comes to R code is the repetitive use of bind operations with `dataframes`. On a large scale, such code can increase your execution time significantly.

For that, let's explore an example with some random data. The next chunk of code will create several `dataframes` and aggregate them into a single object with two strategies: 1) binding within the loop and 2) using lists within the loop for later binding.

```
library(tidyverse)

n_dfs <- 1000 # number of dataframes to bind
n_obs <- 1000 # number of observations in each dataframe

tic('Binding dataframes within the loop')
my_df <- tibble()
for (i in 1:n_dfs) {
  temp_df <- tibble(x = runif(n_obs),
                    y = rnorm(n_obs))

  my_df <- bind_rows(my_df, temp_df)

}
toc()

tic('Using lists within the loop, bind it later')
my_l <- list()
for (i in 1:n_dfs) {
  temp_df <- tibble(x = runif(n_obs),
                    y = rnorm(n_obs))
```

```
  my_l <- c(my_l, list(temp_df))
}

my_df <- bind_rows(my_l)
toc()
```

```
R> Binding dataframes within the loop: 5.092 sec elapsed
R> Using lists within the loop, bind it later: 0.362 sec elapsed
```

As you can see, the difference is significant. As a rule of thumb, **do not bind dataframes repeatedly**. A better approach is to save the result in a list and bind all elements in a single call to dplyr::bind_rows.

13.2.3 Using C++ code (package Rcpp)

Package Rcpp (Eddelbuettel and Balamuta, 2017) is a great example of how R can interact with other programming languages in a seamless way. With it, you can write and run the C++ code within your R script. The main benefit is speed and access to numerical libraries. The C++ language is well known for speeding up numerical operations in a significant way. Not surprisingly, Rcpp is used in more than one thousand packages in CRAN, an impressive achievement.

Have a look in the next example, where we write a simple "sum of elements" function in three different versions: using loops, using function sum and using Rcpp.

```
library(Rcpp)
library(tictoc)

sum_R_looped <- function(x) {
  total <- 0
  for (i in seq_along(x)) {
    total <- total + x[i]
  }
  return(total)
}

sum_R_vector <- function(x) {
  total <- sum(x)
  return(total)
```

13.2. OPTIMIZING CODE SPEED

```
}

cppFunction('double sum_C(NumericVector x) {
  int n = x.size();
  double total = 0;
  for(int i = 0; i < n; ++i) {
    total += x[i];
  }
  return total;
}')
```

Using `cppFunction` is straightforward. Its input is a C++ function definition as a character object. Once it is executed, the function `sum_C` will be available in the current R session.

Now, let's test all three functions with a large vector:

```
x <- 1:5000000

tic('Sum with R loops')
out1 <- sum_R_looped(x)
toc()

tic('Sum with R (vectorized)')
out2 <- sum_R_vector(x)
toc()

tic('Sum with C++ (rcpp)')
out3 <- sum_C(x)
toc()
```

```
R> Sum with R loops: 0.334 sec elapsed
R> Sum with R (vectorized): 0.001 sec elapsed
R> Sum with C++ (rcpp): 0.014 sec elapsed
```

The results are as expected. The case with the least execution time is the vectorized version. This happens because of the low-level function `base::sum` is already highly optimized. Nonetheless, the function `sum_C` significantly decreased the time from the looped version of `sum`.

Whenever you have a numerical bottleneck in your code, consider using package `Rcpp` to decrease execution time. Some time will be spent learning and writing a C++ function but the benefits can be significant. We only scraped the surface of this package. Advanced users should know that you can also call C++ libraries for scientific computing such as eigen[4] and Armadillo[5] straight from your R session. More details can be found at the official Rcpp website[6].

13.2.4 Using cache (package `memoise`)

A very underestimated feature of R is the use of local caching – saving the results of function calls in local files. For better understanding what caching stands for, think of it as a large lookup table that is being built as code runs and all function's output is being memorized. For every group of inputs, there is a single output that is saved in a local file. Whenever you want a result, which has been computed previously, you can simply search your lookup table (load the local cache file) and get the same result without actually executing the function.

Moreover, caching works perfectly with deterministic functions, those that, given a particular set of input arguments, will always bring back the same result. The greatest benefit of caching is speed. Instead of performing lengthy computations, cut corners and simply load the result from memory. **Caching makes your code faster, it's easy to implement, at a very low cost of disk space**.

Particularly, caching works very well in the importation of datasets. As you should have noticed from chapter 4, packages `BatchGetSymbols`, `GetQuandlData` and `simfinR` for example, use a custom local caching system so repeated data queries are imported from local files and not the internet. The decrease in execution time is very impressive.

While you can write your own caching system by saving and reading local files, an easier approach is to use package `memoise` (Wickham et al., 2017). As an example, let's create a function called `sleeping_beauty` that will proxy some execution time by pausing for one second and just returning its inputs.

```
sleeping_beauty <- function(arg1, arg2) {
  # Simple example function that will sleep for one second
  #
  # ARGS: arg1 - anything
```

---

[4] http://eigen.tuxfamily.org/index.php?title=Main_Page
[5] http://arma.sourceforge.net/
[6] http://www.rcpp.org/

13.2. OPTIMIZING CODE SPEED

```
#         arg2 - anything
# RETURNS: A list

profvis::pause(1)

return(list(arg1, arg2))
}
```

The first step in using `memoise` is setting the local path for the cache files with function `memoise::cache_filesystem`. Here we'll use folder mem_cache. You can also set a temporary cache in the RAM memory with the function `memoise::cache_memory` or Amazon S3 cloud service with `memoise::cache_s3`.

```
library(memoise)

my_cache_folder <- cache_filesystem(path = 'mem_cache')
```

The next step is telling `memoise` that we have a function called sleeping_beauty that we want a cached version. We will call the new version of the function as mem_sleeping_beauty.

```
mem_sleeping_beauty <- memoise(f = sleeping_beauty,
                               cache = my_cache_folder)
```

Now, let's call the function with different arguments and check the resulting execution times with `tictoc`.

```
library(memoise)
library(tictoc)

tic('    sleeping_beauty:\t arg1 = 1, arg2 = 2')
out1 <- sleeping_beauty(1, 2)
toc()

tic('mem_sleeping_beauty:\t arg1 = 1, arg2 = 2')
out1 <- mem_sleeping_beauty(1, 2)
toc()

tic('    sleeping_beauty:\t arg1 = 1, arg2 = 2')
```

```
out1 <- sleeping_beauty(1, 2)
toc()

tic('mem_sleeping_beauty:\t arg1 = 1, arg2 = 2')
out1 <- mem_sleeping_beauty(1, 2)
toc()
```

```
R>     sleeping_beauty:  arg1 = 1, arg2 = 2: 1.002 sec elapsed
R> mem_sleeping_beauty:  arg1 = 1, arg2 = 2: 1.007 sec elapsed
R>     sleeping_beauty:  arg1 = 1, arg2 = 2: 1.002 sec elapsed
R> mem_sleeping_beauty:  arg1 = 1, arg2 = 2: 0.033 sec elapsed
```

Function `sleeping_beauty` is the original code that will always take around one second to run, no matter how many calls we make. Function `mem_sleeping_beauty` is the `memoise` version that memorizes the output every time we call it. Notice that, in the first call to `mem_sleeping_beauty(1, 2)`, it took approximately one second. In the second call with the same input arguments, it took far less than one second. This is due to the read of the cached files with the saved outputs, instead of executing the actual R code in the scope of the function.

Going further, if we change the arguments of `mem_sleeping_beauty`, we'll find the same dynamic. The first time it makes a call with the pair of arguments, it saves it locally. In the second and repeated call, it just loads the locally cached file:

```
tic('mem_sleeping_beauty:\t arg1 = 2, arg2 = 2')
out1 <- mem_sleeping_beauty(2, 2)
toc()

tic('mem_sleeping_beauty:\t arg1 = 2, arg2 = 2')
out2 <- mem_sleeping_beauty(2, 2)
toc()

tic('mem_sleeping_beauty:\t arg1 = 5, arg2 = 1')
out3 <- mem_sleeping_beauty(5, 1)
toc()
```

```
R> mem_sleeping_beauty:  arg1 = 2, arg2 = 2: 1.003 sec elapsed
R> mem_sleeping_beauty:  arg1 = 2, arg2 = 2: 0.002 sec elapsed
R> mem_sleeping_beauty:  arg1 = 5, arg2 = 1: 1.003 sec elapsed
```

13.2. OPTIMIZING CODE SPEED

Looking at folder `mem_cache` we find the actual files with cryptic names:

```
mem_files <- list.files('mem_cache/')

print(mem_files)
```

```
R> [1] "67f3a17aa3168441" "9f54d3972877ed8b"
R> [3] "d4ca327bdead9d90"
```

These are just *rds* files with the content of the output. Since we made only three unique calls to `mem_sleeping_beauty`, there are only three files with data in this folder. As new calls, with new inputs, are made, the number of cache files increases.

Caching is one of the best techniques for improving code execution. It is very easy to implement – as we saw in the previous example –, its very cheap since disk space is primarily abundant, and it can improve code execution time significantly. A piece of final advice, if you combine R cache with file storage cloud services such as Dropbox[7] and Google Drive[8], you'll be able to expand the benefits of caching to different workstations. In other words, your R code will run much faster, independently of where you are working.

13.2.4.1 Using parallel processing (package `furrr`)

Whenever you are running an R script, a single core of your computer is used by default. However, modern computers are equipped with at least four cores or more to handle the increasingly complex computational demands of today's operating systems.

Parallel processing relates to using more than one core of your machine to run R code. In its typical use, a whole problem is divided into smaller chunks, which is then fed to each core of the computer. As the chunks are "solved", new pieces arrive until the whole problem is resolved. The final stage combines all results into a single object, usually a `list`. Depending on the number of cores of your machine, the gain in speed can be extraordinary.

Before we start, understand that not every problem can be parallelized. The most suited candidates are those problems that are **not recursive** in nature, that is to say, we can break them into smaller, independent, problems without computational loss.

---

[7] https://www.dropbox.com/h
[8] https://www.google.com/drive/

A typical case in data analysis is importing a large volume of files from the computer. The order in which we read the files makes no difference to the final result. We can safely treat each importing operation as an independent process. Let's simulate this programming problem and solve it with parallel programming.

First, let's write a function that will create files.

```
create_file <- function(n_obs, folder_to_save) {
  # Create files in the computer
  #
  # ARGS: n_obs - Number of observations in dataframe
  #       folder_to_save - Where to save files
  # RETURNS: True, if successful

  require(tidyverse)


  temp_df <- tibble(x = runif(n_obs),
                    y = rnorm(n_obs))

  temp_file <- tempfile(pattern = 'file', tmpdir = folder_to_save,
                        fileext = '.csv')

  write_csv(temp_df,
            path = temp_file)

  return(TRUE)
}
```

So, with the function completed, its time to call it many, many times.

```
library(purrr)

n_files <- 1000
n_obs <- 10000
folder_to_save <- file.path(tempdir(), 'many files')

dir.create(folder_to_save)

pwalk(.l = list(n_obs = rep(n_obs, n_files),
                folder_to_save = rep(folder_to_save,
```

13.2. OPTIMIZING CODE SPEED

```
                                n_files)),
        create_file)
```

Now we read back those files with two strategies: 1) sequential R code, 2) using parallel computing.

Before we start, we need to set up our machine for parallel computing. First, we must understand the number of cores available to us. We do that with function `future::availableCores()`.

```
n_cores_available <- future::availableCores()

print(n_cores_available)
```

```
R> system
R>     16
```

The machine in which the book was compiled has 16 cores available. Let's use 10 of them to solve our problem. As a rule, **never use all cores of your machine**. Otherwise, the operating system will come to halt and you'll need to forcibly reboot the computer.

This code will run both versions of the same operations. Many packages allow for parallel computing in R. Here we will use `furrr` (Vaughan and Dancho, 2018), which follows the same notation as `purrr` (see chapter 8), and is very easy to use.

```
library(furrr)
library(tictoc)

# get files
my_files <- list.files(path = folder_to_save,
                       full.names = TRUE)

# setup for multicore
n_cores <- 10

# set the number of cores and type of parallel
plan(strategy = multisession, workers = n_cores)

tic('Sequential with pmap (1 core)')
```

```
l_out_1 <- pmap(
  .l = list(file = my_files,
            col_types = rep(list(cols()),
                            length(my_files)) ),
  .f = readr::read_csv
)
toc()
```

R> Sequential with pmap (1 core): 14.312 sec elapsed

```
tic(paste0('Parallel with future_pmap (',
           n_cores, ' cores)'))
l_out_2 <- future_pmap(
  .l = list(file = my_files,
            col_types = rep(list(cols()),
                            length(my_files)) ),
  .f = readr::read_csv
)
toc()
```

R> Parallel with future_pmap (10 cores): 5.005 sec elapsed

```
identical(l_out_1, l_out_2)
```

R> [1] TRUE

Notice the gain in speed is not tenfold. When calling other cores of the computer to solve the problem, some overhead execution time must be acknowledged. The actual code execution time for each core must be added to a fixed cost of overhead. Also, notice how easy it was to set up the parallel version in the previous chunk of code. We only need to call future::plan to set the type of parallel and number of cores, and use furrr::future_pmap instead of purrr::pmap.

In conclusion, parallel computing works better when you have a large problem that can be independently broken into solvable smaller pieces. The improvement in execution time will not necessarily be a multiple of the number of cores in your machine. Always consider the overhead costs of using several cores of your computer.

13.3 Exercises

1. Consider this code:

```
library(tidyverse)
library(forecast)
library(BatchGetSymbols)

ticker <- '^GSPC'
df_prices <- BatchGetSymbols(tickers = ticker,
                             first.date = '2010-01-01')[[2]]

my_arima <- auto.arima(df_prices$ret.adjusted.prices)
summary(my_arima)
```

```
R> Series: df_prices$ret.adjusted.prices
R> ARIMA(2,0,2) with non-zero mean
R>
R> Coefficients:
R>           ar1     ar2      ma1      ma2    mean
R>        0.1682  0.7717  -0.2184  -0.7571   5e-04
R> s.e.   0.1282  0.1206   0.1357   0.1318   1e-04
R>
R> sigma^2 estimated as 8.558e-05:  log likelihood=8299.73
R> AIC=-16587.45   AICc=-16587.42   BIC=-16552.41
R>
R> Training set error measures:
R>                        ME        RMSE         MAE MPE
R> Training set -1.171766e-05 0.009241832 0.006357013 NaN
R>              MAPE      MASE        ACF1
R> Training set  Inf 0.6712617 -0.0009530639
```

Use `Rprof` and `profvis` to identify the bottleneck of the code. Which line number is taking more time?

2. Use package `Rcpp` to write and use a C++ function that will add elements of vectors x and y, in an element-by-element fashion. The output should be another vector of the same size and with equal elements as x + y. Use function `identical` to test if all elements from both vectors are equal.

3. Use package `tictoc` to compare the performance of the previous function against R's native + operator and a looped version of the function, with preallocation. Who has the least execution time and why? Does the `Rcpp` version win over the looped version?

4. Use package `memoise` to create a memorized version of `Quandl::Quandl`. Use the new function to import data for the Consumer Price Index of the United States (code `'FRED/DDOE01USA086NWDB'`). How much of a percentage speed gain do you get from the second call to the memorized version?

Bibliography

Bache, S. M. and Wickham, H. (2014). *magrittr: A Forward-Pipe Operator for R*. R package version 1.5.

Bollerslev, T. (1986). Generalized autoregressive conditional heteroskedasticity. *Journal of econometrics*, 31(3):307–327.

Brooks, C. (2014). *Introductory econometrics for finance*. Cambridge university press.

Campbell, J. Y., Lo, A. W.-C., MacKinlay, A. C., et al. (1997). *The econometrics of financial markets*, volume 2. princeton University press Princeton, NJ.

Croissant, Y. and Millo, G. (2008). Panel data econometrics in R: The plm package. *Journal of Statistical Software*, 27(2).

Dahl, D. B. (2016). *xtable: Export Tables to LaTeX or HTML*. R package version 1.8-2.

Dancho, M. and Vaughan, D. (2019). *tidyquant: Tidy Quantitative Financial Analysis*. R package version 0.5.8.

Dowle, M., Srinivasan, A., Short, T., with contributions from R Saporta, S. L., and Antonyan, E. (2015). *data.table: Extension of Data.frame*. R package version 1.9.6.

Dragulescu, A. A. (2014). *xlsx: Read, write, format Excel 2007 and Excel 97/2000/XP/2003 files*. R package version 0.5.7.

Eddelbuettel, D. and Balamuta, J. J. (2017). Extending extitR with extitC++: A Brief Introduction to extitRcpp. *PeerJ Preprints*, 5:e3188v1.

Engle, R. F. (1982). Autoregressive conditional heteroscedasticity with estimates of the variance of united kingdom inflation. *Econometrica: Journal of the Econometric Society*, pages 987–1007.

Fox, J. and Weisberg, S. (2011). *An R Companion to Applied Regression*. Sage, Thousand Oaks CA, second edition.

Freitas, W. (2016). *bizdays: Business Days Calculations and Utilities*. R package version 1.0.1.

Garmonsway, D. (2017). *tidyxl: Read Untidy Excel Files*. R package version 0.2.1.

Gentzkow, M., Kelly, B. T., and Taddy, M. (2017). Text as data. Technical report, National Bureau of Economic Research.

Ghalanos, A. (2015). *rugarch: Univariate GARCH models*. R package version 1.3-6.

Gillespie, C. and Lovelace, R. (2016). *Efficient R programming: a practical guide to smarter programming*. " O'Reilly Media, Inc.".

Gohel, D. (2017). *ReporteRs: Microsoft Word and PowerPoint Documents Generation*. R package version 0.8.8.

Gorecki, J. (2014). *Rbitcoin: R and bitcoin integration*. R package version 0.9.2.

Greene, W. H. (2003). *Econometric analysis*. Pearson Education India.

Grolemund, G. and Wickham, H. (2011). Dates and times made easy with lubridate. *Journal of Statistical Software*, 40(3):1–25.

Grunfeld, Y. (1958). The determinants of corporate investment, unpublished ph. d. *D thesis, The University of Chicago*.

Hamilton, J. D. (1994). *Time series analysis*, volume 2. Princeton university press Princeton.

Hanck, C., Arnold, M., Gerber, A., and Schmelzer, M. (2019). Introduction to econometrics with r. *Essen: University of Duisburg-Essen.[Google Scholar]*.

Harrison, J. (2016). *RSelenium: R Bindings for Selenium WebDriver*. R package version 1.4.5.

Hausman, J. A. (1978). Specification tests in econometrics. *Econometrica: Journal of the Econometric Society*, pages 1251–1271.

Henry, L. and Wickham, H. (2019). *purrr: Functional Programming Tools*. R package version 0.3.3.

Hsiao, C. (2014). *Analysis of panel data*. Number 54. Cambridge university press.

Hyndman, R. and Khandakar, Y. (2007). Automatic time series forecasting: The forecast package for r 7. 2008. *URL: https://www. jstatsoft. org/article/view/v027i03 [accessed 2016-02-24][WebCite Cache]*.

James, D. and Hornik, K. (2017). *chron: Chronological Objects which Can Handle Dates and Times*. R package version 2.3-50. S original by David James, R port by Kurt Hornik.

Kleiber, C. and Zeileis, A. (2008). *Applied econometrics with R*. Springer Science & Business Media.

Kleiber, C. and Zeileis, A. (2010). The grunfeld data at 50. *German economic review*, 11(4):404–417.

Lang, D. T. and the CRAN Team (2016). *XML: Tools for Parsing and Generating XML Within R and S-Plus*. R package version 3.98-1.4.

Leifeld, P. (2013). texreg: Conversion of statistical model output in R to LATEX and HTML tables. *Journal of Statistical Software*, 55(8):1–24.

Maddala, G. (2001). Introduction to econometrics.

Mirai Solutions GmbH (2016). *XLConnect: Excel Connector for R*. R package version 0.2-12.

Pena, E. A. and Slate, E. H. (2014). *gvlma: Global Validation of Linear Models Assumptions*. R package version 1.0.0.2.

Perlin, M. (2014). *fMarkovSwitching: R Package for Estimation, Simulation and Forecasting of a Univariate Markov Switching Model*. R package version 1.0/r5838.

Perlin, M. (2016). *BatchGetSymbols: Downloads and Organizes Financial Data for Multiple Tickers*. R package version 1.0.

Perlin, M. S. (2019a). *GetQuandlData: Fast and Cached Import of Data from Quandl Using the JSON API*. R package version 0.1.0.

Perlin, M. S. (2019b). *simfinR: Import Financial Data from the 'SimFin' Project*. R package version 0.1.0.

R Core Team (2015). *foreign: Read Data Stored by Minitab, S, SAS, SPSS, Stata, Systat, Weka, dBase, ...* R package version 0.8-66.

Raymond McTaggart, Gergely Daroczi, and Clement Leung (2019). *Quandl: API Wrapper for Quandl.com*. R package version 2.10.0.

Robinson, D. (2017). *broom: Convert Statistical Analysis Objects into Tidy Data Frames*. R package version 0.4.2.

Rushworth, A. (2019). *inspectdf: Inspection, Comparison and Visualisation of Data Frames*. R package version 0.0.4.

Ryan, J. A. and Ulrich, J. M. (2014). *xts: eXtensible Time Series*. R package version 0.9-7.

Sanchez-Espigares, J. A. and Lopez-Moreno, A. (2014). *MSwM: Fitting Markov Switching Models*. R package version 1.2.

Team, R. C., Wuertz, D., Setz, T., Chalabi, Y., Maechler, M., and Byers, J. W. (2015). *timeDate: Rmetrics - Chronological and Calendar Objects*. R package version 3012.100.

Teetor, P. (2011). *R cookbook*. " O'Reilly Media, Inc.".

Thompson, K. (1968). Programming techniques: Regular expression search algorithm. *Communications of the ACM*, 11(6):419–422.

Trapletti, A. and Hornik, K. (2017). *tseries: Time Series Analysis and Computational Finance*. R package version 0.10-38.

Tsay, R. S. (2005). *Analysis of financial time series*, volume 543. John Wiley & Sons.

Tsay, R. S. and Wood, D. (2018). *MTS: All-Purpose Toolkit for Analyzing Multivariate Time Series (MTS) and Estimating Multivariate Volatility Models*. R package version 1.0.

Vaughan, D. and Dancho, M. (2018). *furrr: Apply Mapping Functions in Parallel using Futures*. R package version 0.1.0.

Vaughan, D. and Dancho, M. (2019). *tibbletime: Time Aware Tibbles*. R package version 0.1.3.

BIBLIOGRAPHY

Venables, W. N., Smith, D. M., Team, R. D. C., et al. (2004). An introduction to r.

Wickham, H. (2007). Reshaping data with the reshape package. *Journal of Statistical Software*, 21(12):1–20.

Wickham, H. (2009). *ggplot2: elegant graphics for data analysis*. Springer Science & Business Media.

Wickham, H. (2014). *Advanced R*. CRC Press.

Wickham, H. (2015). *stringr: Simple, Consistent Wrappers for Common String Operations*. R package version 1.0.0.

Wickham, H. (2016a). *readxl: Read Excel Files*. R package version 0.1.1.

Wickham, H. (2016b). *rvest: Easily Harvest (Scrape) Web Pages*. R package version 0.3.2.

Wickham, H. (2016c). *tidyr: Easily Tidy Data with spread() and gather() Functions*. R package version 0.6.0.

Wickham, H. and Francois, R. (2016). *dplyr: A Grammar of Data Manipulation*. R package version 0.5.0.

Wickham, H., Hester, J., Müller, K., and Cook, D. (2017). *memoise: Memoisation of Functions*. R package version 1.1.0.

Wuertz, D., with contribution from Michal Miklovic, Y. C., Boudt, C., Chausse, P., and others (2016). *fGarch: Rmetrics - Autoregressive Conditional Heteroskedastic Modelling*. R package version 3010.82.1.

Xie, Y. (2016). *bookdown: Authoring Books and Technical Documents with R Markdown*. CRC Press.

Zeileis, A. (2004). Econometric computing with hc and hac covariance matrix estimators.

Zeileis, A. and Hothorn, T. (2002). Diagnostic checking in regression relationships. *R News*, 2(3):7–10.

Index

[[ ]], 182

adding column to dataframe, 163
assign, 39

base
    !=, 241
    ::, 67
    <-, 213
    ==, 240
    %*%, 193
    %in%, 350
    |, 241
    and, 241
    apply, 298
    as.character, 235
    as.Date, 245
    as.factor, 239
    as.list, 189
    as.matrix, 195, 196
    as.numeric, 216, 237
    c, 41
    cat, 45, 113
    cbind, 197
    class, 43, 220
    coef, 438
    colMeans, 198
    colnames, 159, 192
    complete.cases, 178, 262, 275
    cumprod, 218
    cumsum, 218
    cut, 214, 258
    data.frame, 152
    dim, 49
    do.call, 296
    else, 284
    Encoding, 232
    factor, 233
    format, 46, 48, 252, 254
    function, 266
    getwd, 57
    gregexpr, 224
    gsub, 225
    head, 177
    help, 62
    if, 283
    install.packages, 66
    installed.packages, 65
    is.na, 260, 271
    lapply, 287
    length, 49
    levels, 239
    library, 67
    list, 180
    list.dirs, 74
    list.files, 73, 102, 373
    lm, 380

load, 102
ls, 42
mapply, 296
matrix, 191, 195
matrix multiplication, 193
max, 217
mean, 29, 188
min, 217
months, 257
na.omit, 179, 261, 271, 334
names, 159, 190
nchar, 52, 228
ncol, 49
nrow, 49
numeric, 204
OlsonNames, 258
order, 167
paste, 46, 220
print, 35
prod, 218
quarters, 257
rbind, 197
regexpr, 224
rep, 154, 205
required, 68
return, 267
rm, 56
rnorm, 206
rowMeans, 198
rownames, 192
Rprof, 467
runif, 206
sample, 208
sapply, 188, 290, 438
save, 102
seq, 204, 246
set.seed, 210
setwd, 57
sort, 218
source, 38
split, 239, 293
stop, 269, 270

str, 44
strrep, 221
strsplit, 227
sub, 225
substr, 223
sum, 216
summary, 384, 414
Sys.Date, 125, 255
Sys.time, 255
Sys.timezone, 258
t, 196, 293
table, 238
tail, 177
tapply, 293, 438
unique, 179, 216, 283
unlist, 189
update.packages, 68
warning, 271
weekday, 311
weekdays, 256
which, 240
which.max, 217
which.min, 217
write.csv, 96
BatchGetSymbols, 124
    BatchGetSymbols, 125
bizdays, 243
bookdown, 28
broom, 442
    glance, 442
    tidy, 442

C++, 17
calculating beta, 385
character, 219
chron, 243
code completion, 69
conditional statements, 283
constants
    LETTERS, 222
    letters, 222
    month.abb, 222
    month.name, 222

INDEX

data.table, 177
dataframes, 152
dates, 31, 245
datetime, 250
decimal, 30
describe.vec, 292
devtools, 66
    install_github, 66
diffdate, 248
dplyr, 309
    %>%, 158
    as_tibble, 333
    bind_cols, 170, 172
    bind_rows, 170, 283
    do, 442
    filter, 166
    group_by, 309
    mutate, 163, 442
    select, 163
    summarise, 309

environment, 34

fGarch, 418
    garchFit, 421
    garchSim, 418
    predict, 424
file types
    .R, 32
    .RData, 32, 102
    .Rmd, 32
    .csv, 90, 96
    .rds, 32, 102
Folder structure, 83
folder structure, 83
forcats
    fct_recode, 236
forecast
    auto.arima, 415
    forecast, 417
fst, 104
    read_fst, 105
    write_fst, 105

functions, 29, 265
furrr, 477

Garch models, 418
ggplot2, 342
    aes, 347
    facet_wrap, 359
    geom_line, 347
    ggplot, 346
    ggsave, 373
    labs, 347
    qplot, 345
    scale_colour_grey, 358
    theme_bw, 356

inspectdf, 156

Julia, 17

latin characters, 30
Latin1, 30
LETTERS, 221
letters, 221
Levels, 233
list, 180
logical matrices, 195
logical operators, 54
long format, 317
loops, 276
lubridate, 243
    dmy, 243
    hour, 255
    mdy, 243
    minute, 255
    now, 255
    today, 255
    ymd, 243

MariaDB, 107
markdown, 32
Matrix, 190
memoise, 474
MTS, 422
MyPrices.png, 373
mySQL, 107

NA, 259
NULL, 186

omit, 261
ordering dataframe, 167

plm, 405
    plm, 405
Profiling code, 466
profvis, 468
prompt, 34
purrr
    possibly, 303
    safely, 303
Python, 17

Quandl, 118
    Quandl, 118
    Quandl.api_key, 118

R consortium, 16
R foundation, 16
R language, 16
RBloggers, 22
Rcpp, 472
readr
    read_csv, 93
    read_lines, 111
readxl, 97
    read_excel, 98
recycling rule, 203
regex, 224
ReportRs, 451
Research scripts, 81
reshape2, 321
    dcast, 321
    melt, 321
return, 267
RMarkdown, 18
Rmarkdown, 28, 32, 448
RSelenium, 148
RSQLite, 109
    dbConnect, 110

dbDisconnect, 110
dbReadTable, 108
dbWriteTable, 110
RStudio, 17, 22, 32
RStudio panels, 34
RStudio projects, 32
rugarch, 418
rvest, 145, 148
    html_nodes, 145
    html_table, 145
    read_html, 145

S language, 16
script editor, 34
shiny, 18
source, 37
splashr, 148
SQLite, 107
stargazer, 451
stat
    arima, 414
    arima.sim, 412
stringr, 219
    fixed, 224
    str_c, 220
    str_dup, 221
    str_length, 228
    str_locate, 224
    str_locate_all, 224
    str_replace, 225
    str_replace_all, 225
    str_split, 227
    str_sub, 223, 348

texreg, 451
tibble, 153
    data_frame, 153
    tibble, 153
tibbletime, 177
tidyquant, 138
    tq_exchange, 139
    tq_index, 140
    tq_index_options, 140

INDEX

tidyr, 319
    gather, 319
    spread, 320
timeDate, 243
transpose matrix, 196
tseries, 415
    adf.test, 415

UTF-8, 30
utils
    View, 154
    zip, 114

Vector, 190
vector operations, 470

webscraping, 143
wide format, 317
writexl
    write_xlsx, 100

x11, 343
XLConnet, 97
xlsx, 97, 99
    write.xlsx, 99
XML, 148
xtable, 448, 451
    xtable, 448
xts, 175
    xts, 175

yield curve figure, 351